SECOND EDITION

SOCIAL WORK PRACTICE

Problem Solving and Beyond

Tuula Heinonen
University of Manitoba

Len Spearman
University of Manitoba

THOMSON NELSON

Australia Canada Mexico Singapore Spain United Kingdom United States

Social Work Practice: Problem Solving and Beyond, Second Edition

by Tuula Heinonen and Len Spearman

Associate Vice President, Editorial Director:
Evelyn Veitch

Executive Editor:
Rod Banister

Executive Marketing Manager:
Don Thompson

Developmental Editors:
Sandra de Ruiter
Glen Herbert

Senior Production Editor:
Natalia Denesiuk

Copy Editor:
Kelli Howey

Proofreader:
Karen Rolfe

Indexer:
Edwin Durbin

Production Coordinator:
Ferial Suleman

Creative Director:
Angela Cluer

Interior Design:
Sarah Battersby

Cover Design:
Roxanna Bennett

Cover Image:
A Summer's Day by Tuula Heinonen

Compositor:
Nelson Gonzalez

Printer:
Webcom

Printed and bound in Canada
1 2 3 4 08 07 06 05

For more information contact Nelson, 1120 Birchmount Road, Toronto, Ontario, M1K 5G4. Or you can visit our Internet site at http://www.nelson.com

Library and Archives Canada Cataloguing in Publication

Heinonen, Tuula
Social work practice : problem solving and beyond / Tuula Heinonen, Len Spearman ; with a chapter by Michael Anthony Hart. — 2nd ed.

Includes bibliographical references and index.
ISBN 0-17-641412-6

1. Social service—Canada—Textbooks. 2. Social service—Vocational guidance—Canada. I. Spearman, Leonard B. II. Hart, Michael, 1965– III. Title.

HV40.S673 2005 361.3'2'0971
C2005-900471-1

Brief Contents

Contents

Chapter 8

Chapter 9

Preface

Finally, a Canadian social work practice textbook that both students and instructors can look forward to! This new edition of *Social Work Practice* includes new content, enhanced presentation, and an instructor's manual that is rich in case material, exercises, reflection questions, and ideas for assignments. Instructors can select from the manual what they will use in group or class discussions and for assignments. Our students have told us that this book, even after they have graduated, remains an important source book to be re-read, marked-up, and drawn from. We think that this new edition offers much food for thought for both students and their instructors.

A few years ago we had the challenging task of developing a print-based and teleconferenced distance education course in social work practice. In writing the course manual, we were constrained by the fact that generalist social work practice textbooks were invariably limited to traditional problem solving, often within a systems or ecological frame, and by lack of content based on the Canadian experience. The first edition of *Social Work Practice* was the result of our experience in writing the distance education manual.

As teachers of social work practice, we believe that social workers need a broad understanding of the foundations of and approaches to practice. One of our goals is to present a view of social work that incorporates—not without criticism—problem solving as a foundation of traditional practice with a conception of practice that takes us beyond problem solving. Newer approaches both critique and enrich generalist social work practice. These are the strengths, Aboriginal, structural, and feminist approaches, and they need to be incorporated into generalist social work practice.

Our second goal is to write a book that uses perspectives that are relevant to modern social work practised in North America. This book emphasizes Canadian social work experience and developments because the Canadian experience, often without fanfare, has greatly enriched the profession. We have formulated a model of generalist practice that we believe can work in other societies that have comparable social work education, social welfare, and social policy environments.

This book is intended for several groups of readers. Most directly, it is designed for social work students, mainly at the undergraduate level, who need to understand the principles, values, and knowledge behind generalist social work practice. While much of the book is drawn from the Canadian experience, all social workers will find the book useful as both a description of generalist practice and a reference source. Another group that will find the content helpful consists of people from other fields who need to know or are interested in social work practice that draws from the strengths, structural, Aboriginal, and feminist approaches and from cross-cultural social work.

The decision to write the second edition was based on feedback from students and social work professors from across Canada. We and they believed that the book captured social work practice in the Canadian context and also reflected good practice anywhere. While most of the organization and content of the first edition remain, we have added significant sections on anti-oppressive practice and community development. Most of the chapters include new and/or revised case examples useful for classroom discussions. The chapter on social policy in health and mental health makes a stronger connection to practice. Based on comments from colleagues, we have re-shaped and focused Chapter 7 on culture and social work to more closely reflect practice issues, rather than broader contexts of multicultural and immigrant policies. Chapter 11, on an Aboriginal approach to social work practice, has also been expanded and improved.

To assist educators who use the book in their courses, an Instructor's Manual has been developed by Len Spearman, Bruce Unfried, and Tuula Heinonen. The manual includes a "day in the life of a child protection social worker" vignette, chapter highlights, teaching tips, reflection questions for small group and class discussion, and suggested exercises and assignments.

ACKNOWLEDGMENTS

Many people have contributed directly or indirectly to this book. Some have been our colleagues and students in the Faculty of Social Work, University of Manitoba, and those at the Universities of Tampere and Helsinki in Finland. Others are social work practitioners we have come to know through collaborative work. We would also like to acknowledge Bob Mullaly for his encouragement of this book project.

To Michael Hart we give special thanks for again collaborating with us to enhance this book and for framing Aboriginal concepts on helping for our readers.

Thank you to Anne Williams and Rod Banister, our acquisitions editors, and Glen Herbert and Sandra de Ruiter, our developmental editors at Nelson. For formatting and carefully reviewing the manuscript to correct grammar and enhancing its style, we thank Natalia Denesiuk, our senior production editor, and Kelli Howey, our copy editor.

It is important that any new book have good reviewers who can bring an instructor's perspective in reading each chapter. We were fortunate to have received constructive and useful suggestions from a number of reviewers, to whom we owe a debt of gratitude for the thoughtfulness and care evident in their reviews. We are very appreciative of the help and guidance that we received from our reviewers: Donna Bell-Rachmistruk at Keyano College, Keith Brownlee at Lakehead University, Michael Crawford at University College of the Cariboo, Anne Spilker at Malaspina University College, Karen Stewart at Sheridan College, and Janice Wiens at Yukon College. They provided many helpful suggestions and ideas.

We thank those colleagues who offered their ideas, suggestions, and criticisms to make the first and second editions of this textbook more responsive to instructors' and students' needs: Brenda Bacon, Esther Blum, Ann Charter, Lyn Ferguson, Kathy Jenson, Leonard Kaminski, Kathy Levine, Don Lugtig, Eveline Milliken, Grant Reid, Ranjan Roy, and Sharon Taylor-Henley. We also thank the many students from our classes and in other social work classes who gave us comments on the book.

Thank you to the Yarmeys for use of their computer and to Aiti for the space to spread out materials and write these chapter revisions. It is nice to know that there is always a place to work away from Winnipeg.

Tuula Heinonen

I would like to thank my wife, Marietta, for her diligent efforts and patience in editing and critiquing my writing and for excusing my many late nights. I would also like to apologize to my border collie, Heidi, who could not understand why we missed so many outings.

Len Spearman

ABOUT THE AUTHORS

Len Spearman and Tuula Heinonen are associate professors in the Faculty of Social Work, University of Manitoba. Both have played a major part in developing the social work practice curriculum, and together they wrote a distance education course manual that became the framework for this book. Most of their teaching is in the social work practice courses and with practicum students.

Dr. Heinonen's background is social work in health care, use of health care services, and international social development. Her current interests are women's health and experiences of immigrants in Canada. She has collaborated in health and social work–related projects in Finland and in social development research in the Philippines. Currently she co-directs a large social work training project in rural China. She has been active in both undergraduate and graduate curriculum development.

Dr. Spearman has practised in the field of mental health in both Canada and the United States. At the University of Manitoba, he has played a major part in designing the Bachelor of Social Work (BSW) curriculum and the northern off-campus and distance education programs. He chaired the BSW Curriculum Committee during most of the 1990s.

Michael Hart, guest author of Chapter 11, "An Aboriginal Approach to Social Work Practice," and a former colleague at the University of Manitoba, has had much experience teaching and working with Aboriginal and northern peoples in Manitoba. He has taught a variety of courses on Aboriginal peoples and social welfare policy, social work practice, and northern social work at the University of Manitoba's Faculty of Social Work in Thompson. He has also held positions in policy development, program management, and practice, primarily with organizations that provide services to Aboriginal peoples. Mr. Hart has conducted research and written articles and book chapters on sharing circles and Aboriginal approaches to social work.

chapter 1

Introduction

Chapter Goal

To set out key themes of the book and introduce the context for what follows.

This Chapter ▼

- presents a view of generalist social work practice at the undergraduate level of education
- distinguishes between and defines generalist and specialist social work practice
- describes each chapter in the book

WHAT IS SOCIAL WORK?

Social work is a profession that has two very broad and overlapping dimensions. On the one hand, social work is a helping profession: it focuses on helping people solve or prevent the occurrence of personal or social problems. Social work practice, on the other hand, also aims at social change. The foundation of professional practice is built on humanitarian and egalitarian ideals, the right to **social justice,** and the elimination of oppression and exploitation in society.

During the past 40 years or so, social work has developed and honed a process called *problem solving.* In its simplest form, problem solving means identifying a client's problems, understanding them, and then engaging with the client in a process to solve the identified problems. In practice, problem solving is a sophisticated means of helping that is based on a purposeful set of values and assumptions and a broad set of knowledge about human and social behaviour, the social environment, the connections between people and the environment, and methods of helping. The first nine chapters of this book address principles that are common to most social work. Chapter 8 describes the problem-solving process itself.

In recent years, ideas have emerged that challenge, critique, inform, extend, and enrich traditional problem solving. Many of these new ideas have strong Canadian roots and connections. We develop four approaches in this book that have important practice implications and extend social work beyond problem solving: the strengths, Aboriginal, structural, and feminist approaches.

We accept problem solving as a basis of social work but argue that we must also move beyond it. To understand this and to place this book about generalist social work in the context of current practice, we need to distinguish between generalist and specialized practice.

THE CONTEXT OF SOCIAL POLICY

Social work practice takes place in the context of social policies, often reflected through legislation. Most agencies, public and private alike, operate within the framework of social policies that refer to family, health, criminal justice, child welfare, mental health, and many more fields. Social workers need to understand and analyze (for some, policy analysis is a highly specialized form of practice) the social policies that are relevant to their practice. For example, a child welfare worker who is mandated to carry out child protection must be intimately aware of child and family social policy and legislation. The community health social worker can effectively counsel people with health problems only if the worker understands the social policies that drive the health care system.

The other part of the social work/social policy equation involves knowing how to facilitate social change. Promoting social change almost always involves influencing policy. To illustrate, obviously a social worker who works directly with clients has an obligation to provide them with quality service. Inevitably, the worker will encounter a policy or regulation that she or he views as a problem. The worker not only must have the ability to understand the problem and the related policy but also must begin to enable and mobilize resources to address the policy.

GENERALIST AND SPECIALIST SOCIAL WORK PRACTICE

In Canada *generalist* practice is associated with undergraduate social work education, while *specialist* social work is the primary domain of graduate work. The Canadian Association of Schools of Social Work *Board of Accreditation Manual* makes it clear that undergraduate social work must be general practice:

> Curriculum at the first university level will ensure that graduates will be broadly educated and prepared for general practice and have sufficient competence for an entry level social work position. Competence is evidenced by an ability to arrive at professional judgements and practice actions, based on integration of theory and practice within the context of professional values and the relevant social work code of ethics. (CASSW, 2003, Sec. SB 5.3)

The Canadian standard holds that "Curriculum at the second university level will prepare students to have sufficient competence for advanced, specialized or supervisory social work roles" (CASSW, 2003, Sec. SM 5.2). The "second university level" means an MSW.

In this book, we focus on generalist practice that is aimed at bachelor's and community college–level students who are beginning their studies in social work. Some examples or case situations may, however, draw on more specialized fields of practice, such as mental health, child welfare, health, and corrections.

What Is Generalist Practice?

Generalist practice underpins and is the foundation of social work and is part of all accredited Canadian entry-level social work programs. Yet the accreditation standards do not clearly define what constitutes generalist social work, but leave it up to each individual school of social work to determine the substance of practice within a set of guidelines. "The [individual] school shall have agreed upon core content with coherence, consistency and sequence within the curriculum" (CASSW, 2003, Sec. SB 5.6).

Theorists began to articulate generalist practice in the 1960s (e.g., Bartlett, 1970; Gordon, 1962). Early conceptions of a common base of practice were unclear and divergent. Nevertheless, North American universities began to offer degrees based on generalist practice.

Probably the most important characteristic of generalist social work is that while the concept refers to the ability to practise in a wide range of settings it also refers to incorporating and understanding a particular set of principles, values, and knowledge. Explication of generalist social work practice is a central theme of this book.[1] The core elements are outlined below. Some are central themes of specific chapters; all are discussed and illustrated throughout various sections of the book. Generalist social workers (not in order of importance)

1. work in a wide variety of fields and settings and intervene using a number of different roles (Chapter 4)
2. incorporate a common set of values and principles (Chapter 3)
3. strive to eliminate oppression

4. use assessment and intervention knowledge and skill that
   a. ranges from micro to macro (Chapters 4 and 8)
   b. includes but goes beyond problem solving (Chapters 9 to 13)
5. incorporate principles of cultural diversity and engage in culturally appropriate intervention (Chapter 7)
6. recognize that intervention depends upon a helping relationship between worker and client (Chapter 6)
7. have a wide practice knowledge base (Chapter 8)
8. practise in the context of social welfare policy and view influencing social welfare policy as a form of practice (Chapter 5)
9. work with people's abilities and capacities as opposed to deficits

What Is Specialized Practice?

Most specialized practice, as required by the accreditation standards of the CASSW (2003), is built upon the generalist base. Practice may be specialized according to the method of practice, the field of practice, the system size, the level of position held (usually distinguished by the degree of responsibility involved), or a combination of these features.

Specialization by method means that one's practice is essentially driven by the application of a set of specific helping techniques. During the first half of the 20th century there were three major methods, each of which involved a set of helping techniques (for example, see Perlman, 1957; Konopka, 1983). These were *casework* (one-to-one work with individuals and sometimes families), *group work,* and *community organization* (social work in communities and neighbourhoods). Nowadays, social workers generally do not identify themselves solely with these categories. New or different specializations by method have emerged, some of which include solution-focused therapy, mediation and conflict negotiation, community development, and others.

Fields of practice are the settings of social work—the areas within which practice takes place. Examples are child welfare, family services, health, corrections, mental health, social assistance (welfare), and addictions.

Another way to think of specialization is by system size. For example, some types of practice involve working with individuals, while others involve working with families and groups, and still others with organizations, neighbourhoods, and communities. In recent years the term *micro* social work practice has been used to refer to small systems that include individuals and usually families. *Macro* systems refer to large units, such as organizations, communities, and neighbourhoods. *Mezzo* practice is in between: working with small groups.

Finally, specialization may be according to the level of position held. Social workers may work in direct practice as line workers or, in some instances, as private practitioners. Some social workers are supervisors, while others are coordinators and administrators. These positions generally involve greater responsibility over staff and for organizations.

Most social workers, as their careers develop, specialize in one or a combination of the above areas. For example, a social worker may become a family therapist in child welfare; another may devote his or her career to using methods of community development to work with young people in transitional or core areas of cities.

Specialization is the product of considerable social work education and experience. Often it is a lifelong endeavour. Many social workers begin their careers as generalists, and most undergraduate social work education programs are designed to train generalist practitioners for career entry.

LOOKING AHEAD

Previously we connected principles of generalist practice to the content of this book. Keeping in mind the connection to generalist practice, we now present a chapter-by-chapter overview of what is to come.

This book will first describe traditional social work, which is primarily reflected in the problem-solving model of practice and its current emphasis on person-in-the-environment, systems, and ecological perspectives, and the older, but only recently articulated, strengths approach. The book stresses that building reciprocal helping relationships is at the core of the social work process. However, good practice must go beyond these traditional ideas. Newer approaches, partly shaped by the Canadian experience, not only make major contributions to social work practice but also critique and inform more traditional ideas. The newer approaches that we argue enrich generalist social work practice are Aboriginal, structural, and feminist approaches, in addition to anti-oppressive and cross-culturally appropriate practice.

Much of this book addresses practice with individuals and small groups. However, working with communities is also very important. In numerous places in the book we emphasize community development practice both through discussion and case examples.

In the past decade or so, social workers have understood that oppression is often a huge factor in explaining why people have difficulties. Oppression is frequently a factor in all kinds of problems ranging from abuse to criminal behaviour to mental health problems. Sometimes oppression is a causative factor in explaining difficulties. For example, the residential school system forced upon Aboriginal children in the first half of the 20th century has oppressed not only the children, but also their families. At other times people who have difficulties must deal with programs and systems that are oppressive; for example, a mental health system that demeans people. In a variety of chapters in this book we discuss anti-oppressive practice and show, through illustrations, how social workers can engage in anti-oppressive practice.

Also, recent social work writing has brought postmodern ideas to the profession, capturing the attention of scholars and practising social workers alike.[2] These ideas challenge established theories in social sciences—for example, ideas about how knowledge is shaped, created, and used (see Pease and Fook, 1999).

Modern practice did not just happen. Current practice cannot be fully comprehended unless it is understood in a historical context. A variety of events and social forces led to the development of modern social work. Chapter 2 summarizes many of these forces and describes the emergence of social work in Canada.

Chapters 3 through 9 present the basic principles and concepts in social work that are foundational to generalist practice. Chapters 10 to 14 extend practice beyond problem solving.

Chapter 3 sets out the ideology and values that are central to social work, influencing and giving perspective to practice. Social work is situated within the ideological context of helping that emerged primarily in the 20th century. Social work values, often expressed through codes of ethics, guide social workers; particularly important is the value of self-determination. The connection between values and culture in social work is also central in that culture shapes our values and beliefs. Resolving ethical dilemmas in social work is of primary importance in today's environment.

The nature of the social work profession and the roles that social workers take on are discussed in Chapter 4. Whether and how social work is a profession and how professionalization presents benefits and conflicts for social work are considered. In everyday practice, social work integrates a wide range of practice roles from micro to macro—individual to organization or community.

Chapter 5 explains the connection between social welfare policy and social work practice by using the health and mental health fields as illustrations. Social work roles in health and mental health are similar to those in other fields of practice; today, the changes in our health care system have in turn changed the emphasis on some roles over others.

Chapter 6 describes the nature of the social work relationship and the importance of building a partnership between worker and client based on trust, acceptance, respect, and the inherent right to self-determination. The professional relationship is seen as the core of the helping process. The difficulty of establishing helping relationships with people who do not want help is recognized, but the chapter argues that working with all people is an essential part of social work.

The importance of practice that is anti-oppressive has brought renewed attention to the need to critically reflect on our work, examine how oppression occurs at individual and societal levels, and ensure that we do not contribute to oppression but strive to counter it. Social workers, through their codes of ethics, aim to eliminate discrimination and inequality in society. Culturally appropriate and anti-oppressive practice is discussed in Chapter 7. Recognizing and responding to cultural diversity in ways that value and respect uniqueness is also a focus in Chapter 7. Culture offers social work a lens to look through, one that adds depth and breadth to practice.

The problem-solving process, detailed in Chapter 8, offers a rational, step-by-step way to help people solve problems. It is a person-in-the-environment approach—that is, it emphasizes the individual's relationship with the environment rather than, for example, concentrating on the inner psychological experiences of people or the social structure.

The theories and approaches that provide social work with its knowledge base are discussed in Chapter 9. Several forms of social work assessment are described and we suggest that assessment needs to be guided and focused by a broad base of knowledge that includes theory. Life experience, culture and tradition, observation, and testing also contribute different forms of knowledge for social work, and the ecosystems framework is useful in conceptualizing assessment.

The strengths approach presented in Chapter 10 focuses on people's resilience and capacity for dealing with problems in everyday life by drawing on their strengths, abilities, and internal and external resources. This approach stresses empowerment of the client as an important goal.

Chapter 11 presents Aboriginal perspectives on healing, helping, and social work. Culturally specific ways of dealing with human situations and problems have only begun to make inroads into social work. Although there are similarities between some social work models and Aboriginal approaches, there are also many differences. Recognizing the importance of the relationship between an individual and the natural and spiritual worlds is one major Aboriginal contribution to social work.

Structural social work uses ideas from socialism and critical theory to focus on the structures and institutions in society that oppress people. Through the structural approach, described in Chapter 12, we appreciate that people are not solely responsible for the difficulties encountered in their lives, and that the broader social environment plays a significant role.

Feminism has shed light on sexism in society, social policy, and the social work profession, offering alternative ways of understanding and practising that seek to eliminate the constraints of rigid social roles and expectations for both women and men. Chapter 13 explains how some of these ideas have been integrated by social work into various settings; however, feminist practice has been less well integrated into social work practice areas such as child welfare, income security, hospital-based health care, and so on. Although a core of common principles can be identified in feminist social work, there are numerous strands to feminism that reflect the realities of diverse groups of women, and not necessarily all in the same way.

Chapter 14 illustrates key components of the problem-solving process and the strengths, Aboriginal, structural, and feminist approaches, comparing the similarities and differences among them.

The Glossary at the end of this text defines all **boldface terms** that appear within the chapters.

NOTES

1 Most definitions of generalist practice are similar but with differences. We consider the definition in this chapter to be reflective of Canadian social work practice. For comparisons, refer to Johnson, 1995; McMahon, 1994; Compton and Galaway, 1999; and Kirst-Ashman and Hull, 1999.

2 During the past few years, a new, sometimes controversial perspective called **postmodernism** has begun to filter into social work. There are ongoing debates as to the usefulness of postmodernist ideas. For this book, we felt it was impossible to discuss the development of postmodernism in the depth it warrants. Instead, we refer to some ideas that stem from postmodernism, which will be defined as they are used. A number of recent works explain and delineate postmodernism as it relates (or does not relate) to social work: Sands and Nuccio, 1992; Chambon and Irving, 1994; Taylor-Gooby, 1994; Peile and McCouat, 1997; Smith and White, 1997; Pease and Fook, 1999; and Chambon, Irving, and Epstein, 1999.

and *settlement houses* were started (Daly, 1995; Lieby, 1978, pp. 71–89; Pumphrey and Pumphrey, 1961). There is no doubt that social work is the product of industrialization and urbanization.

The predecessors of social work in Canada emerged at the end of the 19th century, later than in both Britain and the United States, mainly because urbanization and industrialization occurred later in Canada. For example, the population of Toronto in 1834 was about 9,250 and in the 1880s to 1890s was only about 100,000, when London's population was about 4,000,000 and New York's about 1,500,000 (Irving, Parsons, and Bellamy, 1995, pp. 4–8). "Canada's economy was largely agricultural rather than industrial, and urban problems were not pressing in the 1880s and 1890s as they had been for more than a hundred years in Great Britain and had quickly become in the United States" (Irving, Parsons, and Bellamy, 1995, p. 8).

THE CHARITY AND SETTLEMENT HOUSE MOVEMENTS, 1850–1930

Social work has its roots in many sources, including, for example, the development of child welfare, the social gospel movement in Western Canada, and the cooperative movement in Nova Scotia led by Moses Coady (Bellamy and Irving, 1986). However, early social work was probably influenced most by two social movements that originated in the last half of the 19th century: the *charity movement,* epitomized by the Charity Organization Society, and the *settlement house movement* (Brieland, 1995, p. 2249; Camilleri, 1996; Daly, 1995; Ramsey, 1984). The two movements occurred during approximately the same time period, initiated first in England and then spreading to the United States and Canada. Both social movements were responses to industrialization and urbanization. While the ultimate goals of the early charity workers and the settlement house workers were similar, their view of the world and their approaches to helping were radically different.

The charity movement, based on religion and religious thought (Daly, 1995; Lieby, 1978, pp. 111–12; Wills, 1995), was the product of a belief that held that it is better to help (treat) people with problems than to banish, punish, or ostracize them. (See Chapter 3, which explains how much of social work ideology is bound to an ideology of helping.) The movement's supporters assumed that the new industrial system was fundamentally sound and that their task was to help disadvantaged people adjust to or cope with their surroundings. *Casework* can trace its direct heritage to the charity movement.

Others viewed the industrial system as badly flawed. These were settlement workers and other reformers who saw such problems as poverty, poor working conditions, and unhealthy living environments in industrial parts of cities as products of the capitalistic industrial system. These reformers and social activists generated and promoted new ideas, such as workers' compensation, unions, social insurance, and public and universal health insurance. Some settlement workers also saw an immense need for a variety of social, health, and recreational services in slum areas of large cities. Many settlements organized or provided services to meet such needs. Much of group work, community development, and community organization can trace its beginnings to the settlements. As we will discuss later, the methods of casework, group work, and community organization subsequently became known as methods of social work.

The Charity Workers

The first Charity Organization Society (COS) was established in Britain in 1869. A leading spokesperson for the charity movement was Thomas Chalmers, a Scottish minister who is credited with leading the charity movement toward the goal of providing aid, based on strict religious principles, to people in distress. The first North American COS opened in Buffalo, New York, in 1877. The Toronto COS opened in 1888 (Kidneigh, 1965; Lieby, 1978, pp. 111–16; Wills, 1995). The society expanded rapidly, with 92 cities in North America reporting a COS by 1892. In the early 1900s, the numbers would have been in the hundreds. Through a process that unfolded during the first half of the 20th century, which included a name and function change, the COS evolved into the modern family service agencies that continue to thrive in Canada and the United States. In 1965, for example, there were more than 300 such agencies in North America (Kidneigh, 1965, p. 5), and many Canadian cities today have an agency.

At first the charity workers—almost always women, and from the middle and upper classes—were volunteers called "friendly visitors." Wills (1995) writes, "The COS was notorious for its rigid moralistic stand, which rested on a firm belief that poverty was the hallmark of a sinful life and its relief a matter of Christian uplift" (p. 14). Charity was provided on the basis of moral character. People in need were more likely to get friendly advice from the COS than any kind of tangible aid such as goods or cash. The COS organized or coordinated relief but generally did not provide direct relief services (Brieland, 1995, p. 2247; Carniol, 1995, p. 24).

Later, while still called friendly visitors, these volunteer workers became paid staff, albeit poorly paid. These workers were the first to suggest that the key to personal helping was the interpersonal relationship formed between helper (usually a friendly visitor) and person in need. The friendly visitors also firmly believed that sound assessment would lead to good advice. As a result, they began to articulate a process of helping (Lieby, 1978, pp. 116–23; Pumphrey and Pumphrey, 1961, pp. 341–43).

By 1910 many were calling the friendly visitors *caseworkers.* They were beginning to be viewed as professionals, and some were taking leadership roles in society. Probably the most notable from a social work point of view was Mary Richmond. A caseworker at the Baltimore COS, Richmond was the first person to attempt to formulate a theoretical base for social work. In 1917 she published her famous and highly influential book, *Social Diagnosis.*

In her book, Richmond outlined a process for social work practice that has had considerable influence on the profession. According to Richmond, the process of casework is study, diagnosis, and treatment, with the concept of helping—treatment—at its centre. But the process she outlined is the same as that used in medicine. Diagnosis implies that after examination (study), a person's problem can be diagnosed just like a disease, and the treatment that follows must be based on the diagnosis. Thus, Richmond's process was a medical model. This simply stated process set the **theoretical framework** for all casework for the next half-century. It finally evolved, another half-century later, to the social work problem-solving process that is still in widespread use today (see Chapter 8). Richmond's work also articulated and shaped two cornerstones of current social work practice: first, that intervention depends on an assessment process (which Richmond called diagnosis), and second, that the key to social work intervention (treatment) is the relationship between client and worker.

In 1928, J. H. T. Falk, then General Secretary, Council of Social Agencies in Montreal and in 1918 the first director of the McGill University social work program (Wills, 1995, p. 20), presented a paper at the First International Conference of Social Work held in Paris. In his paper, Falk clearly, but almost apologetically, connected Canadian social work with the charity movement and then distanced social work from the charity view that social ills are the responsibility of the individual. He wrote that social workers in Canada

> would be frank to admit that they have inherited from past generations ideas and practices which are part of the programme of charities established in the nineteenth century, and which at the best are well-meant attempts to relieve want and suffering prompted by the sympathy and conscience of the well-to-do. (p. 28)

He then defined social work as follows:

> Social work therefore concerns itself in the main with the prevention and cure of diseases physical and mental, the prevention and cure of poverty, and the prevention and cure of delinquency; for any of these conditions implies maladjustment to society for which social and economic factors are often responsible. (p. 28)

Falk's definition on the one hand is a clear reflection of Richmond's concept of social diagnosis and the medical model. He even seemed to view poverty and delinquency as things to be cured like a disease. But, importantly, he also saw social and economic factors as often responsible for problems that people face; unlike the charity view that people's deficits are responsible for their problems, Falk saw as important—and even emphasized—social and environmental factors.

The impact of the charity movement on social work was enormous. The concept and process of the professional delivery of personal helping were becoming rooted in society. People began to believe that poor people had the right to a minimum acceptable standard of living. While poverty continued to be viewed as a moral issue, it was felt that help in the form of relief and guidance could be offered based on an assessment of worthiness. If the poor person passed this kind of "morality means test," then relief would be given. More important to the emergence of social work, the advice and guidance provided by caseworkers of the time were early forms of counselling.

...ed to the development of social work was the settlement house movement that began in the late 1800s. Much of this movement was very critical of the charity movement and the COS. Settlement house workers saw the charities as a form of social control. Giving people charity and advice only perpetuated poverty and the ghetto structure of industrial urban centres where most immigrants lived. They offered people no real way out of their plight. What was needed, it was argued, were reforms and services that would help poor people shake the bonds of poverty and industrialization so that they could enjoy a better quality of life. In Canada and the United States, the settlements focused much of their work on immigrant populations.

The Early Settlement House Worker

Some of the early settlement house workers were activists and service providers. Others tried to understand and study the nature of the slums, poverty, and the effects of industrialization. Often the latter were university students and professors, intellectuals, and union and political leaders, frequently socialists (Camilleri, 1996, p. 33). Some settlement houses, like University Settlement in Toronto and Chicago Commons in Chicago, became closely connected with leading universities and were influential in establishing major social policies (Irving, Parsons, and Bellamy, 1995). The settlement that probably had the most political and social policy influence was Toynbee Hall in London (Barnett, 1950; Camilleri, 1996, p. 33).

Many of the early workers were women, and some were the daughters and wives of industrialists. Historical literature clearly shows these women as idealists (Addams, 1910, 1930; Chambers, 1986). However, they were more than that. They were highly skilled, often well-educated, competent people in their own right who had limited avenues for using their talents. These women found an important niche in the settlements. They decided to do something about the plight of the poor; ironically, this poverty was often a result of the low wages paid by companies owned by some of the women's own families (Addams, 1910, 1930; Barnett, 1950; Chambers, 1963). Many found satisfaction in their work because it challenged their skills and because they observed real progress as the conditions experienced by immigrants did improve (Irving, Parsons, and Bellamy, 1995, pp. 211–12).[2]

The word "settlement" means to settle in, as in settling into a new home. The settlements were houses in the slums in which many of the workers lived. Imagine living 24 hours a day, 7 days a week in the inner-city social agency in which you work—that is exactly what the settlement workers did!

The settlements had two general functions. Some settlement houses had strong reform agendas and were heavily involved in social and political action. In Canada this was less true than in Britain and the United States (Irving, Parsons, and Bellamy, 1995).[3] Their second function was to provide services to people who lived in the poor areas of cities. These services varied greatly according to such factors as demographics, community needs, and available resources.

The Reformers

Consider a teeming slum in the late 1800s and early 1900s. The streets were grimy. Pollution from industrial smokestacks darkened the sky at noon on otherwise bright, sunny days. Men, women, and children worked in the factories for wages that perpetuated their poverty. In Britain, the low-paid factory workers were members of the lower class. In North America many, if not most, were immigrants, often of Irish or Eastern European background. Many immigrants had difficulty with the English language, and there were few schools where they could learn it. Few kindergartens existed to enable immigrant children who did not understand much English to begin to attend school.

There were few social services that these people could turn to for help. Adequate medical care was generally not available, let alone health insurance. If a person was injured on the job, it was unfortunate; workers' compensation programs were not yet in place. In most jurisdictions, if a child committed a crime he or she was treated by the justice system as an adult. There were no unions to protect workers. In short, there was no **social safety net.** In North America, particularly the United States, the settlement house workers contributed greatly to reforms that led to the establishment of kindergartens, social insurance, public health insurance, workers' compensation, labour unions, juvenile courts, and more (Addams, 1910, 1930; Chambers, 1963; Daly, 1995; Lieby, 1978, pp. 127–35). In this role, the settlement workers were social reformers.

Probably the two most famous and most reform-minded settlement houses were Toynbee Hall (the first settlement, opened in 1884 by Samuel and Henrietta Barnett) in London, England, and Hull House (opened by Jane Addams in 1889) in Chicago. Most major Canadian cities had at least one settlement house (Valverade, 1991). The first in Canada was Evangelia in Toronto, which opened in 1902. However, the movement did not really become established in Canada until a series of events in Toronto between 1910 and 1912, including rapid growth and industrialization, led to the development of several settlements (Irving, Parsons, and Bellamy, 1995, pp. 26–33).

The early settlement workers recognized that the root of many of the problems facing people in urban areas was social conditions. The causes, in their view, were not due to personal defects, as the charity organizations assumed, but to the economic and social structure of the industrial and capitalist systems (Addams, 1910, 1930; Barnett, 1950; Chambers, 1963; Daly, 1995).

The truly activist characteristics of most of the settlements waned with the First World War.

The Service Providers

In both Canada and the United States, many settlement house workers provided services, mainly to immigrants. Some of the workers who performed these functions became known as *group workers,* while others were called *community organizers* and *community developers.*

Providing services accounted for most of the settlements' functions. According to Irving, Parsons, and Bellamy (1995) this was the primary role of Canadian settlements from the beginning, although many individual workers were socially and politically active. Often they acted as advisers or consultants to help people in the neighbourhood address a social injus tice or some other issue. Settlement workers are credited with starting kindergartens in mar urban centres.

Group workers would often use a task as the backdrop to accomplish an important g For instance, they might start a sewing group for a few immigrant women with the real of helping them learn English. Community organizers from Toronto settlements sta..ed, among other services, a well baby clinic in 1914, a library for local immigrants, ice rinks, and hundreds of other such community projects, all designed to improve the lives of disadvantaged people (Irving, Parsons, and Bellamy, 1995, p. 80).

Irving, Parsons, and Bellamy (1995) also report that during the Great Depression the settlements in Toronto, while still neighbourhood-oriented, tended to focus on providing relief in kind (food, clothing, and other goods) rather than in cash. "During the 1930s the Toronto settlements ... did not initiate or participate in much political action directed at changing the inadequate relief structure" (p. 126). During the Second World War, many services were directed to people who were affected by the war. By 1960 there was still another change, and the settlement as originally conceived was gone forever. Most of the remaining settlements in Canada and the United States became neighbourhood or community centres (some complete with swimming pools and gyms) where people in inner cities could meet their neighbours and spend leisure time with others.

THE SOCIAL GOSPEL MOVEMENT AND J. S. WOODSWORTH, SOCIAL WORKER AND SOCIAL WORK EDUCATOR

The Canadian settlements were different from those of the United States in other respects. First, they started later—largely because industrialization and urbanization also occurred later in Canada.

Unlike their U.S. counterparts, the Canadian settlements had strong ties to the Protestant churches. Irving, Parsons, and Bellamy (1995) go so far as to use the word "dominate" to describe the influence of the churches over the development of social services in Canada, and write that "the social gospel was behind much of the social reform of the time" (p. 36). For example, J. S. Woodsworth—a powerful social reformer and Methodist minister—in 1907 became superintendent of All Peoples Mission, a settlement in the north end of Winnipeg (Ziegler,[4] 1934, p. 37) and was a major leader in the social gospel movement (Irving, Parsons, and Bellamy, 1995, p. 36).

The social gospel movement—with strong roots in the Prairie provinces but a force throughout Canada—was a social reform movement built on Protestant religious thinking and a form of Christian socialism. The movement began in England in the mid- to late-nineteenth century, and viewed the problems of society "as the result of flaws in the institutions of society" (Bellamy and Irving, 1986, p. 33; Wills, 1995).

Unlike the British experience, "the Canadian movement developed a radicalism through exposure to Western populism and industrial unionism" (Wills, 1995, p. 17). The social gospel movement influenced the settlement workers. For example, All Peoples Mission in Winnipeg, with J. S. Woodsworth as superintendent, supported the ideology of the social gospel movement (MacInnis, 1953; Ziegler, 1934). Woodsworth was also influenced by other settlements and received much of his education about the poor while visiting missions and settlements in London and the United States in 1899. "His appointment as superintendent of the All Peoples Mission in Winnipeg enabled him to develop institutes, settlements, clubs and hospital-visiting and relief programs" (Bellamy and Irving, 1986, p. 34).

Woodsworth, an important political leader in the social gospel movement, was a primary force behind the establishment of the Co-operative Commonwealth Federation (CCF) in 1933, the forerunner of the New Democratic Party (NDP) of Canada. First elected to Parliament in 1921, he held his seat for 21 years until his death. He is credited with many ideas that later formed the basic foundation of Canadian social policy, health care, and the social safety net. Woodsworth was instrumental in the "implementation of many reforms championed by the CCF and adopted by the Liberal government of Prime Minister Mackenzie King. These included old age pensions, health care benefits, unemployment measures, and a great many environmental programs that were intended to humanize modern society" (Bellamy and Irving, 1986, p. 34).

Before his political career began, Woodsworth was a social worker and social work educator. Mann (1968), in a short monograph, reports that in 1914—the same year that the University of Toronto initiated its Department of Social Services (Yelaja, 1985, p. 18)—one of the first training programs for social workers in Canada started in Winnipeg under the aegis of the Canadian Social Welfare League, a social research organization that Woodsworth founded and served in as secretary (Bellamy and Irving, 1986, p. 34; MacInnis, 1953, p. 90; Ziegler, 1934, p. 62). Woodsworth was the director of the training program as well as a committed social activist and a strong supporter of social welfare services (MacInnis, 1953, pp. 85–95; Ziegler, 1934, pp. 27–77).

The Winnipeg social work training program continued for two years. Woodsworth gave a number of the lectures. Interestingly, Falk, quoted earlier in this chapter, also gave several lectures. This was a very early training program and probably one of the first that used the term "social work" to describe social service, welfare, and charity work. Exhibit 2.1 shows the reproduction of a brochure that describes the curriculum of the training program,[5] almost certainly under the authority of the University of Manitoba,[6] that was given in 1915, the second year of the program. The brochure gives a sense of social work in at least one Canadian centre in 1915. The training program dates from before professional social work is generally considered to have been well established.

The social work training program is illuminating for a number of other reasons. Woodsworth, a major political figure in the establishment of Canadian social policy, clearly saw social work as important and was an early social work educator. His use of the term "social work" to describe the course of studies was unusual in that the term was really not widespread until the 1920s and 1930s. Also somewhat surprising for the time period, the description repeatedly uses "social work" to describe a professional activity.

The curriculum reflected a balance between charity work and reforms. While we have no solid information on the content of the courses, probably what is most important is that the curriculum covered the range of casework and work in charities, to social reform, to social and economic policy, to community organization. It is not a big leap to conclude that this range probably reflected Woodsworth's conception of social work, the views of the Social Welfare League, and social workers in the various community agencies that sponsored the program. Certainly it would have been influenced by the social gospel movement.

Exhibit 2.1 ▼ Winnipeg Training Class in Social Work

SECOND SUMMER SESSION, 1915

In view of the success of the Training Class last year the University authorities have authorized the holding of a session this summer.

The course is designed to help (a) those already professionally engaged in social work; (b) volunteer social workers, members of Boards of Charitable Institutions and Associations, and church workers; (c) University graduates or senior students looking to further study in special service.

Special attention will be given to the needs of out-of-town students.

The course is divided into three Institutes of two weeks each: (1) Community problems; (2) Modern Philanthropy; (3) Neighborhood workers.

Arrangements are made to visit the institutions described in the classes and others of special importance to social workers.

Instruction in Playground Supervision may be substituted for visits of inspection and group discussions.

DATE—July 5th to Aug. 13th.
HOURS—10 to 12 noon—Visits of inspection, and group discussion held in Board Room, Industrial Bureau.
5 to 6 p.m.—Lectures held in University.
8 to 9 p.m.—Lectures held in University.
FEES—$5.00 for course; $2.00 for one Institute.
LIBRARY—A specially selected library will be arranged for.
EXAMINATIONS—In lieu of, an essay will be expected on one subject in each Institute.
CERTIFICATE—At the conclusion of the course any student may obtain a certificate stating the work covered and an estimate of his fitness for Social Work.
REGISTRATION—Should be made at once to the office of the Secretary, Miss Elinor Mitchell, Room 10, Industrial Bureau, Winnipeg, Phone Main 6091.

I. Institute on Community Problems.

JULY 5–16

A Statement and Interpretation of Modern Social Developments—*J. S. Woodsworth*

July 5th 5 p.m. —The New Era.
" 6th " —Modern Industry.
" 7th " —The Twentieth Century City.
" 8th " —The Rural Problem.
" 9th " —Social Reconstruction.

Special Problems—

July 12th 5 p.m.—Municipal Ownership *A. W. Puttee.*
" 13th " —Unemployment—*J. H. T. Falk.*
" 14th " —Recreation—*H. R. Hadcock.*
" 15th " —Town Planning—*Prof. Stoughton.*
" 16th " —The School and the Community.

July 5th 8 p.m. —Education—*Pres. Maclean.*
" 6th " —Organized Labor—*Alderman Rigg.*
" 7th " —Agriculture as a Solution of the Unemployment Problem *Mayor Waugh.*
" 8th " —The Health of the Community *R. T. Riley.*
" 9th " —The Relation of Economic Problems to Health and Disease *Dr. H. P. H. Galloway.*
" 12th " —Recent Tendencies in City Government—*Theo. Hunt.*
" 13th " —Municipal Finance —*Theo. Hunt.*
" 14th " —Housing—*William Pearson.*
" 15th " —Public Services *Controller Cockburn.*
" 16th " —Charities Endorsement *N. T. McMillan.*

Remarkably, many undergraduate social workers in Canada today are educated in universities and community colleges covering the same breadth of material as in this early training program. These social workers are now usually called generalist social workers.

Many of the issues and titles covered bear an uncanny resemblance to twenty-first-century issues (and modern curricula): unemployment, underemployment, immigrant issues, feminism, organized labour, health, volunteer work, and delinquency, to name a few. On the flip side, topics like unmarried mothers, the inefficient, and the backward child would raise many red flags in today's schools of social work. Most modern university-based social work programs also do not emphasize the role of the church in social work.

Finally, note the emphasis on the problems of immigrants. Much of early Canadian social work focused on immigrant populations and, based on the titles of some of the lectures, attempted to assimilate them into Canadian society. This, of course, is contrary to today's Canadian policy. (Chapter 7 explores these ideas further.)

II. Institute on Modern Philanthropy.

JULY 19–30

Organized Charity—

July 19th 5 p.m.—History of Organized Charity—*J. H.T. Falk*

" 20th " —Technique of Family Investigation—*G. B. Clarke.*

" 21st " —Special Cases—The Unemployed; The Underemployed; The Inefficient; The Delinquent *G. B. Clarke.*

" 22nd " —Special Cases—The Sick; Widows; The Deserted; The Unmarried Mother *G. B. Clarke.*

" 23rd " —The Volunteer in Social Work *Rev. G. H. Broughall.*

" 26th " —The Homeless Transient *Roy Austin.*

" 27th " —Social Resources—*J. H. T. Falk.*

" 28th " —Hospital Social Service *Miss Inga Johnston.*

" 29th " —Laws Affecting Social Workers *J. H. T. Falk.*

" 30th " —Standards of Living and Labor *J. S. Woodsworth.*

The Promise of Politics

—Prof. Harold Laski, McGill University.

July 19th 8 p.m.—Methods of Politics.

" 20th " —Materials of Politics.

" 21st " —Orthodox Sins and Heretic Dangers.

" 22nd " —The Necessity of Transformation.

" 23rd " —The Promise of Feminism.

" 26th " —The Promise of Labor.

" 27th " —The Meaning of Industry.

" 28th " —The Reconstruction of Party.

" 29th " —The Organization of Education.

" 30th " —The Will to Succeed.

III. Institute for Neighborhood Workers.

AUGUST 2–13

Special Problems—

Aug. 2nd 5 p.m.—Problems in Connection with Boys' Club Work—*W. Finnegan.*

" 3rd " —How to Help Working Girls *Miss M. Tweedie.*

" 4th " —Instruction in Sex Hygiene *Dr. J. Halpenny.*

" 5th " —Causes of Juvenile Delinquency *Rev. H. Atkinson.*

" 6th " —The Backward Child *Miss M. H. Kelly.*

The Church and the Community—

Aug. 9th 5 p.m. —The Church and Changing Conditions— *J. S. Woodsworth.*

" 10th " —The Development of a Community Conscience *Dr. A. G. Sinclair.*

" 11th " —A Constructive Programme for the Local Church *Dr. A. G. Sinclair.*

" 12th " —Organization and Training of Christian Forces *J. S. Woodsworth.*

" 13th " —The Rural Church *J. S. Woodsworth.*

Immigration Problems—*J. S. Woodsworth.*

Aug. 2nd 8 p.m.—The Immigrant.

" 3rd " —Maintaining Canadian Standards.

" 4th " —Conserving Immigrant Resources.

" 5th " —Forces Canadianizing the Immigrant.

" 6th " —Elements of a Constructive Policy.

Immigrant Groups—

Aug. 9th 8 p.m. —The Slavic Peoples *Rev. A. O. Rose.*

" 10th " —The Poles—*Louis Kon.*

" 11th " —The Hebrews—*E. A. Cohen.*

" 12th " —The Ruthenians *P. H. Wojcenko.*

" 13th " —The Russians *Joseph A. Cherniack.*

This type of information is important to us as social workers almost a century later: our past helps us to understand and appreciate our current knowledge and practices, and shows us how "everything that changes remains the same."

THE DEVELOPMENT OF PROFESSIONAL SOCIAL WORK, 1925–2005

It is clear that early social work was strongly influenced by religious values and theology. This was true of the charity, settlement, and social gospel movements. There is no doubt that current values in social work are influenced by these pioneer movements (Wills, 1995).

By 1920, many methods of practice existed. There were group workers and community organizers, who tended to come from the settlement movement, and caseworkers, who came from the COS. And each of these methods was even further specialized. For example, there were, among others, medical caseworkers, public welfare workers, psychiatric caseworkers, corrections workers, and child welfare workers. Each branch tended to be an entity in and of itself, and there was no professional body for people who called themselves social workers. Many of these specialists had their own professional associations and were not yet organized as a social work profession. Falk (1928) adds another dimension to this fragmentation, suggesting that in 1928 the practice of social work in Canada varied greatly from province to province: "As to the methods [of social work] in vogue, they differ so greatly in different Provinces that any attempt to generalize is impossible" (p. 28).

By the mid-1920s, however, some began to argue that there were common threads between the various specialties, using such phrases as "a common base" or "generic social work."

In 1926, the Canadian Association of Social Workers (CASW), a federation of provincial associations, was established (Graham, Swift, and Delaney, 2000). The CASW, through its provincial branches, remains the primary professional social work organization in Canada. From the 1930s to the mid-1960s, Canadian social work was strongly influenced by its American counterpart, the National Association of Social Workers (NASW). The first Canadian university-based social work program began in 1914 at the University of Toronto, 11 years after the first American programs (Chandler, 1986, p. 335; Graham, Swift, and Delaney, 2000, p. 29). In 1918, McGill University in Montreal followed suit. But it was not until 1947 that the University of Toronto graduated the first master's-level student in Canada (Yelaja, 1985, p. 18). In comparison, the United States had developed many graduate programs in the 1920s (Brieland, 1995, p. 2249), and in 1939 the accrediting body of the time decided to accredit only university-based, master's-level programs (Frumkin and Lloyd, 1995, p. 2239).

Until the late 1940s and early 1950s, although social work training programs were offered in Canada, students often had to attend an American university for professional education and certainly for advanced training. In fact, the lack of training in Canada was so acute that in 1960 the CASW requested that the federal government grant special funding to universities so that more students could enroll in social work programs (Akman, 1972, quoted in Yelaja, 1985, p. 18).

As social work began to mature, the fledging profession became closely connected with the social sciences (Lieby, 1978; Pumphrey and Pumphrey, 1961). Canadian social work was influenced by several, sometimes divergent, disciplines. One of the most important was the theory from psychology and psychiatry, most notably **Freudian** and **neo-Freudian** theory. For nearly half a century, beginning in the 1920s, Freudian and neo-Freudian theory greatly influenced much of social work practice and education (Johnson, McClelland, and Austin, 2000; Leighninger, 1987).

Both Canadian and American social work were also influenced by interactional theories that focused on the environment. In Chapter 9 we discuss two of these: role theory and labelling theory. However, Canadian social work, unlike mainstream American practice, was also influenced by British socialism, which developed the intellectual foundations of the welfare state (Wills, 1995, pp. 19–20). The roots of this influence can be traced to the London School of Economics and Toynbee Hall (Barnett, 1950; Wills, 1995).

By the 1950s the emphasis of practice on the inner person was waning. In 1957 Helen Perlman published her seminal book *Social Casework: A Problem Solving Process*, which tied casework practice to role theory and, although within the context of ego psychology, shifted practice emphasis toward the environment. In the late 1950s the NASW established a commission to re-examine a common base of practice. This commission became the starting point for the important contributions of Bartlett (1961, 1970) and Gordon (1962, 1969). They began to lay the framework for a theoretical, common foundation in social work based on the interaction of a person with the environment. Others, including Meyer (1983, 1988) and Germain and Gitterman (1980, 1995), later articulated an ecosystems view of social work that some argue should be the common base of all social work (see Chapter 9).

The Generalist Emerges in Canada

By 1960, master's-level social work education was common in Canada. However, most of the Canadian schools were accredited by the American-based Council on Social Work Education (CSWE). Canadian social work education mirrored its American counterpart.

Several events of the 1960s and 1970s dramatically changed Canadian professional social work. During the 1960s, Canadian universities were in a period of rapid expansion, prompting some to look seriously at the long-standing contradiction of how a professional graduate program (Master of Social Work) could be offered as a beginning degree. Further, many in the 1960s viewed the content of some MSW programs to actually be of an undergraduate calibre. For instance, even though an MSW was offered at the University of Manitoba, it was part of the Faculty of Arts and not the Graduate Faculty.

Most MSW degree programs specialized in one or any combination of casework, group work, and community organization methods. Many believed that this distinction did not reflect the reality of social work practice. Educators and practitioners agreed that many workers actually practised in all three areas. Also, there was a shortage of university-educated social workers in Canada. Canadian social workers and educators viewed all of these problems seriously enough to change the conception of practice and chart a course that led to a different social work educational system than that of the United States.

By the early 1970s, many Canadian universities with social work programs had established a three- or four-year Bachelor of Social Work (BSW) degree as the first professional degree. Some of these universities then established a graduate-level MSW degree based on the undergraduate BSW. (A few, including the University of Toronto and Wilfrid Laurier University in Waterloo, Ontario, retained the MSW as a graduate degree without a BSW.) This was a marked departure from the American educational system. At the time, the accrediting process of the American-based CSWE did not accommodate a professional BSW and a one-year MSW. Also, the development of the BSW meant that Canadian schools needed a new curriculum. As a result, the Canadian Association of Schools of Social Work (CASSW) was established in 1967 with the goal of setting curriculum standards and accreditation processes for the new BSW and MSW programs as well as the existing two-year MSW programs. The accreditation process, under the aegis of the CASSW, was in place by the early 1970s (Yelaja, 1985, p. 19), with several schools admitting BSW students as early as the mid- and late 1960s. Yelaja reports that in 1969, 460 MSW students graduated from Canadian universities; in 1972, a total of 1,058 BSW and MSW students graduated (1985, p. 18). The new BSW programs accounted for nearly all of this increase.

As the BSW in Canada grew, social work programs in community colleges also gained strength. Some community college programs have a full social work curriculum with a generalist orientation. Graduates of these programs usually earn a diploma and work in many fields of social work practice including health, mental health, child and family services, and corrections. Other community college programs offer a certificate or diploma in a specific field of practice, often child and family services. These programs tend to be specialized but most offer a number of social work–related courses.

University-based BSW programs normally require, according to accreditation standards of the CASSW (Canadian Association of Schools of Social Work, Standards of Accreditation), that between 40 and 50 percent of their courses be in the liberal arts, humanities, and social sciences. The strong rationale for this is that social workers need to be broadly educated professionals. Often this is referred to as professional education with a liberal arts base. On the other hand, "There is a sense that college courses tend to be more closely linked [than university-based BSW degrees] to meeting labour market demands" (Canadian Association of Schools of Social Work, 2001, p. 3). Generally, community college programs emphasize skill development, often in a specialized area such as child and family services. In recent years, these programs have formed linkages or partnerships with universities so that college graduates can transfer a considerable portion of their credits to a university-based BSW degree program.

At the university level, the pattern of BSW education followed by graduate-level MSW education is now the norm in Canada and has flourished and grown since the late 1960s. The development of an MSW graduate degree based on a professional undergraduate BSW led to a major change in the conceptualization of social work itself. Before 1970, most social workers were trained in a particular method. Many of the new undergraduate programs did not use a methods-based curriculum. Instead, these universities offered a BSW generalist degree (Wharf, 1992, p. 31). The MSW, building on the professional undergraduate degree, then offered specialized studies, but not necessarily by method. Part of this decision to develop a generalist undergraduate degree was based on the principle, often expressed as a belief, that social work has a common base. Second, and importantly, many in the professional community argued that social workers of the 1960s and 1970s needed to be able to practise using multiple methods and across a variety of fields (e.g., child welfare, corrections, health). This posed a problem because there was no agreed-upon common base or a clear way to articulate generalist practice.

A number of Canadian schools elected to conceptualize generalist practice based on work in systems and ecology begun by Gordon and Bartlett but used in some new textbooks (for example, Meyer, 1970; Pincus and Minahan, 1973; Germain and Gitterman, 1980) that integrated the various methods and saw people as being very closely connected with the environment (see Chapter 9). While in retrospect these first attempts at conceptualizing generalist social work practice were in many respects flawed,[7] they did offer an important framework for initiating generalist practice in Canada.

Until the mid-1980s, social work theory used in Canada was mostly imported from the United States, but Canadians are now making major contributions to practice theory, particularly to the development of three emerging perspectives of social work. These are the Aboriginal (Chapter 11), structural (Chapter 12), and feminist (Chapter 13) approaches, which not only take us beyond traditional problem solving but also are well suited to Canadian practice.

Employment Opportunities

The first social workers in the late 19th and early 20th century were mostly volunteers. These included the early settlement workers and the friendly visitors. As society became more industrialized and urbanized, social workers increasingly took over helping functions that were formerly the domain of informal **institutions** such as the family or more formal structures such as churches. Because of the serious social problems caused first by the Great Depression of the 1930s and later the Second World War, the need for social workers increased dramatically. As need increased, social workers became employed in more and more settings. At first this was mostly charity work, which during the Depression became public (government-financed) welfare. Social workers found jobs in health and mental health settings. (See Chapter 5 for a brief history of social work in health.) Many of the early workers concentrated their services in child welfare. This work was particularly important during the Depression. Workers were employed in prisons and the justice system, public schools, centres for the elderly and disabled, and a number of other areas. Historically, social work services have been concentrated in different fields in different eras.

By the end of the 1940s most social workers were paid for their services. As emphasized in Chapter 5, the professionalization that was in its infancy in the 1920s was beginning to mature. Today almost all social workers are paid employees.

The Future

The future is always difficult to predict. However, in the late 1990s a partnership of major Canadian social work associations and Human Resources Development Canada initiated what came to be known as the *Social Work Sector Study* (Canadian Association of Schools of Social Work, 2001). This large and comprehensive study examined the "state" of social work in Canada and attempted the difficult task of developing a Canada-wide human resources strategy. Some of the study's major findings are cited below.

> Future employment growth in the social services sector will continue to be a balancing act between societal needs and public policies as to how best to meet those needs. High growth of the geriatric population will require extensive, innovative social services programming. The rapidly growing Aboriginal population, with its significant needs and commitment to developing appropriate service delivery models, will account for even higher demand for social services. In some provinces, new areas of service need are emerging from the significant

> immigrant and/or visible minority populations. Policies to support social services are expected to be somewhat more expansive, but also to continue to emphasize cost-contained community based responses. The sector is expected to show overall employment growth that at least matches the overall Canadian population growth rate. Within social services, the occupations that are expected to be higher than the overall population growth rate are social workers (usually defined as having a BSW) and—even more so—specialists in a range of counseling services. (p. 2)

Social work will continue to be needed in Canada, as is clear from the Sector Study; however, the fields of employment and mandate for service provision are subject not only to the needs in society, but also to the response by governments and other organizations in meeting perceived needs. In sum, the study concludes

> All in all, the social services sector is a vibrant, dynamic field, occupied by dedicated individuals and organizations. Employment opportunities are good, but employment conditions are increasingly taxing and professional recognition is less robust than it has been. The societal support of the field is weakening, as a part of the weakening of societal commitment to support the most vulnerable in society. The link between labour market demand and the supply side as related to educational preparation of future workers is seen as not being as strong as it should be to sustain and even increase the sector's viability. The need for the profession to clarify its identity, its goals and objectives is evident. In doing so, it will enable the sector to meet changes from a position of well-founded, well-documented strength. This sector study should provide an important foundation for the strategies the sector will develop to meet the changes to come. (p. 3)

Two studies (Spearman, 2004; Westhues, 2004) have examined employment of social workers from another angle. Both are longitudinal studies, one in Ontario and one in Manitoba, that show the number of graduates of social work programs who are employed. The Ontario study (Westhues, 2004) tracked MSW graduates of Wilfrid Laurier University for each of the years 2000 to 2002. The Manitoba study (Spearman, 2004) traced the employment status of BSW and MSW graduates from the University of Manitoba for the years 1990 to 2000. Both studies, using different methodology, concluded that 95 percent of MSW graduates found a job in a social work or related position. The Manitoba study found that the BSW employment rate was approximately 92 percent. In both studies there was very little variation between years, even though the Manitoba research was carried out over an 11-year span that included four or five years of an economic downturn.

In short, we conclude that it is likely social workers will continue to find employment, but as shown in the historical past and as predicted by the Sector Study, the nature of the jobs will change.

WHAT WILL THE FUTURE BE IN A PRIVATIZED WORLD?

One of the factors that could change future social work is privatization. In the past 20 years it seems that Canadian scholars and practitioners have been making increasingly important contributions to social work, much of this work emphasizing environmental and structural issues related to society as a whole rather than focusing on the person and inner self. This has occurred at a time when American social work may be heading in the opposite direction. The force that may well determine the future direction of social work in North America is privatization of services.

At least part of American social work seems to be rapidly privatizing, particularly for those who have an MSW and are working in health, mental health, or related areas, including individual and family counselling (Skidmore et al., 1997). The move toward private practice is being given a jump-start by the system of **managed health care** in the United States and the emerging system of contracting out social services (Schram and Mandell, 2000, pp. 228–29). (Managed health care involves a health insurance program that frequently pays for services of licensed social workers.) Because insurance programs can now pay the fees for social workers, **private practice** is very attractive to some and an often lucrative enterprise.

In 1995 there were more than 28,000 social workers in private practice in the United States (Skidmore et al., 1997, p. 387). This means that social work practitioners focus more and more on various forms of **therapy.** Along with this therapeutic, clinical focus goes the need to use theories that centre on the person and pathology (see Chapter 4 for a discussion of therapy in social work). No doubt, this reduces the impetus to explore perspectives that challenge the existing social structure and systems such as those highlighted in structural and feminist approaches. Work that focuses on community in a private world seems to struggle to find both a theoretical and a practice base (Fisher and Karger, 1997).

This trend toward privatization has not reached nearly the same proportions in Canada. Managed health care, at least in the year 2005, is not on the Canadian horizon, and public insurance programs tend to exclude social work services (this may change, however, as pressure is placed on public social service agencies to reduce programs, cut costs, and purchase selective private services). Canadian social work practice remains primarily agency-based and publicly funded, and there is still room for emerging Aboriginal, structural, and feminist approaches that challenge existing services and systems. However, if privatization of health care services takes hold in Canada, then the push toward private social work practice may begin in earnest.

CHAPTER SUMMARY

The emergence of social work as a profession has been the product of many forces, probably the most important of which were industrialization and urbanization. Social work grew as the institutions of agrarian societies dramatically changed and could not adequately cope with many of the industrial and urban problems of the day. Early social work filled gaps left by failed social institutions.

As a response to urbanization and industrialization, the charity and settlement house movements were born. They were both highly influential in the development of social work. Casework can trace its genesis to the charity movement, particularly the Charity Organization Society. Group work and community organization/community development were highly influenced by the settlements.

Social work developed later in Canada than in Britain or the United States, an important reason being that industrialization and urbanization occurred much later in Canada. Social work did develop somewhat differently in the three countries. It seems, for instance, that in Canada (particularly Toronto) the settlements emphasized providing services and focused less on reforms, whereas in both Britain and the United States the settlements had a strong social reform goal. The 1915 social work education program developed by J. S. Woodsworth and influenced by the social gospel movement is an important example of the breadth of social work in Canada in the early part of the 20th century.

During the middle part of the 20th century, Canadian social work borrowed heavily from American practice. Many Canadian social workers were trained in the United States. It was not until the 1950s that advanced training was generally available in Canada, and it was the late 1960s before Canadian social work education began to chart a course that was somewhat different from its American counterpart.

Beginning in the late 1920s, social work began to search for a common base. Over the past 70 or so years, social work has changed from a set of independent specialties to a profession that is tied together by a set of values, a mission, goals, and an emphasis on the professional relationship. Since the 1970s, some have held that the person-in-the-environment view (systems perspective, ecological perspective, or what is now called the *ecosystems perspective*) should be seen as the common knowledge base for social work and hence generic to practice. This view is shared by many, but it can also be argued that systems/ecological frameworks are too narrow and limiting to serve as standards for generic knowledge.

Finally, in the future social workers will likely find jobs but the nature of social work will evolve and change, as it has in the past. The future of private social work practice in Canada is still a question mark. While Canadian social work is predominantly agency based, if health care is privatized and social work becomes increasingly defined as a "therapy" then private practice will probably expand considerably.

NOTES

1 While social work in Quebec and English Canada developed in parallel, the roots of social work in Quebec are somewhat different. For instance, the Catholic religious orders in Quebec were instrumental in the development of early social work in the province (see Bellamy and Irving, 1986). This chapter mainly discusses the roots of social work in English Canada.

2 The role of women in early social work, including those who worked in the settlements, is controversial. There is little dispute that women made huge contributions to the development of early social work and took leadership roles in the reforms of the late 19th and early 20th century. Some, such as Chambers (1986) and Walton (1975), as suggested by Camilleri (1996), go further and argue that social work "was a movement and an occupation, from 1890 to the 1920s, created for and with women" (p. 36). This view holds that women occupied positions of some power and professional responsibility and were able to create important careers for themselves in a patriarchal world.

Feminist and radical thinkers present an alternate view and suggest that many of the early women social workers were exploited. Carniol (1995) holds that the women who were charity volunteer workers (friendly visitors) and early caseworkers were low-paid staff who served to mask the problems of poverty from men in power and "confirmed [the men's] views about being superior mortals and gave them a clear conscience about their relationship to the poor" (p. 25). In 1929, J. H. T. Falk, like many settlement house workers and social reformers of the time, took a similar position that charity was a way to ease the conscience of the industrialists.

Some also suggest that settlements and charity agencies were usually run by men but staffed by women. This meant that the role of women was undervalued and that "women in social work would play an important but secondary role in the professional hierarchy" (Daly, 1995, p. 11).

3 Historical information on American settlements is considerably more abundant than that on Canadian settlements. One of the best Canadian sources is Irving, Parsons, and Bellamy (1995), who generally describe the settlement movement in Canada but focus on examining in detail three settlements in Toronto. Of the three, only one had a clear social reform agenda. The other two were service-oriented.

4 Olive Ziegler was an influential settlement house worker and social activist in Toronto.

5 This document was obtained from two sources. Professor Len Kaminski of the Faculty of Social Work, University of Manitoba, discovered the brochure in the Welfare Supervision Board papers, File # GR 1557, Provincial Archives of Manitoba. We also received a copy from Professor John Cossom, School of Social Work, University of Victoria.

6 The reference sources refer to the "University," which in 1915 would have meant the University of Manitoba. Wesley College and Manitoba College also existed in Winnipeg at that time (later they merged to become United College and still later the University of Winnipeg), but neither were considered universities.

7 Wharf (1992) identifies one important flaw in these person-in-the-environment views (usually referred to as an ecological or ecosystems perspective, as discussed in Chapter 9): "[W]hile [ecological theory] allows and indeed pushes practitioners to consider the impact of societal and community factors on the lives of individuals and families, it fails to come to grips with how change occurs at the community and societal levels. The consequence is that individuals and families must adapt to or otherwise cope with their environment rather than the reverse" (p. 33).

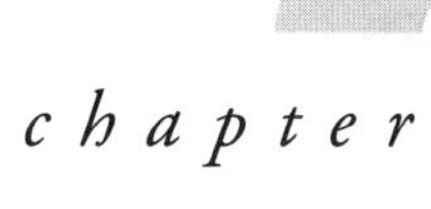

chapter 3

Ideological Foundations and Values of Social Work

Chapter Goal ▼

To explore and establish the importance of the ideology and values of social work that both shape and filter practice.

This Chapter ▼

- connects social work practice with the ideological foundations of professional helping that have emerged mostly in the 20th century
- distinguishes between knowledge and values
- suggests that social work is strongly influenced by an ideological lens that filters and shapes the way that social workers approach practice
- articulates a set of social work values, much of it based on the CASW and NASW codes of ethics, that guides social work practice
- shows how values are applied in practice by
  - illustrating the usage of the important but complex value of self-determination
  - connecting social work values with culture
  - addressing the issue of clashes between values
  - exploring ethical dilemmas

A NEW IDEOLOGY: HELPING PEOPLE

To understand values in social work, one needs to appreciate the importance of the ideology of helping and that the concepts of treatment and rehabilitation in Western societies are barely 150 years old.

Up until the latter half of the 19th century, public policies dealing with vagrancy, deviance, and morality were punitive. People who could not fend for themselves or who were defined as deviant were generally punished, ignored, or forgotten in institutions. Often people who committed crimes were given corporal punishment. Vagrants, orphans, paupers, and elderly people were placed in institutions, sometimes called almshouses or poorhouses, that provided minimal levels of care and no attempts to rehabilitate. Similarly, asylums were built to care for people referred to as insane, usually without any real hope that those admitted would ever leave. Frequently, conditions in these institutions bordered on squalor, conditions that certainly would not be tolerated today.

During the last half of the 1800s, major social reforms in North America and Western Europe changed all of this. Mental hospitals replaced insane asylums. This was much more than just a name change—it reflected a commitment to treatment. Penitentiaries were built as prisons with a rehabilitation focus. In many places, corporal punishment was abolished. Orphans were placed in foster homes or adopted, and orphanages largely disappeared. Programs were provided for disabled and elderly people that gradually focused on building a better quality of life. It is interesting to note that often families tried their best to care for their frail and disabled members; it was when they could no longer cope, or when the person's situation worsened to the extent that family resources were no longer adequate, that families turned to institutionalization (Montigny, 1997). Slowly but surely over the next century, society began to accept the ideology of helping in the form of treatment, rehabilitation, and therapy for people with personal and social problems.

Out of this change in society's view emerged the helping professions, which include social work, psychology, and psychiatry, all well established in 21st-century North America. Around 1900, however, the ideology of professional helping was new. Professions were being established to provide the treatment and helping services that flowed from the emerging acceptance of a helping or rehabilitation ideology. Freud was just beginning to publish. Psychologists, social workers, parole officers, probation officers, psychiatrists, personal counsellors, marriage counsellors, and other human service workers either did not exist or their respective fields were just in the formative stages. The "professional" helpers then were family physicians or members of the clergy. In understanding social work at the turn of the 21st century, one should realize that the use of professionals to help others with personal and social problems is a practice that is barely a century old.

The concept of "helping" implies a certain kind of relationship involving a professional expert providing help to a client or person who asks for or needs such help. In some approaches and **practice perspectives,** professional helping is problematized—that is, the approach assumes that the client has a problem and that the task of the worker is to help the client fix the problem.[1] What does this have to do with ideology? Our position is that ideology is important because it influences our approach to practice.

IDEOLOGY AND SOCIAL WELFARE (MACRO) POLICY

Ideology shapes values, assumptions about social issues and how they affect people, and the public provisions that are necessary. Simply stated, social welfare policy is developed according to the prevailing ideology of government and influential actors (e.g., business, unions, and professions) with input from various groups and organizations (e.g., business, unions and professions) and the voting public. Social welfare policy deals with "concrete issues such as the quality and effectiveness of social service programs, citizen participation in policy and service issues, the role of the community and the actual impact of public policies on people" (Graham, Swift, and Delaney, 2003, p. 14). The human service professions, including social work, implement social welfare policies at the front line where services are delivered. A conservative, liberal, or socialist lens (among others) filters the ways in which social issues, the role of government and economic markets, causes of people's problems, and appropriate methods to deal with them are seen.

Conservative ideology is characterized by a belief in individual interest and responsibility, personal freedom, and acceptance of unequal power and resources in society. This lens tends to shape approaches to social welfare that see individuals as responsible for their own problems and solutions. For example, if Nina, a mother with two children subsisting on an inadequate social assistance income, finds it difficult to pay her rent each month, she may be seen as a poor planner who needs to be more resourceful and work harder to budget the money she receives. Policies related to workfare (requirement to work in exchange for social assistance benefits) and courses in household budgeting and parenting might be used to solve Nina's problem. Rather than examining why social assistance benefits are kept low and why caring for children is not worth more, it is assumed that there is nothing wrong with the system, only with people like Nina who can't manage well.

Adopting some features in the conservative position, a liberal lens includes a more humanistic view that people need to have a social safety net in case they become unemployed or face health or other crises. As Steve Hick (2004) explains, liberals "believe in a mix of targeted programs for those in need as well as universal programs, such as Medicare, that are available to all Canadians" (p. 61). Liberal social welfare, in the case of Nina and her children, adopts some conservative principles such as social assistance and food banks but also advocates that community programs and self-help groups targeted to those in need, and particularly universal supports such as child benefits, government-funded income security programs, and basic health care, also comprise part of their available social safety net. Drawing from this mix of programs and services, a liberal approach strives toward greater social equality, but without much tampering with the system.

Moving away from individualism and minimal social service provisioning is the Fabian socialist (or social democratic) position, which Fiona Williams (1989) sees as including "equality, collectivism and social harmony" where "social policy influences economic policy to become more socially responsible" (p. 21). This social welfare ideology holds that universal programs and a just distribution of social goods are necessary in society to ensure equality. Important values in this social welfare ideology include equality, cooperation, and justice in society. In this type of social welfare environment, Nina would find herself in a better situation where her income would be sufficient to allow her to meet her family's needs for shelter, food, clothing, and other basic requirements of life, and other public programs (e.g., family holiday programs) would allow for a better quality of life. Many social workers might view this alternative as their preferred ideal scenario. Ideology influences social welfare policy, which in turn influences social services delivery and the practice of social work (see Chapter 5).

IDEOLOGY IN SOCIAL WORK PRACTICE

The social work profession has also developed its own ideology, one that shapes, in varying degrees, the practice of social workers. As the use of professionals, often social workers, to provide personal and social helping services gained acceptance in society (and in the social welfare system), they began to provide more and more services. An ideology of social work emerged, consisting of a set of ideas, knowledge, values, and principles that help shape the thinking and characteristics of social work, which has matured during the past century. It has been influenced by social change over time and by movements such as the women's movement and the peace movement beginning in the 1960s. In social work, a major part of the ideology is expressed as values. Over the years social work has spent considerable effort—perhaps more than any other profession—articulating a set of values, much of it embedded in the ideology of helping, to guide practice.

WHAT ARE VALUES?

Values cannot be proven. Gordon (1962, pp. 8–9) distinguishes between values and knowledge statements (see also Bartlett, 1961, pp. 21–37; 1970). Both values and knowledge statements are assertions of truth—assertions that something is so. Values, however, are based on a belief system. As the word "value" implies, we make an assertion because we like (value) it; it is desirable and important. We *believe* the statement to be true.

A statement of knowledge may also be valued. We may also believe it to be true. However, we have also either tested or intend to test its validity through research. We do not intend to test the validity of a statement of a value.

For example, "We believe in egalitarian ideals" is a statement of a value. For whatever reason, we hold this ideal to be important. It is so because we think it is so. It is a belief and we do not intend to rigorously test it. Now assume that we believe that a new intervention will benefit clients. We may like the new intervention and think it is a good idea, but it is not a statement of value if we intend to test (or have tested) whether it works. It is an assertion of a knowledge statement.

Many assertions of truth contain elements of both knowledge and values. In fact, the two can be conceptualized on a continuum ranging from "pure" knowledge on one end to "pure" values on the other. Making this distinction between knowledge and values can help us understand practice.

IDEOLOGY AND THE CORE VALUES OF SOCIAL WORK

In the late 1950s the U.S. National Association of Social Workers initiated an intensive effort to establish a definitive working definition of social work. In 1962 William Gordon, as part of his work on values, crafted what is considered a social work classic: *A Critique of the Working Definition.* In his critique, he articulated his view of "the most nearly primary and ultimate value in social work. ... [T]hat it is good and desirable for man [sic] to fulfill his potential, to realize himself, and to balance this with essentially equal effort to help others fulfill their capacities and realize themselves" (p. 9).

This definition, while dated, continues to be meaningful, reflecting a widely held view of the essence of social work. It captures the rights of individuals and the responsibilities that people have to each other. The emphasis on growth and collective responsibilities is generally part of all statements on core social work values.

A feminist ideal postulated by Bricker-Jenkins (1991), while in a different era and context, also emphasizes growth. She argues that an important principle is to "identify and mobilize inherent individual and collective capacities for healing, growth, and personal/political transformation" (p. 277; see also Chapter 13 of this book). However, very different from Gordon, at the centre of a feminist approach to social work is the right to social justice and the elimination of oppression, domination, subordination, and exploitation.

The Ideological Lens of Social Work

Earlier we suggested that the lenses of different worldviews filter how we establish social welfare policy. Here we want to expand the analogy of a camera lens. Think of a camera lens that uses different filters. For instance, a polarizing filter accents the contrast between a deep blue sky and white, puffy clouds. An ultraviolet filter reduces the effect of atmospheric haze outdoors. Filters can correct the distortions created by artificial light indoors. Other filters create special effects.

The image that is created on the film is partly shaped by the lens and its filters. Helping professions also develop an image[2] that shapes their practice and defines their understanding of people to whom they provide services. An image is the product of an ideological lens that filters a view. The essence (reality) of the view is still there, but its interpretation (the image) is partly shaped or coloured by an ideological lens.

Members of helping professions, through their socialization in the profession and their education and acceptance of professional values and knowledge, develop an ideology. The view of the world as seen by members of any profession is filtered by an ideological lens that most members of that profession share. This ideology shapes the way that clients are viewed and, as discussed earlier, the way that social welfare policies are conceptualized, developed, and implemented. It also shapes the nature of practice, including assessment and intervention. Different helping professions may have a different image of clients because the ideological underpinnings of the professions are different. The concept of an image has further importance because often clients and social workers view things differently based on the ideological lens through which they view the world.

As an example of the differences in the ideological lens among professions, psychiatry is steeped in the medical view that defines people as patients and in terms of disease and pathology, and includes a strong commitment to treat and eradicate disease. These ideas fundamentally shape psychiatrists' view of the people they serve. They are in contrast with social workers' view of the people they serve, which is discussed below.

Social Work Values

The ideology that filters social work's view of people is different. Social work is essentially based on humanitarian and egalitarian ideals. This view is consistent with Mullaly (1997, p. 27), who argues that these two abstract ideals are the fundamental or primary values of social work. Humanitarian ideals are based on fundamental respect for the worth, dignity, and inherent rights of all people. Social workers use the term "egalitarian" as a synonym for equity. All people are equal and should have the same rights and privileges despite differences in race, culture, spiritual beliefs, sexual orientation, ability, gender, or other characteristics. In Mullaly's view, instrumental or secondary values flow from these two fundamental values. Examples are self-determination, acceptance, and respect for the client. To Mullaly, Gordon's ideals of fulfilling potential, realizing oneself, and helping others fulfill their potential are instrumental values that help us reach the more abstract humanitarian and egalitarian ideals.

The Canadian Association of Social Workers' code of ethics expresses these fundamental and more instrumental values in a single statement:

> The profession of social work is founded on humanitarian and egalitarian ideals. Social workers believe in the intrinsic worth and dignity of every human being and are committed to the values of acceptance, self determination and respect of individuality. They believe in the obligation of all people, individually and collectively, to provide resources, services and opportunities for the overall benefit of humanity. The culture of individuals, families, groups, communities and nations has to be respected without prejudice.
>
> Social workers are dedicated to the welfare and self-realization of human beings; to the development and disciplined use of scientific knowledge regarding human and societal behaviours; to the development of resources to meet individual, group, national and international needs and aspirations; and to the achievement of social justice for all. (CASW, 1994a, Preamble)

These core values guide practice, and from them a set of moral principles or ethics emerges.

Summary of Fundamental Social Work Values

The list that follows both synthesizes the above discussion of social work values and represents the core of social work's ideology in a globalized world. It draws heavily from the Canadian Social Work Code of Ethics and is influenced by person-in-the-environment, structural, and feminist social work thinking.

The foundation of the profession is built on humanitarian and egalitarian ideals. Within the frame of these two fundamental ideals, social work emphasizes and is characterized by the following values, which are applied to practice:

- the right of every person to be safe from harmful and abusive environments
- the importance of the acceptance and intrinsic worth, integrity, respect, and dignity of every human being
- the right to self-determination
- the right to social justice, which includes the elimination of oppression, domination, subordination, and exploitation
- the individual and collective empowerment of people who are vulnerable, oppressed, or living in poverty
- a commitment to individuality, self-realization, growth, healing, and well-being of people
- the belief that all people have the responsibility, individually and collectively, to provide resources, services, and opportunities for the benefit of one another and humanity
- the belief that people's culture should be respected

These same values are held by many people, maybe the majority in our society, and are not characteristics solely of social work. There is also some disagreement among individual social workers about which principles are most important in our practice, and these principles are applied differently by social workers in different practice situations.

Dilemmas between these practice principles in real-life situations are well known and require careful thought and considered action. For example, the right to self-determination of an angry man under the influence of crack cocaine who aims a gun at his family conflicts with the right of his family to a safe environment. It is clear to most of us that in this case the family's right to safety is uppermost. This means that we must override the man's right to self-determination in this instance to help his family. If he is later requested by the court to seek the services of a social worker for assessment and treatment, the social worker would treat him with dignity, respecting his right to self-determination as much as possible given the circumstances.

All of these principles speak to values that are related to people's rights and responsibilities. Mullaly (1997, pp. 29–30) presents a different **paradigm** that agrees with these principles but adds a set of values that outlines the responsibilities of social institutions. His paradigm offers a challenge to current practice in that it raises the point that it is not possible to have equality or equal rights in a society that is characterized by vast differences in access to the resources that provide people with a good quality of life. Underlying Mullaly's view is the idea that social equality, in which "every person is of equal intrinsic worth and should therefore be entitled to equal civil, political, social, and economic rights, responsibilities, and treatment" (p. 28), does not rest on a uniform division of resources among all. Instead, his view takes into consideration individual differences and potentials. This, Mullaly says, is necessary so that people can voice their ideas and wishes and participate in making decisions about a wide variety of issues and concerns in which they have a stake. For social equality to be realized, it is necessary to address the responsibility of social institutions to promote justice for citizens. In practice, this requires a serious re-examination of social, economic, labour, and other policies. To illustrate, the right to self-determination of a poor, lone mother with two young children is meaningless unless she has available to her the resources that allow her to be self-determining—adequate shelter, food, clothing, and childcare. Only then will she realistically be able to express her views publicly and participate in the decisions that affect her, her children, and her community.

APPLYING SOCIAL WORK VALUES

The principles summarized above are expressions of values. These values are general and some of them are rather abstract. Applying them in practice raises many issues.

Limits to Self-Determination

Social work holds as very important that all people have the right, within socially defined limits, to the democratic principle of self-determination. This is presented as a value, a belief, and a right. However, in actual practice it is not that clear. Often the right to self-determination conflicts with other rights and obligations, is limited by external reality, and sometimes is both a value and a principle based on knowledge. In fact, as explained below, self-determination is very complex.

Clearly, in our society self-determination of individuals is limited by social codes, laws, and normative expectations. When the decisions of individuals impinge on the rights of others, society sets limits that require individuals to make responsible decisions. The following example illustrates one of the limits to self-determination and a dilemma that social workers often face. Suppose you are working with a homeless client who has few social skills and whose decision-making capacity is limited. Your goal is to help the client find suitable housing within her means. You are considering two strategies. One is that your client's need for housing is the highest priority and you will scour the area until you find suitable housing for her. The advantage of this plan is that you will likely be able to find the housing, your client will not have to experience the stress of the search, and you reduce the risk that her limited social skills will result in the failure of her own search, which for her could be traumatic. However, this approach would eliminate some of the client's choices and her own ability to make decisions. Her right to self-determination would be thwarted. Yet, these may be acceptable costs if the search successfully ends with finding suitable housing. If you choose this option for the client, you will have decided that the limit to client self-determination is justifiable. The primary goal is to find suitable housing, and you do not want to risk failure.

Your other option is to support the client in her own search. While you believe this option has a higher risk of failure, you think a more important goal is to help the client make decisions for herself. The goal of finding suitable housing is secondary to the primary goal of enhancing her decision-making capacity. In this instance, your strategy is to maximize her self-determination.

This option illustrates an additional point. In much of the social work literature, self-determination is seen as an expression of a value. But often social workers use self-determination as a strategy of intervention based on knowledge and **theory.** In the second option, self-determination is both a desired end (a value) and a strategy of intervention (based on knowledge). In part it is a value because the worker holds that all have the right to self-determination. However, it is also an assertion of knowledge because the worker will test the efficacy of self-determination by finding out whether the strategy of assisting with self-determination is successful if suitable housing is found and the decision-making abilities of the client improve. In this sense, self-determination is not a value but an outcome—a specific, testable strategy of intervention, and therefore a form of knowledge.

Thus the principle of self-determination that at first may seem straightforward is really very complex. However, distinguishing between the elements of assertions that are values and those that are knowledge can often help us understand the focus, direction, and nature of our own practice. In turn, this helps us understand our own value positions and select those that require testing.

Limits from External Sources

Since the concept of self-determination is a slippery one, it is worth discussing some of its limits and how it poses problems in practice. For example, to what extent can a woman and her two children who live on a meagre social assistance income be self-determining about their lives? The low income very likely limits many of their choices in life. How can a community where plant closures have created mass unemployment be self-determining about its future? The community is limited by the problems caused by the closure. Can a man who is hospitalized for a serious mental illness determine that he will be able to care for his young children? Is a 12-year-old child who has become a ward of the court able to determine whom she will live with? All of these examples suggest how self-determination may be constrained. This doesn't mean that there is no room to make any choices, but that the areas in which choices can be made are limited by circumstance.

Social workers may also face situations where clients do not want to be self-determining. Clients sometimes want social workers to make decisions for them. For example, a refugee family fleeing persecution in another country may not yet understand how to get things done in Canada, or may not be accustomed to open communication with people in authority. They may want the social worker to make decisions for them about how and what help is to be secured.

Rarely can any kind of choice in life be made without some constraints to free and independent selection. People can make choices only when they perceive that they have a range of options to select from and when the rights of others are not diminished by their decisions.

Values and Culture

Sometimes the core and other values held by social workers can conflict with the values of various cultural groups. For example, Ross (1992) points out how some of the important values of Aboriginal groups conflict with some white European values and how frustration and misunderstanding can occur. In social work, we learn from our clients before we know how we can be of help. We need to begin our work with an awareness that there are different ways of seeing the world and the people in it. In the urban, white environment, some important values include independence, skills in verbal communication, acting quickly ("taking the bull by the horns"), and being assertive. In the practice of social work in Western cultures, we are trained to view client independence and, in some cases, assertiveness (not aggressiveness) as strengths that are to be encouraged. Our profession is highly dependent on verbal communication, provision of expert help, efficiency in decision making, and confrontation when it is deemed helpful or necessary. Furthermore, we encourage clients to show their emotions, verbalize their feelings, and assert their needs when appropriate, often during a time-limited intervention.

Particularly when working with clients of different cultures, social workers must clearly understand those clients' values and how they conflict with the social workers' professional and ethnocultural values. To illustrate, many of the values and behaviours mentioned above conflict with those of some Aboriginal peoples (recognizing that there are differences among different Aboriginal peoples as well). For example, in some Aboriginal communities assertiveness and independence are not revered; instead, cooperation and collective experiences are valued. Mores that dictate acceptable means of communication may differ; ways of showing emotions also differ.

Another example relates to the concept of noninterference. People in some traditional Aboriginal communities do not interfere with another's decisions or behaviour and consider it inappropriate to confront others by criticizing their behaviour or giving advice. Ross (1992) suggests that it is important in these communities not to embarrass people by showing in front of others that they are wrong. He also notes the need to forget grief and sorrow as quickly as possible, even destroying evidence that could bring back such feelings (e.g., a picture of a loved one who died). Talking about such things is seen as burdening others; thus, communication about these events is often indirect. This principle is different from that of most European-based cultures.

Another common Aboriginal principle that shapes behaviour is the need to carefully weigh all the facts available before doing anything. This may involve periods of physical immobility and silence, not the intense dialogue that is often a strategy of the non-Aboriginal person.

One's culture contributes to what is seen as right, true, or desirable. There may be similarities across cultures and individuals with different cultural backgrounds, but these can never be assumed. In situations where the client's ethnocultural background and identity differ from the social worker's, values that guide thinking and behaviour may not be similar. For example, in some South Asian cultures, traditional values and practices define the status of men, women, children, and extended family members. Sometimes the eldest male determines what will be done by others in the family. Young females may be protected by the family until they marry. Dominant North American (and social work) values that stress an individual's right to self-determination can fly in the face of values that clearly limit what less influential family members can say or do. In cases where a daughter is seeking increased freedom to date or travel like her peers, value conflicts can create dilemmas for families adhering to another set of values. Social workers must recognize these differences and try to find a way to work across worldviews or to negotiate between them in a given situation. To illustrate, the social worker providing services to a South Asian family facing such a value conflict can help by understanding the place of such values within the family's and each individual's cultural context. Then the social worker can work with family members to discuss the source and meaning of the conflict, ease tension, and help them to find an acceptable solution. Chapter 7 discusses the role of culture in social work practice in detail.

Clashes in the Priority of Values

People differ in how they prioritize values. As social workers, we come across situations in which our personal and professional values clash with those of clients, other professions, or the **agency** that employs us. Our work in a particular agency may pose problems for us if our values cause us to disagree with some aspect of service provision or agency functioning (e.g., when client benefits are cut in order to save money).

Frequently, the personal values of social workers clash with those of clients. A social worker may personally disagree with the plans of a woman who is fully capable of making decisions for herself to return to an abusive partner. The worker may have as her highest priority the safety of the abused client. While the client may be fearful, she may value the maintenance of the family unit above all else. If the client chooses to carry out her plan with full knowledge of its implications, most would agree that the worker should respect her right to make her own choice. Of course, the social worker would assess the safety risks, offer ongoing help, and help the woman plan what to do if she or her children are in danger.

In general, the social worker must respect the values of the client, and when there is a clash in values or a difference in priority of values the client's values must take precedence over those of the worker. This is particularly important when the client and worker are from different cultures. However, there are exceptions to the precedence of the client's beliefs over that of the social worker. The primary limiting factors are the safety of the client and others, and beliefs that advocate breaking the law. One example is seeking a physician's services for the purpose of circumcising a female child. Female circumcision has continued for centuries in a number of cultures, but in Canada it is illegal and is seen as a form of child abuse.

In some situations, social work principles go against those in authority, such as when government decisions to pay off national or provincial debts decrease the available health and social services for people who need them. Social workers may choose to challenge through legitimate channels laws they consider wrong.

Some guides can help us prioritize values. Obvious ones are the professional codes of ethics. However, the codes recognize that resolving conflicts is highly dependent on the specific circumstances. In the case of disagreements between a worker and her or his employing agency, the CASW code of ethics suggests that the worker take the first step of making reasonable and responsible efforts to solve the problem in a way that favours principles outlined in the code. The CASW code argues that if there is an ethical disagreement between a professional social worker and an employer, then professional obligations supersede agency or employer obligations (1994a, Chapter 8.2).

ETHICS AND ETHICAL DILEMMAS

Ethics has to do with what is right and wrong in human actions, one's duty to others, and striving to understand what underlies ethical behaviour. Mowrer (cited in Freeman, 2000) posits that although morals and ethics are closely related, "moral refers to the goodness or badness of a behaviour while ethics is an objective inquiry about behaviour" (p. 30). Ethics is "concerned with living a good life, being a good person and doing the right thing" (p. 30). It attempts to apply abstract principles of what is right or good, apply them to specific situations, and use reason to determine what actions need to be taken. The study of ethics is concerned with identifying standards that can be applied in practice (see, for example, Reamer, 1995; Freeman, 2000). There are numerous ideas that are important in ethics and in ethical decision making. These are helpful to social workers, who daily face many situations that involve ethics and the need to employ ethical practice principles.

Another issue related to values and ethics that sometimes faces social workers is that of ethical dilemmas. Bond (1993), writing about ethical issues in counselling, distinguishes between an ethical dilemma that belongs to the counsellor and one that belongs to the client. The counsellor (or social worker) may be caught between two courses of action, both of which involve certain beneficial or adverse consequences. For example, a social worker is given a beautiful and expensive emerald bracelet by a wealthy female client, who insists that in her culture such gifts are expected and represent mutual respect and a good way to end any effective partnership. What should the worker do? Accept the gift? Return it and risk offending the client and perhaps hurting her feelings? Discuss the incident with and seek advice from her peers or supervisor? What consequences could the social worker's quietly slipping the bracelet into her desk drawer have on the social worker, the client, and the organization? There are gentle ways to explain to clients that it is thoughtful to offer such a gift, but a "no, thank you" along with the gentle explanation is sufficient and most appropriate.

Ethical dilemmas are experienced by clients in many situations. Often we don't hear of them until after they have been dealt with, for better or worse. At other times, a client's ethical dilemma may be the reason for seeking help from a social worker. Consider the situation of a young woman who is to be married in two weeks. She has just found out that she is HIV positive. She is fearful that her fiancé will call off the engagement when he learns of the diagnosis, but she is also concerned about already having passed the infection to him. What should she do? Pretend she doesn't know, but start taking precautions? Put off the wedding until she can tell him? The social worker can begin by helping the client to explore the options available to her and the potential consequences of each.

Of course, other ethical dilemmas take place within the social worker–client relationship. Often these have to do with issues of confidentiality and preserving autonomy. Ethical dilemmas occur when a social worker cannot simultaneously meet her or his obligations to two different parties without violating an ethical commitment to one or the other (Compton and Galaway, 1994, p. 240). Often, social workers can avoid these situations by clearly stating the limits to confidentiality and the helping process. (Of course, respecting client confidentiality as a general rule is fundamental to social work practice.) For example, not giving a client information about situations in which confidentiality cannot be guaranteed can pose serious problems in cases where a report must be made (e.g., if the client confides that her child is being abused by her partner).

Ethical dilemmas are often best approached using some systematic way of sorting out the characteristics of the dilemma. One could use the code of ethics as a guide to what principles are important in each potential course of action, and then attempt to weigh the positive and negative consequences of each. The code can be a good resource for resolving a dilemma for a number of reasons. First, it is written by and for social work practitioners. Second, it is accountable to social work and is recognized by our professional associations and most agencies as a guide for practice. Third, it has been revised over time to respond to the current practice environment. The difficulty in applying the code of ethics to an ethical dilemma is that it does not help determine which value or principle is uppermost in a given situation. It guides the social worker in identifying the relative importance of certain ethical principles. Further, the code has not incorporated many values or principles from Aboriginal, structural, or feminist approaches and may not adequately address aspects of working across cultures.

Some have attempted to prioritize a list of values that can be used as a guide for practice and as a way to help handle social work dilemmas (e.g., Reamer, 1995). The hierarchy of needs put forward by Maslow (1970)[3] is reflected in the first four ethical principles for ethical decision making set out by Loewenberg and Dolgoff (1985, p. 114). For social workers, these principles require that

- Basic human survival requirements are addressed, such as shelter, food, air, water, and the sustenance and protection of life.
- Independence, human rights, and self-determination are promoted to the degree that these do not curtail others' freedom to enjoy the same. The CASW code of ethics refers to the need for clients to be treated with respect and so that their dignity, uniqueness, and human rights are safeguarded (CASW, 1994a).
- Equality of opportunity and access for everyone are promoted in social work practice. In addition, the ethical responsibilities for social change set out in the CASW code of ethics prompt social workers to advocate for a fair distribution of society's resources and elimination of discrimination (1994a).
- A better quality of life is fostered for all. The promotion of social justice and a healthier environment for all is also to be fostered by social workers (1994a).

Other ethical principles are also important in social work practice. Respect for privacy and confidentiality is particularly important in a profession that works with problems that are personal and private. Disclosing information truthfully (and appropriately) is also necessary in social work practice. This refers not only to information provided to a client regarding social work services, but also to supervisors and authorities such as the courts, and in research activities (CASW, 1994a; Loewenberg and Dolgoff, 1985).

Most of us can understand the primacy of the right to basic needs (life itself, food, shelter, and safety). Social workers support this principle by delivering, for example, programs and services that help people when they lose a job or become ill or disabled. Addressing social inequality and injustice that adversely affect people who are most vulnerable—those who are old, homeless, young, or ill—is a duty of social workers. Social workers have an obligation to ensure that vulnerable people are given the aid they need through public policy so that people are treated fairly and not subjected to discrimination.

Basic survival needs also take precedence when there is a conflict between them and maintaining confidentiality. Suppose a social worker is in a counselling relationship with a client. In the course of counselling, the client describes how she has been upset by the way the Smiths, her next-door neighbours, abuse their three-year-old daughter. Even though the client may ask the social worker to keep this information confidential, the worker has the responsibility to take appropriate action to protect the child from abuse, even though the worker is not part of a child welfare agency. In fact, in many jurisdictions the worker has a legal responsibility to report to the appropriate authorities (likely the local child welfare agency) the possibility that the Smiths are abusing their daughter.

Assume now that the child welfare worker seeks to determine whether the Smiths are actually abusing their child. The principle of self-determination would hold that if abuse is taking place then the worker must act in the best interest of the child and protect her even if this means that the right of her parents to make their own decisions about parenting is restricted.

As discussed earlier, an important principle in social work is self-determination. A person has the right to self-determination, even when it means risking well-being (e.g., injecting drugs with dirty needles, or engaging in more socially acceptable activities such as skydiving or mountain climbing). Self-determination assumes that people have choices in the actions they pursue and can make their own decisions. Young children or people who are cognitively impaired (e.g., debilitated by Alzheimer's disease) usually cannot make important decisions for themselves, limiting their self-determination.

However, an individual's rights to basic survival and safety take precedence over someone else's right to self-determination (Reamer, 1995). When one person's activities jeopardize another's well-being, such activities cannot be condoned. In social work we would not, for example, turn away a client who discloses suicidal thoughts, even if it is time to close the office for the day.

When we accept the code of ethics as social workers, we agree to abide by certain rules and laws that we are usually not free to break (Reamer, 1995), even when we may have some personal conflicts with them. For example, a law that requires social workers in a social assistance (welfare) agency to refer clients to a job placement program that forces them to work as street cleaners, tree planters, or in other public works jobs may seem demeaning and punitive to a social worker, but the worker cannot simply refuse to participate. Instead, he or she can seek ways to act that don't break laws, such as requesting and evaluating the program's results or seeking alternatives. A final option for the social worker would be to seek other employment if no other solution can be found.

To understand an ethical dilemma adequately, questions need to be asked about the factors that have created it. Robison and Reeser (2000, p. 9) suggest that in each case, social workers ask themselves who are the participants or actors and who else is affected, what it is that these people do or do not do that might cause harm, and why the participants act or don't act in these ways. Making a decision about which course of action to take involves weighing the possible consequences to the participants to select the option that minimizes harm for those involved.

To resolve the ethical dilemma, a social worker can adapt the problem-solving process (see Chapter 8): assess the situation from various perspectives, determine the key values and principles, examine possible courses of action and their consequences (seeking consultation when needed from peers or supervisors), select and implement a course of action, monitor and review the process, and follow up and conclude. It may be useful to step back and consider the situation from a distance to ensure that an ethical dilemma, rather than a disagreement or emotional response, actually exists (Robison and Reeser, 2000).

CHAPTER SUMMARY

Social work practice emerged as the idea of professional helping took hold during the 20th century. Practice is based on a complex ideological foundation that includes a set of values that guide the nature of practice and help set the goals for intervention.

Values are assertions that we believe to be true. Knowledge consists of assertions that we may believe but that we either have tested or intend to test to determine whether the assertions are true. Understanding the difference between knowledge and values can help us understand our practice.

Social work's view of the world is filtered through an ideological lens that most members of the profession share. This ideology shapes the way that clients are viewed and social policies are conceptualized, developed, and implemented. This, in turn, shapes the nature of practice, including assessment and intervention.

A major part of social work ideology consists of a set of values based on humanitarian and egalitarian ideals. Within the frame of these two fundamental ideals, social work emphasizes and is characterized by the following values that are applied to practice:

- the right of every person to be safe from harmful and abusive environments
- the importance of the acceptance and intrinsic worth, integrity, respect, and dignity of every human being
- the right to self-determination
- the right to social justice, which includes the elimination of oppression, domination, subordination, and exploitation
- individual and collective empowerment of people who are vulnerable, oppressed, and/or living in poverty
- commitment to individuality, self-realization, growth, healing, and well-being of people
- the belief that all people have the responsibility, individually and collectively, to provide resources, services, and opportunities for the benefit of one another and humanity
- the belief that the culture of persons is to be respected

This statement of social work values is based on the Canadian and American social work codes of ethics and is influenced by person-in-the-environment, structural, and feminist social work thinking.

The chapter continues by illustrating how values are applied in practice, partly by illustrating usage of the important but complex value of self-determination. While we assert its importance, the right to practise self-determination is limited by many factors.

The chapter ends by connecting social work values with culture, showing clashes between values, and highlighting the problem of ethical dilemmas.

NOTES

1 We recognize that a variety of forces have shaped social work ideology. All of these did not come from the acceptance of professional helping. For instance, in 1963 Clarke Chambers published a seminal book, *Seedtime of Reform,* that shows how the ideals of early-20th-century social reformers—some predecessors of modern community development and community activists—strongly influenced social policy, including the development of social insurance programs. It is beyond the scope of this book to fully explore these forces.

As will be discussed in much more detail later in this book, the problem-solving approach (Chapter 8) makes the traditional assumption that the social worker is the expert who, often in partnership with the client, helps the client fix her or his problem. The strengths perspective (Chapter 10) also often assumes that clients have problems that need to be solved but attempts to mitigate the expert–client dichotomy by, for instance, viewing "clients" as consumers or perhaps even "partners" with social workers. Feminist approaches (Chapter 13) also attempt to diminish the expert–client dichotomy by using techniques such as self-disclosure, reducing power differentials, and stressing the commonalities among women.

A structural perspective (Chapter 12) would view the notion of "helping" as linked with conventional social work practice. By contrast, structural social workers would see the personal as connected to the political (as in feminist ideals), which would mean not dealing with social problems as residing in an individual's purview. A social analysis that gets to the social and political roots of people's problems means that relationships with people in trouble are collectivized (Mullaly, 1993, p. 168) so that groups of people are joined together and the worker acts to facilitate collective efforts. In this way, social workers work with oppressed people in dialogical relationships (p. 173) so that critical reflection can be facilitated. "To be able to engage in a meaningful dialogue the structural social worker must develop a dialogical relationship with service users—are relationships based on horizontal exchange rather than a vertical position ... all participants in the dialogue are equals, each learning from the other and teaching the other (pp. 173–74). An Aboriginal perspective (Chapter 11) also sees a relationship with people in trouble as an egalitarian one, where the social worker provides support rather than expert helping.

2 This observation is similar to the notion of deviant imagery that British sociologist Geoffrey Pearson articulated in his book with the intriguing title *The Deviant Imagination: Psychiatry, Social Work, and Social Change* (1975).

3 Maslow's well-known model hierarchy of needs is usually pictured as a triangle divided into five levels. Beginning from the widest, bottom level are (1) the basic survival needs (food, water, and sleep), (2) the need for security (a safe environment), (3) the needs for belonging and love (caring relationships), (4) feelings of self-esteem and individual worth (through accomplishments and competency), and (5) self-actualization needs (optimizing potential and experiencing personal growth).

chapter 4

The Social Work Profession

Chapter Goal

To explore the professional nature of social work and to outline a variety of common roles that social workers perform.

This Chapter

- attempts to answer the question "Is social work a profession?"
- explores the benefits and problems of professionalization
- discusses regulation (licensing) of practice in Canada
- describes a wide range of common social work roles according to system size (micro, mezzo, and macro practice)

PROFESSIONALISM

When we think of the practices of medicine and law, it is evident that they have certain characteristics enabling us to categorize them as professions that organize individual professionals into associations. For example, they have some type of governing and licensing body sanctioned by legislation (e.g., in medicine, the College of Physicians and Surgeons), guidelines for professional practice, disciplinary procedures for breaches of professional conduct, and a shared foundation of knowledge and professional language that makes it easier for members to communicate with one another. All of these factors contribute to defining an occupation as a profession.

In 1915, Abraham Flexner asked the question "Is social work a profession?" after doing work in medicine. His conclusion was "probably not" (Flexner in Garvin and Tropman, 1992, p. 463). Forty-two years later, Ernest Greenwood (1957, pp. 45–55) caused a stir in social work circles by asking the question again. He listed five attributes of a profession: (1) a systematic theory, (2) authority, (3) community sanction, (4) ethical codes, and (5) a culture. He then proceeded to suggest that on most of these criteria social work fell short, particularly on having a systematic theory, authority, and sanction. Greenwood's article led to a serious debate in social work that was instrumental in the 1958 effort of the American NASW to produce a definitive working definition of social work.

In 1992 Garvin and Tropman undertook a similar analysis, and their conclusions were similar to Greenwood's. They listed seven criteria for a profession based on what they called their "overall review": (1) a common body of knowledge, (2) a theoretical basis, (3) university training, (4) production of income, (5) professional control of practitioners (e.g., provincial sanctioned **licensing**), (6) internal moral or ethical control of professional activities (i.e., a code of ethics and licensing), and (7) measurable or observable results. They concluded that social work clearly meets the criteria of university training, income production, and internal moral and ethical control, but only partly meets the remaining four criteria (Garvin and Tropman, 1992, pp. 457–63). From this analysis one might conclude that little has changed since 1915 and that the status of social work as a profession is still limited.

What does this mean to social workers? It is important not to get caught up in a debate about the status of social work as a profession. First, consider the criteria used by Greenwood and by Garvin and Tropman. Neither identify the single most important and obvious characteristic of a profession: providing a service. Medicine, law, engineering, teaching, and so on, like social work, provide a service that carries out the mission of the profession.

Social work clearly provides a **human service,** usually defined as helping. Thus the real issue is not whether social work is a profession—the issue is the quality, efficacy, and relevance to society of the service that social workers provide.

Professional Regulation

There are two fundamental ways that provinces regulate social work practice. These are use of protection of title, and regulation or control of practice.

Use of protection of title means that only those who meet certain qualifications can use a professional social work title. All provinces have a professional licensing procedure that protects title. The strength of title legislation varies widely among provinces. Usually the title "social worker" or "registered social worker" is licensed and can be used by professionals who meet certain qualifications and standards of practice set by a provincial social work licensing body.

Some provinces also have more rigorous legislation that controls social work practice. Regulation or control of practice means that provincial legislation defines and regulates practice by having jurisdiction over what activities a professional social worker can perform.

Qualifications for licensing vary among provinces but most require a professional BSW, MSW, or doctorate in social work, work experience, and evidence that the worker meets provincially defined standards and ethical practice. Some provinces accept a community college diploma in social work as an educational qualification.

Regulation procedures are subject to change. For detailed, up-to-date information we direct readers to the specific provincial associations or colleges of social workers or the Canadian Association of Social Workers (CASW). The CASW Internet address is www.casw-acts.ca; the site provides a useful summary of each provincial regulation, or users can follow the links to find addresses for the provincial associations. See also Hick (2002, pp. 67–69).

Even though provinces are moving to establish criteria to regulate social work practice, regulators find it difficult to set rigorous and common standards. Social work clearly has a common base, but the types and fields of social work practice vary widely; maybe more than in any other profession. Some workers provide community services, such as community development, while others work with groups and still others, engaged in clinical social work practice, provide personal counselling or therapy. Clearly, community development and clinical social work are very different types of practice. Further, while practice in different fields may have commonalities, work in, for example, child welfare differs greatly from practice in health. Hence, regulators find it very difficult to set standards that can apply to all social workers. This is evidenced by a trend in the United States in which licensing applies only to clinical social work practice.

The type and extent of regulation of social work practice also remains contentious. There are persuasive arguments for strong regulation. Probably the most common is that legislated regulation leads to uniformly high standards of practice quality and ethics. Hence, regulation or licensing protects the public. Some also contend that licensing raises the perceived status of the profession. These views are widely shared by social workers.

However, some people suggest that licensing leads to unwanted characteristics. They argue that regulation forces social workers to "look inward." Licensing helps protect the profession from external threat. It does this by claiming its territory and then arguing that it is better equipped than others to provide the service. This limits ventures into new areas and distracts from social work's time-honoured function of social change and community action.

Meeting the criteria of professions, as outlined above by Greenwood and Garvin and Tropman, can help standardize professional practice. Yet some of these criteria may also be seen as an obtrusive means of controlling practitioners by setting standards of education and behaviour that must be followed by all. Not all social workers are in favour of this type of regulation, even though they practise ethically and view the well-being of clients as uppermost. Those who practise using an approach that is less well known or integrated within the social work profession might prefer to maintain the principles and methods that are external to any standard guidelines. At this time in our history, there is a need for social work to explore new approaches that extend practice to new populations and use innovative methods of social change.

Features of the Profession

There are many subtle features in professions, such as a professional environment or culture. A culture is the sum total of ways of living into which we are socialized and that provides guidelines for appropriate behaviour. In the same sense, members of a profession are socialized through similar kinds of education in professional schools and through training and activities in their workplaces, such as peer review and supervision of practice. There is also a kind of internalizing process that occurs over time that leads people in a profession toward a shared orientation or common approach to their work—think about groups or associations to which you have belonged and how members learned to become part of them.

In social work, we are informally guided by our professional culture and formally guided by our codes of ethics (see Chapter 3). Other types of codes of behaviour may also be important—for example, the ethics of Aboriginal cultures that guide the healing practices of their helpers (see Chapter 11). Most social workers would likely agree that a strong commitment to applying helping principles and values in practice and the ability to heal or help are critical to ensuring that the needs and interests of clients remain the highest priority. Professionalism refers, then, to applying accepted principles and using the qualities and skills deemed necessary in the practice of a profession.

Social workers do not practise in a vacuum, guided only by their knowledge and ethics. They work in agencies and organizations, many of which are bureaucracies connected with and often funded by federal, provincial, or municipal governments (although public social service funding is being challenged in many fields of social work). These bureaucracies are complex and do not always view things in the same way as social workers. For example, bureaucracies are interested in efficiency and standardization. These aims may help the organization to do its work without much waste of time and money. Social workers, on the other hand, are trained to appreciate individual differences in clients, which means being flexible to these differing needs and interests and not trying to ensure the same type and level of services for all. Furthermore, establishing a good relationship and striving for quality in intervention with clients is often seen as more important than serving many clients efficiently in a given time period. This is important in a profession that values human relationships. In a bureaucratic organization, where efficiency is a priority, the social worker often feels pressured to carry a large caseload of clients. Preserving a high quality of service is extremely difficult when there are many to be served. Of course, even organizations that are not large bureaucracies may constrain social workers from practising in the ways in which they have been trained—due to limited resources, for example.

The roles that social workers perform are not unique to social work, nor are they unique to any other profession. For example, nurses and psychologists frequently act as case managers and counsellors, and a variety of professionals may be mediators. However, what each professional brings to his or her role helps to determine how he or she performs it. For example, a nurse brings a different orientation to the role of case manager in the mental health field than does a social worker or psychologist. The personal and professional values of social workers thus shape the manner in which they perform their roles.

SOCIAL WORK ROLES AND FUNCTIONS

Generalist Social Work Practice

Social workers perform many different roles, yet there are important commonalities. Much of the basic skills and knowledge required are similar, while the emphasis, context, tasks, and focus are different.

One way to describe social work roles is according to **fields of practice** (see Garvin and Tropman, 1992). For example, the role of a social worker in a hospital differs considerably from that of one, say, in a family agency that specializes in marriage counselling. The hospital worker might work with people who have long-term illnesses and require considerable help in **discharge planning.** The marriage counsellor would most likely define her or his role as helping people to resolve marital difficulties.

Another way to view the roles of social workers is according to system size—that is, to identify roles in the context of **micro, mezzo,** and **macro systems** (see Kirst-Ashman and Hull, 1993). These designations are general categories with blurred boundaries. Micro social work practice generally focuses upon individuals and draws upon knowledge from psychology. Mezzo practice is aimed at small groups such as families or other primary groups such as peers. Macro practice centres upon helping communities, neighbourhoods, or organizations. For example, a caseworker who works with individuals is engaged in micro practice. The role of a case advocate acting on behalf of an individual or family is a common social work role that is used in micro or mezzo settings. A different form of advocacy—sometimes called class advocacy—is used in macro practice, such as community organizing (Sheafor, Horejsi, and Horejsi, 1997, pp. 59–60). In class advocacy the worker acts on behalf of a group of people or an organization. For example, a class advocate may argue the case of a group of welfare recipients who have lost benefits due to government cutbacks. (See Chapter 9 for further discussion of micro, mezzo, and macro practice.)

While social work roles are partly shaped by the field of practice environment and system size, they also have a common, generic base. In this book, we describe various generic social work roles that cut across all or many fields of practice and system sizes, recognizing that the context is very important in how these roles are implemented (see DuBois and Miley, 1992; Miley, O'Melia, and DuBois, 1998; McMahon, 1994).

Social workers in generalist practice perform numerous roles. In fact, there are too many and they are too diverse to expect that any one person can become competent in all. In practice, social workers develop different roles and related sets of skills and competencies. The roles to learn and hone depend on the interests of the individual, the fields in which the social worker will practise, the requirements of unique client situations, and factors such as the sociocultural, economic, and political contexts of practice. Generalist social work practice is too fluid and broad to circumscribe or define its functions or limit its roles. In fact, it is likely that as new opportunities and challenges arise over time, new social work roles will emerge. The social work roles that we describe in this book comprise not an exhaustive list, but rather a range of roles on the micro to macro continuum.

COMMON GENERALIST SOCIAL WORK ROLES

Although the following list of roles is divided according to system size, this is not intended to suggest that social workers limit their work to a single domain size. On the contrary, it is possible for an individual's activities to involve work in all sizes of systems. For example, intervention may take the form of direct practice with individuals, families, or groups, and may take the form of social policy analysis related to family services. The following roles, which describe functions of social workers, are not in any particular order of importance or frequency of use.

Micro and mezzo systems: working with individuals, families, and groups

- counsellor and therapist
- case manager
- group worker

Micro, mezzo, and macro systems: roles for all levels of practice

- advocate
- enabler or facilitator
- educator, teacher, or coach
- mediator
- outreach worker
- social broker
- evaluator

Macro systems: roles in community development and social policy

- community practice or organizing
  - community developer
  - social planner
  - social activist
- policy activist and analyst

The Story of Kim and Ann

The story of Kim and Ann begins in this chapter and continues through later chapters, spun into scenarios used to illustrate various roles, theories, and approaches to social work practice.

Case Example

Kim and Ann

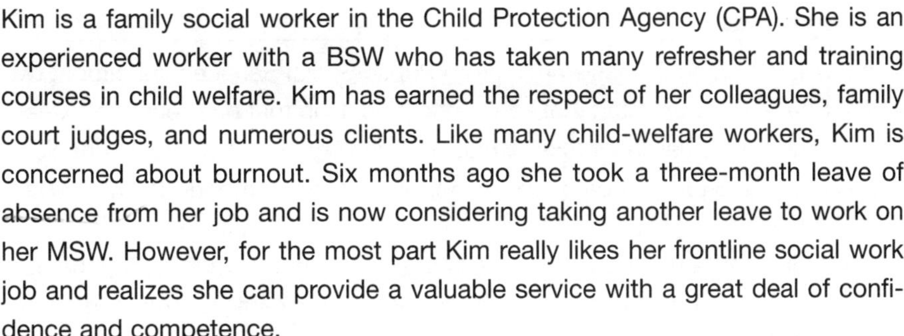

Kim is a family social worker in the Child Protection Agency (CPA). She is an experienced worker with a BSW who has taken many refresher and training courses in child welfare. Kim has earned the respect of her colleagues, family court judges, and numerous clients. Like many child-welfare workers, Kim is concerned about burnout. Six months ago she took a three-month leave of absence from her job and is now considering taking another leave to work on her MSW. However, for the most part Kim really likes her frontline social work job and realizes she can provide a valuable service with a great deal of confidence and competence.

Ann is a 27-year-old lone mother of three children (Jim, aged 9, John, aged 4, and Amy, aged 18 months) with a grade 10 education. A child of Dutch immigrants, Ann was raised with her two older brothers and one sister in a working-class section of the city. The family is Protestant but rarely attended church.

Jack and Ann were married when he was 18 and she was 17. Ann was pregnant with Jim at the time of their marriage. Jack left the family just after Amy was born. He pays very little child support even though the family court has ordered him to increase his contribution.

Brief History of Events

Recently the CPA nightshift worker placed Ann's three children in temporary custody. The worker had received a call at 1:30 a.m. from a neighbour that the children were home alone, unattended by an adult. He discovered that Ann was at a party and indeed had not arranged for adult care of her children.

The nightshift worker found the three children alone. Amy was crying and needed her diaper changed. Jim did not want to do it. All three had colds and runny noses, and looked like they had been wearing the same old, torn clothes for days. Food was scattered all over the house, and the sink and kitchen were cluttered with dirty dishes. Amy had a bottle, but when Jim filled it he had spilled much of the milk and it had run under the refrigerator. Jim was still awake watching TV, but John was asleep. Ann was a smoker, and there were several packs of matches scattered around the house. Three or four used matches were on the floor. The nightshift worker wondered whether Jim or John had been playing with the matches.

The family is known to the agency, and neglect has been suspected, but there has been no evidence of direct physical abuse. The nightshift worker placed the children in a temporary shelter, and the next day Kim was assigned to work with the family. Ann was initially an involuntary client (required to accept social work services), but over time Kim and Ann have formed an amiable relationship.

Circumstances ▼

Ann has been on social assistance (from Public Social Services) for almost two years. She is very frustrated that she cannot find a job that pays enough to feed, clothe, and house her family. Her stress level is very high, and she is unable to cope with both a job and parenting. Her problems are compounded by the fact that she has only a grade 7 education and no vocational training.

Ann and her family live in the core of the city in an area that, during the past five years, has deteriorated badly. There are many vacant houses, and neighbourhood kids have set fire to several of them. Youth gangs have grown rapidly in the last two years, and the neighbourhood is covered with graffiti. Banks and grocery stores have moved out. Many people are afraid to venture outside at night, and some worry about safety even during the day.

Ann lives on the upper floor of an old house, next to a vacant one that has been burned. The house is divided into three apartments. Some of the windows have no screens. The toilet is not working, and the family has been unable to use it for more than a day. The house is badly run-down, and Ann has a lot of difficulty getting her landlord to make even basic repairs. One of the main reasons that he does not want to make the repairs is that he has not been willing to pay the high cost of fire insurance on the house.

As a youth, Ann had hoped to continue schooling so she could have a career but found herself pregnant. Her parents insisted that she marry, and she did not give abortion any real consideration. Jack was an exciting and fun-loving young man and she liked to be with him, but neither of them really wanted to be a parent. At first Jack took his parenting responsibilities seriously. He held a fairly good job as a highway maintenance worker for the provincial government. His wages met the family's basic needs with some left over for a few extras. Then, three years ago, Jack began to drink and to resent the responsibilities of being a parent. He became abusive. While Ann was never afraid of him, she was often glad when he was not around.

Despite these problems, Jack would often take over parenting tasks that reduced some of Ann's stress. While the relationship between them was not really close, they often complemented each other. About two months before

Amy's birth, Ann discovered that Jack had a new woman friend. Marriage breakup followed very quickly. Jack is now living in a common-law relationship with his new partner.

While Ann often feels relieved that she does not have to contend with her ex-husband's drinking and abuse, the marriage breakup has caused other very serious strains. Now she is on social assistance and cannot make ends meet. Jack does not make the support payments that he is supposed to. Before the breakup, the family lived in reasonable accommodations. Now, because of the lack of income, Ann and her children live in inadequate housing. Her stress has mounted over the years.

Ann is close to her older sister and often confides in her. On occasion she has been able to get her sister to take care of the children in order to give her a break. Ann sees little of her parents, who are elderly; her mother is in poor health. Ann still has a couple of high-school friends that she sees occasionally but has no really close friends.

In the past year, Ann had more trouble with parenting, and Public Social Services had referred her to Family Counselling and Assistance Services, a sister agency of CPA, for help in developing parenting skills. The family counselling worker thought that Ann was under considerable stress. Some of it was caused by her environment, some because she felt trapped by her children, and some because she believed she would never be able to achieve any of the goals of her youth. Her workers at Family Counselling were concerned that Ann sometimes neglected her children, yet they were also convinced that she was capable of providing a loving and quality home life for her children. Over the past nine years, Ann has grown to love her children and deeply wishes she could be a good parent, but she feels overwhelmed by the stress of her living conditions and the frustration of not being able to attain a better quality of life.

Several times in the past three months CPA had reports that Ann had left her children alone. However, each time the agency investigated, her children were with an adult and Ann denied ever leaving her children unattended. Nevertheless, it was clear that sometimes Jim would prepare meals for himself and his two younger siblings, and the children were often dirty and unkempt.

Kim's Initial Assessment

Ann is very upset that her children have been taken away from her and badly wants them returned. Kim, aware of the assessment of Family Counselling and Assistance Services, quickly recognized the stress that Ann feels and concurred with the family counselling workers that Ann, with coordinated help, does have the potential to provide a good home life for herself and her children. It seems likely that the neglect of her children is not due to an uncaring attitude but to the mountain of stress Ann faces, which has been constantly rising. While long-term foster care will not be necessary, Kim is unmoved in her decision that Ann must prepare to have her children returned to her. Kim's essential task will be to help Ann get her life in order before she resumes her parenting functions.

Micro and Mezzo Systems: Working with Individuals, Families, and Groups

There is a controversy over the use of the term *direct practice* as opposed to *clinical practice* (Hepworth, Rooney, and Larsen, 1997, pp. 24–25). Many social workers, particularly those with MSW degrees in the United States, now call themselves *clinicians* or *clinical social workers.* As some authors point out, the terms "clinical social worker" and "direct practice worker" mean the same thing—both provide services directly to clients. The role of clinicians or direct practitioners is central to micro practice and may be the most frequently performed role in social work (Sheafor, Horejsi, and Horejsi, 1997, p. 61). Clients of clinicians may be individuals, couples, families, and small groups.

While the terms may be used interchangeably, they do have different implications. Clinical practice implies the medicalization of social work. Specht and Courtney (1994) argue that by emphasizing the clinical and psychotherapeutic functions of social work, we are in danger of losing our focus on fundamental humanitarian and egalitarian missions of **social justice** and elimination of oppression and poverty. This is so even though direct practice with individuals, families, and groups on problems that are psychological or developmental in nature is an essential part of social work. Further, the idea of clinical social work implies a focus on disease and pathology rather than on strengths, growth, and development (Hepworth, Rooney, and Larsen, 1997, p. 25). For these reasons, this book uses the term "direct practice" instead of "clinical practice."

Counsellor and Therapist

Two major functions of direct practice are, with considerable overlap, counsellor and therapist. The word "counselling" usually refers to exchanging opinions or ideas, with the implication that one party helps the other. The meaning of "therapy" is quite different—it refers to a remedial and directed process, usually the cure or treatment of an illness or disease. However, in practice the distinction is blurred. In a field study reported by Rothman and Sager (1998), social workers used the words interchangeably. The authors explain, "Several factors explain this lack of differentiation: both functions deal with emotional and cognitive processes; they share some of the same theoretical knowledge base; and they use many similar techniques" (p. 92).

Generally the purpose of both counsellors and therapists is to help individuals, families, and sometimes small groups maintain or stabilize their social or psychological well-being. Counsellors and therapists perform a variety of tasks including, for example, enabling clients to more effectively cope, helping them establish meaningful relationships, assisting them to make constructive decisions, helping them better understand their feelings and behaviour so that they can gain more control over their lives, and establishing an environment in which people can empower themselves. This form of counselling and therapy involves a direct service role that helps people solve problems with a variety of techniques but with a clear focus on growth and development. It is a voluntary arrangement that depends heavily on the relationship between social worker and client. The social worker applies basic, generic skills such as interviewing, communication, and relationship skills.

Social workers can learn many specialized types of counselling and therapy through advanced education or training, and adapt these for their practice. Examples include a variety of cognitive therapies, **solution-focused** therapy, feminist therapy, and an array of **family therapies.** Most, if not all, of these therapies focus on enabling clients' growth and development. In this sense, they fit the generic meaning of the word "counselling" rather than therapy.

However, all too frequently, therapy in social work refers to remedial cure of a problem defined as if the problem is an illness. The focus is on deficits. In a narrow view of therapy, the object of the therapy is cure or treatment of a presumed pathology or disease process (faulty psychological or **psychosocial** functioning or deficits). The goal is to eliminate the pathology or to stabilize the symptoms. The practice reflects a medicalization of social work (see Chapters 8 and 10). Such therapy is often performed in mental health settings and in private practice.

By its very nature, this type of social work therapy is **restorative**—focused on treating a problem to restore the client to his or her prior state (see Specht, 1988). Such therapies typically draw on theories of personality, including ego psychology and **psychoanalysis,** that examine **intra-psychic** dynamics. Often these, as well as other therapies, are called **psychotherapies.**

Social work practice should support therapies and treatments that promote growth and development. But therapies used by social workers that focus solely on restoring and treating a pathology shift social work away from its primary mission—whether they are called psychotherapy or not (see Specht, 1988, and Specht and Courtney, 1994).

Case Example

Tamar and Ann

Tamar, a social worker with Family Counselling and Assistance Services, had been providing direct counselling services to Ann with the primary goals of helping her learn better parenting skills and how to manage stress. Tamar helped Ann practise a number of stress management exercises and deal with specific problems she was having as a parent. The clear focus of the counselling was to promote Ann's growth and development. However, three months ago, Ann abruptly stopped coming for counselling. Tamar had attempted to reach Ann but was unsuccessful.

A few months ago, during one of the counselling sessions, Ann had talked about the noticeable change in behaviour in Jim, her 9-year-old son. All Jim seemed to want to do was watch TV and play video games on an old machine they have. He used to play with friends almost every day, but since his father left he no longer asked them over. His schoolwork had also deteriorated badly. Tamar was concerned enough to refer Jim and Ann to Local Child Guidance. There they would assess Jim for psychological and possible learning problems. If they found that Jim was suffering from major psychological problems, one course of action might be to engage him in play therapy with the goal of helping him deal with his negative feelings and psychological difficulties. However, along with this restorative goal, the agency would focus on activities to help Jim grow and develop in school and with his friends. While part of the treatment provided by the agency is usually restorative, it is also oriented toward growth and development.

Case Manager

The role of case manager, another direct practice role, is very common and is often referred to in the social work literature. This role arose almost overnight in the 1970s as the result of mental hospital depopulation. As people were discharged from hospitals, community professionals were needed to help them access scarce and fragmented resources. These professionals, not necessarily social workers, became known as case managers in programs specifically developed by the influential National Institute for Mental Health in the United States (Gerhart, 1990, p. 206).

In less than two decades the use of case managers drastically changed. The title "case manager" has now become so broad and varied that it is difficult to clearly define. To illustrate the ambiguity of the role, the index in Dennis Saleebey's book *The Strengths Perspective in Social Work Practice* (1997c, p. 250) cross-references case management with the helping process, indicating that the two concepts have similar meanings. Zastrow (1996) writes, "Recently a number of social service agencies have labelled their social workers case managers. The tasks performed by case managers are similar to those of caseworkers" (p. 49). In many instances it seems that case management is simply used to refer to the entire helping process. Gerhart (1990) makes a similar point: "Today, the articulated goals of social work remain strikingly similar to those of case management, reflecting the profession's dual focus on the individual and his or her environment" (p. 207).

Case management can be misused. Governments, in times of cutbacks to services, seem to use case management as a new way to classify what social workers do. This opens the door for many poorly trained and less expensive personnel to qualify for positions that formerly required higher levels of expertise. In turn, this can—and does—reduce helping to simply coordinating resources and services required by clients. Some see "case management as a convenient device to save money by emptying out large and expensive physical facilities and dumping clients on the streets without ample service back-up. According to this view, case management is used by canny politicians to protect the public coffers while giving the illusion of meeting the needs of the people" (Rothman, 1994, p. 277).

Despite these problems, case management can describe a useful helping role. For the most part, case managers work with clients who are very vulnerable and have to overcome significant challenges. They often require coordinated services that meet several areas of need, such as physical care, counselling, financial assistance, and home-based support. Examples of such clients are frail elderly people, people with serious mental illnesses or physical disabilities, and children requiring foster care. To manage all of the complex needs and ensure that the services required are provided in a satisfactory manner and at the appropriate time, someone must take responsibility. Clients contribute by mobilizing some of the supports and resources they are able to access. This is the proper realm of case management. Thus, good case management consists of much more than just administrative tasks. The fundamental purpose of case management is to provide supports and resources to clients so that they can maximize the use of these services and, to the extent possible, mobilize their own resources, skills, and capabilities. This requires that each client receive maximum benefit from each resource and use only those that are beneficial. Case management is really a collection of roles. In a sense, a case manager wraps some of the other roles into a single package. To mobilize and coordinate resources, case managers must be advocates, brokers, sometimes mentors, counsellors, facilitators, mediators, and perhaps more. The role of case manager is not merely case coordination but a sophisticated helping role with particular emphasis upon building client supports (see Moxley, 1989).

To illustrate the point, assume a case manager is working with an elderly man who has recently had a stroke, has trouble walking, and has slurred speech. He is on the road to rehabilitation and is seeing, among others, a speech therapist and a physiotherapist. He is also receiving homemaker services. The case manager ensures that the man receives these services effectively and efficiently and that his recovery proceeds smoothly. However, suppose a few days into his recovery the man's home is invaded and, while he is not hurt, he is badly traumatized. A good case manager educated as a social worker can provide immediate, on-the-spot crisis counselling and help to mobilize the man's social support network (family members, friends, and neighbours). Further, the case manager can assess the need for longer-term counselling and decide whether referral to other services is best or whether the case manager should undertake the counselling.

The role of case manager is not unique to social work, but is often performed by a variety of professionals. In the above example, a registered nurse might be the case manager. If so, she or he would likely bring a different set of skills and another orientation. For instance, a nurse might immediately refer the man to a crisis counsellor. But suppose that on a home visit the nurse finds that the man has cut himself and needs medical attention. She might provide the required treatment without any referral, while a social worker would most likely seek medical help.

Case Example

Kim and Ann

One can see Kim's primary role as that of case manager. As she attempts to determine the course of action to take regarding the temporary custody of Ann's children, she needs to work with many agencies and the court system. After consulting with agencies that previously provided services to Ann (including Family Counselling and Assistance Services, Public Social Services, and Local Child Guidance) and assessing the circumstances of the events that led up to Ann leaving her children unattended, Kim decides that she will ask the court to keep the children in temporary custody for three months. During this time she will help Ann develop a plan to achieve more independence and a better quality of life for her family. Kim needs to prepare documents for court presentation and also coordinate services among various agencies. The case management function of coordination is and will be a major role for Kim.

Kim recognizes, contrary to common belief, that case coordination is difficult and has pitfalls that are often not considered. It will not be enough for her to assume that each service is being carried out. If, for instance, an important part of the plan is for Ann to receive some form of adult education, it will be necessary for Kim to ensure that this education meets its intended goals and even to ensure that Ann is regularly attending classes and receiving passing grades. If Ann is not, then this might make it very difficult to help her achieve her goals of independence and a reasonable quality of life for her children and herself.

However, there is more to Kim's case management role. Above we argue that good case management is not just case coordination. Probably Kim's most important function is to help Ann plan how to get her family back together. Kim is convinced that Ann's desire to have her children returned is genuine.

As mentioned in the initial summary of the case, Kim's assessment is that, with coordinated help, Ann is capable of providing a loving and quality home life for her children. Kim will spend the next few months helping Ann get her life in order first so that she can resume her parenting functions. Fortunately, Ann has already developed working relationships with two important resources: Tamar at Family Counselling and Assistance Services, and Local Child Guidance.

Group Worker

Group work has a long, established history in social work and is used by nearly all social workers at one time or another. The social worker can lead or facilitate groups in many different social work settings and for different purposes. Therapy, support, and self-help groups are often found in direct practice when counselling, emotional support, and/or education may be desirable. Often, the sharing of experience and ideas in the company of others dealing with similar life problems can be very powerful and helpful. A good group worker can play a key role in creating a safe space to talk and encouraging a positive experience for members. As Johnson and Johnson (2003) claim,

> [S]trengths and positive interpersonal behaviour will be revealed in a setting in which they can be enhanced. In creating a microcosm of the outside world, groups provide an arena for participants to interact freely with others, help them identify and understand what goes wrong and right in their interactions, and ultimately enable them to change maladaptive patterns and use their strengths more effectively. (p. 525)

Group work is also important when working with interdisciplinary professional teams, task committees, boards of directors in organizations, workplace peers, and many more. The group worker's skill in balancing the dual roles of keeping to task and attending to group process is critical (see Johnson and Johnson, 2003). Community organizing can offer a good site for group work where a worker can use skills in facilitating meetings, building capacity for leadership in others, mediating in conflicts, brainstorming ideas for action, and many other activities (see Sullivan et al., 2003).

Micro, Mezzo, and Macro Systems: Roles for All Levels of Practice

Advocate

As advocates, social workers act on behalf of others primarily to improve social conditions and promote social justice. Sheafor, Horejsi, and Horejsi (1997) suggest there are two kinds of advocacy: client or case advocacy, and class advocacy (pp. 59–60).

Case advocacy refers to action undertaken on behalf of individual clients. Usually the advocacy is directed toward a bureaucracy that the client needs to access. Often the client is perceived as being treated unfairly. Sometimes the social worker's action is directed at the worker's own agency.

Ordinarily, **empowerment**—helping people to help themselves—should be a primary goal of intervention. But advocating on a client's behalf probably does not aid empowerment, even if it significantly improves a client's situation. Advocacy is frequently justified on the basis that many of the clients for whom social workers advocate are vulnerable or in difficult circumstances and unable to take action themselves. These include frail elderly people, people who are seriously mentally ill or disabled, people affected by natural disasters or crimes, and children. As a general rule, case advocacy should be used in situations in which the client cannot advocate for herself or himself or the social worker and client agree that the skills of the worker will more likely achieve the desired results.

It is important to carefully consider whether the needs of the client are better served by encouraging or supporting her or him to advocate or act on her or his own behalf. For example, a woman who has been battered by her spouse and has experienced increasing feelings of powerlessness in her marriage may feel that only another person who has more power can change her situation. Some advocacy on her behalf may be required, say, for legal protection, but it would also be necessary to support and encourage her to begin to draw on and use her own resources and strengths to effect change in her life. The social worker would then be helping the client to increase her own agency (capacity and initiative), which can lead to greater feelings of personal empowerment.

As in all social work, the worker and the client (except small children and others who are unable to make decisions for themselves) must agree on the need for and goals of advocacy and who should carry it out. One of the goals can be to use advocacy to help create better conditions for the client to take further action by himself or herself. In this limited sense, advocacy has an empowering function.

Class advocacy is direct action taken by a social worker on behalf of a group of people. Usually class advocacy is aimed at the policies of social institutions or legislation. More than case advocacy, class advocacy is a political process that takes place in the public arena.

Case Example

Kim and Ann

Kim presents the family court with the position that Ann's children should be kept in foster care custody for three months until Kim and Ann can develop a workable parenting plan. Kim is acting as an advocate for the three children and sees the children as her clients. Often social workers advocate on children's behalf without the children agreeing to this action. However, if the client is an adult, the social worker and client must agree that case advocacy on behalf of the client is an appropriate intervention.

The court has agreed to place the children in custody for three months. While Ann is very upset with this decision, Kim and Ann have learned to respect each other and Ann is beginning to trust Kim. A week after the court grants temporary custody of the children to foster care, Ann learns that her social assistance payments will stop. While she expected a decrease in the payments, she did not expect complete denial. Both Kim and Ann believe this is very unfair, is probably against the policy and related rules of Public Social Services, and will make it very difficult for Kim and Ann to develop a workable plan that will help Ann's family. Kim and Ann agree that Kim should advocate with Public Social Services to get the organization to reverse its decision. They decide that Kim should do the work because she is most familiar with the bureaucracy, she knows the staff at Public Social Services, and she is skilled in advocacy. The risk of failure is too high if Ann acts on her own behalf. Kim knows that Ann's basic survival needs are threatened without the support income.

Enabler or Facilitator

The role of an enabler is incorporated in many of the other social work roles. "In the enabler role, you assist clients to find coping strengths and resources within themselves in order to produce the changes required by the objectives of the service agreement. Change occurs because of client efforts; your responsibility is to facilitate—or enable—the client's accomplishment of a defined change" (Compton and Galaway, 1999, p. 310). For example, a teacher, a therapist, or a mediator might also enable. Empowerment is an enabling process. Compton and Galaway further suggest that the purpose of enabling may be not only client change but also to help the client change the relevant physical or social environment.

The enabler role is often used in micro, mezzo, and macro practice. Some see the enabler role as being particularly useful in work with small groups (Connaway and Gentry, 1988). Group enabling is characterized by four factors that enhance group interaction: "(1) member involvement; (2) decision making about norms, goals, and roles; (3) group discussion skills; and (4) structuring of meetings" (Johnson, 1995, pp. 204–5). The role of the worker is to help the group strengthen and develop these skills.

Suppose some teenaged girls from the inner city have formed a group at a local community centre. Their main goal is to initiate and implement organized weekend activities at the centre. They are a diverse group from a variety of cultural backgrounds. While enthusiasm is high, the group does not have a good bond, and they do not know how to organize themselves to accomplish their goals, which remain vague. The role of the social worker is to enable the group so that they can first clearly define their goals and then meet them. To do this, the social worker might ensure that all members are involved in the group. They must all feel important and that they are contributing. This will likely enhance their discussion skills and group bonds. The social worker may also provide some leadership to help structure the group; a solid structure will enhance decision making.

The enabler does not do the work for the girls. That is, he or she does not organize the weekend activities. In the end, the girls will do the work and make the effort to meet their own goals. The worker only helps them to make this happen. These same enabling principles can be applied to work with individuals, families, and, particularly, communities and neighbourhoods.

Case Example

Kim and Ann

In the previous example, Kim agreed to advocate, on Ann's behalf, with Public Social Services. Kim and Ann have agreed that their priority is to have Ann's social assistance reinstated, albeit at a rate lower than if her children were living with her.

Now Kim and Ann agree that there is a goal of higher priority. While the social assistance is very important, Ann has considerable difficulty in doing things for herself. This causes her to rely too much on others and leads to some of her parenting problems. Both women recognize this as a problem. Instead of agreeing to advocate on Ann's behalf, Kim encourages Ann to do the work herself. Kim stays behind the scenes helping, encouraging, and sharing her expertise (coaching) with Ann. Kim's role is no longer advocacy but enabling Ann to do the work for herself. The advantage of Kim taking this role is that if Ann is successful, she may develop improved self-esteem and confidence as well as meeting the goals of the immediate task.

Educator, Teacher, or Coach

The social work role of educator or teacher is an empowering and enabling role that has a number of functions. Frequently clients need information or need to learn a skill before they can take action themselves. Some see the function of education as part of the enabler role (Parsons, Jorgensen, and Hernández, 1994, pp. 196–97). In the enabling example of the teen group, the worker needed to teach the girls how to structure a group so that they themselves could make effective decisions toward goal attainment. Social workers frequently help clients change unhelpful behaviour by teaching them effective ways to interact and cope (Sheafor, Horejsi, and Horejsi, 1997, p. 60).

Teaching involves a number of functions that range from micro to macro practice. Some of these are modelling, public education, teaching daily living skills, coaching, and role-playing. Note that all of these examples assume empowerment—that the teaching is provided so clients can take effective action by themselves.

Modelling, a common intervention technique, is teaching by example. It may be a natural spinoff of the helping relationship. For instance, if a client is shown acceptance and understanding the client may, in turn, show tolerance to others in her or his own life, thereby improving the client's relationships with others. Modelling may also be a complicated technique, such as what might be used in child therapy to help a child learn a new behaviour or develop different attitudes.

Public education is a role practised by social workers in the health care field, sometimes with other health professionals. Health education and promotion are useful strategies that assist people in developing healthy lifestyles and improving their quality of life in the face of health concerns. In this type of work, social workers can be especially helpful in tracing and identifying the roots of poor health when they are related to social and structural factors such as unemployment, discrimination, or lack of security in inner-city neighbourhoods.

Many clients, particularly those who are highly vulnerable, lack necessary social and other daily living skills. For example, lone parents on welfare do not always know how to cope with the limited amount of money they receive. They may not know about programs or additional help to which they might be entitled. When they run out of funds, they may not know what to do. Lack of skill in determining other available help and not knowing how to use local resources such as community kitchens, low-cost programs for children, and self-help groups can add to their difficulties. These limitations in skills and knowledge may even contribute to the fact that these clients see social assistance as their only option for survival. Perhaps they do not know about job training or childcare subsidies. When the money runs out, frustration levels can run high and self-esteem can be low. Social workers for such clients may teach them how to extend their resources, negotiate additional help, and seek other support to enhance their quality of life.

The teacher/coach role can be complex and require considerable specialized skill from the worker. For example, many parents who are clients of the child welfare system may lack fundamental parenting skills. They may not have had good parenting themselves as children, or they may have experienced abuse that hindered their development. Social workers in child welfare agencies sometimes convene and lead parenting skills classes to support these clients.

Coaching is usually undertaken when a client needs to approach something new or is apprehensive or unsure about how to do something. The social worker might suggest or give advice on how to approach the task. For example, a worker could help a client with an upcoming employment interview, coaching the client on how to highlight strengths he or she would bring to the job.

The situations in which role-playing is used are similar to those of coaching. In role-playing, the client acts out, with the social worker or others, a process to learn how to undertake a task. For example, an 18-year-old who has been convicted of a crime needs to find a job but is fearful that his criminal record will be held against him. A worker may coach him on how to approach an employer and how to react if the employer begins to ask questions about his criminal past. Alternatively, the social worker may role-play a job-seeking interview with the client.

Case Example

Kim and Ann

The previous example using enabling is also an example of coaching. Below is a different spin on the case that shows how education is also enabling.

Kim very strongly believes that Ann's parenting skills and responsibilities must greatly improve before her children can be returned to her. Ann agrees that this area needs improvement, but she is not anxious to tie it to the decision about having her children returned to her. Nevertheless, Ann agrees to a program to improve her parenting skills.

Since Ann has had previous experience with Tamar at Family Counselling and Assistance Services, Kim and Ann decide to attempt to make a referral to Family Counselling. Even though Ann has refused Tamar's services in the past, Kim is able to convince Tamar to work with Ann again. This time there is more urgency, and the goal is clearly to develop parenting abilities.

Tamar's agency operates a group program designed to teach young lone mothers parenting skills. Tamar is able to enroll Ann in this program. This educational program assumes that better parenting skills will enable Ann to become a better and more responsible parent. Ann will be able to do for herself rather than depend on others—or, worse, avoid her responsibilities.

Mediator

The mediator is a direct practice role that is used to help people solve disputes and negotiate conflicts. Many mediation situations require advanced education or training on the part of the mediator, and only some generalist social workers learn sophisticated mediation skills.

One way to approach mediation is to think in terms of factors that block interactions and agreements between parties. These include the self-interest of the parties involved; the complexity of systems, institutions, organizations, bureaucracies, and agencies; and the difficulties of communication between the involved parties (Johnson, 1995, p. 331; Shulman, 1984, pp. 9–10). The task of a mediator might be to resolve conflicts by having the parties address each of these blocks.

The social work role in mediation has many similarities with those in education and enabling. In each instance, the work of the professional is to find ways for people to arrive at solutions themselves. In mediation, all parties must do the work. The social worker is the catalyst; the parties who have the dispute must arrive at their own solutions. Note that mediation differs from arbitration. In arbitration, the professional is in a position of authority and may impose a solution for the dispute.

Let's return again to the example of the group of teenaged girls. They had proceeded nicely toward developing a set of activities for Saturday afternoons until they discovered that another group also wanted to book the community centre at approximately the same time. Neither group would change its time, and the executive of the centre would not permit either to book times until the dispute was resolved. In this example, the social worker might mediate the dispute between the two groups. Both groups have their self-interests at stake, and they probably have difficulty communicating. The social worker would likely seek a compromise solution that meets the needs of both. Most social workers who work with groups should have the skill to mediate such a dispute.

Other situations require specialized mediation skills. Miguel is a 15-year-old who has run away from home three times. While away, he spent most of his time on the streets. Miguel and his father do not get along. They fight over trivial things. Miguel's father has threatened to kick him out of the house many times. His mother, while caring, does not want to get into the arguments between the other two.

Your child welfare agency has considered placing Miguel in a foster home. However, his mother begs for one last chance for him to live at home. You have special mediation skills and have been selected to mediate the dispute between Miguel and his parents and, if possible, arrive at an agreement and contract among the three of them (and probably your agency) that will permit Miguel to remain in his home.

This case requires considerable skill in mediating family disputes. Unlike the teenage group example, much is at stake. The mediator needs specialized training to work in this complex and difficult situation in which emotions likely run high.

Case Example

Kim and Ann

The above discussion suggests that mediation often requires specialized skills. All workers must at times help mediate disputes but sometimes, as illustrated above, this is outside their role and expertise—they need to be specially trained. The following illustrates a type of mediation in which most social workers should have sufficient competence.

Ann finds out that her landlord is going to raise her rent by $33 per month. Ann will have a very hard time making this extra payment. Her landlord has told her it is necessary because he has decided to purchase fire insurance on the property despite its high cost.

Kim and Ann agree on two courses of action. First, Kim will try to help Ann and her landlord arrive at a more modest increase. She will attempt to mediate this rather minor dispute, albeit a very important one to Ann.

Second, because Ann lives in a part of the inner city that has badly deteriorated, affordable insurance has been difficult to acquire. Her neighbourhood association has formed an action group to lobby the government and private insurance companies to initiate policies that will protect property in their neighbourhood. This action is a form of class advocacy. Ann agrees to join the association.

Outreach Worker

An outreach worker attempts to extend services to people in the community by defining who is in need and then offering services or referrals (see Hepworth, Rooney, and Larsen, 1997, p. 593). Usually the attempt is to provide a service to people who are not clients; a major part of the work may be defining who should be a client. For example, some agencies assign staff to work with the general population of young people living or working on the street in a downtown core. The service may be as simple as helping a youth locate a friend who has disappeared. Or the social worker may aim to disseminate information, such as how to reduce the risk of illness from sharing needles.

A common function of outreach workers is educating community members. "As an outreach worker, a social worker provides information to the public at large to educate citizens on a variety of social work–related issues. Community education is achieved through the dissemination of public information, including presentations, media promotions and public relations activities" (DuBois and Miley, 1992, p. 293).

Many of the examples of outreach work are about life in the inner city. However, often outreach is undertaken in rural areas. For example, a remote Aboriginal community may be concerned about the extent of communicable diseases such as tuberculosis or AIDS in the community. The government may have a health education program designed to disseminate information, but the leaders of the community do not think this is enough. They need someone who is either Aboriginal or who has a good understanding of Aboriginal culture and traditions to work directly with the people. The work might start with finding out the needs and concerns of the community and who might be at risk. After identifying those at risk, the goal may be to offer information, services, and referral. Note that in this example, the social worker would likely need community development skills. Community development and outreach often overlap.

Usually, outreach services are provided by community and neighbourhood social workers. However, workers in most fields need to reach out to people who are perceived as needing help. Thus, while most child welfare workers would not be outreach workers in the sense defined above, they often are expected to "reach out" to people. In our ongoing case example, Ann lacks many life skills but is essentially loving toward her children and seems willing to take the difficult steps necessary to restore order and quality to her family life. Kim did not have to "reach out" to her.

Often, however, parents who neglect or abuse their children do not want the help of social workers. Suppose Ann did not want help from anyone and showed considerable anger with the social agencies and courts. If so, Kim's initial responsibility would change. Instead of beginning to develop with Ann a plan for the return of her children, Kim would need to spend much more time outlining alternatives and consequences—negative and positive—of decisions, and explaining services that her agency could offer to Ann. Kim would need to work to reach out to Ann and search for ways that she (or others) could be of help.

Case Example

Kim and Ann ▼

Kim feels that Ann's three children badly miss having their father at home. The separation between Ann and Jack had been stressful and involved considerable conflict. However, for many years Jack had been an important figure in the lives of the two older children, Jim and John. Since the separation two years ago, Jack has seen very little of his children. As Kim works with Ann, they decide that Kim should reach out to Jack to see if he wants to resume his parenting role. This may also be a way to get his support payments started again, avoiding possible litigation.

Social Broker

Like the case coordination function of case management, the social broker is a linkage role. The main goal of the social broker is to connect clients with needed resources.

At the micro or mezzo levels, the role is in part a referral function, meaning that the worker simply suggests a resource to a client or arranges an appointment for a client at a different agency. However, the broker role often involves much more (Locke, Garrison, and Winship, 1998, pp. 206–9). Linking a client with services or programs usually requires assessing client needs and available resources. To do an assessment, social workers need a thorough understanding of local resources. In the best-case scenarios, they know and have worked with the group of people to whom they provide the needed service.

As in all of social work practice, the linkage requires that a relationship be established between worker and client. This includes developing a partnership with the client in which referral options are mutually explored. A basic task of the social worker is to ensure that the client has a good understanding of the resources that are available and, to the best of the worker's ability, an understanding of the quality of these services. In most instances, the goal of the social worker is to enable the client to access the resources herself or himself and for the client to make the best possible decisions.

The broker role can sometimes be used to begin to establish a relationship with an involuntary client. Clients who resist the services of a social worker frequently want to access resources that they think they need. Offering to help the client obtain these resources may open the door to further communication between the worker and the client. Of course, the social worker's intention is genuine help, not just getting the client in the door.

Brokerage is also a macro function. Social workers can broker between service organizations or service systems and groups of recipients who need the services but for some reason underuse them. Locke, Garrison, and Winship (1998, p. 208) suggest an example of this in what they call the cultural broker or translator. Ethnocultural minorities can tend to underuse social and health services, often because they face barriers such as confusing customs, an unfamiliar language, and limited knowledge about resources. A social worker can sometimes help a service agency better understand the needs of such groups and, at the same time, help the group learn how to better use needed services.

Case Example

Kim and Ann

Some time ago, before Ann left her children unattended, she had been referred to Tamar at Family Counselling and Assistance Services. However, this had been more than a simple act of referral that provided Ann with a name, address, and phone number. At the time Kim knew Ann but did not have a strong professional relationship with her. Nonetheless, when Kim suggested to Ann that she might find counselling in parenting skills useful, Ann's response was positive. Kim agreed to explore with a variety of agencies the services that they provided and then outline each of them to Ann. After Ann made her preference known, Kim made the referral to Family Counselling and Assistance Services. Kim further brokered the referral by providing (with Ann's written permission) to Family Counselling and Assistance Services a report of services provided to Ann by the Child Protection Agency, and made sure that a first appointment was made.

Evaluator

The evaluator role is not often referred to explicitly as a social work role, but it is a necessary part of the repertoire of social work practice. Most social workers are required to evaluate their practice, not only in their day-to-day reflection on their work with clients, but also as a way of showing what they have achieved through their actions and how effective these actions have been. The evaluator uses **research methods** to understand and describe practice, program, or other change efforts and to make sense of the related processes (what happened, who participated, what was learned, and other information).

There are two kinds of evaluation. The first is evaluation of direct practice, sometimes called **clinical evaluation.** Social workers evaluate their direct practice using various methods that measure change in clients (see Fischer and Corcoran, 1994; Grinnell, 1993), observing progress, or looking at outcomes at the end of activity with clients. A simple model of evaluating everyday practice is provided in Chapter 8.

The second type is **program evaluation.** The program evaluator may need to establish the efficacy of a particular program by finding out how many clients used the services; what workers saw as achievements; how much money was spent; whether clients were satisfied with the services, program, or agency; and other criteria. For example, a funding body might include as part of the requirements for continued support of an agency or organization a yearly evaluation of all services provided. The funders make their decisions about the achievements of the agency based on statistical and other information. Sometimes an outside evaluator is called in to ensure an unbiased view of the organization's work.

Macro Systems: Roles in Community Development and Social Policy

Community Practice or Organizing Roles

Community organization work is actually a field of practice that many consider to have three subsets: community development, social planning, and social action (Fisher and Karger, 1997, pp. 117–25; Hardcastle, Wenocur, and Powers, 1997, pp. 1–4; Rothman and Tropman, 1987). Over the years the impact of community organization has waxed and waned in social work; in recent years it has come under mounting criticism. For instance, some argue that in the United States social activists have little to show for their work during the last quarter of the 20th century (Cloward, 1994). The same people suggest that this is primarily due to the economic emphasis on the free market system and private enterprise coupled with good economic times. As a result, social work has become "de-politicized," retreating to an emphasis on restorative practice, particularly psychotherapy, and has abandoned public-sector employment (Fisher and Karger, 1997, pp. 126–30; Specht and Courtney, 1994). This situation appears to be more the case in the United States than in Canada. The Canadian public sector still plays a key role in employing social workers.

Regardless of the economic times, social work is a political enterprise. Oppression and poverty continue to exist, and conditions will not improve without social change. Community (macro) practice is an important way to address social change, particularly in local neighbourhoods (Chavis and Wandersman, 1990). Social work practice needs to incorporate community and social change. This is a fundamental position emphasized throughout this book, but particularly in Chapter 12. The roles of community developer, social activist, and social planner are important vehicles necessary for carrying out social change (see Fisher and Karger, 1997; Hardcastle, Wenocur, and Powers, 1997; Rothman and Tropman, 1987; Rothman, 1994, pp. 255–78).

Community Developer A community developer (sometimes called a locality developer) acts as a catalyst to assist members of a community or neighbourhood to help themselves. The emphasis is on a democratic process in order to build a community. The developer does not do the actual work but acts as an adviser, resource person, and catalyst to promote and mobilize self-help, indigenous leadership, and action. Many community developers work in core areas of cities and rural areas in North America and in other parts of the world (Campfens, 1997).

Social Planner The role of a social planner is very different from that of a community developer. A planner typically identifies problems in a community, studies them using various research methods, and then takes action toward a solution. Sometimes a planner acts as a technical adviser to groups such as governments or political parties. This type of work is aimed at informing or supporting the activities of governments or political parties, perhaps in dealing with a local social problem. Other forms of social planning are located outside the domain of governments and more at the frontline or grassroots level. Often a planner will attempt to mobilize segments of a community to take action and advocate on behalf of others. Examples of places where social planners find employment are local governments, neighbourhood associations, social planning councils, and advocacy groups.

Social Activist History brims with old-style activists. They were at the foundations of the profession in the early part of the 20th century and included such notable people as Jane Addams, a major leader in the settlement house movement in the United States, and J. S. Woodsworth, active in government and social policy in Canada. Their aim was to directly implement social change through a variety of tactics, usually aimed at powerful social institutions such as industrial firms. Often the goal was to redistribute power or resources. Unlike community developers, social activists often devise and directly implement strategies for change. While social planners tend to work "behind the scenes," activists are often champions of causes and work on behalf of those whose lives are adversely affected by unjust or exploitative practices and policies.

Moses Coady—not a social worker, but an activist priest—was instrumental in initiating the cooperative movement in Nova Scotia. He targeted the large companies that controlled the lives of fishers and miners, introducing cooperatives to change the exploitative practices that shaped the workers' lives. By using cooperatives in single-industry communities, workers not only were able to buy products at reasonable prices, but also were able to shake the authoritarian bonds of the large companies. Modern cooperatives today can be traced to Coady's pioneering work (Trecartin, Tasker, and Martin, 1991).

Today, many social activists work through self-help groups and grassroots community organizations with limited funding and uncertain futures. Individuals do not seem to have the high visibility in social change they once did. Instead, their work, like that of the community developers, is more behind the scenes and involves mobilizing action groups. This does not mean that community development and social action are unimportant—on the contrary, they are more essential than ever, given the current conservative trend toward cutting costs and reducing services, which creates gaps in **social welfare** provision. The quality of life for many people is and will be diminished by regressive policies and practices that remain unchallenged. Most child welfare workers in frontline practice engage infrequently in community development and planning and in activist and planning roles. However, opportunities often arise in which skills in these roles are important and even necessary.

Case Example

Kim and Ann

Kim has helped Ann become involved in an organization that is lobbying for lower property insurance rates for its inner-city neighbourhood, which is deteriorating. Kim has recognized this neighbourhood deterioration as a growing problem. She often works in this area and believes that incidents of child abuse and neglect are partly due to the condition of the neighbourhood. She believes that action must be taken and that she needs to get involved in a way that uses her skills effectively but does not draw her away from her primary job as a child protection worker.

Recently, a nongovernmental organization that provides funds for voluntary and community services has funded a new agency in the area called Neighbourhood Services, which has a mandate to help the community organize in order to combat the problem of decay. One of the agency's first steps was to establish a board of directors, made up mostly of local residents but also including some experts in problems associated with poverty and urban deterioration. The board is to set policy and oversee operations of Neighbourhood Services. Kim was quick to agree to be on the board even though this will involve one evening of her time per week for at least the next six months, or until the agency establishes itself. She has considerable knowledge of the area and can use her social work skills to help set effective policies.

Policy Activist and Analyst Brian Wharf (1992, p. 14), quoting Richard Titmuss, suggests a broad definition of social policy that covers the range from micro to macro work:

> Social policy is all about social purposes and the choices between them. The choices and the conflicts between them have continuously to be made at the governmental level, the community level and the individual level. At each level by acting or not acting, by opting in or contracting out, we can influence the direction in which choices are made. (Titmuss, 1974, p. 131)

Wharf refers to three elements in the definition of social policy, stressing the involvement of purpose, choice and conflict among choices, and participation. The purpose of a policy implies that a direction is involved that is characterized by a set of preferred values and ideas. For example, the choice between universal, free services and user fees in health care means different policy directions, and likely conflicts among these choices. People who prefer universal and free health care may see it as a right and as a service that should be available to all. Others who want some user fees introduced may feel that individuals should pay for certain health care services to reduce the unnecessary use of these services by citizens. Universal access (no user fees) may be less of a priority in this position, but it does not mean that health care services made available for all is not important. As Wharf (1992) states, "[C]hoice emphasizes that the direction for policy is frequently far from clear and that firmly held values and ideologies compete for attention; participation reminds us that there are opportunities to influence the policy process" (p. 14).

Wharf's last phrase is an important reminder to all practising social workers, regardless of their primary roles. Everyone, social workers and clients included, has the right and sometimes the responsibility to influence the policy process. Whether this takes place through writing letters to newspapers and government representatives, taking part in a public meeting, forming a coalition, conducting research that studies and gives recommendations about proposed policy options, or protesting in a public place, people often voice their opinions and views in most Western (and many non-Western) countries. Through these and other methods, they participate in social policymaking. In some places and at different times throughout history, participating in public debate or even expressing one's views was (and still may be) risky and dangerous (e.g., during a crackdown on public displays of dissent).

Two related social policy roles are part of social work practice: policy analysis and policy activism. Policy analysis is a highly specialized role that includes functions ranging from research to advocacy. Analysis involves three essential steps: (1) policy development and design, (2) policy implementation, and (3) evaluation that determines whether policy goals were met (Fisher and Karger, 1997, pp. 110–11). Policy activism involves advocating for a social policy, often using research and skills based on policy analysis. Examples of the functions of a policy activist are lobbying, acting as an expert and giving testimony regarding proposed legislation and policy, and monitoring policy (Fisher and Karger, 1997, pp. 111–12).

The roles involved in policy analysis and policy activism are specialized ones that require a number of technical skills, some of which entail advanced education. Yet there is an important place for policy as practice in all social work. In the context of Wharf's and Titmuss's broad and inclusive conception of social policy, all social workers must both recognize and understand the implications and impact of the social policies that affect their work and their clients. Further, they must have the skill and knowledge necessary to begin to take action to effect change in policies that the social worker considers detrimental to her or his clients or others. This action may be taken, within the scope of the worker's abilities, directly by the worker alone or in alliance with service users (Wharf and McKenzie, 1998), or by referral to other resources, such as planning councils, community action groups, or advocacy groups, so that they can assess the policies and take action (see Siegel, 1994, for more on this view).

CHAPTER SUMMARY

This chapter began by asking whether social work is a profession. It examined both the benefits of a profession and some of the pitfalls of professionalization. Among others, an important benefit is that a strong profession can more easily establish quality standards. On the other hand, established professions often become inward-looking, and this tends to thwart arguments and initiatives for change and social action. It is important not to get caught up in a debate about the status of social work as a profession. Social work will continue to develop and change as a profession, responding to new theories, events, processes, environments, needs, and populations. Social work's responsiveness is a positive feature, one that is necessary in a rapidly changing world.

The second section organized the roles of social workers according to micro, mezzo, and macro practice. While there are other ways to organize social work roles, we suggest that this is the best way to view roles of generalist practice. The following is a list of roles that are described in the chapter. This list is not exhaustive, and the roles are not in any particular order of importance or frequency of use.

Micro and mezzo systems: working with individuals, families, and groups

- counsellor and therapist
- case manager
- group worker

Micro, mezzo, and macro systems: roles for all levels of practice

- advocate
- enabler or facilitator
- educator, teacher, or coach
- mediator
- outreach worker
- social broker
- evaluator

Macro systems: working in community development and social policy

- community practice or organizing
  - community developer
  - social planner
  - social activist
  - policy activist and analyst

All of the roles described in this chapter—which are by no means the only ones—are vital to social work practice. They offer the worker different possibilities for work among diverse situations and groups of people. Many roles might be taken on by a generalist practitioner in daily frontline practice. Social workers apply their skills in flexible ways, adapting to events and opportunities in the practice setting and in a client's situation. It is not customary for social workers to keep track of the roles they take on each day in whatever field they practise, but if they did, it would likely be evident that these are many.

chapter 5

The Connection between Social Welfare Policy and Social Work Practice: Health and Mental Health as Illustrations

Chapter Goal

To describe social work practice in health and mental health in relation to developments in health and mental health policy.

To show, using the example of health and mental health, the connection between social work practice and social welfare policy.

This Chapter ▼

- shows that social welfare policy is filtered through the professional lens of social work
- describes the historical development of health and mental health in Canadian society
- identifies the common social work roles found in health and mental health practice
- reviews the development of selected social welfare policies in health care and how they have shaped practice
- illustrates the impact of large-scale (macro level) and small-scale (micro level) social welfare policies on social work practice through examples
- describes current developments and future trends and their implications for social work

INTRODUCTION*

The ideological lens discussed in Chapter 3 can help us understand how social welfare policy can be interpreted through a filter or lens. Just as helping professions develop a picture of clients and their situations as filtered through their social work lens, they also develop an understanding of social policy as seen through an ideological lens. Most professional groups, including social workers, tend to filter social welfare policies through a similar lens. This occurs as a result of professional education and socialization (see Chapter 3). The values and ethics of social work (based on a code of ethics) are an important feature of this lens, framing how social welfare policy is viewed. For example, the trend toward privatization of public services and cuts to social programs is generally seen negatively by social workers because those who are poorest will likely suffer additional hardship, an inequitable and unfair outcome. However, additional provisioning for women or families on social assistance is viewed positively because it can be seen as promoting social work values such as dignity and respect of persons, social equality, and justice. Other groups in society hold different sets of values that in turn influence how they see social policy through their ideological lens. Later in this chapter, we make use of an ideological lens based on these values to interpret social welfare policy in health and mental health.

SOCIAL WORK IN HEALTH CARE FACILITIES

Historically, women have been the main actors in helping the sick and frail, not only in the home or community but also in health care facilities. Social services in hospitals began in the early 1900s. In the United States, the Massachusetts General Hospital was the first to respond to the requests of nurses and other women volunteers who said it was not enough to attend only to the physical health of patients, especially those who were poor (Rehr, 1998). At the time, there was a sense that poverty was a sign of moral weakness and that charity meant helping people who were perceived as deserving—for example, those suffering from an illness. Rehr (1998) points out that at New York's Mount Sinai Hospital in the early 1900s, not only social services but also programs that responded to the needs of hospital patients—such as hospital volunteer assistance, patient libraries, homecare, and support services for children—were established. These initiatives marked a new understanding of caring for ill people that went beyond medical treatment alone.

In Canada, social work in health care has had a similar history. Winnipeg and Toronto General Hospitals established departments of social work in the early 1900s. In Winnipeg, historical accounts suggest that most of the services provided were for basic needs, such as arranging transportation, financial assistance, and referrals to "health and welfare agencies" and dealing with mental health problems (MacKay, 1993). Hospital or medical social

* We have chosen to use health and mental health to illustrate the connection between social policy and social work practice. We could have used child welfare, the justice system, income security, or any other field of practice to write this chapter.

workers, once referred to as "almoners"—those who distribute alms—sought to establish medical social work as a profession. They were primarily concerned about the postdischarge needs of patients and how patients could be helped so they could pay for their medical expenses.

Social work in health care facilities was also likely influenced by Mary Richmond's 1917 book *Social Diagnosis,* which stressed a scientific approach and methods that were parallel to medical practice (i.e., diagnosis and treatment) in social work. Richmond's medical model for social work practice fit well in a medical setting.

Group work and community development have become a focus of attention for social workers since the Second World War (Rehr, 1998). Group work is used in health care settings with people who face common challenges or problems. For example, patients in a heart-transplant program might meet with a social worker to discuss health-related issues and concerns about transplantation and aftercare following surgery. In addition, family-centred work has become prominent in hospitals as responsibilities for postdischarge care are increasingly passed on to families and communities. Such responsibilities frequently put additional stress on families and friends (usually women) to provide for the home-based medical and other needs of discharged patients. Social workers use their familiarity with community resources and their knowledge of client situations to draw up a discharge plan that sets out how the client will get the help that is needed and who will be involved.

The challenges that health social workers confront require skills for working in a complex, multi-profession setting, an understanding of the impact of illness on people, and an ability to mobilize needed resources. The importance of collaboration within health care teams and for peer supervision and support must also be highlighted. Client situations are often not only about discharge needs but also involve serious problems that affect well-being. Unemployment, lack of social support, addiction problems, and other concerns may also need to be addressed. Due to more rapid client discharge from the hospital, more efficient service is demanded of the health social worker. The specialized knowledge and skills that a social worker develops over time are assets in health care facilities (Holosko and Taylor, 1992; Spitzer and Nash, 1996; Heinonen and Metteri, in press). In the case example below, you will apply your skills primarily in working with the family.

Social Work Practice: A Case Example in Health

The case example of John Costa illustrates difficulties in communication between John and his family that arise due to feelings of powerlessness and grief. As the social worker in the situation, you have a number of ways in which to work. As the assessment begins, ask yourself who your client is, what is important to consider, and how you will begin.

Case Example

John and His Family

John, 57, is a patient in a hospital where program and staffing changes have recently occurred. He is in the final stages of stomach cancer, and you are asked to assess his situation. John's family members disagree with the health care team about the course of treatment he is receiving. They feel that they are not being listened to and that the staff on the ward do not help their loved one as much as other patients. The nurses, in particular, have become upset due to frequent questions and demands for action by family members, who approach the staff at different times. The family members have come from different parts of the country to be with John. He is visibly tired and distressed by what he overhears his family members saying about the quality of care being provided. This situation has been developing for more than six days, but it was not possible for you to visit the ward until now, as it is not your assigned area. The social work position for this ward was cut some months before due to hospital budget constraints. However, due to the rising tension you are asked to intervene.

When you enter John's room, you are faced with a group of people who do not seem to be communicating well with the person who is ill. They avoid talking about the seriousness of his illness and instead discuss practical concerns and the lives of friends and family members. You are concerned about John and his feelings and wishes at this time. You wonder how his well-being is affected by what is going on among those closest to him.

Since you note that the family members are avoiding discussing their feelings—particularly when they are together in John's room—you would likely want to explore this area. Perhaps you can find a private family room to use for your work with the family, where you can ask about their relationships to John, their understanding of his illness and treatment, and any cultural perspectives that might play a role in how they deal with serious illness and impending death in the family. Although you are not yet sure, you suspect that this family is having trouble talking about cancer and dying. Instead, they seem to focus on what people are doing and what is going on today. Certainly no one talks of the future or of their feelings about John's situation. Instead, there is criticism of the care he is receiving and what has been done to date, as if these are the central problems. The family may feel helpless about not being able to do more for John. It seems to you that they are in distress and are having difficulty expressing their feelings to one another.

At the same time, John expresses concern about his pension benefits and payment of outstanding bills for rent and utilities. He wants to have these taken care of while he is in hospital, but finds it difficult to ask his relatives for help. John also tells you that he has applied for disability pension as his doctor felt he was eligible for this. He is not sure if any decision has been made about it yet.

Clearly there is a need to help the family members talk to one another and to John. As a social worker, you can facilitate this process. The family may need assistance in acknowledging John's impending death. If appropriate, you might assist in helping them talk to one another about their relationship with John. John and his family may want to explore the possibility of another setting in which he may prefer to die—for example, a hospice or palliative care unit or his home. He may also want to discuss his funeral wishes. The family may need support to discuss these issues together and individually.

These topics should come about naturally through gentle questions and sensitive approaches that are learned through social work training. You may also need to advocate with the staff for adequate pain and symptom control, and to work with the other members of the health care team to help them understand and interpret the family's criticisms and angry behaviour.

In this situation, there is much that a health social worker can do. You want very much to help John and his family, even though you know that patients on other wards also need you at this time. You are stretched, but believe that the Costa family's situation could deteriorate further, affecting John, his family, ward staff, and other patients. It is a tough time to be working as a hospital social worker.

SOCIAL WORK ROLES IN HEALTH CARE FACILITIES

There is a wide range of roles in hospital-based social work. In the case example of John Costa, as the social worker you could be

1. an enabler, helping the family members address their feelings together
2. an educator, discussing the course of treatment and its outcomes with family members who may not fully understand it
3. a mediator, attempting to resolve conflict between staff and the family and handling the criticism that has been levelled by the family
4. an advocate, interacting with wider systems or even across hospital departments and/or health professions
5. a counsellor, listening and intervening appropriately and sensitively to the issues and needs of both family and patient during the course of time you work with them
6. a social broker, linking family members to a program for families facing loss
7. a case manager, providing resource coordination and management (e.g., regarding a disability pension application and grief counselling)

You might discover that one of the family members has herself had a life-threatening illness and is now having panic attacks thinking that her illness might be returning. Another family member might be facing some financial problems due to taking time off work to be with John. You could help these people contact community organizations or employers to obtain needed resources. Being an advocate on behalf of the patient might also be necessary so that he receives help in pain and symptom control.

As the social worker in John's case, you need to evaluate the effects of your intervention and its process or outcome as part of hospital policy. At an appropriate time you would then become an evaluator. The data provided by the evaluation could contribute to enhancements in hospital or social work services. Evaluation of social work practice has increased in recent years, particularly as facilities need to demonstrate that the outcomes of services are beneficial and worth funding.

HEALTH POLICY: CONTEXT AND ORIGINS

Social work practice takes place in the context of social and economic policies. In this chapter we do not examine the range of social policies in Canada, nor do we provide a detailed account of how policies are developed or changed. Rather, we limit our discussion to exploring the connection between practice and policy by examining some health and mental health policies. However, we encourage readers to review other works to develop a deeper understanding of policies and social welfare policymaking. Numerous books will provide readers with in-depth and detailed information about Canadian social welfare policy (e.g., Kirwin, 1996; Armitage, 1996; Evans and Wekerle, 1997; Wharf and McKenzie, 1998; Broad and Antony, 1999; Tester and Case, 1999; Rice and Prince, 2000; Turner and Turner, 2001; Hick, 2002; Westhues, 2003; Kufeldt and McKenzie, 2003; Hick, 2004).

The literature does not clearly distinguish between health and other social welfare policies. Many writers, such as Titmuss (1974) and Rein (1974), see the essence of policy formulation as making choices between competing social values and goals. This broad use of the term "social welfare policy" encompasses health policies. T. H. Marshall, a British scholar, is a little more specific (as quoted in Graham, Swift, and Delaney, 2000): "The central core of [social welfare policy] consists, therefore, of social insurance, public (or national) assistance, the health and welfare services, and housing policy" (p. 8). Thus, we are using the term **"social welfare policy"** to encompass both health and social welfare services.

Understanding the connections between macro and micro policy and social work practice is essential for students studying social work. The processes of policymaking involve social workers not only because they see the effects on their clients, but also because they interpret policy every day and advocate for changes in it. Social workers have opportunities to participate in policymaking through the activities of their professional associations, their workplaces, in public meetings, and through research and writing.

The history of health care policy in Canada is lively and interesting, replete with political struggles, strikes, and personalities. According to Sears (1995), health measures in the early 1900s involved preventing and treating communicable diseases, such as tuberculosis and sexually transmitted diseases, and home visits by nurses concerned about household hygiene and children's health (p. 177). These activities, often targeted at new immigrants and poor families, aimed to prevent illness and promote good health at a time when Canada was still developing as a nation (Sears, 1995).

Northcott (1994) explains that before the Second World War Canadians paid for health care out of their own pockets or with help from relatives, friends, or charitable organizations. This created hardship for patients and their families, who often found themselves in serious financial difficulty when illness struck. Clarke (1996) notes that several provinces attempted to initiate health insurance programs in the 1930s and 1940s, but failed (pp. 256–57). In 1946, a conference of the provinces and the federal government was held to discuss a possible Canadian national health care insurance system. Although the conference goal wasn't achieved, it did move forward the process of federal–provincial cooperation in health care (Armstrong and Armstrong, 1996). In the late 1950s, medical insurance that primarily covered hospital care and some medical tests was introduced (Clarke, 1996). The birthplace of Canadian medicare is Saskatchewan, where in 1959 the social democratic government led by Tommy Douglas spearheaded its adoption by the Saskatchewan government. Douglas was committed to public social services and health care that would be available to all regardless of ability to pay. The tumult of a subsequent doctors' strike in 1962 and numerous public demonstrations either for or against universal health care are an important part of Canadian health policy history. By 1970, all provinces took part in the federally and provincially cost-shared health insurance scheme (Clarke, 1996).

The Canadian public health care system was established at a time when people had a high regard for and great faith in medical technology and physician-provided care as the keys to good health. Many communicable diseases had been conquered, and antibiotics and other drugs had been discovered to cure numerous serious health problems. The efficient, professional, modern hospital with the latest equipment epitomized a good health care system (Rachlis and Kushner, 1994), giving people the confidence that they would be well cared for when they or their family members became ill. This period in health care policy also instituted the medical model as the optimum approach to care, and physicians as the gatekeepers of many health care services (Clarke, 1996).

Quebec pursued its own course in 1966 by appointing the Castonguay-Nepveu Commission, also known as the Commission of Inquiry on Health and Social Welfare, in opposition to the religious leaders who essentially controlled health and welfare services in that province (Lésemann, 1984, p. 48). It is interesting to note that, following the commission's report, Quebec implemented, along with other changes, a model of social and health cooperation. A cornerstone of these initiatives was the local community service centres (*Centres locaux de services communautaires,* or CLSCs), bringing together health clinics and social service offices where psychosocial counselling and community programs took place. Due to some contradictions and conflicts in combining health care services and social development, this did not, however, turn out to be a very successful collaboration (Lésemann, 1984, p. 48). Nevertheless, the CLSCs have been effective in supporting numerous local efforts in preventive health and social services (White, 1994, p. 92), and continue to offer an alternative to institution-based and fragmented service provision.

The acknowledgment of people's right to health care implies responsibility on the part of the state to provide this care in an equitable manner. The *Canada Health Act,* decades in the making prior to its national implementation in 1984, stipulates five principles:

1. Health care must be publicly administered through provincial health insurance plans on a nonprofit basis.
2. Health care insurance plans must cover all services deemed medically required and provided by hospitals and health care practitioners. Where it is permitted, services of dentists or other health care providers may be paid fully or partially.
3. All residents are eligible for coverage by medical insurance.
4. Temporary absence from one's home province or a move from one province to another does not interrupt health care insurance coverage.
5. All provincial health plans are required to provide reasonable access to medically necessary hospital or medical care without obstacles such as cost or distance.

These principles also support the medical model of health care, which is hospital based and physician dominated. Canadians pay for health care not directly to practitioners but through taxes, and, in some cases, to a province's insurance scheme. As a national health insurance program, the government is the payer of the services (Weitz, 1996). Nevertheless, most provinces' plans cover the cost of drugs, eye examinations, eyeglasses, dental care, physiotherapy, and chiropractic treatment only partially or not at all.

Medical practitioners, reimbursed a set amount for each separate procedure or patient visit, are able to adjust the mix or quantity of services they provide to earn a desired income level (Burke and Stevenson, 1994). Hospitals receive annual funding from provincial governments, to be spent according to the decisions of hospital administrators. They are required to provide health care to all in their coverage area who need it. The physicians in a hospital are paid a salary from the hospital's budget (Weitz, 1996).

Hospitals consume the lion's share of the health care budget—primarily the teaching hospitals, which purchase and use expensive, state-of-the-art equipment and techniques and employ a large number of well-paid, specialist professionals. These professionals not only are practitioners but also act as instructors to students in medicine, nursing, and many other health-related professions. Social work students also carry out practicum placements in health care settings supervised by hospital social workers.

The five principles of the *Canada Health Act* are currently being challenged, as the Canadian government has cut funding allocations for social services to the provinces. Terms such as "medically necessary" and "reasonable access" are debated and reinterpreted by provincial governments that have felt the brunt of cuts to health, education, and social welfare and seek to pass them on to their populations. Hospitals and other health care facilities that are facing cuts in their budgets are continuously scrutinized by administrators needing to reduce expenses, increase efficiency, and accomplish more with fewer staff (Sullivan and Baranek, 2002).

In 1995, the Canadian government merged several federal programs that provided payments to the provinces for social programs into the Canada Health and Social Transfer (CHST), which saw yearly cuts to all provinces from 1996 (Armstrong and Armstrong, 1996). This sustained cost cutting forced the provinces to bear increasing financial responsibility for health and social services. As funds from the federal government to the provinces decreased, provinces reacted by prioritizing some social programs and services and reducing expenditures on and even cutting others. Although the federal government has attempted to limit provincial autonomy in health care policy, many provinces have cut expenditures, streamlined and merged health care facilities, introduced some private health care services, and decentralized health care decision making and delivery.

At the same time, Canadians are increasing their use of alternative health care strategies, such as acupuncture, herbal remedies, homeopathy, relaxation therapy, and others that offer different treatment options. People who use alternative health care also demand standards and information to guide them in making appropriate choices as consumers. This is an area in which there is a great deal of room for research and public education. Although the medical profession and the government have been slow to acknowledge the significance of alternative health care and its role in people's well-being, this may be changing due to public pressure. Whether people will begin to demand that alternative health care services be included in medicare coverage remains to be seen.

Forming or Reforming Health Care Policy

Health policies are often construed as public policies in which action involves governments and their representatives. However, other nongovernmental organizations, businesses, and institutions often play key roles. Health policy is characterized by

> courses of action that affect the set of institutions, organizations, services, and funding arrangements of the health care system. It goes beyond health services, however, and includes actions or intended actions by public, private, and voluntary organizations that have an impact on health. (Walt, 1994, p. 41)

Those who analyze social policies in order to change them are concerned about the content of policy but also are actors in the policymaking process. For example, a citizen's coalition that wants to take action against imminent threats to publicly funded homecare programs will want to be familiar with governmental policies about eligibility criteria, included services, and standards for these services. The members of the coalition and their supporters will likely study how the new policies will affect homecare users and their families or others involved in caring for them and how they fall short of intended goals and purposes. The coalition might also determine any gaps in the policies and how policies could better serve users and those who care for them, with the purpose of preparing a position paper or presentation to policymakers.

The pieces that make up a social welfare policy—its purpose, aims, intent, target population, and methods of implementation—are central. Important as these are to our understanding of how policies become practice, we also need to consider how policies reach the level of public debate. Politicians, bureaucrats, professionals, organizations, and other groups may be drawn into the debate, offering their views on the best way of doing things (Fraser, 1989; Mackintosh, 1992; Walt, 1994). The processes by which policies are formed and reformed require attention, as do the context or environment in which these occur and the actors who exert influence (Walt, 1994). How are different views given weight in the shaping of social welfare policy? Is the policy thought out, put into practice, and implemented by those who have the position and power to make decisions, or is it the result of state or organizational response to certain interests (say, physicians, insurers, or facilities that provide services)—or is it both? What brings about a change in an existing social welfare policy? For example, how is it that health care programs or services covered by medical insurance come to be deinsured—no longer eligible for coverage?

We often think of policymaking in social welfare as something that is aimed at the public good. But what does "public" really mean? Is it everyone, or a category of people—say, a target group, such as poor older people? Fraser (1989) points out that publics can be "large, authoritative, and able to set the terms of debate for many of the rest. Others, by contrast, are small, self-enclosed, and enclaved, unable to make much of a mark beyond their own borders" (p. 167). Many social work clients can be seen as fitting into the second category. This would include, for example, people who live with a chronic illness and require homecare or other supports that a social worker might arrange. Of course, such groups are not necessarily small, but they may not be organized or powerful enough at a particular time to make their views known in the public sphere (for example, the media), where they can be heard. Nevertheless, this doesn't mean that they don't try. When there is a threat to an existing program, such as subsidized homecare, the voices of those affected in our society may be picked out by the media. In this way the views of concerned citizens become known. Depending on how well the issue pulls others into the debate—such as like-minded groups, politicians, organizations, the state, or other key players—governments may feel pressured to either defend the policy or consider changing it. The issue may also involve people who previously had little input into policy decision making, experiencing it as an exclusive process that involves mainly politicians and civil servants.

Due to rapidly increasing pressures on health care and how it is delivered, policy on health care has had to respond to new challenges. Reforms of existing policies have been introduced and implemented, and other initiatives are likely being considered. Moving away from views that stress technical approaches to health care reform to those that centre on a broader perspective, including the roles and interests of actors and the context (people and environments), is useful. Walt and Gilson (1994), referring to health care, suggest that there are four components to policy reform: its content, actors as individuals and groups, the context, and the process. They emphasize that it is not enough to understand how social welfare policy is made by simply focusing on what changes occur in a program or service. Instead, they assert, a better understanding of policymaking comes from stepping back and looking at how the policy came to be in its historical, political, social, and economic environment. One could also extend understanding of the process of policymaking by examining who promoted the policy and who was against it, and for what reasons (Walt, 1994). In addition, the content of the policy itself needs to be examined to see how it has changed and what potential it has for other changes in the future. Many variables need to be considered together to form a comprehensive picture of policymaking.

Important in social work activity, whether with individuals or groups of people or in social welfare policy, is understanding the conditions and determinants related to an issue (Berkowitz, 1996; Heinonen and Metteri, in press). For example, a policy that enables poor families living in inadequate rental housing (cold in winter, crowded, and needing repair) to own a subsidized house potentially affects these families in other ways. Having a comfortable home of one's own can add to family members' physical health, sense of safety, security, self-esteem, and belonging in a community. As a result, health status may be improved and well-being is positively affected. Although housing policy may not appear to be linked to health, there are connections.

The same can be said for a transportation policy that keeps bus fares low, allowing those with low incomes to seek jobs, go to school, attend health clinics, and visit friends and relatives more easily. Such a policy may enhance quality of life, including social support and health, for many. Child protection policy is important to social work practice. Children whose parents cannot care for them, whether due to poor physical or mental health or other problems, may experience delayed development that may pose mental health and other barriers for them in growing up. Social policies that aim to deal with adverse impacts of serious family problems on children include those related to the provision of early childhood education, supports in school, community recreational activities, and social service programs. These can improve children's health and well-being at important periods in their lives. All these, although not specifically health or mental health policies, may have effects on both the physical and mental health of children.

For some First Nations populations (i.e., those who hold treaty rights), health care is a federal jurisdiction that includes payment of bills for health care as a treaty right (referred to as the "medicine chest") and financing of public health care for First Nations people. It is a complex arrangement of services and programs, delivered provincially, which tends to lead to service gaps among those who move from reserve areas to cities. Health care services are uneven and sometimes do not exist for remote Aboriginal communities (Shah, Gunraj, and Hux, 2003; O'Reilly, 1999). Postl (1997) holds that Aboriginal people's health could be advanced by establishment of an Aboriginal Health Institute "that would play an advocacy role and replace existing functions within Health Canada" (p. 1657). The promotion of education and training of more Aboriginal health workers and the initiation of a network of Aboriginal health centres and other facilities for healing could advance the health of Aboriginal people.

Questions must also be asked about the values and assumptions that underlie particular policies, who influences and controls the decision-making process, who will benefit and who will not, how the policy will be implemented, how much it will cost, and who pays (Wharf and McKenzie, 1998). In addition, the short- and long-term effects of the policy and its impact on diverse groups of people need to be considered.

It is apparent that a shift has been occurring in health policy in many parts of the world (Walt, 1994; Ham, 1997; Green and Thorogood, 1998). Those nations that have benefited from a high standard of health care and relatively good access to services for their citizens are now experiencing the impact of cuts to state health budgets and the reform of health care services and delivery. The context in which budgetary decisions occur is linked to international and national events and processes. Falling currency values and increasing national debt, along with an environment that favours more conservative economic policy and measures to reduce publicly funded programs, have resulted in many governments cutting back on social welfare and health provision (Ham, 1997). The cuts have often affected those who are the most poor and vulnerable.

Many people have spent much time and energy examining what is and isn't good about health care. Health care is political because there is always a perceived need for more, and rarely does the level of care please everyone. When under threat, health care is a policy area that creates a lot of debate, since changes affect us all in some way. That is why many feel passionately about preserving quality physician-provided and hospital-based care. Although people are also concerned about preventing illness and promoting health in daily life, these issues attract far less attention than policies that determine medical insurance coverage, prescription drug programs, and access to acute health care services in hospitals. When we are ill or injured and need support to regain our health, we want to be assured that help will be available, services are nearby, and health care insurance will cover the needed care. Thus, the closing of a hospital or a reduction in health insurance coverage raises strong feelings in most people.

Walt and Gilson (1994) warn that when conservative economics drives policy reform, we lose much more than just services. Our humanitarian values and beliefs and the feelings of responsibility that we have for people, especially those who are ill, poor, frail, and otherwise vulnerable, are eroded. Although social workers as a professional group within the health care system have not been at the forefront of health care policy development, they have been concerned about the impact of changes on clients. Social work's professional mission and mandate call on us to promote the interests of those who are least able to do so for themselves.

Public Participation in Health Policy

The environment in which health policy has been formed and reformed is changing. The medical profession has had, and continues to have, a great deal of influence on health policies, but the voices of health care users are becoming more prominent. Today, the heated debates about health care attest to increasing tension and divergent views. Not only costs, but also concerns about what constitutes and determines health and well-being have become central issues. With the rise in heart disease, cancer, diabetes, and arthritis, among other health problems, has come the realization that medicine is not without limits. It is less able to help, for example, those who suffer from chronic illness.

The major actors in Canadian health care appear to be government health departments, physicians through their medical associations, and regional administrators. Various groups and individuals, such as senior citizens' coalitions, health care workers' unions, social activists, and people with particular health care needs also act in their own interests to influence health care. The federal government's National Forum on Health (1994) and the Romanow Commission (2002), which called for Canadian citizens to come forward and speak about health care, involved people in consultation processes. Although many people across the country had opportunities to voice their ideas, it seems likely that in the future the provincial governments will be the bigger players in health reform while the federal government will play an overseer role, ensuring that the principles of health care are maintained.

Health care users have generally become more demanding, asserting their right to good health care and information about treatments. They also want a greater say in health care policy decision making. The aim of the National Forum on Health was to involve Canadians in advising the federal government on ways of improving health and health care (Health Canada, 1998). This initiative came at a time when the provinces were being forced to pay a greater share of health care costs due to federal reductions in health and social welfare funding. The Romanow Commission prepared its final report in 2002 after hearing from a large number of Canadians across the country. The report was launched by Roy Romanow on November 28 at the National Press Theatre in Ottawa and included some key recommendations for change, including (1) modernization of the *Canada Health Act*; (2) establishment of a Health Council of Canada that collaborates with multiple stakeholders to monitor the performance of the health care system; (3) increased funds to help provinces cover the cost of insured health services in 2006 and continuing, sustained support over time; (4) a national home care program, including help for unpaid caregivers to care for ill family members and for provision of mental health care at home; (5) prescription drug coverage for those with serious need and creation of a National Drug Agency to control costs, conduct tests, and review drug patent laws; and (6) formation of partnerships with Aboriginal peoples to better serve their health needs. Some of these recommendations are being implemented (i.e., benefits for unpaid caregivers), but the fate of others remains to be seen.

Although views from citizens have been sought, public reaction and protest about health care decisions are often heard, and health care has become an important issue for political parties. In Canada, the professional unions and associations of health care workers have been particularly active in voicing concerns about what they see as deteriorating health care services and working conditions (Armstrong et al., 1994; Armstrong et al., 1997; Sullivan and Baranek, 2002). Health care policy decision making needs to include people who represent diverse groups in society; it must also include those who are especially sensitive to changes in health services, access, waiting periods, insurance coverage, timing, cost, and other factors.

Determinants of Health and the Role of Prevention

Important as medical care is, increasing attention is being paid to the links between poverty and illness, between homelessness and mental health, and between unemployment and changes in well-being. People's health has also come to be seen in relation to social, economic, and environmental factors (Health and Welfare Canada, 1986). This understanding has in turn given rise to the idea that poor health needs to be addressed, not only through medical care, but also through social interventions in housing, income security, neighbourhood safety, and early childhood education programs. Burke and Stevenson (1994) warn, however, that we must guard against reductions in health care spending that are carried out in the name of increasing funds for other social services that, it could be claimed, are health related. This strategy could end up reducing acute-care services to provide more preventive social programs. We need both in order to protect the health and well-being of citizens.

Recent health promotion campaigns have encouraged people to adopt healthier lifestyles (for example, quit smoking, eat healthy foods, exercise, breastfeed). Less attention has been given to promoting the physical and social environments that enhance health and well-being, although these play significant roles in our quality of life. Addressing substandard housing, dangerous workplace conditions, air pollution, unhealthy drinking water, and other problems that are linked to poor health is necessary (see, for instance, Armstrong and Armstrong, 1996). The healthy communities approach (safe streets, neighbourhood projects such as community gardens, and other local programs to enhance the quality of life) overlaps with ideas about creating healthy lifestyles. Connections can be seen between community participation, belonging in a neighbourhood, and residents' well-being. As Armitage (1996) notes, "The consequence is a convergence between the concepts of community welfare and health. The convergence is marked by overlapping interests of health and social agencies" (p. 105). This implies that collaboration between these agencies and organizations would be useful for better-coordinated services and programs. Some examples might include safely disposing of toxic or dangerous waste, increasing park space for children's play areas, promoting neighbourhood vegetable gardens, and others. In these kinds of endeavours, government departments might work with community organizations and citizens. Social workers in community development work, in other fields of practice, or as citizens can play roles in helping to initiate and support community projects like these. With skills in facilitation, communication, group work, policy analysis, advocacy, and social brokering, there are many opportunities for social workers to partner with community resident groups to advance or effect change in local social policies.

EFFECTS OF MACRO POLICIES

New hospital policies have meant cuts in equipment purchases, patient programs, and staffing that have demoralized and constrained health care staff. These facility policies can be traced to broader macro-level social welfare policy changes, including macro-level federal budget reallocation that affects the provinces, which have resorted to regional downsizing and reducing some health care services and programs to save money.

In thinking about the macro level, we know that government cuts that are a direct result of the CHST policy have meant reductions in spending on health and social welfare. These budget allocations are typically large and often are the first ones to be reduced. Cutting from these budgets also assumes that other areas cannot be cut. Conservative values and assumptions that underpin state provision of health and social welfare are also involved. Such trends support a focus on less government support and more individual, family, and community-based efforts in providing for people's needs, including health care. The drive for fiscal efficiency and an ideology of individual responsibility (see Chapter 3) tends to be central in these measures. There may also be more stringent eligibility criteria and longer assessment processes; for example, to receive disability pension benefits. This ensures that only those who receive no other support or benefits and whose disability is deemed severe are helped.

What all of this means at the local level is that hospitals, health care programs, and perhaps other social welfare measures are constrained. Managers in these organizations strive to provide services with reduced resources. In some health care facilities, for example, the services of allied health professionals (e.g., occupational therapists, psychologists, and social workers) are reduced so that nursing staff levels can be maintained. Some facilities have experienced the closing of beds or entire wards as a result of health policy reforms.

Despite the changing shape of political and economic forces on cost containment, cost rationalization, and increased community responsibility for people's health and welfare, there continues to be a need for social workers in the health care system. This is so due to the effects of shorter hospital stays, acute health problems, complexity of client problems (biological, psychological, social, and structural), and the recognition that family or other supportive help and client advocacy are needed during hospitalization and after discharge. The ways in which social workers can draw on client and family strengths and understand health and other problems from a combined biological, psychological, environmental, and structural perspective as effective team members working with other practitioners is of value in the health care system (Sulman, Savage, and Way, 2001).

Social Welfare Policy: Effects on John and His Family

If it weren't for budget cuts at the hospital in response to federal and provincial budget cuts, John, his family, and the ward staff might have received help earlier, which could have helped avert or reduce the problems that are now occurring. Having a social worker assigned to a particular ward would also mean that he or she might have brought specialized knowledge and expertise to the situation. She could have mediated between the family and staff to facilitate better communication and understanding, explore appropriate resources in the community as they were needed, and, with the health care team, been available to deal with ongoing issues of concern to John and his family. If there had been a social worker dedicated to this busy ward, other patients, families, and health care team members could benefit from the resources of an additional staff member. This worker would not be so overextended that she could respond only to crises.

The stress created by changes may also affect staff, which can limit their resilience in handling difficult patient situations. Over the long term, job stress can lead to time missed from work and reduced morale for all staff. If, at the same time, community-based resources are also being reduced, there might be gaps in the help available to clients after discharge from hospital. This affects the social worker's capacity to do her or his job well and forces clients to manage without needed help.

Changing Organizational and Social Welfare Policy in Health Care

It is important for social workers in the health care system to contribute to change at both the organizational and social welfare policy levels when they feel it is in the best interests of clients. In fact, our professional values and principles as articulated in codes of ethics require it (see Chapter 3). We can return to some of the roots of social work and use our skills and knowledge for change in three ways (Kaminski and Walmsley, 1995): (1) as members of the community and as citizens, we can speak out and write about our views; (2) as agents of change, our workplaces and local organizations offer sites where we could work collectively with colleagues to effect change that will be of benefit to clients; and (3) as activists, we can join with others (e.g., social workers, service users, and others) in a purposeful program of social change. What issue we choose to take up, for what reasons, and for which outcomes needs to be considered. Some kinds of actions involve more risk to individual social workers than others and their consequences need to be carefully weighed beforehand. This does not mean that nothing should be done, but that a variety of strategies and their potential outcomes need to be explored.

Figueira-McDonough (1993) suggested that social workers could promote legislation that corrects social injustice or enhances equity for marginalized social groups, or use the legal system to challenge laws that are unfair or damaging to some. Other potential activities include analysis of social policies to bring to light their assumptions, goals, effects, and other factors, and research projects that examine adverse impacts of particular social policies (e.g., homecare or pharmaceutical programs) on individuals, families, and communities, and dissemination of research findings to bring these to light.

The social worker working with John and his family might decide to raise the issue of cuts to hospitals and their impact on patient care with her professional association in order to collectively explore how this situation has come about and whether action could be taken, whether through meeting health care administrators, a conference presentation, or joint efforts with a health care users' group. She might also consider becoming part of the hospital's research group to study patient care with other staff, and later report to a government body. Social advocacy, policy analysis, community organizing, facilitation, evaluation, and education roles would be prominent in these activities.

Social Work and Health at the Neighbourhood Level

Health is a concern not just for social workers in hospitals and the individuals receiving their attention. The largely female pioneers of social work worked to improve the health and social situations of people living in crowded, unhealthy environments of rapidly growing cities. The settlement house movement (occurring in Canada, the United States, and England) and the social reforms it aimed for brought to light the importance of seeing the individual and his or her problems within a social and physical environment (Berkowitz and Jenkins, 1996). Rehr (1998) suggests that although this knowledge may have been clear to social reformers, it didn't readily become a part of social work practice in medical settings. Instead, social workers in hospitals focused on the clinical aspects of illness and medical care, serving the needs of physicians and hospital administrators in the services provided. Hospital social workers' jobs did not generally take them to poor communities, where they might have been better able to work locally for healthier conditions.

Future practice in health social work may emphasize greater efforts at the community level that focus on promoting health and preventing illness among people who experience poverty, who are chronically ill, or who lack access to supportive resources to improve their well-being (Rehr et al., 1998). These efforts might be based in a facility in which preventive social and health care services are housed, or they may even be based in a community organization that works mostly on social issues or programs, such as improving neighbourhood housing conditions.

A traditional approach to working at the community level tends to focus primarily on the problems or limitations in a community that determine its needs and the actions to follow. Another strategy, described by McKnight (1998), stresses that people who work with communities could begin with the resources and strengths that exist in the community and build on them in the process of shaping desirable activities and projects. This means identifying with community members their strengths and those of the community as a whole. An approach that focuses only on needs derived from identified problems narrows people's vision, makes little use of a community's existing capacities and assets, and limits creative and locally relevant ideas: "Viewing a community as a nearly endless list of problems leads to the fragmentation of efforts to provide solutions. It also denies community wisdom that regards problems as intertwined" (McKnight, 1998, p. 10). It also limits knowledge about the diverse talents and gifts each person, family, and group in a community has to offer. In his discussion of a strengths approach in social work practice, Saleebey (1997a) points out how these features of people's lives are central to working with them and provide a good starting point for community work.

In effective community work, developing relationships that promote the inclusion of all members, especially those whose voices are less often heard, can lead to richer information, a better range of ideas, and greater commitment to action. Professionals in health and social service agencies, working together with local communities, can establish programs to enhance the quality of life for residents. As an example of such an initiative, social workers and health workers could plan and implement a summer day camp that helps children learn interpersonal skills, build self-esteem, and make effective use of leisure time. Of course, there are many other possibilities. There is still some way to go, however, before such collaboration occurs across health and welfare sectors and respective professional fields.

Social Work Roles in Healthy-Community Initiatives

Social workers who have learned about community work and practice methods can apply their skills at the community level to monitor a client's move back home from hospital, or to work more broadly with communities to enhance health and well-being through community initiatives. Social workers in community-based health programs might find themselves acting as community developers in, for example, organizing lone, adolescent mothers in the community; as advocates for elderly people who live in their homes and need help with chores; as facilitators (enablers) to promote community participation for safer neighbourhood streets; or as teachers who model effective communication skills in community meetings. In community practice there is often a great need for information about the community and its people, projects, and activities. An evaluator may be needed to collect and present data for funders or other stakeholders. The evaluator might conduct research to see what changes have taken place since the implementation of a local neighbourhood recycling project, for example.

MENTAL HEALTH POLICY AND SOCIAL WORK

The number of people who suffer from a mental illness is staggering. Statistics Canada reports that the 2002 Canadian Community Health Survey shows "some 4 percent of people interviewed in the survey reported having experienced symptoms or feelings associated with major depression, compared with 5 percent with diabetes, 5 percent with heart disease and 6 percent with a thyroid condition..." in the previous 12 months (*The Daily,*[1] 2003). Further, *The Daily* reports that according to the World Health Organization, five of the 10 leading causes of disability are related to mental disorders. It predicts that in fewer than 20 years depression will be the second-leading cause of disability in the world. Health Canada estimates that in 1998, mental disorders were the third-highest source of direct health care costs, at $4.7 billion (*The Daily,* 2003). Yet, the Romanow Commission's report (2002) labels mental health as the orphan child of health care. This is so not only because of the lack of resources allocated to mental health, but also because people are reluctant to define psychiatric problems as diseases.

In many respects, mental health policy is a subset of general health policy. For example, in Canada medicare pays for both general and mental health medical services. Generally, the health and mental health policies are similar for mental health patients who require outpatient psychiatric services or short-term (acute) hospital services and who are able to live relatively independent lives. For a summary of mental health policy in Canada see Gray, Shone, and Liddle (2000) and Gray (2001).

The Romanow Commission (2002) recommends the improvement of

> the quality of care and support available to people with mental illnesses by including home mental health case management and intervention services as part of the *Canada Health Act*.... Today, mental health care is largely a home and community-based service, but support for it has too frequently fallen short. It is time to take the long overdue step of ensuring that mental health home care services are included as medically necessary services under the *Canada Health Act,* and available across the country. (Executive Summary, p. 12)

As of the writing of this book, little has been done to change mental health services in Canada since the release of the *Romanow Report.*

As with health services, mental health services are provincial responsibilities. These services are mostly delivered in the same manner as other health services. Usually the frontline, first professional contact for a person with any illness, including a mental illness, is with a family physician. If specialized services such as psychiatric help, family counselling, psychotherapy, group therapy, or the like are needed, the family physician usually makes a referral.

Mental Health Policy, Social Work Practice, and Social Control

In one fundamental way mental health services differ from general health policy: patients who suffer from a physical illness almost always are permitted to make their own treatment decisions. In serious illnesses, doctors will often list the treatment options available to patients, usually with recommendations. In the end, however, the patient is presumed competent to make his or her own choices. This policy differs with people who have mental illnesses.

Treatment of mental illnesses is regulated by provincial mental health acts. These acts establish policies that give professionals the power to make treatment decisions *for* patients diagnosed with a mental illness. To illustrate, suppose a worker on a crisis line decides that a caller is potentially suicidal. Most crisis centres have a policy protocol that directs the worker's actions. A likely scenario is for the worker to notify a mobile crisis unit and/or the police. Often, social workers are employed in mobile crisis units. These workers may visit the caller at his home. Such actions are often taken without the caller's consent or knowledge. If the mobile unit or police determine that the caller is potentially suicidal, or even that he needs medical attention (e.g., a suspected overdose of sleeping pills), the responder has the power to take the caller to hospital—usually the emergency room of a general hospital—even against the caller's will. Once in hospital, the attending physician can order the caller-now-patient to stay and receive treatment even if the patient does not want to do so.

This is a short-term temporary order that must be reviewed, usually within one to three days, by medical experts who are most often psychiatrists. They have the power to certify (sometimes called certification or commitment) that the patient is unable to make appropriate treatment decisions by himself and hence order the patient to stay in hospital and receive treatment with or without his consent. For such drastic action to be initiated, generally the patient must be considered a risk to self or others. Certification must be periodically reviewed, and patients do have rights to challenge such decisions through the legal system. Also, some provinces have legislation that requires mental patients who are at risk to receive treatment even though they live in the community and do not want treatment.

Thus, a major difference between most practice in health contrasted with mental health is the ever-present element of social control in mental health. The primary function of social workers in mental health, as in health settings, is to help clients through a variety of means. However, social workers in mental health also must carry out the policies of the respective provincial mental health act or its equivalent. This means that sometimes we must make decisions for our clients even though the clients do not agree with us and do not want our services. While our purpose remains helping, our intervention sometimes is a form of social control. Ethical practice is of critical importance in such situations, and social workers need to carefully follow the Canadian Association of Social Workers' code of ethics. As discussed further in Chapter 6, these clients are often called nonvoluntary clients.

The function of social control is not limited to mental health. In other fields, such as child welfare—particularly child protection—and the justice system, provincial legislation establishes mandates that social workers must carry out.

Social Policies and Mental Health in a Historical Context

This section on mental health policy focuses on two historical events that currently shape all mental health policy and then shows how these relate to social work practice. The first, and most important, historical event was the medicalization of mental illness. The other is the rise, and some say fall, of community mental health and the related process of deinstitutionalization. Community mental health is a post–Second World War phenomenon.

The Medicalization of Mental Illness

Medicalization in mental health has not been a result of social welfare policy per se. Instead, policy has changed because of the view that what was previously called insanity or lunacy is really a disease, and hence is now called mental illness. Medicalization reflects a societal view that began late in the 18th century but did not spread to North America until the mid-19th century. Until that time, people who were "mad" or "insane" were seen as moral misfits, sometimes thought to be possessed (Conrad and Schneider, 1980, pp. 38–72; Gerhart, 1990, Chapter 1).

Reforms in mental health began in France in 1793 with the enlightened work of Phillippe Pinel, a doctor who worked in an asylum for the "insane." He advocated what came to be known as the moral treatment approach. "Pinel believed that patients should be treated with humane, sympathetic, and personal care in a hospital or asylum setting. The name given to this approach to care of mentally ill persons came from the French term, *traitement moral,* which did not mean 'moralistic content,' but 'psychologically oriented therapy'" (Fellin, 1996, p. 57). Remarkably, two centuries later the field of mental health still reflects Pinel's legacy.

Pinel, like all mental health reformers until the early 1900s, believed that institutional care was better than community care. Pinel's ideas did not spread to North America until about 50 years after he began his work. Most believe the reforms in North America began in the mid-1800s with the work of Dorothea Dix, an activist who also had a major influence on the social reform movements of the early 1900s, including the settlement house movement. Dix, drawing on the work of Pinel, successfully argued for a humane form of hospital care for people who were mentally ill. As a result, large numbers of mental hospitals were built in the last half of the 19th century (Fellin, 1996, pp. 54–56).

Despite the reforms in mental health care, up until about 1900 the emphasis was on care rather than treatment. Treatment implies that people can get better, while care does not. In the early 1900s the mental hygiene movement began to show that mental illness could be treated through an emphasis on psychology and **psychodynamic** psychiatry (Fellin, 1996, p. 59). This movement began to reverse Dix's argument that institutional care was better than community treatment. In an influential book that is still interesting to read (*The Mind That Found Itself,* 1908), Clifford Beers, a man who suffered from serious mental illness, wrote about his experiences as a mental patient. By openly discussing his experiences, he was able to show how he and others could successfully be treated. The mental hygiene movement established that medical intervention based on science, humane treatment, and principles of psychology and psychiatry could effectively treat some people who are mentally ill. Treatments that replaced custodial care in large institutions were initiated. The use of the term "mental illness" truly reflected a major shift in society to one of treatment, helping, and tolerance from custodial care of moral misfits.

These reforms and changes in attitude meant that mental illness began to be conceptualized as a disease in much the same way as physical illness. The medical model was used in the treatment of mental illness. The study of disease (pathology) is an outgrowth of science as a method of inquiry. A disease conceptualization means that the emphasis is on understanding *etiology*—the causes of mental illness. The logic of the medical model is that if a disease and its pathogenesis (development) can be understood, an effective treatment or even prevention can be developed. This model of the treatment of mental illness is the dominant way that we now approach the disorder. As in general health, mental health policy spelled out in provincial mental health acts reflects the medical model, where the physician is in charge and mental illness is accepted as a disease.

Community Mental Health and Deinstitutionalization

To medically treat the growing population diagnosed as mentally ill, most health policies led to the building of large hospitals in the last half of the 19th century, some with 2,000 or more beds. Even though the mental hygiene movement was influential, the population in mental hospitals grew, continuing through most of the 1950s. Many of the institutions built before the Second World War were grand in design, with very high ceilings and huge halls for eating and recreation. The wards were large, with almost no privacy. Often the treatment of choice for mental illness was hospitalization, usually in one of these large mental hospitals. Social welfare policy was to treat the seriously mentally ill in large, publicly funded hospitals.

However, in the 1950s and 1960s some began to seriously challenge the merits of mental institutions. They saw them as places that, because they confined people, thwarted effective treatment (Goffman, 1961; Rochefort, 1993, pp. 213–40; Sommer and Osmond, 1961; Spearman, 1971).

Deinstitutionalization began in earnest in the early 1960s. Several forces seemed to drive it at that time. The most powerful was likely the recognition that thousands of people were suffering from the sterile life in institutions. All of the patients' daily routines were scheduled, and individual needs and interests were usually not supported if they made demands on the administration of the organization and the work of its staff. Further, many argued that community care was much less expensive than hospital care. Also, during this time period antipsychotic drugs were introduced, which meant that many seriously ill mental patients no longer needed the confines of a hospital for treatment.

The movements toward deinstitutionalization in Canada and the United States began at about the same time and followed parallel paths. While working at the provincial mental hospital in Weyburn, Saskatchewan, Robert Sommer and Humphrey Osmond (1961) published a pioneering and influential journal article arguing that symptoms of psychiatric patients in mental hospitals were often the result of the hospitalization experience itself. Their work affected thinking in the field across North America and was instrumental in the deinstitutionalization of patients in Saskatchewan in the early 1960s.

Partly because of the particular interest of then United States President Kennedy, by 1963 large amounts of money were flowing into programs that put people who had been hospitalized for long periods back into the community and set up community-based programs to treat mental illness. These programs were new and exciting at the time. Treatment was to take place in the community, and quality outpatient services were to be provided to those patients discharged to boarding and foster homes.

The social welfare policies that established community-based programs had two goals. One goal was to provide quality community and supportive services to seriously mentally ill, long-term, and previously chronically hospitalized patients who, without the services, would likely remain in hospital for the rest of their lives. Most patients were discharged either to group boarding homes or to foster homes. This model of deinstitutionalization was adopted by many jurisdictions throughout North America.

The second goal of these policies was to make available to consumers mental health services in the community. In this model, the policy shifted from promoting large-scale institutional programs to local mental health centres. Community general hospitals added psychiatric wings, and a wide range of outpatient services were set up. The large institutions were used only as a last resort, partly to keep people connected to their communities so that they did not become dependent on the hospital. A major goal of community programming was to help consumers of mental health services maintain the best possible quality of life.

The success of these policies has been mixed. No one effectively argues that mental hospitals are good places in which to live; for most people, community programs are better than those based in institutions. Most also agree that the original goals of deinstitutionalization were noble. However, in the 1970s and into the 1990s cost cutting overshadowed the treatment-based goals. To make matters worse, many governments in Canada and the United States did not proceed with the necessary second step envisioned by President Kennedy—namely, that hospital resources would be diverted to the community. In most instances this did not happen. One of the main reasons many people have become homeless since the 1980s is the result of mental hospital depopulation and the fact that many people who need mental health services have not had and do not have adequate access to them (Grob, 1991; Halpern et al., 1980; Fellin, 1996, pp. 52–53; Rochefort, 1993, pp. 213–40).

Often, consumers of mental health services and their families experience marginalization and stigma. They may have difficulty in securing supportive and caring help, and services sometimes don't adequately meet their needs. The kind of communication that mental health service consumers and their caregivers can offer each other is important in breaking down isolation from and misunderstanding of mental illness. Through self-help groups, people can meet some of their needs by sharing information, resources, strategies, and methods to change social views of mental illness and its effects. Self-help groups can extend the potential for support and practical assistance among consumers and their families. In his 1986 report *Mental Health for Canadians,* Jake Epp identifies the roles of self-care and mutual support as necessary components in Canadian health promotion (Dickinson, 1994).

Social Work Roles in Mental Health

Social work seems to have an increasing presence in the mental health field. While it appears that most mental health professions bring to the field a medical, disease-oriented perspective, social work's focus generally centres on improving the client's quality of life and viewing the illness as a life event that affects functioning in other areas. By improving their quality of life and maximizing their strengths, people learn to manage their disabilities in the same way that people with physical disabilities develop quality in their lives (Spearman, in press). (See Chapter 10 on the strengths approach.)

Social workers in mental health settings frequently work with clients who are very dependent on the mental health system for support and services and who have many associated problems. With these clients, social workers often provide active supportive roles in which the worker takes the lead in initiating service and providing help. This includes case management, education, brokerage, and advocacy.

Work with clients who are more independent is usually different. Enabling supportive roles include case management and brokerage but also a major emphasis on enabling, counselling, empowerment, and some forms of therapy, such as family therapy. Usually counselling is related to a specific issue, such as employment, establishing better reciprocal relationships, and problem solving (e.g., solution-focused therapy). There may also be some use of the educator role, perhaps in coaching a client on how to approach a potential employer for a job interview. The worker's main goal is to help the client gain sufficient independence so that the client can make life decisions without depending on others. The emphasis is on helping clients develop the best possible quality of life.

Social Work Practice and Teamwork in Mental Health: An Example of How Policy Affects Practice

This example is intended to show how macro social welfare policy, laws, and agency policy greatly affect the delivery of service. Over the past half-century or so, researchers have shown that many mental illnesses have biological roots. To underscore this point, visit the myriad websites that describe mental health and mental illness.[2] However, most professionals also recognize that many, if not all, mental illnesses have psychological and/or social triggers, or the illness itself may result from stress. An example is depression that occurs because of a specific event, such as a death in the family. Further, there is general agreement that there are many social and psychological consequences to a mental illness. These consequences appear in many forms. A few examples are stigma, loss of job and hence income, reduction of life skills, loss of support from family, feelings of shame, and so on.

Thus, a team of helpers often treats mental illness (Toseland, Palmer-Ganeles, and Chapman, 1986). The expertise of this team is usually intended to emphasize the medical, psychological, and social aspects of the illness. Ideally, mental health teams consist of psychiatrists, psychologists, social workers, nurses, occupational therapists, and sometimes others such as physical and recreational therapists. Composition greatly depends upon factors such as setting, resources, and treatment orientation.

Consistent with mental health policy and law (Gray, Shone, and Liddle, 2000; Gray, 2001), psychiatrists are almost always responsible for prescribing medication, medical diagnosis, and major treatment decisions such as hospital discharge. However, given the recognition that mental illnesses involve social and psychological factors, mental health agency and hospital policy usually broadens the scope of intervention to include a variety of allied health professionals. Social workers, nurses, and psychologists often play key roles. For example, social workers commonly help with family relationship issues, assist in accessing community resources, and help with discharge planning if a patient is hospitalized. Psychologists, social workers, and psychiatrists—and sometimes nurses—provide psychotherapy and counselling. Psychologists are usually responsible for psychological testing. All disciplines provide input into patient assessment. Nurses are generally responsible for medication distribution. Clearly, roles differ from team to team. A good team attempts to maximize the skills of each person on the team; yet, their general roles are cast by macro mental health policy and local agency or hospital policy.

Social Work Practice and Social Welfare Policy: A Case Example in Mental Health

All social work professionals practise in the context of social welfare policy, which shapes and defines the character of practice. Often, however, those new to the field have as their primary interest the development of direct practice skills. They have difficulty understanding how and why practice depends on policy. The story of Sonia will help in appreciating the importance of social welfare policy and underscore much of the previous discussion.

Sonia, as a person, did not exist in real life. All of the events described in her story are ones that can be observed happening repeatedly to a variety of people. Many of the things that happen to Sonia are the direct result of social and mental health policies.

The social welfare policy issues raised by Sonia's story fit into two categories. The first category is large-scale (macro) social policies, often expressed in legislation. Obvious examples are policies of deinstitutionalization and community-based mental health services. The second category is program policies—those of specific organizations, which are usually made by administrative and supervisory personnel. Examples of these include policies that routinize hospital life, such as rigid scheduling of activities.

Case Example

Sonia

Sonia was only 66 when she died in 2000. Most of the last 45 years of her life were spent in a mental hospital. She had seen it all.

A daughter of a working-class family, Sonia was diagnosed in 1955 as having paranoid schizophrenia and depression. At the time, she was 21 years old. There was nothing out of the ordinary in either her childhood or her high school years. She attended a teachers' college for two years and was home on summer holidays when her illness struck.

When Sonia first arrived home for the summer, she was withdrawn and uncharacteristically quiet. She did not go out with her friends and did not date. Sonia began to hear voices. Sometimes the voices were muffled and she could not make sense of them; at other times, they were clearer and seemed to warn her that her life was in danger. Sonia usually heard a man's threatening voice.

At first Sonia kept her voices a secret. But they frightened her. Her mother could not understand what was happening to her daughter. The episodes increased during the month preceding Sonia's hospitalization. The voices became louder and more threatening. One evening after dinner, Sonia fled the house screaming. In the early hours of the next morning she was brought, dishevelled, shaking, and incoherent, to the local hospital by the police. Later in the summer of 1955 she was committed to the mental hospital by court order. This hospital was the closest one to her home, but it was 140 km away. In the hospital, Sonia was diagnosed as having schizophrenia.

Her parents did not understand her behaviour. They were ashamed because schizophrenia carried with it a social stigma, and they felt guilty because they thought Sonia's illness might be their fault. No staff member at the hospital contradicted this possibility. To compound problems for the family, Sonia's father died in the spring of 1959, and her mother and two younger siblings had to go on welfare.

At the time of her first admission, Sonia was considered a risk to herself. No one during the 1950s really knew what to do with people who had problems like Sonia's, other than to provide them with a safe, secure, and supportive environment and some interventions such as electroshock therapy or psychotherapy. No medications available at that time were effective, and psychotherapy was rarely provided in public mental hospitals. However, unlike only a few decades earlier, the purpose of institutionalization was treatment, not merely custodial care. If the patient did not go willingly, then often the policy prescribed action that usually resulted in legal commitment to an institution. The policy to treat people diagnosed with a mental illness in hospitals and to force hospitalization on some patients is a macro social welfare policy that reflects the views of a society and, in this instance, is expressed through legislation. This policy greatly affected the life of the individual in our case example, Sonia. Such policies continue to be in effect.

Case Example

Sonia

After about 10 days Sonia felt better, despite being confined in an institution and surrounded by other patients, some of whom had been there for years. Many people would think that living in such a place would cause depression rather than make her feel better. Quite the contrary.

Her new environment helped. Almost every minute of Sonia's life was scheduled for her. She did not have to think for herself. Sonia quickly learned that others could make decisions for her. This gave her a feeling of security and safety and permitted her symptoms, including hearing the voices, to subside. But it was a two-edged sword.

The routinized life was a form of dehumanization. Sonia no longer had to make decisions that were necessary for normal living outside the institution. She lost critical community living skills. This dependence on the institution would make it very difficult for her to find the courage to leave the hospital.

Hospital mental health policy, then and now, is designed to provide a secure environment that assists in reducing symptoms. These policies include the regimentation of everyday life. A major reason for the deinstitutionalization policies of the 1960s through the 1980s was to avoid the effects of dehumanization in large mental hospitals. However, thousands of patients had become so dependent on the protected environment of the hospital that they lost normal life skills required for community adjustment.

Social workers, like all professionals in related disciplines, should not only fully understand the effects of institutional life and the policies that guide it, but also be prepared to advocate for change when such policies work to the detriment of clients.

Case Example

Sonia 

The die was now cast. Sonia was now not only ill but also had become dependent on the institution. Sonia's mother was not well. Her life was hard, and by 1962 she had stopped visiting Sonia altogether. Sonia had no other relatives and no friends outside the hospital. She had lost the life skills she needed to function in everyday community life, partly due to her mental illness and partly because of the institutional life. Sadly, she would never regain these critical life skills.

Things continued without change until 1963. In that year, Sonia began taking new antidepressants and antipsychotic drugs that were quite helpful. She felt better than she had since she was a teenager. Partly because of a new public policy emphasis on community mental health, the hospital decided to help Sonia find a place to live in the community. After considerable coaxing, the social workers convinced her to move to a small boarding home.

At the boarding home, Sonia could no longer visit the few friends she had at the hospital. Further, no recreational services or occupational therapy were available. She became very sad and stopped taking her medications. The frightening voices returned. Within two weeks, Sonia threatened suicide and was returned to the hospital.

In the summer of 1968 the hospital hired a young social work student for a summer position. His job was to help long-term, chronic clients re-experience life outside the hospital by taking small incremental steps. One of his first interventions was to organize a shopping trip into the city. Since it had been nearly 14 years since Sonia had been downtown, the student worker realized this trip would be a frightening and stressful experience for her.

However, the trip was a success for Sonia. She even made a small purchase—a coin purse in which she could keep the money that she used in the hospital canteen. For the next two months Sonia made many trips to town, some of them without hospital staff supervision. The treatment team in the hospital thought she was showing improvement, probably because of the medications that she was now taking. At summer's end, the team believed that they should begin developing a discharge plan with Sonia. After all, it was government policy to discharge all patients who did not require active treatment.

When Domenic, Sonia's social worker, approached her with the plan, Sonia reacted with horror. She began to withdraw, but after about three months of support mixed with coaxing, Sonia agreed to move to a foster home, a very small group home where patients live with a supporting family.

From the start things did not go well. Domenic had promised Sonia that there would be frequent visits from an outpatient social worker, but this did not occur. Resources had not been reallocated from the hospital to the community.

Sonia was not keeping herself clean. She stayed in her room most of the time and often missed meals. She was lost, even in the foster home, without the rigid routine of the hospital.

Within six weeks of her discharge, Sonia began holding her medication under her tongue until the foster mother left the room. Sonia then flushed the pills down the toilet. The voices and depression quickly returned, and Sonia was readmitted to the hospital. (Note that many foster or group home placements were "successful" in that they lasted a long time, with some patients thriving in such protected environments. Sonia, however—like thousands of others—had become so dependent on the hospital that she had lost the ability to perform the normal life skills that community adjustment required. Often group homes were really mini-hospitals, but without any meaningful stimuli to keep the boarders' attention.)

Over the years, Sonia was placed in four group homes, the last one in the summer of 1984. None of them improved her quality of life, but they did prevent rehospitalization.

As time passed, Sonia began to spend more and more time on the streets with her small bag to collect things that she found. She enjoyed the independence and even started spending the odd summer night sleeping in a splendid park that bordered the downtown area. Sometimes she would panhandle in order to purchase a small item that to her was a luxury. While Sonia returned to the boarding home to spend most of her nights, she spent considerable time living on the streets. Some would say that she had regained some of her lost life skills.

Sonia continued with this lifestyle until her death 16 years later.

Sonia's story shows how policy affects all aspects of a client's life and greatly affects intervention. The purpose of telling her story is to challenge you to consider implications of social welfare policies and the possibility of different outcomes of different policies. While the example is from mental health, the principles apply to all social work.

The policies of depopulating mental hospitals and moving toward community mental health services were the primary reasons that the hospital made four attempts to move Sonia to community living. While these attempts were laudable, the fact that adequate resources for community programs were not provided ensured Sonia's failure to adapt to and grow in the community.

Why did Sonia move to the streets? Did the fact that she found independence and a sense of identity on the streets mean that they were a better place for her than the group home? Was this a positive step for her? Or is it a terrible indictment of the failure of the social safety net? Regardless of your view, there is no question that the social and community mental health policies of the 1980s and 1990s contributed to the rise of street living, large-scale soup kitchens, and homelessness (Halpern et al., 1980; Rochefort, 1993, pp. 213–40).

Suppose that you were Sonia's mental health worker during the last 15 years of her life. What would you have done? Challenged the policy that encouraged people to live on the streets? Supported her small moves to independence, which could have meant supporting her decision to live on the streets? Attempted to bring her back to the secure hospital environment? Or something else? These questions and others like them pose enormous practice dilemmas for social workers in mental health.

Consider Sonia's life from another policy angle. As explained earlier in this section on mental health, the mental health policies of the 20th century were based on treating mental illness as a disease. When treatment fails or other factors, such as limited life skills, prevent real progress, the medical model assumes that the symptoms should be treated and life should be made as comfortable as possible for patients.

Now consider an alternative policy. Without minimizing the importance of treatment and prevention, suppose policy also focused on helping clients build a life that acknowledges the illness but emphasizes other parts of life that are rewarding and productive (Anthony, 1993; Saleebey, 1997c). For instance, imagine what could have happened to Sonia if, in the 1950s, the mental health system focused not only on treating her illness but also on helping her retain and improve life skills. Possibly she would have had choices among alternatives such as continuing her education or training for a job. While these possibilities were likely open to her, the system did not provide sufficient supports to attain such goals. Even without the helpful drugs that came along later, it is possible that if appropriate supports and policies had been in place, Sonia might not have become so dependent on hospitals for most of her life and may have been able to achieve a better quality of life.

Few programs and policies focus on human growth, with some exceptions—such as those of the Canadian Mental Health Association, which stress **consumer**- and growth-oriented mental health policies.

We can extend the principle of growth-oriented policies to other fields of practice. Policies that focus only on problem solving are insufficient, as we show in the last five chapters of this book; they also need to help people reach their maximum potential.

CHAPTER SUMMARY

This chapter has described social work practice and roles in health and mental health, using case situations to illustrate social work intervention. We have shown how social welfare policy is used as a lens to filter practice and give practice its mandate.

A central thrust was to explore social welfare policy development in two related areas: health and mental health care services. To explore the developments in these areas, we have located them in their social and historical contexts, traced some of the actors and processes involved, and looked at the content of the policies. Perhaps more importantly, we have discussed, through the use of case examples, how social welfare policy changes at the macro level (e.g., national governments and health institutions) contribute to those at the micro level (e.g., the interface between social workers and clients). It is at the micro level that most social workers carry out their work and directly experience social welfare policy that, in turn, affects their clients.

In health policy, the environment of health reform and downsizing of programs and facilities has forced change, adversely affecting some people, especially those whose health status and social situations are complex and challenging. Canada may be experiencing a trend away from universal health care. The public funds that have supported health and mental health programs are being more carefully distributed, and in ways that may not help some groups of people and may in fact diminish the quality of their lives. Corporate donations, private funds, and even lotteries are being sought for services that once were not required or that had government support. Consider the rapid proliferation of food banks, places where people on low incomes (no longer only social assistance recipients) go to supplement their food needs (Riches, 1985, 1986, 1997; Bidgood, Krzyzanowski, Taylor, and Smilek, in press).

In mental health, practice is partly mandated by provincial mental health acts, which place social workers in positions of control. Deinstitutionalization initiatives were driven, in part, by economic factors, since keeping people in large hospitals was expensive for the state. The shift from facilities to communities and families has been portrayed as more caring, responsive, and effective, although the effects of this shift need to be evaluated. Increased care in the community has been supported by both the state and community groups, as it is clear that most people want to be in their own homes and communities with their families and friends rather than in hospitals, unless they require specialized or urgent care. Nevertheless, it is important that caring for people in communities and within their families is supported by adequate and appropriate programs and services.

Roy Romanow's report (2002) provides recommendations that could sustain Canada's health care system. Provided there is political will and sustained interest in making policy changes in our complex federal–provincial health care system, everyone will gain through better quality, integrated care that substantially improves the lives of Canadians into the future.

NOTES

1 The Daily, a report from Statistics Canada, is a useful and handy resource for social workers. It can be accessed from the Statistics Canada website, www.statcan.ca/english/dai-quo/. Data are archived and can easily be searched.

2 For example, see www.mentalhealth.com, www.webmd.com, www.healthcanada.ca, and www.mayoclinic.com.

chapter 6

The Client–Social Worker Relationship: Voluntary and Involuntary Relationships

Chapter Goal

To describe the nature of the professional social work relationship, both voluntary and involuntary.

This Chapter ▼

- defines the social work client and distinguishes between voluntary and involuntary clients
- defines the nature of the professional helping relationship and describes key components of this relationship
- describes social work relationships with involuntary clients and suggests ways that social workers might form relationships and work with resistant clients

DEFINING THE SOCIAL WORK CLIENT

Fundamental to social work practice is the professional relationship that social workers develop with clients in order to provide a helping service to them and to effect change. Much of the remainder of the book elaborates on this relationship, particularly Chapter 8 on problem solving, Chapter 10 on the strengths approach, Chapter 11 on an Aboriginal approach, Chapter 12 on structural social work, and Chapter 13 on a feminist approach to social work.

The client is not necessarily the person the social worker is working with. What may seem obvious at first is, in fact, rather complicated. Suppose you are a child welfare worker working with a one-year-old child who has been abused. Is the child the client? One or both of the parents? Or is it the society or state, represented by the child welfare agency that is responsible for protecting children? What if the community in which the child lives with his family has been involved and wants to voice some ideas about the situation? Is the community also a client?

The Canadian Association of Social Workers' (CASW) code of ethics defines a client as "a person, family, group of persons, incorporated body, association or community on whose behalf a social worker provides or agrees to provide a service" (CASW, 1994a, section on Definition of Client). The service may be provided on request or in agreement with the client, or as the result of a legal mandate received from legislation or from "a judge of a court of competent jurisdiction who orders the social worker to provide to the Court an assessment" (CASW, 1994a, sections a and b on Definition of Client). In this conception, the client is presumed to be voluntary if the service provided is sought by the client and is the result of agreement with the client concerning the nature of the problem and the action required to address it. In the case of an involuntary client, the relationship is voluntary if the client and worker agree to work on a problem (establish a contract) beyond what was originally mandated (CASW, 1994a, sections a and b on Definition of Client). (Some provincial social work associations have adapted wording that slightly alters that of the national association.)

The word "client" implies a power differential between the social worker and the client, particularly if the client is involuntary. Those who advocate a strengths approach (see Chapter 10) often prefer the word "consumer." Other alternatives might be "partner" or "helpee." However, "client" is the most common and generally accepted word used by social workers, and is the term used in this text.

Helping versus Social Control

The function of **social control** and its impact on involuntary clients are important issues in social work. Social control is an action of a professional worker, agency, representative of a court, or other legally **mandated organization** that is intended to regulate, govern, or restrict the activities and behaviour of a client. Often the action is taken to protect a third party, such as children in abuse cases or the public when the client has been convicted of a crime. Other times, as in the case of mental illness, social workers (and other professionals) may make treatment decisions in the best interest of a client even if the client objects. Importantly, in all situations, the purpose of social work intervention remains to help, and the social worker must always act in the best interest of those with whom she or he works.

Many social workers are employed in fields in which strong mandates for social control are attached to their work. Probably the three fields at the top of this list are corrections; child welfare and family services (particularly work in child protection); and mental health. Ivanoff, Blythe, and Tripodi (1994, p. 2), using data from Epstein (1985), contend that in the United States "it is believed that involuntary clients may number in the millions; yet there is no precise estimate of their numbers and location."

There are two types of involuntary clients, but they are often difficult to separate. Some are involuntary because the justice, mental health, or child welfare system or other social institution takes some form of action toward the client. This group includes clients who are or have been convicted of a crime, those who have neglected children, and those who are mentally ill and are forced to seek treatment. Such clients might be called *mandated involuntary clients.* Probably most mandated involuntary clients are also unwilling. However, an unwilling client can also be one who seeks help because of pressure from family, social agencies, the police, or other outside sources. The classic example is a partner in a troubled marriage who reluctantly sees a counsellor at the insistence of the spouse. Another example is a person who displays eccentric behaviour that is not harmful to anyone but that some consider a sign of mental illness and who resists treatment even though others think it is important.

The second group of involuntary clients, then, are unwilling clients. They are involuntary because they do not want a service when others think the service would benefit them. An example is a hospital patient who needs some help before being discharged to go home but refuses the services of a hospital social worker. Unwilling clients are frequently resistant or reluctant.

Often social workers work with openly resistant clients. An example is a parolee who wants no part of the treatment program developed by her or his parole officer at the order of a parole board. Or, it could be the parents of an abused child who aggressively reject help. Social workers in the mental health field often treat people who are forced by the legal system to undergo treatment or are coerced by others, such as family or police, to seek help. They may lack many social skills but refuse to recognize this as a problem. The fact is that much of social work involves working with people who do not want help. Yet material on intervention with these people is missing from many books that outline generalist models of social work practice (Rooney, 1992). (In Chapter 8, we address the ethical principle of best interest and the involuntary client.)

Case Example

Kim and Ann

Our ongoing story about Kim and Ann can be used to illustrate how social work conceptualizes clients.

Since Kim is a child protection worker and Ann's children are under the legal care of the Child Protection Agency, the children are Kim's clients. Ann is, on the one hand, a mandated involuntary client because the agency removed her children from her without her permission. However, since Kim and Ann agree that Kim will provide a useful service to Ann and they agree on the problems and a plan for solving them, Kim has been able to form a voluntary relationship with Ann even though Ann did not ask for service in the first place.

Now suppose that Ann views herself as a victim of the agency and the courts and, as often happens, actively rejects help from Kim or any other child welfare worker. Using the concept of client as presented above, if Kim still provides a service to Ann (for example, to help Ann understand the legal processes and alternatives available to her), Ann is a mandated and unwilling involuntary client. The children would still be clients because Kim is working on their behalf.

Suppose that the judge requires that Kim file an assessment report with the court after 60 days of custody. In this instance, the court or judge, representing society, is also Kim's client.

DEFINING SOCIAL WORK RELATIONSHIPS

Throughout our lives, human interaction and the quality of the relationships that develop from them provide meaningful experiences for us. We learn from childhood how to get along with people, how to meet our own needs, and how to give in to the needs of others in relationships. Through social and cultural experiences we become aware of how conflict and reciprocity feel and what methods and skills we can draw on to make relationships work—or leave them altogether. In social work, this learning forms a foundation on which we build professional relationships that exist for a specific purpose and in a particular organizational context. There are differences among relationships between friends and family members and those between clients and social workers. Deliberate effort and considerable skill are needed to initiate, develop, maintain, and end client–social worker relationships.

A relationship in social work practice can be thought of as an exchange at the emotional level and a dynamic interaction between people in a professional meeting. It also connects people in a mutual process (Biestek, 1957; Compton and Galaway, 1994, p. 264). Relationships involve process (the quality and flow of interchange) and content (what is being discussed), both of which are necessary to attend to. Above all, relationships are connections between individuals based on some expectations of shared rules of conduct. These rules may be contested in practice, where the different parties in the relationship may negotiate for more flexibility in them and for other changes.

The duration of a relationship depends on the level of commitment, will, and purpose in keeping it going. In social work, some relationships can be long term, continuing over years with the same clients, whereas others are limited to the short term. Relationships are built and shaped over time by the shared rules, purpose, roles, expectations, and needs of those involved. In any client–social worker relationship, you can identify certain points where changes take place in the relationship. To be effective, "it is necessary to attend to the ebbs and flows of the process" (Locke, Garrison, and Winship, 1998, p. 113). For example, when clients have achieved some identified goal that has been a focus of work, the purpose of the relationship will shift to different issues and interests. To illustrate, a social worker's relationship with a family whose crisis situation has resolved changes in its intensity and focus, perhaps to longer-term issues or other underlying problems. Both parties may then renegotiate the purpose, roles, and expectations of their work together.

Social workers have clear responsibilities in helping relationships with clients. Using oneself in a purposive or disciplined way is a feature of this relationship (Perlman, 1957). The need to respect (not necessarily to like), to be concerned about, and to care for clients in ways that acknowledge that they will decide their own actions is central to the relationship. Social workers also strive to communicate integrity and honesty while maintaining client confidentiality and privacy (e.g., not seeking information from the client that is not essential and relevant to the problem or situation being discussed).

We cannot overestimate the importance of the relationship in social work—and we may not realize its importance in the client's life. The client may not either. Here's an example: A social work researcher conducting interviews with women who have experienced addictions, abuse, and other issues is told that the person who really cared when no one else did was a social worker. The interviewee said the social worker listened to her, didn't judge, and carefully guided and encouraged her to decide for herself about a course of action. The few sessions she had with the social worker helped her to take the first steps to change her life for the better. The research participant told the researcher that several years passed until she was able to reflect on the changes in her life and how they came about. Her social worker never knew what an important role she played at that very difficult time in the woman's life. The social worker's compassion and belief in the client and the client's capacity to respond to these helped build a strong, caring relationship between them. To the interview respondent, this relationship was more important than any information given, referrals made, or actions taken by the social worker.

Communication is a key feature of any helping activity. Communication can involve speech or sign language and gestures or it can take a written form, including memos, letters, reports, records, position papers, or articles. The form of communication depends on what is needed in the situation. For example, in community work, a social worker may communicate the community members' need for a children's daycare centre through facilitating a petition and letter to city hall.

There must be a purpose for both the social worker and the client in maintaining a relationship. The benefit for the client is, for example, the hope or expectation that something beneficial will ensue. For clients, the purpose in establishing a relationship with a social worker is to gain access to certain resources or to seek help in making changes in their lives. Clients must view the relationship as an important part of the helping process.

For both the social worker and the client, the relationship is a means to an end. If the worker is able to establish a caring and empathic relationship, then the helping process will more likely be successful. Perlman (1957, pp. 64–83), in her writing on the problem-solving process, clearly recognized this and saw the growth of clients, particularly in their ability to solve their own problems, as a major purpose of helping. She wrote, "[T]hroughout his life each person seeks (and feels secure only when he has found) a relationship with one or more other human beings from which he can draw nourishment, love or sustainment and the stimulus of interaction" (pp. 64–65). She goes on to argue that the purpose of the professional relationship is to help engage the helping process, which "like every other process intended to promote growth, must use relationship as its basic means" (p. 65). The fact that social workers agree, through an employment mandate and a professional ethical code, to work with people to achieve certain ends provides them with a purpose for and a direction to the relationship. This relationship is structured according to its purpose, which may take the form of a written contract, an informal agreement, or some understanding of what is to come (Brammer and MacDonald, 1996, p. 65).

COMPONENTS OF THE CLIENT–SOCIAL WORKER RELATIONSHIP

The relationship between a client and a social worker is a partnership. The partnership conception of the relationship is strengthened in feminist social work, where clients and workers share power and create a nurturing environment (Chapter 13). The importance of sharing the responsibility of helping clients solve their own problems is emphasized in feminist social work.

Social work texts identify the components that are most common in social work relationships with clients. They include care and concern; empathy and honesty; acceptance of people; acknowledgment of the client's capacity for change; self-determination and autonomy; confidentiality; power, authority, and control; purpose and commitment; and context and structure (Biestek, 1957; O'Connor, Wilson, and Setterlund, 1995; Compton and Galaway, 1994; Johnson, McLelland, and Austin, 2000; Kirst-Ashman and Hull, 1993, 1999).

Common Components

Care and Concern

Showing care and concern toward others is basic to social work values and practice, and refers generally to caring for people and what troubles them. Although we may not approve of clients' behaviour (for example, in the case of an abusive parent), we need to respect and value each person's humanity and affirm his or her right to be heard, understood, and helped. Canadian Association of Social Workers' code of ethics also stresses this requirement. The well-being of others is necessarily one of the most fundamental concerns of client–social worker relationships. This means ensuring the safety and security of clients, not only in their own social and physical environments, but also in the social work process. It also means expressing interest in and concern about their well-being by, for example, helping them to feel comfortable in our first meeting with them.

The tendency to want to be helpful and the human need for professional success or esteem can sometimes be obstacles that hamper a helping relationship. As O'Connor, Wilson, and Setterlund (1995) state succinctly, "Concern for others involves responding with our skills, knowledge and time—within, of course, certain limits of purpose, available time and place—as the client system needs [us to help] rather than as our need to help demands" (p. 80). Social workers must consider the goal and purpose of their actions to ensure that they focus on the client's needs.

Empathy and Honesty

Empathy refers to the ability to understand clients in their situations and from their perspectives, and it is integral to social work. It also means that each individual client's uniqueness is appreciated. In explaining empathic skills, Shulman (1999) writes: "The acceptance and understanding of emotions and the worker's willingness to share them by experiencing them frees a client to drop some defences and to allow the worker and the client more access to the real person. The worker also serves as a model of an adult with empathic ability" (p. 155). (See Shulman, 1999, pp. 155–61, and Hepworth and Larsen, 1993, pp. 92–114, for a more detailed discussion of empathy.)

We demonstrate empathy by listening actively and communicating understanding of the client's story. Although the concept of empathy might seem simple, it draws on the skill and experience of the social worker. Without a good grounding in knowledge about human behaviour across the lifespan, stress, crisis, resilience, responses to problems in living, and other elements that affect a range of people in diverse situations, a social worker is less able to empathize with clients. Empathy occurs at the feeling level but also requires cognitive understanding of people's problems and their reactions to them.

Empathy also means being honest with yourself and the client (O'Connor, Wilson, and Setterlund, 1995). There is no sense in telling a client, for instance, that you can help her resolve her problem and that "everything will be okay" if it might not be. Expressing honestly, without destroying any hope, what seems realistic in a situation promotes better practice relationships.

In a helping relationship, it is also important not to lose perspective on the client's situation and to react only emotionally. Consider, for example, what might happen if you became completely focused on the emotions and obstacles faced by a young disabled man who has come to you seeking help with life choices. You might feel unable to help him in dealing with his problems. For the beginning social worker, it is often difficult to keep oneself sufficiently separate from the client's situation, yet it is necessary to find a balance between empathy and separateness. This takes practice and is usually helped by additional experience in drawing on skills and knowledge to avoid getting "stuck on" or overwhelmed by problems presented by clients.

Demonstrating empathy can involve appropriate and timely verbal or nonverbal affirmations. Showing that you empathize with clients, however, does not mean constantly nodding or saying "Mm-hmm," since such behaviour can seem mechanical. With practice, it is possible to change most distracting behaviours that impede empathy and good communication in social work.

Acceptance

Acceptance of people, even when their behaviour is difficult to understand or is repulsive to the social worker, is necessary in effective social work practice. Acceptance is related to concern and empathy. It means not judging, idealizing, or assuming what people are, were, or should be. Sometimes assumptions about a person or group of people have harmful effects in social work practice. This can certainly occur in cases where the worker and the client come from different cultures. For example, a non-Aboriginal social worker who has little knowledge about Aboriginal helping methods might not see an Elder as a useful resource for a traditional Aboriginal client (see Chapter 11).

Not being able to accept and work with certain clients poses problems in a practice situation and can create serious barriers in developing a relationship. Recognizing and appreciating the rich diversity in people and the uniqueness of each individual can help social workers approach and work better with clients. It can also prevent them from judging others' actions hastily when they do not really know what it is like to be in the client's shoes. This does not mean that social workers excuse behaviour—such as criminal behaviour—that they and society cannot condone, but that they seek to understand the whole picture from a client's frame of reference (Kirst-Ashman and Hull, 1993, 1999).

Consider how people's **constructions** of their own realities guide their decisions and actions. Striving for a holistic appreciation of people in their situations discourages stereotyping and labels like "the welfare mother," "the schizophrenic," "the juvenile delinquent," and so on. Listening to the experiences of people from their own viewpoints can be useful in opening up, for example, "the possibility of beginning to hear other voices: those of women, gays, blacks, and other visible minorities, colonized peoples, the working class, religious groups that were forced into silence for so long" (Irving, 1994, p. 28). The ways in which people construct meaning from their life situations and difficulties can reveal differences in what they and their social workers interpret as problems. In social work, there is more than one kind of knowledge; there is the body of knowledge that is derived from theories and research that inform social work practice, and there is knowledge that is local, subjective, and rooted in people's daily lives.

Weick (1992) stresses that it is important to "incorporate and honour people's own experience. In taking this tack, people's own knowledge of their lives is treated as a natural resource. ... [There is] the recognition of a multiplicity of knowledge" (p. 24). In fact, our ideas about a person and his or her situation may prove quite different from those who actually live the experience. For example, a boy of 14 who is receiving cancer treatment tells a social worker that his biggest concern is how his classmates will react to his changed appearance. He explains that his hair was what he liked best about his looks. Due to chemotherapy, he has lost it all. The social worker is surprised to hear about this being so important to him; she expected him to identify other problems, which she perceived as much bigger.

Client Capacity for Change

Acknowledging client capacity for change and client resilience is a key feature of client–social worker relationships. The strengths perspective outlined by Saleebey (1992; 1997c) stresses the importance of actively seeking with clients the range of strengths and resources open to them in the external environment and within themselves. When people's difficulties obscure the fact that they have strengths on which to draw, their capacity for change is also hampered. Recognizing one's strengths can increase self-esteem, hope, and motivation for change. A strengths perspective to social work thus takes the position that people have natural internal resources that can be harnessed for healing and growth: "It is the life force, present in all living things, that pushes for expression. ... [It] expresses itself as an emotional resilience that helps us absorb and reflect on the hundreds of interactions present in our daily lives" (Weick, 1992, p. 23). Articulation and expression of care, concern, hope, and the value of clients' strengths, gifts, and capacities is done through the client–social work relationship.

Consider the situation of an unemployed, despondent woman who has fled Bosnia as a refugee, having had her schooling interrupted. In her new country, she has had trouble finding a job due to her limited education and poor English-language skills. It is apparent to the social worker that the client faces many barriers and feels unable to deal with them. At the same time, the woman has survived war and found the courage and resources to leave her home and extended family for the hope of a more safe and secure life in a foreign land. The social worker identifies and explores with the client some of the many strengths that her experiences suggest. The social worker's knowledge helps him understand that capacity for change is inherent in all humans. They move toward growth and development. He takes the time to get to know her experiences, fears, and hopes as he begins to build a relationship with her. The social worker also works with the client to draw out and find specific strength areas that can be used to improve her current situation. Thus, believing in clients' capacity for change can encourage them to see at least some of their obstacles as surmountable.

A person's capacity for change, according to the strengths perspective, comes from within. We cannot, however, ignore the fact that client situations are often complex and require more than tapping inner resources and capacities. People face many constraints that often call for an examination of the structural features in society that contribute to or create difficulties, such as discrimination based on class, ethnocultural background, ability, sexual orientation, gender, and so on, and that call for interventions that reach beyond the client. To illustrate, imagine the situation of a homeless young man with a heroin addiction. Although a search for his internal strengths may be helpful, many other external resources will likely be needed to help him. He may be able to use his own resources to some extent to secure his own safety and security, since he has survived considerable difficulties until now, but these will likely not be enough to deal with his current situation. There are many issues to deal with, such as how he can be safe, find shelter and food, and begin to regain his self-esteem (see Buchanan, in press). Acknowledging the client's capacity for change is important and can be an impetus for building a relationship and sustaining the client's life changes.

Self-Determination and Autonomy

As explained in Chapter 3, self-determination refers to clients' right to make life choices for themselves. Hepworth and Larsen (1993) write: "Basic social work values embody the beliefs that clients have the capacity to grow and change and to see and develop solutions to their difficulties, as well as the right and capacity to exercise free choice responsibly" (p. 71). One of the most important elements in establishing professional relationships with clients is ensuring that, within the limits of agency and societal mandates and client capabilities, they have the opportunity to make free choices. Social workers may generate and explore options, opportunities, and constraints and their potential consequences with clients, but they cannot select a course of action for clients or take responsibility for it.

Often one of the goals of intervention is to help clients make choices for themselves. A free exchange between client and social worker on courses of action, their potential consequences, and how to select among them can be of great benefit because the client may realize new options and strategies that he or she had not considered before. This can be both empowering and motivating.

However, self-determination in any organized society has many constraints. For example, there are considerable limits on the rights of children to make free choices. People who are incarcerated or in mental hospitals have many of life's "normal" decisions made for them by people in authority, including social workers. Frequently, social workers in child welfare settings often severely limit the choices of parents who neglect or abuse their children (see Hepworth and Larsen, 1993, pp. 71–75).

People can make choices only when they perceive that they have a range of options to select from. When clients and social workers meet, there is often an exchange of ideas and information that may influence the client's decision making. As a result of this process, client autonomy may be reduced, especially when the social worker is seen as an authority. The client may have very little interest in establishing or maintaining a relationship with the social worker, yet it may be in the client's best interest to do so.

The concept of self-determination reflects *individual agency,* where a person makes autonomous decisions and takes action according to personal wishes and motivations. For some people, collective needs and wishes are more important than an individual's. This may be the case in many ethnocultural communities, where family aspirations or collective goals are seen to be more prominent than those of an individual. For example, many Asian families rely on the earnings of older daughters or sons to pay for the school fees for younger children or the purchase of a new home for the whole family. In such cases, individual autonomy of the son or daughter is sacrificed for the common good. It is recognized that self-determination is a Western notion, one that may not be relevant for some. We need to understand whether it is of primary importance to a client and, if not, be open to different perspectives. Thus, personal and cultural values can affect self-determination.

Confidentiality

Confidentiality in social work relationships is a central concern due to the often sensitive personal information clients provide. The client's right to confidentiality and privacy is very important and social workers, like all helping professionals, must make every effort to protect it. The Canadian Association of Social Workers' code of ethics holds that all information provided by the client or others during the helping process must be, within limits, kept confidential (see discussion later in this chapter). Provincial laws (e.g., the Manitoba *Freedom of Information and Protection of Privacy Act*) also regulate access to personal information and the protection of private information by public bodies (Government of Manitoba, 2003). These generally affect all social work agencies.

Some of these provincial laws set stringent requirements in health and human service organizations that govern to whom professionals can release information about clients. They tend to be more specific—and sometimes in the fields of health and mental health, even more rigorous—than those in the CASW code of ethics. All social workers need to be acutely aware of the provincial legislation that governs their practice. Also, in some jurisdictions and some fields, such as health, clients have a legal right to see all or a portion of their files.

Social work deals with intimate details and private difficulties that people do not want revealed to others: social workers hold this information in trust. However, information can be shared if the client gives permission to do so in writing or if statute or a court so authorizes (CASW, 1994a, Chapter 5-5). For example, if a referral for mental health services is to be made, or if advocacy on behalf of a client is needed for housing or residential care, it is important to discuss with clients and receive their permission as to what will be shared and why. When the client is unable to act on her or his own behalf, social workers can talk to designated trustees or guardians. Most often, clients agree to information being shared with others who need it or when this is in their best interest. In some organizations and in some cases, signed consent forms are used to permit social workers to discuss clients' situations with others. It is also possible that consent to share client information need only be verbal in some circumstances. **Organizational policy** and legislation will determine the practice in most social work settings.

Limits to Confidentiality There are important limits to clients' rights to confidentiality. In a number of circumstances, courts can and do subpoena records of workers even if the social worker has promised the client that all information will be kept confidential. If abuse of a child or other vulnerable person is reported, most jurisdictions have legislation that requires professional helpers to share the information with proper authorities. In such situations and in a client–social worker relationship, client self-determination and confidentiality are superseded.

Importantly, social workers need to discuss the limits to confidentiality with their clients when they begin their relationship and agree to work together (see Brill, 1998, p. 237). (This is also the case in social work research.) For example, a worker in a family service agency may help partners in a marriage resolve relationship difficulties. Even if there is no history or indication of child abuse, the worker is obligated to set the limits of confidentiality. Many agencies have protocols that specify how to do this. It should include informing the couple that if they make mention that abuse of a child is occurring, then the worker is required to take certain steps that usually involve reporting to proper authorities. The worker should describe limits to confidentiality honestly, as a matter of fact, in a manner that is clearly understood by clients, and as part of the relationship-building process. Such discussion helps define the relationship between worker and client and helps establishes its boundaries. This discussion seldom harms the helping relationship, and often enhances it because it promotes honesty and transparency.

In general, when the social worker has cause for concern about a client's or another person's safety, he or she has a moral, ethical, and often legal duty to act. For example, if a client tells a social worker about an active suicide plan, requesting that this be kept confidential, the worker is obligated to try to prevent the suicide by mobilizing emergency, and, within the boundaries of the client's legal right to privacy, supportive assistance and other resources, and following up during and after the crisis (Reamer, 1995, p. 165; DuBois and Miley, 1996, p. 225; Draucker, 1993, pp. 52–53). Client confidentiality in this case is not the primary concern.

There is another exception to confidentiality that must be shared with clients. Most social workers are employed in agencies and have colleagues and supervisors. Often other professionals are also part of the organization, such as in hospitals. All agencies should have policies regarding who has access to confidential information. Usually this right is extended at least to colleagues and members of the social worker's team, regardless of the team member's profession (Brown, 1991, p. 77). At the beginning of the relationship, the social worker needs to tell clients who within the agency has access to client information.

Power, Authority, and Control

Social work is not a profession associated with the same degree of power or authority as, for example, medicine or law. Nevertheless, social workers do exercise authority in direct practice situations. In fact, sometimes they find themselves dealing with "grey areas" in which they need to make judgments and determine actions autonomously (e.g., in child protection). This authority may be seen as a threat by clients in cases where the actions taken by a social worker determine access to their children or the return of a probationer to prison. The control function (covered in more detail later in this chapter) of social work should, however, be carried out in a caring and respectful manner (Callahan, 1993). One could say that social work is a profession with some inherent contradictions.

Fields of practice in which social workers are sanctioned to provide services—for example, to people who have abused their children—call for the appropriate use of power and authority. The state gives social workers the right to use their mandate to protect children at risk and to prevent potential or continued abuse (Armitage, 1993). It is critical to acknowledge to ourselves and to our clients what kind of authority we have and how it is to be used (Compton and Galaway, 1994, p. 285). This is not easy, since social workers often experience conflicts that inhibit their use of authority, particularly when it is seen as counterproductive to the helping process (Taylor, 1995). We understand the importance of empathy, respect, and concern for clients, recognizing that often people's issues or problems are not completely of their own making but reflect structural inequalities in society based on class, gender, ethnoculture, age, sexual orientation, or disability (Carniol, 1995; Mullaly, 2002). At the same time, our mandates in many fields of practice (e.g., probation services or the criminal justice system, child protection, and sometimes health care) guide us to use the authority and sanction of the state in our work with clients (Fusco, 1999, p. 53). The control aspect of social work is especially evident in relationships with involuntary clients, creating a source of conflict for both parties when clients don't want to receive services from the social worker, for reasons that may make sense from their perspective. Most people feel intruded upon in circumstances where they are required to tolerate the scrutiny of the state or its agents. The issues of authority and power between an involuntary client and a social worker thus must be addressed honestly and openly (Compton and Galaway, 1994, 1999). Although building a relationship with clients in such situations may be difficult, it is best to be frank and clear about the purpose of social work involvement and communicate in a way that is respectful and understanding of the client's reluctance to engage with the social worker. In all social work relationships, whether or not the client wants the services of the social worker and whether or not the social worker likes the client, the Canadian Association of Social Workers' code of ethics must guide the practice relationship.

Purpose and Commitment

A relationship between a client and a social worker requires purpose and commitment from both to sustain it. However, the social worker must take the lead because it is his or her mandate to provide help. Thus, there is a purpose or intention for initiating the social worker–client relationship. Commitment in a relationship occurs when there is agreement that working together for a specific purpose and goal is possible and desirable. Often the initial contact, whether on the phone or in person, begins a tentative relationship. A longer-term relationship can then be explored. At this early stage, there is no agreement to continue working together. This is so even when clients have been ordered by a judge to accept social work services. A decision by an involuntary client to reject social work services may invoke intrusions into the client's life (e.g., court proceedings, criminal charges, or other actions). Although difficult, it is possible to build commitment in such a relationship, but much depends on the success of discussion, conflict management, and negotiation.

The assessment stage of the client–social worker relationship includes the early, exploratory work that precedes any agreement to work together. It is at this point that a client decides whether she or he will accept the help of the social worker or agency. The client may choose not to pursue the relationship if, for example, she perceives that the kinds of services available are inappropriate for her; the waiting period for help is too long; the organization's mandate, principles, or service delivery is unacceptable; the distance is too far; or some other reason. Likewise, a social worker and agency might determine that they cannot offer services for some reason (e.g., they have no one with the required knowledge).

If, however, the client and social worker establish that they will work together, a relationship can be developed. The social worker commits to helping the client, bringing to the relationship her concern, caring, genuineness, and communication skills (Compton and Galaway, 1994, pp. 272–87; Hepworth and Larsen, 1990, p. 29). Commitment involves concern for and acceptance of the client's uniqueness and humanness within a process of helping. Our responsibility to clients, as described in our codes of ethics and often in agency policies, means that we "spell out the terms of our commitment and obligations to the consumer [client] as explicitly as possible, so that we can be responsible and accountable for what we say and do with the consumer or consumer group, to the system that employs us, and to ourselves" (O'Connor, Wilson, and Setterlund, 1995, p. 82).

Context and Structure

Social work practice occurs within a context, usually a social agency, characterized by organizational policies, values, regulations, and practices. An agency context gives structure to some aspects of the relationship, such as how, where, and when meetings occur, what resources are available for use, which other professionals work with the social worker and the client, and other factors. The context also limits what social workers can do and the kinds of help clients can receive from the social worker and agency.

Sometimes the structure of such a relationship becomes clearer to clients after an initial meeting with a social worker. It is important, however, that expectations and limitations stemming from agency context and structure and that shape the social worker–client relationship be discussed whenever possible (Brammer and MacDonald, 1996). Such discussion can help to reduce anxiety, provide information on client rights, and clarify what is to happen, who has which responsibilities, and how the client and social worker will work together.

RELATIONSHIPS IN STRUCTURAL, FEMINIST, AND ABORIGINAL APPROACHES

The qualities that a social worker needs to bring to client relationships are the same in Aboriginal, structural, and feminist approaches (see Chapters 11–13). However, the nature of the relationship may differ from more conventional approaches, since acknowledging that subordination, oppression, and exploitation shape human experience gives rise to other dynamics in relationship building (Bishop, 2002). Acknowledging and using one's authority and power in the social work relationship, as discussed by Compton and Galaway (1994, 1999) and Brill (1998), tends to conflict with Aboriginal, structural, and feminist approaches, in which the social worker aims to reduce power differences. This may occur when a social worker and client share some experiences in a conscious effort to find common ground and better understanding. The social worker strives to become an ally or partner of the client in order to foster a collective consciousness with those who experience oppression. In feminist social work, sharing and validating a woman's experiences, in which sexism and gender inequality may have shaped those experiences and access to resources, are important. Although power differences between female clients and their social workers exist, feminist social workers attempt to reduce them (see Chapter 13).

RELATIONSHIPS WITH INVOLUNTARY CLIENTS

Relationships with involuntary clients merit specific attention. Earlier in this chapter we defined involuntary clients, and we talked about the use of authority and power as a control function of social work. Chapter 8 will describe how the principle of best interest, widely accepted by social workers, provides a rationale for working with involuntary clients.

People sometimes become involuntary clients through court mandates in fields such as corrections and child protection, and are required to accept social services. Some are involuntary clients because they are hospitalized, often in mental hospitals or in residential facilities, and targeted for social work intervention (O'Connor, Wilson, and Setterlund, 1995, p. 154). Some involuntary clients shun any effort to develop a relationship with the social worker. Probably most, as well as being fearful and angry, are reticent, want to avoid contact, and may be resistant. Yet they still leave room for the worker to attempt to negotiate a helping relationship. In other words, there are varying degrees to which clients are involuntary.

Particularly in fields like forensic psychiatry and corrections, a major responsibility of the social worker is to the public. The public, as represented by the judicial system, is really the primary client in a sense. The service that the social worker provides is usually to both protect the public at large and to help rehabilitate persons charged with criminal offences. Nevertheless, social workers have the responsibility to provide services to offenders and to consider them clients, albeit usually involuntary ones.

Helping in social work is presumed to depend on a working relationship between the worker and the client. The first sections of this chapter have shown that all of the essential helping tools that social workers have at their disposal require meaningful communication between worker and client. The nature and quality of the relationship and the communication contained within it will determine the success or failure of the helping attempt. Social work helping depends on the nature of communication with clients.

We have also shown that to develop this helping relationship, social work practitioners must form partnerships with clients who seek help. All of the approaches used in this book tend to make the assumption that the client is seeking or willing to accept help. This includes the problem-solving, strengths, Aboriginal, and feminist approaches.

Still, developing helping relationships with unwilling clients who do not want our help is not an easy task.

Assessing Involuntary Clients

While assessment frameworks such as those presented in Chapter 9 and other chapters in this book are applicable, there are other approaches to assessing involuntary clients. The social worker needs to see the involuntary client through a different set of lenses, to understand that he or she has probably experienced many difficult, stressful, and possibly even traumatic problems in life. There are important reasons for the client having these problems. The client has probably been a victim in the past, even though others may currently see him as deviant. The client may have committed serious crimes or may be a danger to others. While using the lens of assessment to understand the client, one does not make excuses for his behaviour but seeks to set the stage for a helping process. It may be very challenging, for example, when a social worker experiences strong feelings of dislike for a client who has seriously injured a young child or killed someone. In such situations, it can help to consult a colleague or supervisor for help. It may also be useful to regard the client as someone who, rather than being a victim, has survived adversity in life.

Assessment *must* include both how others see the client and how the client sees herself or himself. For example, a criminal justice worker who is assigned to work with a man who has a long record of violent crime must understand how others view him. These others include a wide range of people, including those close to the man, those responsible for the legal system, and perhaps even his victims. But the worker must also attempt to understand the man's point of view and his story. The same principle applies to working with a young woman who has recently had an episode of schizophrenia, threatened close family members, and been forced into hospital. The worker needs to understand the implications of the views of the mental health staff (including diagnosis and prognosis), the woman's family, and other relevant systems. But, primarily, the worker needs to understand the client from her own viewpoint.

Why are people who experience personal and social problems often unwilling to seek help? There are many possible answers. Some people may not feel that their problems are surmountable given time or luck. Most pride themselves on their independence. They like to be able to handle their own emotional, social, and financial affairs and to meet their own basic needs. If they are unable to do so, they often view this as a failure, as may their friends and family. To ask for help is not only an embarrassment but also an acknowledgment of failure, and may open the door for stigma.

Many clients of social workers in the justice and child welfare systems particularly have had numerous previous encounters with those referred to as "helpers." Often these encounters have had negative consequences. Think of the impact of the abuse that many Aboriginal people experienced in residential schools. Few teachers and religious leaders served as role models and earned the trust of the students, and some of them abused their students (Milloy, 1999). Certainly, this experience would lead to mistrust of those people who purport to help.

Think of the fear that a small Aboriginal community would have of child welfare workers when it was common (as it was in the 1950s and 1960s) for them to apprehend children and place them in non-Aboriginal foster homes in Canada or the United States. Often members of the community did not understand the reasons for the children being sent away, let alone the need for placement in a different cultural environment. The deep grief, pain, and anger felt by parents and communities can only be imagined.

Or think of the embarrassment that some people feel when they wait in line to receive groceries from a food bank. They may also worry about running out of food before they are eligible for more and how to manage until then (Bidgood, Smilek, Kryzanowski, and Taylor, in press).

There are many more possible examples. However, most of them have at least two common threads. First, people have often had negative experiences with a system that was supposed to provide them with a service and earn their trust. Second, all of these people have been defined as deviant.

Social Labelling

Understanding the labelling process is important in working with involuntary clients. The concept of labelling helps us understand how the perceptions of others and their actions toward a client affect him or her. It also helps us understand why some people have been defined as deviant and ultimately why some clients are unwilling to accept help from social workers.

Most clients who are involuntary are also seen as deviant (Rooney, 1992). Likely they have broken a social rule, and possibly the law. Many social rules or norms are not codified in law. Often rules set by families and other primary social groups are more important than cultural or legislated rules. Deviance is a category of behaviour that does not conform to normative expectations and toward which others take negative sanctions. These negative sanctions often take the form of stigma, ostracism, punishment, and other means of social control.

Deviance covers a wide range of behaviours. Probably all who enter the criminal justice system are seen as deviant by society, even if they are only charged with or merely suspected of a crime. Parents who have a child removed from them may be seen as deviant. The behaviour of a person who is psychotic and threatens others or seems "mad" will be seen by others as a rule breaker and hence deviant, even if the psychosis has clearly been defined as an illness. It is not necessary for this person to break the law—she or he has broken a commonly held social code that prescribes "normal" behaviours (Becker, 1963; Kitsuse, 1962; Lemert, 1951; Schur, 1971; Suchar, 1978, pp. 165–242).

Labelling theory holds that the label or tag by itself is of relatively little consequence. Such a tag, a name for a deviant activity, is sometimes called the *primary deviance.* What is critically important is how others react to the tag and how this reaction affects the person who is labelled. Social labelling is the process of defining someone as deviant and condemning that person for a behaviour or trait that she or he has or expresses.

A gay man who has just found the courage to "come out" to his coworkers after five years of working with them may be seen as deviant by some at his workplace. They avoid him because they are unsure how to relate to him now. They may be homophobic and fear that they too might be seen as gay by association, so they do not join him for coffee or lunch any longer. (Others, however, might be encouraged by his openness, sharing their own identity issues or providing him with the validation and support he needs at this time.) This example illustrates differences between primary deviance and subsequent labelling. The primary deviance, according to labelling theory, is the man's homosexuality. Labelling theory holds that there would be no consequences in being defined as homosexual if others did not label his behaviour as deviant.

However, the man's family may be embarrassed and possibly ashamed of him. Former friends might not want to continue to associate with him. Fellow employees may shun him. He may be passed over for promotions at work, or even his job may be in jeopardy. If such reactions occur, then the man has been labelled. According to labelling theory, these are the factors that are important. The labelling process has defined the man as deviant, and he must now contend with this as part of his life.

The labelling process can have devastating effects, causing severe stress, guilt, defensiveness, fear, anxiety, and a host of other emotional and social problems. If the response to the labelling is further deviance, this response is called *secondary deviance* (Lemert, 1951; Rooney, 1992, pp. 121–24; Schur, 1971; Suchar, 1978, pp. 165–242).

Labelling theory can help us work with involuntary clients. Most involuntary clients (and many voluntary clients) have experienced labelling. If the labelling was perpetrated by professional helpers, as frequently happens, this often helps to explain some of the problematic behaviours of clients and why clients do not want help. Assessment must include a clear understanding of the social labelling process (not just the tag) and a clear understanding of how it affects clients. This understanding may provide clues on how to engage involuntary clients in a helping relationship. An acknowledgement from the social worker that she or he understands how the labelling happened and its effects may be a starting point, helping to validate the client's past experiences. A social worker trying to develop a relationship with a client who has been labelled needs to acknowledge the effects of such labelling for the person, including the impact on his or her current situation.

Case Example

Tom ▼

Tom is an 18-year-old Aboriginal boy who moved to the city from a reserve at age 7. When he first enrolled in school he was behind the other students in his grade. Teachers quickly labelled him "slow." Other students taunted him because he was different, and he was often the butt of teasing that had racial overtones. Tom's teachers and fellow students defined him as deviant. At that young age, he began to believe that he was not as good as or equal to the other children.

By age 9 Tom had begun his delinquent career. At first it was petty shoplifting. Then he began to sniff solvents. His parents, who were both unemployed, were having difficulty controlling him. At age 10 Tom was placed, by the courts, in the first of four foster homes. The first home was very strict. The people there had no understanding or appreciation of Tom's Aboriginal heritage. Like his teachers, they considered Tom incapable of keeping up with others in school. His social worker visited only when there was a crisis and, in Tom's eyes, was cold and uncaring. The school considered him a troublemaker, and he was expelled twice. After nine months, Tom ran away and was placed in yet another foster home. Four years later, the police arrested him after he was caught shoplifting. They took him to a group home for delinquent boys.

The negative experiences in foster homes were repeated three times. Tom's teachers and social workers continued to believe that he had little potential. As the years passed, the severity of his delinquency increased. Tom, now 18, has been convicted of armed robbery and trafficking in heroin.

You have been assigned to the courts to complete a pre-sentence report. As you interview Tom, you discover that he has little use for professionals, particularly teachers and social workers. You find that he is not only a mandated involuntary client but a resistant one as well.

In the case example, Tom has been labelled almost all of his life—at least since he moved to the city. The psychological and social consequences of labelling are huge. This may be particularly so because those who were supposed to help him—teachers, foster parents, and social workers—either actively dehumanized him or displayed an uncaring attitude. The system had failed him. Understanding the dynamics of this process of labelling often helps explain the difficulties in working with involuntary clients. Tom has learned not to trust others. There is good reason for him not to want to seek help. Why should Tom seek help from professionals who dehumanize him?

This process is not uncommon. Aboriginal people often experience labelling because they are Aboriginal. When they encounter the social service system, like Tom, why should they trust it? Their experience may tell them not to do so. Likewise, people living in poverty who have been dehumanized by their plight may have difficulty trusting those who wish to help. Labelling can occur as the result of many social processes, including intolerance, racism, and prejudice.

It is best to avoid communication or action that labels. While avoiding labelling completely is probably impossible, its effects can be mitigated. For instance, it is possible to separate condemning certain behaviour from condemning the person. If the goal is to establish a helping relationship, it is all right to appropriately condemn a behaviour, but it is not all right to condemn a person. Think of how such condemnation has affected Tom throughout the course of his young life. How can we begin to establish a relationship with him that is built on respect and trust?

To further illustrate, assume a young woman has been given a diagnosis of schizophrenia. When her illness is active, she is paranoid and sometimes threatening and potentially abusive. Also, assume that your goal is to begin to engage her, an unwilling client, in a helping relationship. There is a subtle but big difference between defining her as a schizophrenic and seeing her as a person who has schizophrenia. The former implies that schizophrenia is the person and the person is deviant because of the paranoid and threatening behaviour. The second limits schizophrenia to a disease and implies that it is only part of the person. This attitude accepts that the person has dignity but suffers from a significant disease. If the disease leads to irrational behaviour, such as threatening actions, you can show that the behaviour is unacceptable and will certainly affect how others relate to the woman.

It is important to help clients deal with labels. For example, a social worker might offer to speak for a client who is fearful of seeking employment because she has been convicted of a crime. A social worker might also intervene directly with those who label—for example, by helping a teacher understand that a student is not unintelligent but has a learning disability that gives him trouble in school. He needs specialized help to adapt, and his family has not been able to afford this. Offering to help clients who have been labelled can open the door to a stronger helping relationship.

Reaching Out

Most social workers recognize that attempts to help a hostile client will not succeed unless the worker and client agree that a problem needs to be solved. On occasion, a client needs to be convinced that there is a problem. While the client may reject help, often the worker needs to continue trying to establish a helping relationship. This process is sometimes called *reaching out* and is often a major part of work with involuntary clients. (See Shulman, 1999, pp. 107–17, for a good illustration of contracting with resistant clients. Also see Chapter 4.)

Decision Making, Assessment, and Best Interest

Most social workers who work with involuntary clients make decisions that affect clients' lives. However, unlike working with voluntary clients, these decisions are generally made *for* the client rather than *with* the client (Ivanoff, Blythe, and Tripodi, 1994). Consider the decision of a social worker to support a family's attempt to force a member who suffers from bipolar disorder to be hospitalized. Think about the approach of a child welfare worker working with a mother who has apparently abandoned her child, requiring that the worker seek temporary custody of the child. Another example is a parole officer who reports that his client has broken the rules of probation.

In one sense, the assessment process for involuntary clients (see Chapters 8 and 9) is the same as for voluntary clients. However, the assessment with an involuntary client is often not a dialogue between social worker and client. Instead, it is usually more like detective work in which the worker tries to deal with conflict, establish what is wrong, determine the client's problems, and develop a treatment plan. Assessments of involuntary clients can involve completing official assessment forms for agencies or individuals with authority, such as court officials, the medical staff of a hospital, a child welfare agency, or a parole board. Often these documents not only assess the client but also include recommendations for action. The purpose of such assessments is to help the proper authorities, often courts, to make treatment or other judicial decisions, such as sentence length. In providing the information, the social worker is acting in the best interest of the clients, who are often both an individual and the public.

Case Example

Ravi and Maria

Maria had left her children at home alone while she visited friends, and the local child protection service agency apprehended her children. Maria is very hostile to Ravi, the child protection worker assigned to her case. Ravi realizes that despite Maria's hostility and rejection of his help, he may need to make decisions that could have a profound effect on her family's life. Ravi also understands that he is acting in the best interest of both Maria and the children, but that his highest priority is ensuring the safety and well-being of the children.

Ultimately, Ravi believes Maria will get her children back, so it is very important that he think in the long term. Ravi hopes that eventually he can establish a helping relationship with Maria. His current challenge is to begin to reach out to Maria.

As suggested above, working with clients who do not want services often requires the social worker to make decisions that affect the client's life but without the client's consent. Of course, these decisions must be made within the boundaries of the worker's and agency's mandate. The worker should be clear about the decisions and not withhold information from the client. Further, the worker needs to carefully explain the reasons for the decisions, the exact nature and content of the decisions, and the likely effects of the decisions on all those involved. The social worker must make a considerable effort to keep the decision making transparent and open, with no hint of deception or dishonesty. By keeping everything above board, showing how the social worker is acting in the best interest of a variety of stakeholders, the worker sets the stage for the later formation of a helping relationship with the client. The social worker must make known that she or he is available to the client if the client so wishes. This fact needs to be outlined clearly and regularly in order to open the door to future contact.

Negotiation and Contracting

Suppose, in our case example, that Ravi has clearly told Maria that he is going to petition the court for temporary custody of her children. Ravi has discovered that Maria has a history of abandoning her children. He is honest with her and lets her know that custody will be reviewed in 90 days, but that it is unlikely that the children could be returned to her then. Ravi emphasizes, however, that he is available to help Maria. After the end of the first month, he receives a phone call from Maria asking to meet with him. Ravi sees this meeting as a possible opening for forming a helping relationship. His ideal goal is to form a contract (see Chapter 8) that outlines a plan and method to help Maria decide the best course of action, which probably, but not necessarily, includes return of the children.

Ravi may use this opening to begin negotiations with Maria. Unlike most voluntary relationships, engaging with involuntary clients usually requires substantial negotiation. Since Maria suggested the meeting, a good place for Ravi to begin might be to invoke the old social work adage "Start where the client is."

Case Example

Ravi and Maria

Ravi meets Maria at her home. This is Maria's own environment, where she likely feels most comfortable and in control. Ravi lets Maria explain what she wants and tries to clearly understand her point of view before reacting. As Maria talks, it becomes clear that she wants her children back immediately. She also says she is willing to attend a parenting group and accept counselling for herself. Once clear about Maria's position, Ravi makes explicit the non-negotiable items. For instance, Maria has to show progress before a decision to return her children can be made, and there is no chance of their return before the review date. However, within these confines Ravi is willing to help Maria enroll in the parenting group and seek counselling in addition to helping her develop a plan to get her children back. Maria still does not trust Ravi, the person who in her mind has taken her children from her. But she does ask him to help her get started with the parenting group and counselling.

In the case example of Ravi and Maria, the two negotiate a starting point—a limited contract. Neither Ravi nor Maria get what they want. Ravi is unable to develop a plan, and Maria does not get the immediate return of her children. But they do have agreement on a starting point. Most helping relationships formed with involuntary clients involve considerable negotiation, and most are much more complicated than our example. (See Rooney, 1992, pp. 175–200, for further discussion of negotiation and contracting in involuntary relationships.)

Involuntary Relationships and Social Supports

In mandated practice, clients often feel a lack of power and autonomy because they are not in charge of important parts of their lives. The social worker is usually in a clear position of power and control over the client. Instead of the relationship being a supportive one, it is controlling. However,

> All too often, individuals in the mental health, child protective and criminal justice services became involuntary clients, in part, because they did not have enough sources of social support. In other instances, these individuals had used up these supports by asking for too much help too many times, or by disappointing these sources of support. Without these supports, they were not able to hold things together and committed actions that brought them into one of these systems as involuntary clients. (Ivanoff, Blythe, and Tripodi, 1994, p. 92)

Ivanoff, Blythe, and Tripodi (1994) argue that social workers need to focus interventions with involuntary clients on building both formal and informal support networks. Support networks can include mutual aid (self-help) groups, friends, volunteer organizations, and professionals.

Sullivan (1994), in a study that examined factors that contributed to recovery from mental illness, found that community and case management support was second (out of eight factors) only to the benefits of medication. Community support and case management were ranked five places higher than mutual aid groups and supportive friends. While the study sampled only people diagnosed with a mental illness, it suggests that providing professional support is very important in initiating recovery.

Social workers need to be innovative in building supports, even if clients are resistant. While they may reject efforts at support, resistant clients often appreciate them. In addition, support building may depend upon the ingenuity and resourcefulness of the worker. Support of client strengths and goals by social workers can have important benefits for involuntary clients.

We have attempted to outline some principles designed to engage mandated and unwilling involuntary clients. This is in reality a very complicated and, to some extent, controversial process. Further, exact processes are different depending on the field of practice. For example, forming relationships with someone who has a psychosis and displays paranoid thinking is very different from engaging with an angry man who has abused his spouse. A major part of our thesis is that good social work practice must account for work with both voluntary and involuntary clients. The strategies and methods discussed above can help in the development of a social worker–client relationship, but the skill, compassion, and commitment of a social worker in beginning, establishing, and maintaining a relationship with a client, even when doing so is very difficult, is of critical importance in any field of practice.

CHAPTER SUMMARY

Social workers must work with both voluntary and involuntary clients. Involuntary clients may be mandated, unwilling, or both. While all client–social worker relationships are important, the nature of professional relationships with voluntary and involuntary clients is different.

The features that are most important in forming relationships with clients are care and concern; empathy and honesty; acceptance of people; acknowledging client capacity for change; self-determination and autonomy; confidentiality; power, authority, and control; purpose and commitment; and context and structure.

There are challenges in working with different kinds of people in diverse problem situations; social workers need to understand how social labelling can create feelings of shame, reduced self-esteem, and anger in people. Social workers' professional experience, knowledge, and commitment will help them in using the problem-solving process and other social work **practice approaches** for work with voluntary and involuntary clients.

chapter 7

Cultural Diversity, Cultural Awareness, and Social Work Practice

Chapter Goal

To understand how culture provides a lens for social work practice.

This Chapter ▼

- examines the meaning of culture, ethnicity, race, and racism
- describes anti-oppressive and antiracist social work in relation to immigrants, refugees, and visible minorities
- discusses etic and emic stances and ethnocultural competence in social work
- applies the above concepts to case situations and explores the implications for social work practice at the micro, mezzo, and macro levels

INTRODUCTION

This chapter uses the lens of culture in relation to values, assumptions, orientation, and actions of social workers in their work at various levels. It also examines the meaning of concepts that are used in social work; those that often are not clear until applied to practice situations. For this reason, we introduce a number of case situations to illustrate their application. This chapter does not describe ethnocultural (pertaining to an ethnic group) demographics in Canada or the development of laws and policies regarding immigration or multiculturalism, as these are covered in other works (e.g., Driedger, 1996; James and Shadd, 2001; Li, 1999, 2003; Driedger, 1987; Halli, Trovato, and Driedger, 1990; Halli and Driedger, 1999).

Honestly exploring who you are and what you stand for, what has advantaged and disadvantaged you in relation to others, and how you have found strength to overcome challenges in your life are important for social workers. In the first part of this chapter, we define and discuss concepts such as culture, ethnicity, race, racism, and antiracist and anti-oppressive social work, among others, in order to explore how they influence people's lives. We also discuss their significance in social work practice with individuals, families, groups, and communities, primarily but not solely in relation to immigrants, refugees, visible minorities, and people from diverse cultural backgrounds. We acknowledge that some in these groups may also experience oppression due to disability, age, sexual orientation, or poverty.

CULTURE, ETHNICITY, AND RACE

North Americans are either Aboriginal peoples, immigrants, or descendants of immigrants. In the early 1900s, settlement house workers at St. Christopher's House and other settlements in Toronto headed by clergy and academics had a dual purpose—to Christianize and to assimilate newcomers (Irving, Parsons, and Bellamy, 1995; O'Connor, 1986, p. 6). Their work aimed not only to educate the poor but also to help them in accepting the dominant morality and culture. These activities reflected the social policy of the era. Settlement house workers later noted, however, that most newcomers maintained an affiliation with and followed the cultural practices of their countries of origin. We now recognize that culture and cultural practices are important to many immigrants and often provide a source of strength and grounding in families and communities. It must, however, be noted that some cultural practices can be harmful and may conflict with laws or practices in Canada. One example is the practice of female circumcision, which can have serious health consequences for girls and women.

Awareness of Ethnoculture and Identity

Clearly understanding your own cultural background, whether or not you are a first-generation immigrant, can help you to empathize with and recognize the considerable and different challenges faced by newcomers, whether they are people who have come here through planned immigration or for refuge from a situation of persecution, war, or conflict.

For all social workers, self-awareness about identity and background is important, as this is part of who you are as a person and how you relate to others. It may be that you view your own background or identity as significant in your life experience or that it has little significance for you, perhaps because it is taken for granted. As helpers, we often work with members of cultures that differ from our own. In order to fully understand people from another culture, we need clarity about our own backgrounds. This is necessary so that we can appreciate and understand similarities and differences between ourselves and clients and how we mutually react to each other's cultures.

Consider some of the ways in which cultural heritage has been significant—or not—in your life and how important it is to you now. It may even have some relevance in your decision to study social work. It might be useful to draw a family tree or genogram (a map of your family and families of origin) showing the ethnocultural roots of your parents (and/or foster parents), your grandparents, and yourself and other details that highlight the places, cultural contexts, and events that are a part of your ancestry and social history. For example, if one grandparent immigrated to Canada from France and married a person of Cree background, what events and circumstances do you think brought them together in life? What obstacles do you think they had to face and overcome? What legacy are you left with? Has this cultural background been a factor in shaping your values, identity, life goals, and personal relationships? If so, how? Over the course of your life, you may have had many experiences with people from cultural backgrounds different from yours. Think of one or two examples that are particularly memorable. What effects did these encounters have on you? What did you learn from them? What learning can be applied in your work with people or groups whose cultural background differs from yours?

Throughout this chapter, we will look at the benefits of social work that respects and responds to the diversity in clients and in all people.

Culture

Culture includes a shared but not necessarily identical home country, region, or group; customs; language; beliefs; traditions; and worldview, which are expressed in everyday life. Culture has an influence on people's values and behaviour. For example, think about how the culture of traditional Inuit hunters in Nunavut differs from that of a middle-class urban family in Vancouver or the subculture of homeless people living in Toronto's streets. (A subculture represents a distinct group that varies in certain ways from the broader cultural environment in which it is found.) Culture can be shared by people living in a particular region or by a specific community of people who are not necessarily found in the same geographic area, such as Filipino or Somali communities that are scattered in various countries and cities. It can also refer to a common bond or interest between people who may have no other ties (e.g., alternative film culture, gay culture, dog breeders' culture, etc.).

Culture is dynamic, changing over time and place. For example, if you think of the culture of early French-Canadian settlers who lived mainly as farmers in rural Quebec and compare it with the primarily urban French-Canadian cultural context of Quebec today, you can appreciate the degree of change over time. Moreover, the culture and cultural practices of the same French-Canadians, when they relocate to a city in British Columbia, are differently adapted and perhaps differently expressed. Of course, some aspects of cultural life are retained as people adapt to a new environment. "'Culture' is not an item of baggage but a continuous process of renegotiation grounded in specific times and places and affected by other social processes" (Morrissey, 1997, p. 102). For example, immigrants coming to Canada are affected by the culture they left, the culture they enter, and the changes they go through as they settle and make a life in Canada (see Herberg, 1993).

Culture partly consists of a social structure that includes values, beliefs, and expectations. It sets guidelines for what is acceptable behaviour and what is not. People tend to abide by these guidelines if they belong to and identify with a particular ethnocultural group. Culture can also offer a map for understanding what goes on around us and for interacting with others. Barnlund (1988) refers to culture as a "symbolic universe governed by codes that are unconsciously acquired and automatically employed. [We] rarely notice that the ways [we] interpret and talk about events are distinctly different from the ways people conduct their affairs in other cultures" (cited in James, 1995, p. 1).

Culture is also about how people view their world. It is difficult to ever fully understand the culturally embedded beliefs and behaviours of others, at least not from the group's own standpoint. Each person views the world and experiences events from the perspective of her or his uniquely created individual lenses (McIntosh, 1989).

The word "culture" can also be used in reference to harmful aspects in our society. Evidence of this is seen in a shared culture of violence among organized crime groups, or a culture of sexual exploitation on Internet pornography sites or when members of one cultural group seek to destroy those of another due to notions of superiority (e.g., ethnic cleansing). We need to be cautious about portraying culture only as a neutral or positive feature in a society.

To some, culture refers to those who are non–English speaking, perhaps immigrants or members of particular ethnocultural or racial groups. This is especially likely if you are of Western European decent and are at least second-generation Canadian. Importantly, the Canadians who have descended from European settlers do have their own cultures. So do North America's Aboriginal peoples—Inuit, Indian, and Métis—whose identity has been subjected to classification by state legislation and policy. Sometimes, you hear people say that they don't have any special culture; they're just Canadian. It is difficult to experience our culture as unique when it is so much a part of our everyday thinking and living. It is not easily seen because it surrounds us.

Some features in Canadian society might contribute to a broader national culture. We are exposed to the same national laws, attend schools that impart certain common ideas and values, and are integrated through events and processes in which we all share. As James (1995) asserts, "Through acculturation and assimilation, ethnic and racial minority group members come to share the dominant Canadian culture. The variations which exist in Canadian culture do not fundamentally dispute the fact that we must all at some point adhere to, and participate in, the same activities" (p. 21). Despite the shared form of culture in which all people living in a society participate—at least to some degree—there is considerable diversity in how culture is expressed in other areas of life.

Ethnicity

The word "ethnic" is derived from a Greek word that can be translated as "people." It is often used to refer to immigrants, refugees, and foreigners in general, but everyone belongs to an ethnic group. An ethnic group shares a common heritage. It tends to be assumed that ethnic groups also share a common identity, experience, and origin, including aspects such as beliefs, language, and traditions, an assumption that often leads to stereotyping. "To the extent that an ethnic identity is accepted by outsiders, it becomes a convenient way for members of the group to distinguish themselves and for others to distinguish them" (Li, 1990, p. 5). The word "ethnicity" can be viewed as "essentially relative (historically and geographically) and social [in] nature," (Morrissey, 1997, p. 98), making it difficult to define in concrete terms. Individuals may identify themselves as members of a particular ethnic group, but there are variations in the strength of their affiliation. In addition, people's ethnicity may not be the most significant social category in their lives. Perhaps class, gender, sexual orientation, or age is more important to them.

Race

Race is also seen as a feature of ethnicity where a particular racial group might have some common physical features, such as colour of skin. Race is difficult to conceptualize because it has been defined in relation to ethnic groups, biological traits, personalities, nationalities, and particular geographic regions (Li, 1990), creating confusion and distortion. Race is a socially defined category of humans that changes over time and place. In fact, there is more variation among people of one race than there is among people of diverse races, so it is uncommon, especially in Canada, to differentiate people solely by race. Dei (1996) asserts that the notion of ethnicity is now often used in place of race, which does not adequately reflect the diversity among human beings. This book uses the words "ethnoculture" and "ethnicity" rather than race. We do, however, make use of the terms "racism" and "antiracist social work practice" as defined below.

Racism

Attempting to define racism, assert Fleras and Elliott (1999, p. 67), is like "pasting Jell-O to the wall" because its meaning, much like the meaning of race, is difficult to pin down. It is easier to point to actions that are racist than to define racism. Some definitions of racism, for example, do not refer to colour of skin, seeing racism as any act against a group of people. Although we acknowledge these difficulties in definition, we have decided to define racism as a form of discrimination based on ethnicity, which may also include skin colour.

Oppression based on ethnicity and/or skin colour—racism—occurs due to an assumption of superiority by one group over another, whether this is conscious or not. Barker (1991, p. 113) defines individual racism as negative attitudes, such as prejudice, held by a person about those who are members of a particular ethnic or cultural group. These kinds of attitudes can be seen when someone insults or is violent toward a person because of his or her culture. Legal processes offer individuals courses of action to take should they feel discriminated against. A considerable amount of attention has been given to the impact of individual acts of racism, often in the form of books and articles written by the victims (see, for example, *In Search of April Raintree* [Culleton, 1992], the moving story of two Aboriginal sisters who coped with foster home placement and discrimination).

Institutional racism refers to the structural or systemic factors that support unfair treatment of people based on race or ethnic group. Baron refers to the "web of institutional dependencies" in which discrimination in one institutional sector, such as schooling, can "feed into or reinforce distinctions in other institutional sectors" (cited in Ponting, 1994, p. 105), such as employment and housing. A chain of institutional connections affects many spheres of daily life (Ponting, 1994). For example, university admission requirements tend to work against Aboriginal people and other cultural groups whose first language is not English or French or who may have had fewer supports to succeed in high school (e.g., language or other assistance). Some students may drop out of high school due to their feelings of exclusion and isolation.

Racism is not confined to the attitudes and behaviour of white people. Discrimination occurs across many groups of people (Dei, 1996)—for example, when members of one minority group discriminate against members of the same group (or another) according to class or religion. In social work, we recognize cultural racism (and discrimination) as issues that need to be discussed and dealt with in our society, and as concerns in social work practice.

SOCIAL WORK ACROSS CULTURES

The terms "etic" and "emic," borrowed from anthropology, are useful in thinking about intervention when a client and social worker's ethnocultural backgrounds differ.

An Etic Approach

The etic approach involves a perspective from an outsider's position, allowing general comparison across cultures. For example, if an anthropologist wants to compare community-organizing strategies of women in a number of cultural groups in different parts of the world, she or he needs to think broadly of the general features of community organizing by women. The anthropologist might study the issues that women organizers address, who the group leaders are, and how community work is balanced with paid work and domestic chores. These general topics might be explored so that a range of cultural groups can be included in the research. From such a study, the researcher would obtain general findings that tell her or him about these features in a number of countries, but the anthropologist would have little information on the unique cultural context and experiences of each of the women's community organizations. The etic approach filters everything through the lens of the outside researcher.

An Emic Approach

The emic approach refers to an insider's view—one that is local and specific to a cultural group. In the study of women's community organizing, an emic perspective would be one that deals with specific organizing experiences and their relevance to one group, according to the women themselves. This approach offers the group members' or insiders' account. The information would include many details specific to one unit (e.g., people in the group), including experiences in local events, issues, or problems that are of concern to the group in their local environment.

In social work, we strive for an emic approach. We want to know about a client's perception of what has occurred, how he or she understands the situation, what factors in his or her life have played a part, and what the client thinks might help. While we may draw on general knowledge of clients we have worked with in similar circumstances, we cannot assume that the current client's situation is the same as in our past experiences.

For example, consider an Asian family with an elderly member. He is in hospital recovering from a severe stroke. You are the hospital social worker responsible for discharge planning. Past experience and your general knowledge tell you that grandparents in many Asian families (and in other ethnocultural groups) are highly respected and valued; families are usually willing to take care of sick extended-family members in their own homes. In assessing the family situation, you must take into account your past experience but also hold open the possibility that the family cannot care for the elderly member. While guided by your generalizations, you must let the family members tell their own story so you understand how they perceive the situation. This will determine your course of action.

Green (1995) states that in social work we are mainly concerned with the emic perspective because generalization is not helpful when we are trying to communicate with sensitivity and understanding in diverse situations of the people we try to help. This means recognizing that clients and their circumstances are unique, requiring social workers to maintain openness and flexibility as they intervene in each client situation.

Social workers may encounter both new and more established immigrants and refugees as clients in large social service agencies or in organizations that specifically work with these groups. Such work may be carried out, for example, in social service delivery to new immigrants dealing with settlement issues and related needs, such as practical help or emotional support. These needs can arise from "a series of stress-producing events that result in the need for assistance and support; such events include separation from family and community, journeys of different durations and levels of danger, and relocation problems associated with finding housing and employment" (Padilla, 1997, p. 596). Social service programs reflect current immigration policy and may include a variety of public and voluntary social provisioning (e.g., financial help for settlement, access to legal resources, language and job training programs, housing assistance, and mental health services). Of course, this is not meant to imply that all immigrants will require these social services; many will not.

Antiracist Practice

Moving beyond a model that stresses cultural sensitivity is the antiracist approach to social work practice, in which social workers deal directly with attitudes and practices that promote prejudice and discrimination against ethnocultural groups. Writing from the field of education, Dei and Calliste (2000) refer to antiracist practice as "an action-oriented, educational and political strategy for institutional and systemic change that addresses the issues of racism and the interlocking systems of social oppression (sexism, classism, heterosexism, ableism)" (p. 13). This broad definition includes the examination of diverse forms of oppression along with racism. Thompson (1993) agrees, adding that oppression and discrimination are "aspects of the divisive nature of social structure—reflections of the social divisions of class, race, gender, age, disability and sexual orientation. These are dimensions of our social location [where we see ourselves fitting in relation to others in society] and so we need to understand them as a whole…" (p. 11).

Considering our social location means understanding ourselves in terms of our ethnoculture, gender, age, socioeconomic class, ability, and other characteristics and critically examining how these have advantaged or disadvantaged us in meeting our needs and life chances. Recognizing our own social location in relation to that of our clients and others is important for all social workers.

Antiracist practice is inherent in an Aboriginal approach to social work (see Chapter 11). The history of Aboriginal peoples and the policies of assimilation resulted in cultural loss to such an extent that efforts to reclaim traditional teachings and to promote culturally specific practices and languages must now be made (McKenzie and Morrissette, 2003; Morrissette, McKenzie, and Morrissette, 1993). Bringing antiracist practice to one's social work practice can help to promote these aims.

How people feel about themselves has much to do with how others behave toward them. In Chapter 6, we described how Tom's experiences as an Aboriginal student in a school dominated by white students and teachers were characterized by discrimination and labelling that worked to oppress him. His treatment by students and teachers played a role in how he saw himself and subsequently behaved toward himself and others. The example shows clearly how important it is that the development of positive regard for oneself and others begins early in life, and how it can be seriously hindered through the negative actions of peers and authority figures and tolerance of these in our society. Internalized oppression, where a person believes he or she is inferior and unworthy, leading to self-hatred, often occurs. How an individual senses she or he is perceived by others in society, "whether in the media or in history books or among professionals such as teachers, doctors, and lawyers, has an impact on her [or his] perceptions of self-worth and ability" (Lundy, 2004, p. 132).

What we can learn from Tom's experience is that it is necessary to understand how racism diminishes people, not only those who perpetrate it knowingly or unknowingly, but rather all human beings. It is worthwhile for social workers to help people like Tom make connections between their past experiences and current reality so that they can begin to examine their strengths, build their self-worth, and develop hope that their lives can be better. We also learn from Tom's situation that investing time to help children develop self-worth and compassion for others is critical to their continued growth and well-being.

Discrimination and the Role of Social Work

The Canadian Association of Social Workers' code of ethics states: "A social worker shall identify, document and advocate the elimination of discrimination" (CASW, 1994a, p. 24). Some current social work literature reflects a multicultural model, focused on promoting cultural identity and understanding the meaning of people's cultures in social interaction (e.g., Green, 1995; Devore and Schlesinger, 1991; Herberg, 1993). The rise in Asian and African immigration in North America and the attendant social effects have called attention to discrimination based on ethnicity or race and the need for policy responses that are relevant to newcomers and visible minorities.

Mullaly (2002, p. 100), for example, criticizes multiculturalism when it is equated mainly with ethnocultural festivals but pays little attention to the obstacles and difficulties many immigrants face in finding good jobs and gaining access to the resources that enhance the lives of those who are in the Canadian mainstream. Adasme (in Fleras and Elliott, 1999, pp. 278–83) provides an account of her immigration experiences in Canada, noting that for immigrants an occupation is a critical link to who they are in relation to society. She notes that immigrants are found in occupations that tend to be the least valued and most poorly paid in contrast to those in which most mainstream Canadians are employed. She states, however, that, "There is nothing wrong with it if one is allowed to move away from that setting (through educational programs, etc.), if one feels the need to do so. But there is something very wrong if one has to remain a janitor, sewing machine operator, etc., for life ... feeling enslaved." For many immigrants, upgrading and opportunities for training and education in Canada are the means to acquire better jobs, but access to education and training may be difficult because of high cost, lack of affordable childcare, no English-language assistance, and other reasons. Educational equity programs are one way that has been used to level the playing field and allow more access to education for people who may otherwise not be able to participate.

Education Equity and Affirmative Action

There is an ongoing debate as to whether affirmative action and equity programs are working. On the one hand, such initiatives open doors for people who have previously had less access to higher education or good jobs, and aim to better reflect the composition of society in education (Blum and Heinonen, 2001) and the workplace. On the other hand, some people believe that affirmative action threatens standards of excellence and quality in the university or workplace. Referring to the field of education, Dei (1996, p. 38) counters, "The issues of diversity, excellence, quality and equity in education are inseparable," implying that equity programs promote better and richer educational and workplace environments by including all members of society. Removing barriers, offering supportive programs (such as mentorship), and building an inclusive learning environment can help increase the enrolment of students who previously felt shut out of postsecondary education.

Efforts to increase access to education and the labour market (equity or affirmative action) have become common strategies to deal with these problems, but obstacles to recognizing foreign credentials, for example, continue to pose serious barriers. Licensed occupations, including medicine and dentistry, continue to impose restrictions and deny accreditation, which results in blocking the entry into these professions of immigrants with foreign degrees or credentials outside Canada (Fleras and Elliott, 1999, p. 276). Social work is not immune to these practices, although they may vary across provinces. As licensing and standards for practice shape who can practise as social workers in Canada, it seems that Canadian experience and education will be more prominent than foreign experience and education, even when skills and knowledge requirements are similar. This is partly so because employers hire those whose experience and education they know about and can relate to. This is unfortunate because immigrants who bring experience from their own countries enrich social work and add new perspectives and knowledge to the profession, not only about social work practice but also about their cultures and languages. Many will be cultural brokers and service providers for members of their own cultural communities, who often don't use mainstream social services because they are incongruent with what they have known or prefer. Immigrant social workers can also demonstrate alternative methods and unique skills that all in the profession can learn about. We need to critically examine how such practices contribute further to institutional barriers and lead to marginalization of some social workers (personal communication with Esther Blum, June 26, 2004).

In social work practice, we need to work to support the successful settlement and integration of immigrants in Canada and identify the obstacles that stand in the way of full access and promote exclusion of newcomers (and others) from education, occupations, and other entitlements in our society. Doing so is part of our professional responsibility and is referred to as such in our code of ethics.

Intersection of Multiple Forms of Oppression: The Example of Lola

It is necessary to acknowledge and understand the intersections of all forms of social oppression. Leah (1995) asserts, "Anti-racism discourse must incorporate gender, class and sexuality as fundamental and relational aspects of human experience that intersect both in the historical and contemporary reality of people's lives" (cited in Dei, 1996, p. 28). For example, class, race, and gender may work to oppress a Somali refugee woman who is living on social assistance income in Toronto. She may experience the effects of racism or other kinds of oppression when she tries to find a job. McIntosh (1989) also refers to how all systems of advantage (and disadvantage) are interlocking: "Since race and sex are not the only advantaging systems at work, we need to examine the daily experience of having age advantage, or ethnic advantage, or physical ability, or advantage related to nationality, religion, or sexual orientation" (p. 12). The myth of equal opportunity and democratic choice hides the fact that Canadian society and its social structures do not offer an even playing field for all.

To illustrate how racism combined with other types of oppression constitutes intersections of oppression, we draw on the story of Lola. (This example is inspired by research findings reported by Migliardi, Blum, and Heinonen, 2004.)

Case Example

Lola

Lola Mendez, a 34-year-old immigrant woman from a South American city, lives in Calgary with her husband, Alberto, 37, and their two daughters, Nita and Donna. The girls are 8 and 11 and attend school near the family's apartment in an older area of the city. The family has been in Canada for five years. Alberto works as an apprentice mechanic in a gas station, and Lola works in a garment factory sewing jacket sleeves together.

Recently, the situation at home became difficult. Beginning a year ago, Alberto started to abuse Lola. At first he yelled at her and pushed her when he was not happy with her cooking or the way she spent money. Lola at first tried to talk to her husband and say she would try to do better and that it was best not to fight in front of the children. She did not say anything to anyone for fear that the whole community would look down on her and that someone might even report her and have her deported. Lola is fearful of what will happen to her and the children. Already she could see that Nita, the youngest, was slapping her sister and demanding more of her mother's attention. The girls hid in Donna's closet when they heard the arguing start, because they were frightened of what would happen.

After the girls had gone to sleep one night, Lola began to prepare the children's school lunches for the morning. Alberto came in after drinking and began to yell at her, pulling her hair, punching her, and throwing her against the door. Lola fell to the floor. Upstairs, Donna called 911; she had learned about it at school. When the police came, Alberto was still yelling at Lola and trying to get her to stand up. He did not open the door for the police, so they entered by force. The girls were awake and crying at the top of the stairs.

Alberto was taken to the police station to be charged with assault, and an ambulance was called for Lola. An after-hours social worker was called to help place the children temporarily. Both feared that their mother would not recover and had to be consoled for some time.

When Lola was discharged home from the hospital, a friend came to help her, and the children were returned to her a few days later. Lola decided that she would never accept this kind of treatment from Alberto or anyone again. She had been visited by a hospital social worker, who asked if she could introduce her to another immigrant woman who was a volunteer counsellor for immigrants. The volunteer, Sari, had herself experienced physical abuse from her father-in-law and now knew a lot about the rights of women and laws against violence in Canada. The two women spent a number of hours talking as Lola began to recover from her injuries. Sari could see Lola's many strengths and asked if she wanted to work against violence against immigrant women herself someday. Lola agreed, saying, "Yes, because it is one thing I can contribute to my community so other immigrant women don't have to live like me."

After Lola moved to another location, separated from Alberto, and started a better job in a unionized factory, she decided to call Sari. Sari told her that a special training course would be beginning in a month's time where women from different ethnocultural communities were invited to learn how to help other women who were facing the effects of violence in their homes. Lola agreed to participate for one evening per week when she learned that childcare and transportation costs would be taken care of. Donna and Nita would enjoy the many activities in the playroom and the company of other children.

The training course lasted three months. In the course, Lola learned about laws against violence, women's rights, different kinds of abuse, how violence arises and is maintained, myths about woman abuse, effects of violence on children, how some cultural beliefs and practices sometimes work to support violence, how to be supportive of women facing abuse in their lives, and when to call for help. In the training course were many other immigrant women from a range of cultural backgrounds. Lola was surprised that despite so many differences among them, there was so much they shared, too, as immigrants in Canada and as women. The guest speakers and immigrant women leaders who guided the training used visual aids and spoke clearly and explained things when some did not understand. The best part of the course for Lola was sharing experiences and views with the other women participants. Many of the women in the group said things like: "I would never have been afraid of my in-laws if I had known that I could not be deported for getting a job of my own"; "I feel so free now. I have rights and I can use this information, not just for myself, but to help others too. I feel strong"; and "Immigrant women really can understand what it is like. I would like to have another immigrant woman help me if I was being abused, I would be too ashamed to tell most people about it."

The training group helped Lola, a poor, immigrant, visible-minority woman, to use the help she got in the hospital and the knowledge she gained from the training to form a self-help group for women in her ethnocultural community to counter violence in their lives. One of the women's husbands heard of the group and thought something along the same lines would be good for men, too, so they could learn about nonviolent ways to deal with anger, frustration, and relationships with women and children. The men's group was advertised not as a support group for men who used violence, but as a group to support peaceful and healthy ways of being a father. (It was decided that this kind of group would be more attractive to men than a group with some other stated purpose.) Appropriately, the men's group began on Father's Day.

Just as in Lola's situation, the life experiences of some people bring them face-to-face with racism, poverty, and other challenges, often in very difficult ways. Lola's poor job, her lack of access to education, limited knowledge of human rights, and fear in her family situation were related to her being poor, an immigrant, and a woman. These featured as sources of oppression that intersected in her life, affecting her experiences in the home, the workplace, and the community. Her self-esteem, confidence, life chances, economic situation, and social position were adversely affected.

Group and Community Helping in Immigrant Communities: The Example of Lola

Community organizing and mutual help can often be useful where mainstream social services are not available or do not fit with immigrants' needs or ways of helping. In our case situation, the hospital social worker was aware of this and referred an immigrant helper to speak to Lola. If the hospital social worker had not done so, Lola may not have found the power in herself to heal and grow to the point that she could be a resource to others. A community of women, all with the common experience of immigration to Canada, offered her this opportunity.

Lola and her peers felt that it was important for immigrant men to examine violence and its meaning in their lives, since working with women alone was not enough. Men could not be excluded. They found a way to do this by finding a male ally who discussed with them the immigrant men's interests and what they wanted to learn from the group. This was an important means of offering a service that built on men's interests and promoted the prevention of violence in their homes and communities. Methods that fit with Western social work in professional practice may not fit for immigrant clients. It is important to explore what ways of helping are appropriate and most useful in a particular ethnocultural community and, if possible, how these might be adapted in the Canadian urban context. Immigrant social workers could be very helpful in developing such alternative models and methods and enriching existing ones in many social work agencies and organizations that are poorly utilized by immigrant clients.

Anti-Oppressive Social Work

Anti-oppressive social work involves intervention that is not confined to individuals but that spans the social structural level of society (Mullaly, 2002). It involves critical reflection about oppression and its harmful effects on clients and action based on learning from such reflection. As we have seen, social workers mainly provide services to individuals who face issues such as poverty, illness, addictions, and mental health conditions. Anti-oppressive practice avoids adding to existing oppression experienced by clients, viewing the cause of problems as lying outside individual control. Anti-oppressive social workers critically ask questions in their work with clients: "Why does this family need to live in substandard housing? Who gains from this situation?"; "How is it that this 62-year-old, skilled worker was laid off a few years before his retirement and replaced by a younger, inexperienced employee? Who gains and why?"; "What brought this immigrant woman to the brink of suicide after she was beaten by her husband? How has Canadian society failed?"; "Why does this gay man need to fear for his safety when walking alone at night? In what ways is society to blame?"; and "What caused this young woman to turn to crack cocaine and steal from her family? How are social structures to blame?" They strive to understand the "oppressive conditions, processes and practices [that] exist at the personal, cultural and structural levels" (Mullaly, 2002, p. 171) and how these influence or shape an individual's situation. In doing so, anti-oppressive social workers can help clients to search for the roots of their difficulties outside themselves. Dominelli (1997) asserts that new, less oppressive forms of practice can be realized through such understanding. In relation to the clients of social work, Mullaly (2002) explains,

> As awareness of injustice and oppression grows, oppressed people are less likely to blame themselves for their oppression and are more able to identify the social causes of their negative emotions and experiences. These insights, in turn, help them to develop their analyses of their oppression as well as to build confidence and the capacity for seeking social changes. (p. 173)

Anti-oppressive practice and culturally sensitive social work are appropriate for working with all clients, no matter what their background. They also offer an alternative perspective that draws on strengths, assets, and capacities first, rather than a primary focus on problems and limitations. This alternative way of practising is attractive to most social work students because it fits well with the values and principles in social work codes of ethics. (See Chapter 10 on the strengths approach.)

The Practice Relationship

You may see your cultural background, offering some distinct ways of viewing the world, as different from that of your clients or coworkers. On the other hand, you may find yourself in a workplace in which there is a shared cultural heritage between most workers and clients—for example, an organization in which Aboriginal social workers are employed to help Aboriginal teenagers who are experiencing problems in school. Whatever the cultural environment in your workplace, social workers need to use empathy and effective communication to enhance understanding between themselves and their clients.

There may be other differences that, in addition to culture, are significant to the practice relationship. How, for example, does the age or gender of the social worker affect the development of a relationship with the client? Such issues may raise challenges for you in practice. Will you be able to understand the ways in which clients view their situation, identify what strengths and assets they have, and determine what help they will accept and how they'd like to go about dealing with their situation? Is it possible for a middle-aged Scottish female social worker to develop a working relationship with a teenaged Eritrean male client? Can a young social worker of Polish ancestry understand why a Chinese family views their son's failing grades in school as a major problem for his grandparents? Can a new social worker of European descent appreciate the significance of an Aboriginal community's healing practices? In considering these questions, we need to see that social workers, like most people, are generally resilient and can learn to respond effectively in unfamiliar situations. We can also be reflexive in our practice so that we critically and self-consciously evaluate the process of our work and its impact on clients.

Social workers may find themselves in situations where clients or other people make offensive comments about their (or someone else's) cultural background or traditions. For example, ethnic jokes can be insensitive and harmful. Social workers, through their codes of ethics, support the elimination of discrimination and racism, so doing nothing conflicts with our professional ethics. Finding a way to challenge such comments skilfully and appropriately is not easy, but it is necessary. It might be that the offending person lacks awareness about the impact of such comments or believes that her or his views are justified. Letting such comments go without speaking up could reinforce the view that it is okay to put people down. Of course, a social worker needs to be cautious in such a situation to prevent it from escalating and becoming threatening. Focusing on what is said and its effect rather than on the individual who makes the offending comment is useful. Remaining calm and clear, but at the same time empathic and respectful of the other person, can help.

If you know that some or all of your clients will be of another culture—say Latin American or Aboriginal—it is wise to learn something about their beliefs and traditions. Often these contain unique strengths and may offer keys for dealing with obstacles and problems in life. Such learning by a social worker may also provide some ideas (which cannot be generalized to all members of a cultural group) about spiritual practices, family relations, roles of men and women, accepted ways of raising children, importance of extended family and community networks, and other areas. Morrissette, McKenzie, and Morrissette (1993), referring to people who are Aboriginal, point out that people may range between strong and weak cultural identification, which influences their degree of adherence to traditional cultural values and orientation. Some people may even see themselves as belonging to several cultures, such as French and Aboriginal. As a guiding principle, people are viewed as unique individuals first before they are grouped together as Somalis, Chinese, Métis, Inuit, or members of another ethnocultural group.

Gaining Ethnic Competence

Green (1995) refers to the concept of ethnic competence as helpful in social work practice across cultures. Ethnic competence involves a number of factors.

As a step toward attaining ethnic competence, it is necessary to be aware of your own cultural limitations in your work with clients, particularly as you form relationships with them and intervene in their private troubles. Although our profession trains us to encourage clients to express their feelings freely, some cultural groups see such expression to strangers, especially those in authority, as inappropriate. This may deter some from seeking any help from social service agencies.

Morrissey (1997) points out that applying an ethnic category that contains certain static cultural ideas or characteristics attributed to a particular group leads to stereotyping and generalizing, which in turn create misunderstanding and inappropriate practice. Referring primarily to health care practice, he explains that generalizing can lead to imagining relationships between a person's behaviour and culture based on a limited understanding of that culture. It might be assumed that the client's situation is due to some cultural belief when it is actually caused by a social situation that would create distress for most people. If we are to be competent in cross-cultural social work, we need to accept differences among people and relate to our clients openly and genuinely without being patronizing or condescending (Green, 1995).

Although it is not always necessary or even appropriate to ask clients what cultural group they belong to, it is helpful for social workers to consider that differing perspectives—for example, attitudes toward parenting or preventive health care—might be attributed to cultural factors. It is sometimes necessary for social workers to review with clients, for instance, parental responsibilities and obligations, including acceptable ways to discipline children. This information, rather than closing discussion, could be offered in such a way that clients feel able to ask questions, discuss options open to them in various situations, and inquire about any supportive programs or available help. The difficulties newcomers may face because of language barriers and fear of authority figures (e.g., school principals, guidance counsellors, and social workers) may be considerable, so the strengths and resources of parents trying to raise their children in a new environment should also be highlighted. In some cases, there may be distinct differences, some of which may conflict with Canadian laws. These will need to be discussed to prevent misunderstanding at a later time. Clients may be in a position to inform social workers about the best ways to help them with their specific issues or problems. Being empathic and open is necessary, but it is not sufficient.

The strength of a person's cultural beliefs and practices will give you some idea about which resources could be useful. Invoking a client's internal strengths, such as spirituality or previous persistence in the face of hardship, may help. External resources, such as cultural associations or culture-specific health and social services, may also be useful. Clients are the best people to decide whether these are appropriate, and they may have strong feelings about wanting or not wanting to use them.

Clients can help us understand what is most appropriate for them given their cultural traditions and practices. The social worker could learn whether a trusted midwife, godmother, community leader, or other resource person might be preferred for help rather than a formal agency. Helping resources that are most desirable to clients need to be explored so that misunderstanding and frustration can be prevented. Thus, the helping process can become a mutual learning context. Social workers become participants in the cultural worlds of their clients as they interact and build relationships with them (Green, 1995).

The resources to which a person has access (internal and external) vary across cultural groups and according to circumstances. For example, a man who has fled a war-torn area with his young son to settle in Canada as a refugee will almost certainly lack many of the resources others take for granted. Supportive help from family members, friends, and trusted spiritual guides are not available. The man may be dealing with the loss of his spouse, his extended family, and his home. He and his son have many needs as they adapt to life in a new country, and social service agencies and workers may need to become involved.

Expectations of how social services are delivered vary across cultures. For example, in seeking counselling for a depressed young mother, members of some cultures may expect that family members and extended kin will accompany her into the counsellor's office to support her. Most counselling agencies would find this unusual.

The modes of social work practice for specific client situations may call for family, individual, group, or community intervention. Pecnik and Miskulin (1996), in describing their use of group work as a means of addressing the many difficulties of displaced women in Croatia, stress the appropriateness of the group format for women in sharing losses, being understood and supported, exchanging strategies for coping, and building hope for the future. For some ethnocultural groups, connecting with a social network is necessary for survival in a new environment.

Encouraging and enabling access to informal networks can be a key role for social workers helping newly arrived immigrants, as shown in the case situation of Lola. Social work with families and communities may be most effective for new immigrants' success; however, social workers can also use their skills in policy analysis to improve the current situation for immigrants, advocating for inclusion of foreign credentials of immigrants, including social workers and better, more comprehensive social services that respond to immigrants' needs in culturally appropriate ways.

In using an emic approach, we strive to understand how a situation looks from a client's perspective. This involves meanings: those attached to words spoken, gestures, and silences in communication. We need to feel comfortable about asking questions when we do not understand what is behind the client's words or gestures. It may be necessary to work with an interpreter when the client and social worker have no common language. This raises issues such as building the helping relationship through an intermediary, handling confidential material, and ensuring accuracy. In many cases, social workers will need to clearly explain their roles and the kinds of help they can offer, since newcomers may not understand what social workers are or what they do. Clients may fear, for example, that social workers have the capacity to deport immigrants. Or perhaps they may view social workers as having the power to provide all of the material help they require.

CHAPTER SUMMARY

In this chapter, social workers are encouraged to explore their own cultural background and what it means to them. By doing so, one can experience culture as a lens for looking at the world. This is important in order to practise effectively across cultures.

The chapter presents a view of antiracist, anti-oppressive, culturally sensitive, and culturally appropriate practice that emphasizes an emic approach and cultural competence. The significance of culture in social work practice is highlighted in a multicultural society like Canada's. Social work practice has incorporated ways to understand the significance of culture for clients and ourselves by developing cross-cultural practice principles, defining culturally sensitive and culturally appropriate practice and cultural competence. These enrich social work practice when social workers and clients do not share similar cultural backgrounds.

Racism and other related forms of oppression work to keep some groups of people disadvantaged and others privileged. The social work codes of ethics guide the profession and encourage social workers to work at eliminating discrimination and all forms of oppression in society. It is, however, difficult to address institutional racism that pervades organizations and institutions like an invisible mist. For example, the institutional racism and rigid requirements for Canadian experience work to marginalize immigrants with foreign professional credentials. Much can be learned from immigrant colleagues about alternative methods and viewpoints on helping and being helped. Applying such knowledge can enrich and broaden social work perspectives and lead to better, culturally appropriate services. Through mutual exchange and collective effort we can promote respect for and appreciation of human diversity in society.

chapter 8

Problem Solving in Social Work Practice

Chapter Goal

To describe and analyze the problem-solving process in social work and to identify its contributions and limitations.

This Chapter

- outlines and describes the elements of the problem-solving process
- compares the process of assessment in social work with that of diagnosis in medicine
- establishes the importance of contracts with clients
- describes a simple evaluation framework that can be used in almost any direct social work practice with individuals
- addresses many of the important implications of the problem-solving process

INTRODUCTION

The traditional model of social work practice is problem solving. This has been true since at least 1917, when Mary Richmond outlined a framework for casework practice in her book *Social Diagnosis.* The heart of her book described a problem-solving process. Although social work's conception of problem solving has changed, the process remains central to practice.

THE PROBLEM-SOLVING PROCESS

The business of social workers is to help people or communities solve serious, often complex problems. Social workers would not be asked to help if solving problems were easy. Part of solving difficult and complex problems is understanding the process itself.

The elements of problem solving are quite simple (see Exhibit 8.1):

1. Identify the problem.
2. Attempt to analyze or understand the problem.
3. Use the analysis to set goals.
4. Evaluate the appropriateness of the analysis.
5. Take action to solve the problem.
6. Evaluate, through **feedback loops,** whether the action accomplished the intended goals.

If successful, or if the decision is made that the problem cannot be solved, then the process ends. If not, the process begins again. This process is generally the same whether it is used in solving everyday problems of life or in professional practice.

Let's illustrate with an everyday example. Suppose early one cold winter morning a harried student discovers that his car will not start. He has an exam at 9:00 a.m. He has identified the problem and begins to analyze it. Quickly he decides that he must get to his exam at all costs. Within seconds he realizes that he has five choices: he could attempt to fix the car himself, call a tow truck, call a friend, take the bus, or take a taxi to the university. He is not very good at fixing the car, so he rules out that option. Calling a tow truck may take a long time on a cold morning. The frustrated student thinks his friend has already left for work. He has only $2 in his pocket—not enough money for a taxi. So, he decides that his best bet is to take the bus. However, he does not know the bus schedule.

Exhibit 8.1 ▼ The Problem-Solving Process

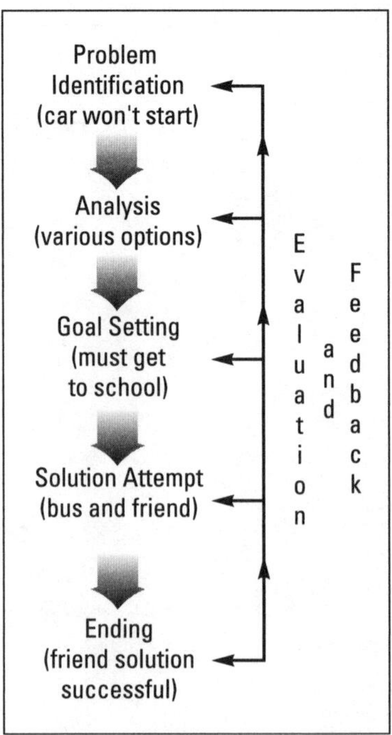

By now the student has established a clear goal. He must write the exam! The analysis has narrowed down his options for action. To his chagrin, he finds that the bus will get him there too late. Quickly he evaluates his remaining options and calls his friend. Fortunately, she is still at home and can get him to the exam on time. The friend brings the process to a successful end.

This example could have taken a different twist. Suppose the student chose to fix the car himself. He could have used the same analytical method to understand the process for fixing the car. Most likely he would have attempted to clearly understand the problem with the car, diagnosed it, and then taken the appropriate action to fix it. The problem-solving process can apply to almost any situation that requires a solution.

THE PROBLEM-SOLVING PROCESS IN SOCIAL WORK

Notice that the process outlined above and in Exhibit 8.1 proceeds in a generally linear fashion with feedback loops. Each evaluation establishes a **feedback mechanism.** If in any of the evaluations an error, mistake, or omission is discovered in any of the steps, then the process will likely revert to a previous step for correction or revision. This was what happened when the student found that the bus was not an option. Evaluating the information related to the bus schedule led him to revisit the action step and devise a new plan—basically, to revert to plan B. Like the steps in the example, in social work each stage of the process is often revisited and reviewed, leading to changes in problem definition, assessment, goal setting, and intervention.

In *Social Diagnosis,* Richmond (1917) outlined a process of social casework that has had enormous influence on today's social work practice. This process is (1) study, (2) diagnosis, and (3) treatment. Richmond established the idea that helping (treatment) is at its centre. The process that she outlined was almost the same as that used in medicine and is the framework of the medical model. Diagnosis implies that a person's problem can be diagnosed like a disease. Emphasis is often on pathology. Further, the diagnosis determines the prescribed treatment. This simply stated process set the theoretical framework for all of casework for the next half-century. Richmond's work also formalized two cornerstones of current social work views of problem solving: first, that intervention depends on assessment, and second, that the key to social work intervention is the relationship between the client and the worker.

In 1957 Helen Perlman published a landmark book, *Social Casework: A Problem Solving Process,* that carefully articulated problem solving in modern social work. Since then, many people have developed variations of the process and used a variety of terms to describe the central ideas (see, for example, Compton and Galaway, 1999; Kirst-Ashman and Hull, 1993; Johnson, 1995). Nevertheless, Richmond's and Perlman's writings laid the foundation for today's problem-solving process.

Social work problem solving involves the following elements (see Exhibit 8.2):

- Define the problem(s).
- Conduct an assessment.
- Set goals and objectives.

- Establish a contract.
- Intervene.
- Evaluate the process.
- End the process.

Exhibit 8.2 ▼ The Social Work Problem-Solving Process

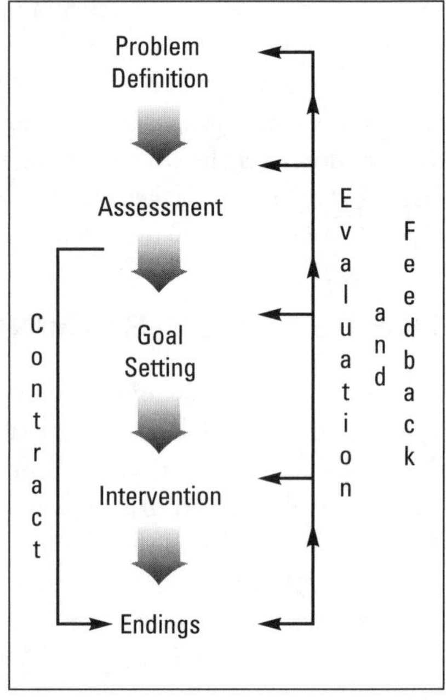

Exhibit 8.2 shows the flow from problem definition to endings, with evaluation occurring during and after each step. When feedback from the evaluation warrants, one or more of the earlier steps may be revisited. Review is frequent and important. Later in this chapter we suggest a simple scheme to evaluate everyday practice. Exhibit 8.2 shows that contracting, like evaluation, is a part of each stage of the problem-solving process. It is very fluid and involves frequent changes.

Chapter 6 discussed in some detail the social work relationship. The problem-solving process depends upon the relationship between worker and client. As emphasized in Chapter 6, the social work relationship is at the heart of all social work practice. Helping almost always is engaged through the relationship.

Certainly the helping relationship is important in all stages of problem solving. It is necessary in order to help clients define and articulate their problems. Effective goal setting and intervention also depend upon the worker–client relationship. There is not a single stage of problem solving that does not depend upon the social work relationship.

The exhibit suggests that the process is smooth and essentially linear with feedback mechanisms built in. In practice this is usually not the case. In real life, problem solving proceeds in fits and starts, is very fluid, and hits many bumps.

Problem Definition

A problem may be that of an individual, group, organization, or community. Often the problem is first identified by the person or persons who are experiencing it. The starting point may be their story. Other times, the problem is reported by someone else—for example, a woman who suspects that her neighbour abuses his child. Sometimes a problem is first reported by an authority such as the police.

The goal of problem definition is to begin to articulate the problem in a way that both the social worker and the client can understand. They need to agree on this definition before the worker can take action to help solve the problem.

This first step of the problem-solving process has several crucial elements. The place to begin is "where the client is." This means beginning with the client's story, and his or her understanding of the problem. It is essential to encourage clients to tell their stories in their own words. Only after the story begins to emerge should the social worker formulate his or her opinion of the nature of the problem.

Case Example

Kim and Ann

Recall that Kim is a family social worker in the Child Protection Agency (CPA). The nightshift worker placed Ann's three children in temporary custody. The worker had received a call from a neighbour stating that Ann's three children were at home alone, unattended by an adult. He discovered that Ann was at a party and indeed had not arranged for adult care of her children. The family is known to the agency, but there has been no evidence of direct physical abuse—only neglect.

Kim's first concern, as Ann's worker, was for the safety of the three children, but helping Ann was also a high priority. Agency workers in the past have felt that, with help, Ann could manage the role of lone parent.

Upon meeting Ann for the first time, Kim explained the reasons for apprehending her children, emphasizing that the children needed adult supervision. Ann was angry with Kim but particularly upset at the Child Protection Agency worker and the neighbour who reported the neglect. Kim let Ann express her anger, and, when Ann began to cool down a little, in a calm and encouraging voice she asked Ann to tell her story. Kim wanted to shift the attention to Ann's needs and problems, to let Ann know that her needs were important, and to let her know that Kim was there to help. As Ann told her story, Kim was better able to understand the stress that Ann felt.

Ann saw her problems as being related to her lack of income and blamed the intrusive nature of the Child Protection Agency for compounding them. Kim gently steered Ann toward telling about other parts of her life, including her relationships with her children and their daily activities. As Ann talked, Kim realized that Ann thought very poorly of herself. She was recently fired from a job in a store when her boss learned that she could not read the labels on products. Ann's lack of work and her family responsibilities were getting her down. When there was enough money, Ann could take care of her children. When there was no money, Ann seemed to drown her sorrows by drinking heavily. Kim, through Ann's story, began to get a different picture of the problem.

Often, the social worker defines the problem differently than the client. In the case example, Kim saw more dimensions to the problem than Ann did. Kim agreed that Ann's lack of income was important, but her limited parenting skills, lack of education, and problem drinking were also factors. To successfully conclude the identification of the problem, the client and the social worker need to agree on the main problems and which ones they will attempt to solve. This is part of contracting, which will be discussed later in this chapter.

Kim successfully merged the function of social control (apprehension of Ann's children) and helping. Often such an approach works when it is perceived by clients to be in their best interest. However, if Ann had refused to discuss her situation with Kim, clarifying the problem would have been much more difficult. Kim would have had to work hard to convince Ann that while her primary intent was the children's safety, she could also help Ann address her own problems that precipitated the apprehension. Helping Ann address her own problems is probably not possible unless Ann decides that she needs and wants such help from Kim.

The establishment of a helping relationship between Kim and Ann is necessary for them to engage in problem solving. Kim took several steps to do this. Of these, probably her encouragement of Ann to tell her own story was most important.

The success of all later steps depends heavily on the establishment of a professional relationship, as discussed in Chapter 6.

This example illustrates another important principle. Kim at first concentrated on Ann's telling of her own story. She listened and did not make quick judgments. Only after Ann and Kim began to be more comfortable together did Kim begin to draw her own conclusions. This principle of social work is often called "starting where the client is."

Assessment

The purpose of assessment is to set goals and devise a means (intervention) to reach these goals. Clarifying and articulating the problem generally leads to better understanding its nature. In a formal sense, assessment is a consequence of problem definition. However, in practice, assessment usually starts as soon as the social worker begins to understand the problem and take in information about the client. Problem definition and assessment are best viewed as sequential, with many feedback loops and constant revisions beginning from the initial client–social worker contact.

Assessment can be seen as having two key elements (Specht and Specht, 1986). The first element has two parts. First, the social worker and client must have a clear understanding of the nature of the problem, and second, they must translate it into a need. For example, suppose the parents of a 10-year-old boy, Tranh, agree with the social worker that the main problem is Tranh's aggressive behaviour. They are also worried about his poor performance in school. To solve the problem, the worker and clients must determine what Tranh needs. This translation of a problem into a need is necessary to begin to take steps toward a solution. Suppose the worker and clients then determine that Tranh, among other things, needs clear rules. They think this not only will help him recognize and set **boundaries** but also will provide him with a feeling of security (another need) that he lacks. To meet these needs, the social worker and parents agree on a plan to set clear rules at home.

The second element of assessment is determining whether the agency can meet the client's needs. For example, do professionals in the agency have the skills to meet the client's needs? Does the agency have the appropriate resources? If the answer to these questions is yes, then the social worker and clients can move on to planning. If not, other action is required, most often a referral to an appropriate resource. When this occurs, it is recommended that the worker follow up to ensure that the referral has resulted in the expected services for the client.

Information for an assessment may come from many sources, including relatives, reports from authorities such as the police, referring agencies, and the like. However, probably the chief source of assessment data is the client's own story. Cowger (1997, pp. 63–64) argues that clients are, most of the time, the best source of information. He holds that they are not only the most reliable source of information but also that their story tells the social worker how they perceive their problems.

Assessment addresses such questions as the following: Why did the problem occur? What are the likely short-term and long-term effects? Does the problem affect other areas? If so, how? What is the context of the problem? What are the perspectives of the problem according to the client, the social worker, and possibly others with an interest in the situation? What goals are realistic? What strategies of intervention might enable the client to reach these goals and solve the problem?

Some might see assessment as simply another word for diagnosis. In medicine, diagnosis means understanding the symptoms of pathology (usually an illness) so that the type of pathology can be identified and hence treated or prevented. The social work conception of assessment is broader: it means analyzing a problem in the context of relevant systems, including the social work agency. This step leads to selecting goals and planning interventions. Emphasizing the strengths of clients and the social context of problems as central to social work assessment is a major departure from the more restrictive notion of diagnosis (see Kirst-Ashman and Hull, 1993, p. 149).

Hepworth, Rooney, and Larsen (1997) call this *multidimensional assessment,* meaning that a wide range of factors, including both strengths and problems, are part of the assessment process. Human problems are always connected, and sometimes one problem affects another. Often a problem has psychological consequences; it is almost certainly connected to the environment and probably affects other people. The problem may also affect other needs of the client.

It goes without saying that if, for example, a social worker sees a person who is very depressed, it is important to understand the nature of the depression. However, it is at least equally important to understand the person as a whole. What, for example, are the key relationships in the person's life? What supports does the individual have? What are his or her needs, wants, and resources? Social work problem solving emphasizes assessment that analyzes the problem in the context of relevant systems, particularly those that add strength to the functioning of the systems. The client's history in her or his social context should also be considered, and is often included as part of the client's story.

Good assessment requires that the worker draw on relevant theoretical constructs (see Chapter 9), not only to help analyze the problem but also to help pose questions that aid understanding. This is why social workers need a good background in social science theories.

Case Example

Kim and Ann

Kim begins contact with Ann by helping Ann tell her story. As the relationship progresses, Kim uses her theoretical knowledge, mostly borrowed from the social sciences. For instance, Kim's knowledge of ecosystems theory (see Chapter 9) helps her to help Ann explore her relationships with key friends, family members, and institutions such as her eldest son's school. By exploring these various systems, Kim discovers that two of Ann's friends could give her considerable support and be valuable resources.

Kim and Ann, both mothers, also discuss Ann's feelings about what is expected of women today and how Ann can't cope with the demands. Kim understands these difficulties and is able to point out that Ann is not alone.

Theory from ego psychology (see Chapter 9) helps Kim understand Ann's low self-esteem. Role theory helps Kim understand that Ann is experiencing a major strain between the expectations for her role as a parent and her role as a worker. This contributes to her low self-esteem, and when she experiences these conflicts, she usually tries to escape the strain by drinking.

During their discussion, Ann tells Kim that her oldest son, Jim, aged 9, has learning disabilities, is hyperactive, and is difficult to discipline at home and at school. Kim's knowledge of these problems helps her understand not only the problems the boy faces but also the stress Ann experiences. Kim is beginning to understand Ann as a whole person in her environment rather than merely as someone facing a problem with the placement of her children.

Kim now has a clearer understanding and analysis of Ann's problems. She realizes the strain in performing the roles of parent and worker (provider) and the challenges of juggling both.

Kim also knows from personal experience that being a mother to young children tends to be valued less than having a job. Increasingly, women face difficulty in obtaining resources to help them combine childcare and paid work.

If Ann is to get her children back and needs to work in order to support them, then it would be very important for Ann to deal with the problems of role strain, ability to cope with the survival needs of her family, and limited personal and social resources. Kim uses her assessment skills to re-evaluate Ann's problems and begin a process to translate them into needs. For example, Ann needs a job in order to get her children back. She also needs affordable childcare and considerable support in parenting. Kim must determine whether and how the agency can help Ann meet these needs or can help Ann locate other resources.

Assessment versus Diagnosis

Sometimes it is easier to understand some of the principles of social work assessment by comparing them with the diagnostic process in medicine, as shown in Exhibit 8.3. As you read the comparisons, note that the process is parallel but the emphasis is very different. Also note that these descriptions represent a standard or ideal. As explained later in this chapter, it is sometimes easy to slip into assessments guided by principles of disease and client deficits instead of by strengths and related systems.

Exhibit 8.3 ▼ Medical Diagnosis versus Social Work Assessment

	MEDICAL DIAGNOSIS	SOCIAL WORK ASSESSMENT IN PROBLEM SOLVING
Purpose	• To provide a basis on which a disease can be prevented or cured	• To help people solve problems by providing a basis for selecting appropriate goals and intervention
Emphasis	• Pathology and disease	• Personal and social functioning, particularly personal strengths and connection with the environment
Problem	• Seen as a disease	• Seen as having psychological and environmental dimensions; may be seen as a weakness or deficit
Process	• Based on examination by an expert, who makes the diagnosis with little or no discussion with the patient	• Usually based on a contract between client and social worker; worker viewed as an expert skilled in helping
Final result	• Diagnostic category and label	• No attempt to condense assessment to a single category • End product is an analytical statement that usually describes person in situation
Goals	• To prevent or cure illness • Are clear and easy to measure • If cure or prevention is not possible, then goal is to reduce the effect of symptoms	• Fluid, with emphasis on improving quality of life • Depends on the assessment and varies considerably depending on needs of individual clients, agency setting, and orientation of helper

	MEDICAL DIAGNOSIS	SOCIAL WORK ASSESSMENT IN PROBLEM SOLVING
Bases of knowledge	• Based on science and scientific inquiry; knowledge is not acceptable if it cannot be empirically verified • Reliability of diagnosis is very important	• Partly based on the social sciences but also on life experiences and culture • Theoretical knowledge often used even though it has not been empirically verified • Research is often experience based, without empirical verification
Types of science	• Life sciences, with emphasis on biology, biochemistry, biomedicine, psychiatry, and psychology	• Emphasis on social and behavioural sciences, including psychology, sociology, economics, and anthropology
Treatment	• Prescriptive with respect to specific treatments, such as type of medication • Diagnosis determines treatment	• Prescriptive only in a general sense; strategy of intervention depends on assessment and goals that derive from assessment • Goals and treatment methods frequently negotiated with clients
Place of	• Generally assumes illness occurs across cultures, so culture is a secondary factor	• Culture shapes personal problems and solutions in very important ways
Causation	• Presumes that illness is caused by biological or psychosocial factors, possibly triggered by environmental stress	• Biological and psychosocial factors play an important part in personal functioning, but so do values, culture, and economic conditions, as well as many other possible factors

Goal Setting

The next step in the problem-solving process is goal setting, though some see this step as part of or an extension of assessment. Goal setting determines the focus of intervention. Goals identify the problems that the client and social worker have chosen to solve. They must be measurable, communicable, and observable. In our case example, suppose Ann tells Kim that she wants a better life. Probably Kim's first question would be, "What do you mean by a better life?" Unless Kim understands what Ann means, they cannot properly communicate. If Ann tells Kim that she would like a new job and to get her children back, and that if she can accomplish these two goals then she believes that her life would be better, Kim will better understand Ann because Ann has stated the goals in observable and hence measurable terms.

The client and social worker *must* specify goals in clear terms. The more clearly and precisely goals are stated, the more likely they can be achieved. In social work, it is not easy to measure all kinds of change—for example, shifts in thinking, attitude, or beliefs. But such changes may be significant in the course of work with clients. Although observable and measurable goals are important, social workers must be aware that because some processes are not easily measurable, this does not mean that no progress has occurred. Some changes are just more difficult to measure in standard ways.

The values of the client and social worker help determine goals. As explained in Chapter 3, a value is an assertion of truth, or belief. A goal is really no more than a valued end. A goal in social work, in simple terms, is the desired end result of the intervention process. A key function of social work values is to guide the worker in establishing goals with the client.

Often, goals must be prioritized. For example, Ann's primary stated goal is to get her children back.

Case Example

Kim and Ann

Kim and her agency are firm. While their goal is also family reconciliation, they will not return Ann's children to her until other problems are solved. Most important to them is Ann's ability to handle her role as parent along with other key life roles.

Kim decides to engage Ann in a process that could lead to the return of her children. They must prioritize their goals. Number one is family reconciliation. When Ann resorts to social assistance benefits, her self-esteem suffers. The two of them decide that she must find a suitable job and appropriate childcare arrangements before her children can be returned to her.

Kim believes there is another, prior step. She convinces Ann that before she gets a job, they must find ways for Ann to cope practically and emotionally with the competing expectations of employment and parenting. They both also realize that Jim's learning disabilities and hyperactivity may pose a long-term threat to his well-being. Focusing on this problem is a high priority. To summarize, they agree that for Ann to get her children back she must first find a good job and show that she can handle her different roles. Kim agrees to help Ann arrange childcare, which is necessary if Ann is to accomplish her goals. They must also find help for Jim. The goals, as in most life situations, are complex, multiple, and dependent on one another.

Finally, goals must be achievable. The ability to judge the difference between goals that are achievable and those that are hopeless or involve extreme risk is key to professional practice. Proper assessment will help ensure that the goals selected are realistic.

The Contract in the Problem-Solving Process

In social work there are a variety of different kinds of contracts. The nature of contracts can be quite complex. There are at least three kinds that are important and that we highlight in this book. A social work "business contract" sets out the administrative details of intervention including length of meetings, payment, responsibilities, and roles of client and worker, among others. This sort of contract is particularly important in private practice or when there are important administrative arrangements that need to be made between worker and client.

We call another kind of contract a "conditional contract." The practice contract, as will be shown, connects directly to the problem-solving process (see also Tutty, 2002). Sometimes social workers need to have the client agree to a certain condition. Usually, such contracts are established when risk is involved. A common example is a "no harm to self" agreement. This sort of contract is very common in crisis work. The worker may even make the agreement conditional. For example, if a client threatens suicide and hence violates the contract, the worker may notify the police. Another example of a conditional contract involves work with families in which violence has taken place. The worker may make "no violence" a condition of treatment.

Probably the type of contract that gets the most attention in the literature is what we have called a practice contract. Exhibit 8.2 shows contracting as an important part of all stages of problem solving. Contracting is the process of client and social worker negotiating and agreeing on the outcome of four of the steps in the problem-solving process. This means that to provide effective help, the social worker and client must agree on the problems to be solved, the understanding of these problems (the broad assessment), the goals and objectives that the worker is to help the client meet, and the means (type of intervention) to be used in meeting these goals.

Case Example

Kim and Ann

A central part of the relationship between Kim and Ann were the agreements—sometimes partnerships—that they reached. For example, both agreed that Ann had several problems that needed resolution. These were limited formal education, loss of job and income, and role strain. Ann agreed with Kim's assessment that she had the capacity to hold a good job, was capable of pursuing formal education and that strain in a variety of her roles hindered her job performance and the possibility of pursuing education. They also concurred that ultimately (primary goal) Ann should regain custody of her children. To reach this goal, Ann first had to upgrade her education, find a job, and work on her parenting skills. Ann reluctantly accepted this process, though she knew it would take at least a year. Kim had reached a contract with Ann.

Establishing a contract usually does not happen easily. Often a client and social worker begin from different positions and must make an effort to narrow the gaps or differences to move toward a contract. Again, the problem-solving process suggests a clear principle that helps this happen: start where the client is. For the social worker, this means using careful listening and other communication skills. She or he also needs a clear and informed understanding of the client's perception of the problems. Kim's task is to understand Ann's problems from Ann's point of view, make her own judgments about the problems, and attempt mutual definition of them. Throughout the problem-solving process, Kim intentionally attempted to arrive at mutual understanding.

Power and Social Work Contracts

Power is a central issue in establishing business, conditional, and practice contracts. This is so both in situations in which clients are voluntary and nonvoluntary. Particularly in conditional contracts, the worker attempts to directly exercise control over clients in order to reduce risk.

Kim, throughout, had both implied and real power over Ann. Ann, for example, was aware that Kim had the power to greatly influence whether her children were to be returned to her. This is power granted to Kim through the mandate of her agency and it gave her a limited right to control Ann's behaviour. It was a form of social control. Kim has the legal (mandated) power to control regardless of whether Ann wants it or not.

Now, consider another kind of power that is also important between Kim and Ann. When a client seeks or accepts the services of the social worker (Ann wants Kim to help her have her children returned to her), there is the expectation that worker will have the expertise and skill in order to help the client. This expertise gives the worker a form of power over clients. If a client accepts and utilizes this expertise and skill, then the client grants the worker the right to influence the client. This is a particularly important type of power because if the client accepts the influence attempted by the worker, then it increases the likelihood of positive change. The result is an implied contract; the client grants the worker the right to use her expertise to help (influence) the client.

The stronger the agreement between the worker and the client at each step of the problem-solving process, the more likely the worker will be able to effectively help the client solve the problems. A later section of this chapter addresses the situation in which a client and social worker cannot agree on fundamental details.

Although not always done, the contract should be put in writing. There are some important reasons for doing so. First, a written contract helps clarify possible misunderstandings. Second, it can be a good reference point for evaluations. Third, it provides documentation if required by the courts. Finally, it is a tool of intervention. Occasionally referring to the contract and updating it from time to time can help keep the intervention process on track.

Intervention

Intervention is the action that the social worker or client takes toward solving the problems. Generally, intervention flows from the assessment and the established goals.

Intervention includes both treatment (action to alleviate a problem) and prevention of a problem's possible reoccurrence. There are two kinds of prevention: primary prevention is an attempt to keep a problem from occurring in the first place, while secondary prevention attempts to stop the development of new problems while working on an existing one. For instance, if one is attempting to help a person with a chemical addiction recover, one might also attempt to prevent the loss of his or her job.

Social work intervention, as discussed in Chapter 3, consists of many roles. The case example describing Kim's work with Ann highlights how a single case manager can perform a number of roles.

Case Example

Kim and Ann

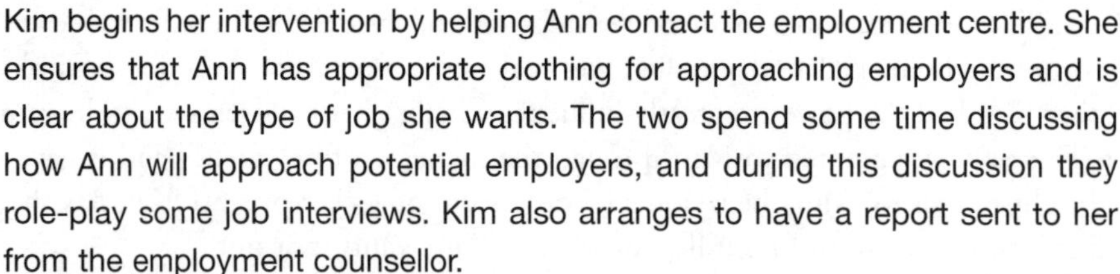

Kim begins her intervention by helping Ann contact the employment centre. She ensures that Ann has appropriate clothing for approaching employers and is clear about the type of job she wants. The two spend some time discussing how Ann will approach potential employers, and during this discussion they role-play some job interviews. Kim also arranges to have a report sent to her from the employment counsellor.

The next time Ann sees Kim, Kim has the employment report and Ann is somewhat dejected. Her employment counsellor told her that without better reading and writing skills, Ann will not be able to get a job that pays enough to support her family. So Ann and Kim are back to square one and must devise plan B.

Kim is there to give Ann support and encourage her to consider alternatives. She helps Ann lay them out, ranging from doing nothing to upgrading her education. The "do nothing" option would mean that Ann's children would remain in foster care. Going back to school would be a long-term effort and would require certain sacrifices. However, by this time, Kim is convinced that Ann has the strength to select this option and senses that Ann is leaning toward making this decision.

Returning to school would mean that Ann would have to go on welfare under a provincial program that encourages training of welfare recipients. However, applicants must first prove that their employment depends on further education. Kim helps and encourages Ann to check out the specifics of the local adult education program. Ann agrees to do this herself.

However, the welfare application poses a bigger challenge. Kim agrees to broker Ann's application with the department of welfare and, if necessary, advocate for her.

Kim also agrees to contact the school for a report on Ann's son, Jim. Ann does not think that Jim has had a good medical and psychological assessment. Kim will find out what resources are available for him and lay out the alternatives for Ann and the temporary foster parents.

Note that in the case example, as intervention proceeds, the goals change. Returning to school was at first ruled out. However, when Ann found out that good employment depended on it, she reconsidered. This meant that there would be a delay in working out how to solve the important role strains and associated problems until her schooling had begun. However, help for Ann's son could not wait.

Let's summarize the interventions from the example. The overall role of the social worker, Kim, is case management. She also acts as a broker and advocate with the welfare department. By showing support and encouragement, she enables Ann. By helping her prepare for and go to the employment centre by herself, Kim attempts to help Ann do for herself. We could call this empowerment. Kim also helps Ann with decision making by listing alternatives for her consideration. All interventions are in the context of building a strong helping relationship and problem solving.

Note how Kim uses multiple roles and interventions. If we were to present the contacts between Kim and Ann in greater detail, we would be able to see even more interventions. Social workers need to be able to use multiple interventions that vary depending on the case situation and relevant circumstances.

Evaluation

Social workers often seem to emphasize assessment and intervention and pay less attention to evaluation of the process. However, evaluation should be viewed as an important step in the problem-solving process, and it should occur at all stages of the process because it is the mechanism for feedback. For instance, as intervention progresses, the social worker and the client should regularly review and update the problems to be worked on.

Evaluation helps social workers decide whether to push on as planned or revisit earlier stages. Often evaluation results in reassessment and new strategies of intervention. It helps in making judgments about the progress and effectiveness of intervention. Another primary use of evaluation is to decide when and how to end intervention.

Direct practice evaluation helps the social worker and the client understand the progress that they have made, the effectiveness of the specific helping process, the need for further interventions, and, possibly, the decision to end the relationship. Evaluating client–social worker contact should take place during each intervention.

Often evaluation is informal. Informal evaluations are usually based on a specific type of formal evaluation but do not have a structured schedule or protocol. Many social work situations do not allow the time for formal evaluations.

It is the responsibility of the worker, with the client, to evaluate the process and effectiveness of intervention. While a formal process is probably best to evaluate practice, we argue that all problem-solving processes with clients should engage in at least an informal evaluation.

Evaluation in day-to-day social work practice is mostly qualitative rather than quantitative. **Qualitative evaluation** is generally a description of outcomes and process. A framework, usually one that is easy to construct, guides such evaluations. It may merely consist of a listing of reference points and goals with agreed-upon ways to chart progress. Quantitative evaluation often flows from qualitative efforts. Quantitative evaluations are methods that allow observations to be measured in numeric terms. For example, a couple that is experiencing nightly arguments might record the number of incidents on a chart over a 12-week course of therapy.

Evaluation of Progress in Everyday Practice

This method assumes general adherence to a problem-solving approach and that all parts of the approach are flexible. This means that as social worker–client contact continues, all steps can be revisited and altered. For instance, during intervention an assessment may change and, as a result, goals may be reformulated and new interventions engaged. The evaluation of practice involves at least two factors: outcome and goal attainment, and process.

An outcome is simply the result of any intervention. Goal attainment is the extent to which goals have been met. Sometimes, outcome and goal attainment are the same thing. At other times, intervention can have an outcome that was not an intended goal. For instance, a couple in family therapy may have as a goal the reduction of hostile arguments. The achievement of this goal is obviously also an outcome. Suppose, because of the intervention, the female partner finds she is getting along better at work. The stronger relationships at work were not a goal set by the social worker or client but, like the improved marital relationship, are an outcome of the therapy.

Process is the means of intervention. **Process evaluation** is an evaluation of the method that the client–social worker team used in attempting to achieve the goals. Usually process evaluation answers such questions as the following: How satisfactory was the relationship building? What ups and downs were evident during the course of intervention? What were the actual methods of intervention? Was the intervention applied as intended? What steps did the worker do right? What steps need improvement? Responses to these questions tend to be qualitative by nature.

The following three steps put these ideas and assumptions together into a working model that practitioners can use to monitor everyday practice:

1. *Establish a clear reference point.* This step ensures a starting point or baseline against which to assess progress. Probably a key to professional practice is experience in judging the difference between goals that are achievable and those that are hopeless or extremely risky. Good assessment helps ensure that goals are appropriate.

   The reference point is a statement of a current problem, in measurable terms, that the client and social worker intend to solve. It is the current state—that is, where the client and social worker are currently in the relationship as opposed to where they want to be.

   The idea of establishing a clear reference point borrows from the concept of baseline as used in **single-subject designs** and **goal attainment scaling,** which are generally **quantitative designs.** The reference point is often part of the **narrative** of the client's story and is frequently expressed in qualitative, or descriptive, terms. Often the reference point is in-depth information about the client's perception of her or his problem and the implied goals of intervention.

   The reference point is usually derived from the connection between goals and problems. In the problem-solving model, goals usually imply a solution to a problem. For example, Ann defines her major problem as losing her job. Ann and Kim agree that this is an important problem and develop two related goals. The first is to upgrade Ann's education and, when this is accomplished, the second is to find her suitable employment. Both of the identified problems of lack of a job and limited formal education are obvious reference points.

In this example, both the reference points and the goals are stated in reasonably specific and measurable terms. Such clarity and specificity make evaluation possible.

Sometimes, however, the problem is not identified in clear and measurable terms. Suppose Kim wants to evaluate progress related to the stress Ann feels in trying to be both mother and worker. Kim, along with Ann, needs to identify the specifics of the role strain that pose problems. For example, Ann may tell Kim that demands at work make Ann so tired that she has no time for the children. However, this may not be specific enough. Ann may need to be clear about what demands she is referring to and articulate what she means by "no time for the children." When the general problem is abstract, it needs to be restated in observable terms. Once stated in specific terms, the problem becomes a reference point against which change or progress is measured at a later time.

2. *Clearly articulate goals connected to the reference point(s).* In the problem-solving process, if goals are not measurable they are essentially worthless. In part, this means that the social worker and the client cannot figure out whether they have successfully applied an intervention.

   Techniques such as goal attainment scaling and small sample designs sometimes require quantifiable (measurable in numbers) indicators. While quantification is usually not necessary for evaluating everyday practice, the language used to describe the goals must be sufficiently clear for the social worker and the client to know when they have or have not reached their goals, and so each will have the same understanding of both baseline and goals.
3. *Evaluate progress: evaluation time-outs.* A social worker should always build into the problem-solving process a way to evaluate the progress being made. Every intervention session should include time-outs to evaluate progress. This may include beginning with, "Where are we today?" and ending with a summary of progress. At the end of each session, the social worker and client should agree on issues to work on at the next meeting or follow up on later.

A direct practitioner should use the evaluation time-outs, whether at the beginning, middle, or end of sessions, in at least three different ways:

1. To evaluate progress on goals in the relationship to the established reference points. This is central and will help both social worker and client determine whether the interventions are working.
2. To evaluate the process or method. The social worker and the client might ask questions such as, "How satisfactory is communication? Are there better ways to achieve our goals? Does the process seem to be achieving our goals?"
3. To decide whether the intervention is having effects other than helping to achieve goals.

Case Example

Kim and Ann

Kim and Ann have not developed a formal evaluation process. When Kim first began working with Ann, she did not see the need. However, it has quickly become clear that evaluation will be important.

A clear and easy-to-state reference point is Ann's lack of education. However, when Kim began to connect the goal of "upgrade education" to the reference point in measurable terms, the goal suddenly seemed less clear. What did they mean by upgrading Ann's education? Together, Kim and Ann begin a process to determine what they mean by "upgrading."

Both realize that, at a minimum, Ann must develop better reading and writing skills. But how long will this take? What level of skills does Ann need? Kim helps Ann to develop a process that leads to making a decision regarding the level of educational upgrading. This involves talking with employment counsellors, administrators of the adult education program, and the local welfare department. This time Kim knows that she must pay more attention to evaluation.

In effect, Kim and Ann identified two new problems. The first was the need to redefine the goal of upgrading Ann's education, and the second was the related lack of needed information. The two new reference points thus became "lack of information" and "no clear definition of upgrading." Kim helps Ann devise a plan to talk to the appropriate people to get the needed information. However, since Ann cannot write well enough to keep notes, they have to schedule several meetings to monitor her progress. Together they lay out the information supplied, the alternatives available to Ann, and the pros and cons of each. By monitoring this process and taking evaluation time-outs, Kim ensures that Ann makes a good decision.

If evaluation is informal, as it often is, the evaluation time-outs may simply be discussions of progress between social worker and client. While it is not necessary to put the evaluation in writing, some find this useful. For instance, a simple way is to list all of the reference points and goals. Then, during each evaluation time-out, chart or write down the progress. This is really a form of ordered recording. If it is made part of the intervention progress, the client should participate. However, the social worker can also record progress for agency purposes after the client has left and to prepare for the next meeting.

Results of the evaluation time-outs can lead to redefinition of the problem (and by implication a new or different reference point), a different assessment, new or revised goals, a new means of intervention, and help in making a decision for ending the relationship. The process will work if the social worker (and client) consciously builds it into the helping process as an ongoing procedure.[1]

An important yet difficult part of any evaluation research is to link process with outcome. It is usually easy to describe process and measure application against some model. Specifying clear goals usually results in the ability to measure outcomes.

Evaluation in Short-Term and Involuntary Relationships

So far we have assumed that the client and the social worker can agree on goals and that the contact extends over at least several sessions. However, similar principles of evaluation apply in short-term contacts.

Crisis intervention is a good example of short-term contacts. In crisis situations, such as calls to a suicide hotline or a mobile crisis team, the social worker may need to act quickly to try to prevent a suicide from occurring. Nevertheless, identifying the problem implies the existence of a reference point. Goal setting may emerge quickly, as does formulating a contract for and an ending to the relationship. For instance, a call on a hotline or a request for face-to-face help from a crisis team worker may primarily be a plea for help (which is always taken seriously). The goal of both client and worker is help. This may never be clearly articulated, yet is usually understood by both parties. Evaluation time-outs may serve to restate difficulties in getting help or to review specific plans for referral to a helping agency that may include such details as transportation to the helping resource.

In involuntary contacts, the social worker's primary role may be to monitor the behaviour of an offender or to protect an abused child rather than to provide personal helping. However, evaluation is still required in these instances, maybe even more so than with voluntary clients. The principles of establishing a reference point, setting goals, and determining outcomes remain important. The differences are that the reference point and goals are from third parties, usually mandated by an agency or the courts, and evaluation is usually done by the social worker alone. However, when possible, it remains important to share the evaluation with the client even though he or she may not agree with it or with the process.

Endings

All problem-solving processes must eventually end. Usually either an explicit or implicit goal of the process is to help the client learn how to engage in his or her own problem solving without further need for social work assistance. When accomplished, ending of the helping process should take place.

Ending is a general concept that means closing the contact between social worker and client. There are many possible endings, including referral, a decision that no further help is needed or warranted, termination, unplanned endings, and combinations of these.

Referral

Referral means connecting the client with a needed resource or service. It may or may not end the professional relationship. However, for many social work interventions, referral does become an ending for the referring source. Referral after first contact is a frequent outcome of many social work interventions.

Sometimes, however, referral is not an ending but simply a need for further service. For instance, Kim referred Ann to an employment counsellor but did not end her relationship with Ann.

Referral involves several important tasks. The social worker must make sure that the referral instructions are clear and the client has the capacity to carry them out. If not, the worker needs to help the client complete the referral. This may range from simply giving verbal instructions to actually taking the client to the referral agency. It is equally important that the client understand the reasons for the referral. Like all parts of social work intervention, the referral process is really a form of contract. Referral is most successful if both client and worker agree not only on why the referral is important but also on the type of referral, the expected service, and the goals of the referral.

Often, the social worker must prepare the referral agency for the client. This may involve arranging an appointment and, with the client's agreement, sending information about the client to the new agency. It is very important that the worker's professional responsibility go beyond simply giving the client a referral source. Further follow-up ensures that the client takes appropriate action. If the referral falls through, the social worker can also intervene.

Termination (Planned Ending)

The process of termination is used to end the intervention after the client and worker have completed the agreed-upon work. It is a planned process that should take place when the worker and the client believe that the client's problem solving can continue without the worker's assistance.

The significance of termination is a direct function of the strength of the relationship between client and worker, their attachment, and the length of service. Often, the process is an emotional one. Sometimes obvious change has taken place and both client and worker readily agree that there is no longer a need for continued service. Other times, progress is less apparent but it seems that the worker has done all that is possible. The social worker sometimes thinks it is time to terminate the relationship while the client does not. The reverse may also happen when the social worker feels that there is more work to be done but the client disagrees and wants to end the relationship. Termination is a process fraught with issues, most of them specific to the particular client–social worker situation.

Successful planned endings often take place when worker and client have met their goals. Goal completion signals the time for them to consider termination. It is important that both agree to end intervention.

The decision for termination should be based on ongoing evaluation. If a client and a social worker have established a process for ongoing evaluation, then the decision for termination should occur as a result of the evaluation.

Brill (1998) suggests that the client and worker must deal with unfinished business and feelings about ending the relationship and plan for the future. Often both agree that termination should occur, but other issues remain. Possibly the client has become dependent on the worker. Maybe, in the process of helping, they have discovered other areas that call for professional assistance. Sometimes both feel a loss when termination occurs, and both need to address this issue and take action to resolve it. Sometimes, when dealing with unfinished business, the social worker refers the client to another needed service.

Kirst-Ashman and Hull (1993, pp. 294–304) also suggest that the termination is a good time to evaluate successes and plan for ways that successes can be sustained.

Unplanned Endings

Unplanned endings occur for many reasons. A client may move, get sick, or even die. She or he may feel there is no longer a need for service or may submit to pressure from a family member or friend not to seek the services of a social agency. A social worker may get transferred or quit his or her job.

The social worker has at least two important functions in unplanned endings. If the ending is the result of the worker's action (e.g., job transfer), then she or he has the responsibility to go through a termination process that will likely include referral. Often the referral is to another practitioner within the worker's own agency.

Most unplanned endings are the result of client action. In such cases, the social worker should try to find out the reasons for the client leaving. If the worker believes that service is still required or advisable, then she or he should take appropriate action. There are no real principles to guide "appropriate action," because the reasons for unplanned endings tend to be unique to each situation. Referral is a possibility. Working through some of the issues identified in the above section on termination is advisable. In many instances the worker should accept the client's judgment that service is not needed or not helpful.

Difficulties of unplanned endings occur when client–social worker interaction is not voluntary. If, for example, the court requires a youth on probation to visit his probation officer weekly and the youth stops the visits without court permission, the worker probably must report that action to the court. Even in such instances, the worker has the responsibility to ensure that he or she extends all possible services to the youth.

IMPLICATIONS OF THE PROBLEM-SOLVING APPROACH

Problem Solving and Pathology

Earlier, we distinguished between assessment in problem solving in social work and diagnosis in the medical model. What was presented were ideals—the way these approaches should be. Social workers have, more often than one would think, attempted to view practice within a pathology framework. Problem-oriented assessments encourage practice based on a framework that emphasizes pathology (disease) and deficits. Saleebey suggests that this can be observed in social workers' everyday use of a language of pathology. Shulman (1999, p. 4) suggests that even social workers who use other models and reject "clinical practice" often, in fact, are using the medical model.

Many argue that social work becomes bad social work if we view our clients in terms of disease and deficits. The foundation of their argument is that viewing personal problems as deficits is counterproductive to personal helping (Goldstein, 1992; Saleebey, 1997a; Weick, 1983). Conceptualizing such problems as poverty, marital difficulties, most criminal behaviour, child neglect, and many more as diseases not only labels but also does not lead to productive helping. We agree with this position.

To appreciate the importance of this concern, we need to understand what it means to view personal problems as diseases. In Chapter 5 we conceptualized disease as a harmful deviation from the normal structural or functional state of an organism. A diseased organism commonly exhibits signs or symptoms that indicate its abnormal state—pathology. If a diagnosis is correct, then diagnosis often leads to effective treatment.

"Social work, like other helping professions, has not been immune to the contagion of disease- and disorder-based thinking. Social work has constructed much of its theory and practice around the supposition that clients become clients because they have deficits, problems, pathologies, and diseases; that they are, in some essential way, flawed or weak" (Saleebey, 1997a, p. 7). To illustrate the problem with this thinking, return to our case example. What is the pathogenesis (method of development) of Ann's problems? What disease represents the cluster of Ann's problems? What are her symptoms? Clearly, neither these questions nor their answers assist in understanding and helping Ann with her personal and social problems.

Now suppose Ann suffers from a mental illness. Likely this would be an inhibitor to her ability to care for her children. However, mental illness is treatable. Kim would help Ann receive appropriate help. All social workers, including those in child welfare, should understand enough of the symptoms of mental illness to at least make necessary referrals. Mental illness would be only a part of Ann's life, but the diagnosis might help her gain access to certain services or supports (e.g., subsidized childcare or counselling). At times, a diagnosis provides the evidence needed that certain social services are necessary or desirable. As we discuss in some detail in Chapter 10, even with clients who suffer from serious and long-term mental illness, the focus of social work intervention should be on the strengths of these clients rather than on their problems.

While the substance of assessment in social work and diagnosis in medicine are substantively different, the processes are both a form of problem solving. It is not much of a leap for social workers using the problem-solving approach to join the rhetoric of pathology. If the leap is taken, there is a tendency, as in medicine, to assume that the disease process leads to a prescribed solution.

Individual Orientation: A Limited Scope

The problem-solving approach tends to be individualistic in practice due to its focus on helping people solve specific, articulated life problems for themselves. The individual is the centre of the process. In the case example about Ann, the problems are Ann's, not her sister's or her social worker's or even society's. This means, much like the medical model, that Ann as an individual becomes the focus of expert attention aimed at solving her problems. While the model does not exclude interventions related to larger systems, problem solving in social work primarily focuses on the individual's behaviours and her or his adjustment to the environment. The problem-solving model generally does not question or challenge current social structures and institutions but implicitly accepts them as part of life. Nor can the paradigm be easily used to address social change. It offers instead a kind of blueprint of logical steps and procedures that can be applied and adapted to different problems in which interventions can be devised and outcomes measured.

The individual orientation of traditional problem solving encourages the tendency to place people in categories, a professional kind of shortcut that tends to pigeonhole. Saleebey (1997a, p. 6) puts it this way: "When we transform persons into cases, we often see only them and how well they fit into a category. In this way, we miss important elements of the client's life: cultural, social, political, ethnic, spiritual, and economic" (also see Holmes, 1997). For example, when youths are convicted of crimes, helpers and others may define them as delinquents. By doing so these youths are put into a category of people who are seen to share similar characteristics instead of being understood as unique individuals. In the context of his or her own environment, the individual youth is partly defined in terms of characteristics that are associated with others labelled "delinquents." Usually this definition emphasizes deficits. The youth is typecast ("pigeonholed") by the category that has been assigned to him or her. The better the perceived fit to the category "delinquent," the more the youth has been typecast and defined by the helper's conception of delinquents.

Restorative versus Promotional Approach

The problem-solving approach, like the medical model, is essentially restorative. Restorative—sometimes called residual—in this context means that action (intervention or treatment) takes place only after the social worker and client have identified a problem that requires solution. Intervention is restorative because it is an action taken to alleviate an identified and existing problem.

Generally, a person must experience a problem before helping takes place. Kim helped Ann only after she left her children unattended. If there had been no problem in the eyes of the Child Protection Agency, there would have been no intervention. Most social and health agencies focus their efforts on residual problem solving, mental health agencies generally treat patients only after they are diagnosed with a mental illness, the criminal justice system usually works with people who are legally defined as offenders, and so on. All of these are examples of treatment after the fact. A problem-solving approach fits restorative programs because they have similar bases.

The flip side of restoration is sometimes called a promotional approach. This approach results in programs that are different from those intended to solve a specific problem. Promotional programs are aimed at addressing wider needs. For example, public health education programs are often designed to promote good health in a large population; the Canadian government's promotion of physical fitness and programs aimed at keeping teenagers in school are examples. Often one of the goals of promotional programs is prevention of problems.

Case Example

Kim and Ann ▼

As part of the effort to help Ann get her life back on track, Kim suggests that she needs to consider her own physical well-being. The local health centre has just established a top-notch wellness clinic that offers a physical fitness and mental health promotion program. Because the centre is government-funded, it is able to defray most of the costs for people on social assistance.

Ann likes the idea and enrolls in the program. The intent of both Kim and Ann is not to solve a particular problem but to help improve Ann's quality of life and possibly, as she feels better about herself, improve her ability to solve her own problems.

Kim also thinks it would be a good idea to put Ann's younger son, John (age 4), into a pre-kindergarten learning centre. First, however, Kim consults with Ann. Ann quickly agrees. All children are eligible to attend, and the purpose of the learning centre is to prepare them for the public school system. The purpose is not restorative but promotional. (If the intent of the centre were to help children "catch up," then one might consider the purpose restorative.)

Social Worker as Expert

The problem-solving model holds that a partnership between the social worker and the client is essential. The professional relationship is built on this partnership. However, this is a relationship with important power differentials.

Even in relationships that are entirely voluntary, the worker is presumed by both the client and the worker to be an expert with good practice skills. Certainly one reason people with problems seek out social workers for help is because they perceive them to have expert knowledge and skills. A marriage counsellor without specialized knowledge and skills would likely not be very effective or helpful.

Thus it is important *not* to assume that in problem solving the client–social worker partnership is one of equality of power. Social workers must know how to effectively, ethically, and judiciously use this power differential in order to engage and work effectively with clients. A major reason social work, and also most other professions, has a code of ethics is to regulate the potential power of the professional and help prevent the abuse of power.

Other approaches to practice are critical of power differentials in the helping relationship and suggest different ways to build helping relationships that minimize power differences. These are discussed in the chapters on the strengths, Aboriginal, structural, and feminist approaches.

Involuntary Problem-Solving Relationships and the Principle of Best Interest

The problem-solving process was illustrated using the case of Ann, a lone mother, and Kim, a family social worker in a child protection agency. Although Ann was initially an involuntary client, she quickly formed a helping relationship with Kim. What might have happened if, as often happens, Ann had not wanted Kim's help? Ann would have truly been an involuntary client and the problem-solving process would have been very different.

The Canadian Association of Social Workers' code of ethics establishes an ethical framework for providing help when help is not wanted (see also Rooney, 1992, Chapter 4). The CASW code of ethics asserts, "A social worker shall maintain the best interest of the client as the primary professional obligation." The code goes on to define best interest, which is

> (a) That the wishes, desires, motivations and plans of the client are taken by the social worker as the primary consideration in any intervention plan developed by the social worker subject to change only when the client's plans are documented to be unrealistic, unreasonable or potentially harmful to self or others or otherwise determined inappropriate when considered in relation to a mandated requirement and (b) that all actions and interventions of the social worker are taken subject to the reasonable belief that the client will benefit from the action. (CASW, 1994a, Definitions, section on Best Interest)

The U.S. National Association of Social Workers' code of ethics states that the

> social workers' primary responsibility is to promote the well-being of clients. In general, clients' interests are primary. However, social workers' responsibility to the larger society or specific legal obligations may on limited occasions supersede the loyalty owed clients, and clients should be so advised. (NASW, 1997, Section 1.01, Commitment to Clients)

The NASW code further holds that "...(s)ocial workers may limit clients' rights to self-determination when, in the social workers' professional judgment, clients' actions or potential actions pose a serious, foreseeable, and imminent risk to themselves or others" (NASW, 1997, Section 1.02 on Self-Determination).

Both codes urge a strong commitment to clients and their best interest, but both provide exceptions, and these exceptions give social workers important responsibilities. If clients are presumed to be at risk to themselves or others, or, in the case of the CASW code, when their plans are "unrealistic, unreasonable or potentially harmful," the right of clients to make decisions by themselves is suspended, but action must still be in their best interest. The worker can ethically intervene even though such action is opposed by the client. Under these circumstances, social workers clearly act as agents of social control.

The codes present guidelines for working with involuntary clients and provide justifications for it. Suppose Ann did not want help from Kim but made it very clear to all that she wanted her children back. Kim or the agency would not have agreed to return them if they could clearly show that the children were at risk. A child protection agency is a mandated agency and is legally responsible for the safety of the children and must protect their interests. Their safety and well-being would have the highest priority.

In our case example, if Ann is an involuntary client, Kim still has an obligation to provide service to her. Kim can still follow the problem-solving process—by, for instance, clearly laying out to Ann the conditions under which the Child Protection Agency will return her children. She can also suggest alternative plans and resources that might be available to Ann. Kim may even make decisions that affect Ann without her consent. Another possibility is to show Ann that the quickest and best way to have her children returned is to problem solve with Kim. Kim may attempt to negotiate a helping relationship with Ann. In mandated practice, the social worker can intervene without the agreement of the client if the worker can justify that the action is in the best interest of the client.

Often probation or parole officers are faced with clients who are assumed to be a potential risk to society but who do not want help. They appear for interviews only because they are forced, by threats of penalty, by the courts. In these cases the best interest is often that of society as well as of the parolee. People in mental hospitals may be treated against their will. This can occur even if the courts have not committed a patient to the hospital. Often patients are "voluntarily" hospitalized because a family member, public agency, or community entity threatens some form of action if they do not seek treatment.

Notwithstanding the intent, the principle of best interest sanctions the social worker to determine what is best for the client as long as the worker can clearly document the reasons for doing so. The principle holds the worker as expert with power over the client in both voluntary and involuntary relationships. Determining best interest is a judgment call made by social workers. Since such judgments profoundly affect the lives of others, the skills to make them are some of the most important that social workers need.

CHAPTER SUMMARY

This chapter has presented an overview of what is often considered the foundation of traditional social work practice. The problem-solving process in social work involves a number of elements, which are graphically displayed in Exhibit 8.2.

The formation of a practice contract between the social worker and the client is central to problem solving. Successful helping depends on agreement on the problems, their nature, and an understanding about them; the goals of intervention; and the action required to meet these goals.

In this chapter we suggest a workable, informal method that frontline social workers can use to evaluate their everyday work. The three basic steps are as follows:

1. establish a clear reference point
2. clearly articulate goals connected to the reference point
3. evaluate progress and take evaluation time-outs

While problem solving is very important in social work, it has its limitations. Several problems are inherent in the process, including concerns about defining problems as pathologies and deficits; power and how it is used; the limited, individualized, and restorative scope of problem solving; and the principle of best interest when it requires making decisions against the client's wishes.

Much of the remainder of this book takes the reader beyond problem solving by critiquing, informing, and discussing enhancements to the traditional social work process.

NOTE

1 The logic used in this example is similar to the research strategy goal attainment scaling and single subject designs. Goal attainment scaling is a formal and sometimes complicated process for evaluating the extent to which practice goals have been met (see Grinnell, 1993; Kiresuk, Smith, and Cardillo, 1994; Tripodi, 1994).

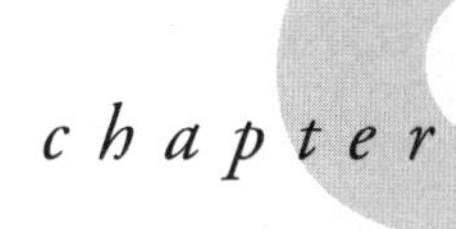

chapter 9

A Broad Knowledge Perspective in Focused Assessment

Chapter Goal ▼

To articulate a broad knowledge-based perspective in social work and explain its relation to focused assessment.

This Chapter ▼

- describes several forms of social work assessment
- suggests that social work assessment must be focused and guided by a broad knowledge base that includes theory
- explains that there are various sources of knowledge, including life experience, culture and tradition, authority, and observation and testing
- links knowledge used in social work to knowledge developed in the social and behavioural sciences
- casts a broad knowledge-based assessment within an ecosystems (person-in-the-environment) framework. The selection of knowledge areas covers the micro to macro continuum
- describes areas of knowledge that are important to a broad knowledge-based assessment and shows how each relates to focused assessment
- directly connects focused assessment with social work's broad knowledge base through the use of examples

INTRODUCTION

The first eight chapters of this book presented basic principles that form the foundations of generalist social work practice.

- Social work practice is strongly influenced by an ideology that is based on a set of values.
- Social work is practised in the context of social policy and social welfare institutions, and social policy analysis and implementation are forms of social work practice.
- Forming professional relationships is a necessary part of social work intervention.
- Social workers must understand cultural diversity, be able to practise cross-culturally, and engage in cross-cultural and anti-oppressive intervention.
- Traditional social work practice is built on a strong problem-solving approach.

In this chapter, we begin to address social work practice beyond problem solving. This chapter discusses how assessment in generalist social work practice must have a broad knowledge base. Part A discusses what social work knowledge comprises and how it is relevant in assessment. Part B applies this knowledge base to focused assessment, providing examples. The remaining chapters on the strengths, Aboriginal, structural, and feminist approaches to social work criticize traditional problem solving and present ways to enhance it.

PART A: SOCIAL WORK KNOWLEDGE AND FOCUSED ASSESSMENT

Assessment Tools

In recent years, social workers have been making considerable use of specific assessment tools. Many different assessment tools are used, most of them specific to a particular field of practice. Many are designed and used as forms by specific agencies. For example, child welfare agencies use assessment forms designed for those particular agencies. Assessments are often specific to a particular type of problem and are used to try to estimate the risk of behaviours such as suicide or violence, or to identify the functional skills of clients.

For instance, Gerhart (1990) describes a way to undertake social functioning assessments in the field of mental health. Social functioning assessment "includes observations of a client's interaction with family and transactions with landlords, friends, schools, employers, shopkeepers, and neighbours" (pp. 101–2). To complete this assessment, Gerhart uses a **rating scale.** Instruments like rating scales are common assessment tools. Such scales attempt to place a risk, a behaviour, or an attitude on a continuum. Rating suicide risk from high to low is an example of a rating scale used to arrive at a specific assessment.

The Specific Level of Function Assessment (SLOF) scale (Schneider and Struening, 1983, cited in Gerhart, 1990) is a good example of an assessment tool that uses a rating scale. The scale assesses on several dimensions the social functioning of people who have a chronic mental illness. These dimensions include interpersonal relationships, social acceptability of behaviours, level of activities, and work skills. Each dimension is rated according to five

Likert categories. For instance, in the "level of activities" category, subjects are rated on a scale ranging from totally self-sufficient to totally dependent on activities such as shopping, handling personal finances, using the telephone, and self-medicating.

Other assessment tools attempt to understand the range of a person's problems in the context of the environment and personal and social strengths. Most often these more global assessments use guides rather than specific instruments like scales. Such guides are listings that suggest areas that need to be explored (Cowger, 1997; Rothman, 1994). Gerhart (1990, pp. 116–19) presents a global guide in an Outline for a Social Functioning Assessment. The outline is simply a listing of categories, such as communication skills, problem-solving skills, and functional skills, for the social worker to review in making a judgment about the level of functioning of a mentally ill person. Unlike the SLOF scale, there is no rating of a dimension or category.

Knowledge Required for Assessment

All assessment processes, scales, guides, and procedures used by social workers and agencies assume that the workers have a basic understanding of social science theory and knowledge. Competent focused assessment depends on the ability to understand, criticize, and use theories about human behaviour, the social environment, economics, and other fields. (See Gold, 2002, for a discussion of the use of theory in assessment.)

What kinds of knowledge are required? Unfortunately, there is no unified theory of social work practice or human behaviour that is useful to social workers (McMahon, 1994, pp. 85–86; Turner, 1999, p. 26). All theories address only parts, rather than the whole, of the human condition. Some are more useful than others, depending on the nature of problems, the setting, the culture, and a host of other factors. One of the important steps in becoming a professional social worker is learning how to select and use theory that best serves, addresses, and focuses the assessment and intervention problems at hand. This skill must be learned over time and honed throughout one's professional life.

Using Theory and Knowledge in Focused Assessment

A theory is simply a network of concepts that are logically or empirically related to one another. A theory explains the world, at least in part, or predicts events. A practice theory is one that helps social workers intervene with clients. A theory about human behaviour usually explains and sometimes attempts to predict behaviour.

Social workers often use theories to help explain different phenomena they encounter in practice. For example, child welfare workers look to theory to explain why a small child has been abused. They may use concepts such as motivation and defence mechanisms from ego psychology to explain how a parent has become abusive. Social workers may also draw on theory from human behaviour to understand how abuse can affect the subsequent development of the child. Clearly, explanations of causation and effect are very important to social work.

However, theoretical knowledge plays an even more important role in assessment. Paraphrasing a common saying, "You can't get the right answer until you ask the right question," helps to explain. The social worker must know what to look for. Good assessment does not use a haphazard approach but is focused. Theory focuses assessment; thus, focused assessment is knowledge-guided assessment.

Let us illustrate. People often seek help because of problems in relationships at home or at work. They may have difficulty coping with the roles that they are required to perform at home (such as parenting or being a companion) or at work (such as getting along with fellow workers). For instance, suppose Jennifer, a middle-aged woman, is depressed and feels that her life is empty. The local counselling centre may assume that her depression is biologically related. A social worker at the centre may agree but also think that role theory (discussed in more detail later in this chapter) may help clarify Jennifer's situation. Role theory tells us that people who experience role-related problems are often experiencing role conflict (conflicting expectations or norms) or role strain (expectations that the client has difficulty meeting). The social worker might find out whether Jennifer has recently experienced significant role conflict or role strain that could help account for her depression. The worker's assessment finds that Jennifer's stressful job has placed considerable strain on her role as mother. Because of the strain, Jennifer is finding it more and more difficult to cope with daily life, and this in turn increases her depression. Without knowledge of role theory, it is unlikely that the social worker would discover the strains and be able to connect them to Jennifer's depression. If the worker is familiar with role theory, it should be an almost automatic response to explore whether role conflict or role strain exists and, if so, how it arose and how it affects the functioning of the client.

If the social worker hears Jennifer say that her life is not worth living anymore, a risk assessment for suicide would be initiated. The social worker will use her knowledge about crisis and suicide and make use of guidelines designed to assess suicide risk (e.g., Shebib, 2003, pp. 276–79). She knows from past experience in her work at a mobile crisis service that when a client seems preoccupied with death, gives away favoured items, appears to be saying good-bye for no known reason, and/or seems unusually satisfied despite feeling down or depressed previously, it is important to assess suicide risk.

The social worker's theoretical frame of reference influences and undoubtedly biases the assessment (Gold, 2002). Assume that the worker has a good background in a feminist approach to social work (see Chapter 13). While she may recognize the importance of biological causes of depression and think role theory helps in understanding Jennifer, the social worker may take a different angle in the assessment because her lens for viewing clients is different. Feminist social work holds that women need to feel validated and be believed and heard. It also sees as important the link between personal troubles and social causes. For example, if Jennifer, a single mother, cannot afford good childcare while she is at work, she may experience guilt and worry about her children's welfare. She may feel that she should not go out to work even if she is the sole support for her family. Due to these stresses in her life, Jennifer's self-esteem might drop. A feminist assessment might look at whether she has any support and the unrealistic expectations she faces as a working mother, determining how these are connected to current problems. Such an assessment would also look at the systemic problem of lack of affordable childcare. Note that while the feminist approach and role theory both suggest problems between Jennifer's roles as worker and as mother, the analysis is different.

The strengths approach and structural social work are still other lenses that filter practice. A social worker operating only from a strengths perspective who works with Jennifer would certainly look for and assess her individual strengths (see Chapter 10). If the worker was also knowledgeable about structural social work (see Chapter 12), he or she would assess collective, or group, as well as individual strengths. For example, a structural social worker would acknowledge the collective strengths of mothers with young children in managing the many demands on their time and resources. Possibly a woman's needs and skills could be validated in collective action with other women in similar situations. A childcare collective based on the needs of lone parents might then be set up through the efforts of women themselves so they can secure affordable childcare.

As these examples suggest, social workers need a broad knowledge base. The filters of different lenses shape the way social workers work with clients, including the application of theories and conduct of the assessment. Achieving this knowledge base and integrating it into assessment and intervention are important challenges for beginning and experienced workers alike. The deeper and more comprehensive the worker's knowledge, the better equipped she or he is to assess clients.

SOURCES OF KNOWLEDGE

Social work is an art, a science, and more. It is an art in the sense that practice includes skills that are learned over long periods of time and are incorporated within one's total life experiences. One worker has suggested such skills are often difficult to articulate, are intangible, and are learned by osmosis—an unconscious process of learning. Many of these skills are in the area of developing meaningful and helpful human relationships. Others rest in understanding, appreciating, and empathizing with the human and social condition.

Possibly the easiest way to define science is that it is a method or way of knowing, a rigorous method to help us understand the world we live in. Research, as a part of science, helps us determine whether something that we assert, say a theory or **hypothesis,** is true. Research also helps us discover new things about the world. For example, a social work researcher might use a qualitative method to discover and understand the meaning of social and recreational activities to elderly people in a large long-term-care facility. Or the researcher may test a hypothesis of the board of directors of the home that residents need a more rigorous physical exercise program. This might be done by using a survey that asks the residents questions. In both cases, the social worker is building knowledge by using research methods.

There are many other ways to gain knowledge. The best way depends on the subject matter and the purpose of knowing. The following are four common ways that all of us use to learn about ourselves, our world, and our environment.

1. *Life experience.* Maybe the most common and important way that all of us learn is through our life experiences.

2. *Culture and traditions.* A critical part of life experience that shapes our understanding of the world is our culture and associated traditions (Chapter 7 addresses cultural issues in detail). Culture is often intrinsically linked with spirituality or religion, and these reflect many of the values of a culture. All religions assert a foundation of truths, many of which are based on articles of faith. The social worker's culture shapes his or her knowledge base. As well, the social worker must understand how the views and knowledge of clients are products of their cultural background.
3. *Authority.* We often accept knowledge because an expert tells us something is so. This is particularly true if we know little about the subject matter. Thus we tend to accept the teachings of those we consider knowledgeable.

   While depending on authority is a quick and easy way to acquire knowledge, it is fraught with problems when accepted unquestioningly; so, it is not a good way for professionals in any field to build knowledge. How can we be sure that the expert is correct? In professional practice it is up to each practitioner to have the tools to evaluate the validity and usefulness of information. Social workers must be able to make judgments about assertions, theory, research, and the like. Without observation and testing, reliance on authority can lead to accepting dogma and incorrect conclusions.
4. *Observation and testing.* While rigorous observation and testing are at the core of science and research, they are certainly not limited to science. Quite the contrary—observation and testing are integral parts of life experience that are practised in all cultures. We all learn them as small children. Observation is the process of perceiving something through one or more of the senses. It can be very simple; for example, a toddler watching a parent and hearing a word that she or he cannot pronounce is demonstrating a simple form of observation.

   Testing is an attempt to validate, or determine the truth of, an observation. The toddler's effort to speak the word is a type of testing. The child may test whether and how others respond when he or she attempts to pronounce the word. If the response is rewarding, the child will likely continue to use the word. Eventually it will probably become part of her or his vocabulary.

   Observing and testing, then, are daily knowledge-building activities of most people and hence part of all life experience.

   Science uses a rigorous process of observation and testing. It attempts to reduce bias in observation and testing by a variety of means. Science is a method of inquiry in which the observers take great pains in order to be objective. Indeed, physicists, sociologists, biologists, psychologists, and many others make considerable use of the scientific method: observing, hypothesizing, testing, and confirming or rejecting. Social workers also use scientific methods to help build theory and knowledge and to evaluate practice and programs.

LINKS TO SOCIAL SCIENCES

Social work is related to psychology, sociology, anthropology, economics, education, and other fields. Social work shares with these social sciences the interest in and need to understand human personal and social behaviour. For example, social workers, like economists, need to understand the effects of such factors as recessions or inflation. Like anthropologists exploring cultural beliefs, social workers are often required to know about individual and group perspectives on areas such as dating, marriage, and child rearing.

There are also substantial differences. Maybe the most obvious is the difference in emphasis between a profession and a discipline. The purpose of a profession is to provide a service, such as teaching, medical help, engineering service, or legal advice. The central purpose of a discipline such as sociology, psychology, or economics is to develop a deeper and better understanding of the world in which we live.

Medicine is a profession and essentially a human service. In order to practise, a physician clearly must possess a wealth of knowledge and skills. However, it is not the main purpose of medicine to develop new knowledge; rather, it is to provide medical services to people. Yet the new knowledge about health is very important to medicine, and many physicians spend their entire career in the pursuit of new knowledge. When they do, they make considerable use of knowledge developed in other disciplines. They may also be trained in a discipline such as biochemistry. Medicine uses biochemistry, a discipline, in order to help develop new knowledge to better meet its main professional goal of provision of health care services.

Psychology offers another example. Some fields of psychology, such as experimental psychology, are clearly disciplines. However, clinical psychology seems to place a nearly equal emphasis on its role as a clinical helping profession and developer of new knowledge.

Social work is a human service profession. While developing new knowledge is important, it is not the main goal of social work. Social work, maybe more than most professions, uses theories and knowledge developed in disciplines. Most knowledge used by social workers to understand human behaviour and the social environment has been developed in such disciplines as sociology, economics, political science, psychology, and the like.

Branches of some disciplines such as psychology provide human services. For example, clinical psychology and counselling psychology are two fields that provide therapeutic and counselling services to people. As in medicine, some social workers devote their careers to knowledge building. But, as in medicine, these social workers are in the minority. As a whole, the emphasis in social work is on providing human services, while in the scientific disciplines the primary but certainly not exclusive focus is the pursuit of knowledge.

ASSESSMENT WITHIN AN ECOSYSTEMS FRAMEWORK

Chapter 1 suggested that generalist social work must include a range of perspectives, approaches, and theories. Exhibit 9.1 describes these terms and their relevance to social work practice methods. In social work, the terms "perspective" and "approach" are used almost interchangeably. "Approach" tends to be used when the subject matter is primarily intervention.

Exhibit 9.1 Knowledge Base of Social Work Practice

Framework	Theory	Perspective	Approach	Methods
Group of theories or other forms of knowledge based on particular ideologies.	A network of related concepts that have at least some empirical verification and are usually used to explain or predict something. More precise and much narrower than a framework, perspective, or approach.	Framework of theories that guide a particular area of practice; based on connected values, sets of ideas, and knowledge.	Applied to social work intervention.	Used in practice situations, the means and techniques a social worker uses in intervention.

"Perspective" usually refers to a broad view about an area of practice. A perspective can be defined as a broad **framework,** based on ideology and knowledge that guides social work practice.

One perspective, ecosystems, plays a major role in broad-based assessment in at least two ways. First, it generates an important set of ideas that helps focus assessment, and second, it establishes a useful framework for assessment based on the range from micro to macro practice.

Background

To understand the use of ecosystems in broad knowledge-based assessment, it is important to understand the basics of ecosystems thinking in social work and how it fits into practice.

In the 1950s and 1960s, social workers began a search for a unifying theory that would be common (generic) to all of social work. Most theories that social workers used focused on understanding the "inner person." The environment was seen as an external force that had an impact on the individual, but, as in inner person–focused theories such as psychoanalysis and ego psychology, could be separated from the person. There were few links that connected these domain-based theories that social workers used.

Some saw major flaws in using these theories. They argued that the person and the environment could not be separated. William Gordon (1969) laid much of the foundation for a new line of thinking. Gordon, a social work practice theoretician, suggested that the uniqueness of social work rested in the transaction between people and their environment—or, as he called it, the interface. What he meant was that the primary focus of social work should not be on psychological forces, the environment, or the social structure, but on the interface or relationship between the person and the social environment. This was very different from the commonly held view that the person and the environment were separate entities.

Beginning in the 1970s, an ecosystems perspective that captured the interface between people and the environment was articulated. This perspective has been developed and honed to the point that today it is frequently seen as fundamental to social work practice; to some, it forms the common base of all social work practice (McMahon, 1994; Meyer, 1983, 1988; Wakefield, 1996b). No other perspective seems more commonly used in social work today.

Ecosystems: A Person-in-the-Environment Perspective

Ecosystems involves a combination of systems concepts and ecological concepts (Meyer, 1988; Wakefield, 1996a, p. 4).[1] Generally, a systems perspective examines the connection between a set of interacting elements. A system is usually seen as a whole with a number of elements. Interaction exists among elements of the whole, and between the system and other systems.

An open system grows and develops by receiving and using input from outside sources as well as contributing to those sources. A system that does not interact with other systems or parts of its own system, does not use input, or refuses input is a closed system, and it is fraught with problems. Closed systems tend toward *entropy* (Rodway, 1986, p. 517), which means they are unable to grow and be productive. According to systems theory, clients who experience problems are often parts of closed systems.

The ecological perspective emphasizes the person-in-the-environment perspective. Ecology is a biological concept that refers to the interrelationships between living organisms and their environments (Dubois and Miley, 1992, p. 58). Social work uses the biological concept of ecology as a framework. "The ecological perspective makes clear the need to view people and environments as a unitary system within a particular cultural and historic context" (Germain and Gitterman, 1995, p. 816). The perspective emphasizes the unity of a person within his or her environment, and the focus of practice is on the interface between persons and their environment.

Germain and Gitterman (1980) base their **life model of social work** on ecology. "In [the life model] human needs and problems are generated by transactions between persons and their environment, and through a process of continuous reciprocal adaptation, humans change and are changed by their physical and social environment" (Dubois and Miley, 1992, p. 59). Central to the ecological perspective is the concept of goodness of fit between the person and the environment (Wakefield, 1996a, p. 3). Clients experience problems when there is not a good fit with their environment. Causation is circular in that the environment and the person affect each other.

The ecosystems perspective accepts the broad principles of the ecological perspective while also borrowing from the systems perspective ideas such as systems are sets of interacting elements, systems can be open or closed, and systems possess states of equilibrium or disequilibrium (Meyer, 1988; Wakefield, 1996a, p. 4).

What Ecosystems Is and Is Not

Ecosystems is not a theory but a perspective or framework borrowed from biology that shapes practice. It is not a practice theory about intervention. However, many claim that it is a comprehensive, unifying, and generic perspective that underpins social work (Dubois and Miley, 1992, p. 60; Meyer, 1983; Wakefield, 1996a, p. 6). Herein lies the source of much debate: is ecosystems really a generic, unifying perspective? Is it even useful in practice? This debate is important because the perspective is very widely accepted in social work. Many schools of social work build their entire curricula around ecosystems, and a large number of standard textbooks on practice assume that ecosystems is fundamental to practice and base their writing on acceptance of this perspective (e.g., Compton and Galaway, 1999; Kirst-Ashman and Hull, 1993).

In 1996, Jerome Wakefield (1996a, 1996b, and 1996c) wrote three thoughtful articles that were highly critical of ecosystems. His work questions the widespread use of this perspective, even its usefulness. Alex Gitterman (1996), well known for his work on the ecological perspective, responded. While we do not summarize the debate here, we do use it to focus on five principles that guide this book's view of the ecosystems perspective. The first two principles explain what an ecosystems perspective is not, and the final three show how it can be used as the framework for problem solving and beyond.

First, ecosystems is not the common or generic base of social work or even a foundation of social work in the sense that traditional practice is based on problem solving. This view agrees with part of the argument put forth by Wakefield (1996b). Like Wakefield, we question whether social work even needs a common theoretical base. Social work practice involves too wide a range of fields to even attempt to bring all practice together under a single theoretical umbrella. While common values, principles, knowledge, and practice skills are shared among generalist social workers in widely disparate fields, it is not reasonable to assume that all should share the same theoretical base.

Second, the ecosystems perspective is not a theory, nor do its proponents claim that it is a theory. Ecosystems is a combination of ideas from general systems theory and ecology that does not have any real explanatory power (Wakefield, 1996a, p. 4; Payne, 1991, p. 150).

Third, ecosystems is a loose connection of ideas, views, and concepts. It is a framework for assessment.

Fourth, while not an explanatory theory, ecosystems spawns many useful ideas, concepts, and hypotheses that are testable and sometimes explanatory. These ideas, concepts, and hypotheses are important in focusing assessment. Some of these are discussed in the next section of this chapter.

Fifth, ecosystems is a very strong and useful perspective that helps us organize assessment and acts as a lens that focuses assessment on the person-in-the-environment (Gitterman, 1996). One important way this perspective organizes assessment is by helping us conceptualize broad knowledge bases along a micro to macro continuum. This helps us link **domain**-specific theories ranging from personality theories on the one hand to structural theories on the other.

The Micro to Macro Continuum

Consistent with the ecosystems perspective, the broad knowledge base for assessment can be classified into three interconnected systems: micro, mezzo, and macro (Kirst-Ashman and Hull, 1999). As explained in Chapters 1 and 4, micro social work practice focuses on work with individuals or primary groups, such as the family. Micro assessment uses knowledge derived mostly from psychology and sometimes sociology and is mainly concerned with inner psychological functioning or relationships between individuals and small, usually primary, groups. The focus in macro practice is large social institutions, such as the health or welfare system, or work with communities or large neighbourhoods, including social policy issues. Macro assessment usually uses theories from economics, political science, and sociology. Between micro and macro systems is work that is carried out with secondary groups, task groups, and small local groups, which is called mezzo practice. Mezzo assessment is drawn mainly from theories from sociology and sometimes psychology or management, which often share both micro and macro elements.

PART B: APPLICATION OF KNOWLEDGE IN FOCUSED ASSESSMENT

Assessment Defined

As developed in Chapter 8, assessment depends on information available to the social worker about a client. Also in Chapter 8, we pointed out that the primary purpose of assessment is to set goals and determine a strategy for intervention. Social work assessment involves the ongoing analysis and interpretation of information collected by the worker about the client and the client's situation. By focused assessment, we mean assessment that is guided and underpinned by knowledge. Often, but not always, the knowledge used in assessment comes from the social and behavioural sciences. The range of knowledge that social workers need to use must be broad based.

A broad working knowledge of appropriate and related theories, approaches, perspectives, and principles about micro, mezzo, and macro systems is necessary in order to engage in assessment as well as intervention. This knowledge needs to capture the person-in-the-environment (or persons-in-the-environment) and also the person herself or himself and the wider social and cultural features that affect (and are affected by) the person. Some components that may be necessary to explore in client assessment (primarily with individuals and families) include the following:

a) material circumstances such as income and assets
b) health and mental health
c) emotional functioning and coping
d) past experiences relevant to current situation
e) client understanding and perspective on problems
f) available support systems and resources
g) shelter and safety of surrounding community

h) effects of age and life stage
i) family relationships and family life cycle
j) gender issues
k) salient aspects in cultural background
l) spirituality and worldview
m) experiences of stigma, discrimination, marginalization, and/or oppression

Depending on the client situation and the knowledge areas, perspective, and approach of the social worker, some components rather than others will be the focus of assessment and intervention. Exhibit 9.2 lists knowledge areas that are discussed in this chapter, according to system size (micro to macro). The rest of the chapter provides an overview of how a number of knowledge areas can be applied to assessment. Note that the list in Exhibit 9.2 is not exhaustive.

Many of the areas listed in the exhibit are perspectives, approaches, or theories that are fundamental to the major theme of this book, a problem-solving approach and beyond. These are the structural approach; anti-oppressive practice and culture, ecosystems, and strengths; Aboriginal perspectives; and the feminist approach. Each of these areas is covered in some detail in other parts of this book but is also important to the broad knowledge base and focused assessment.

Exhibit 9.2 ▼ Knowledge Bases Used by Social Workers in Focused Assessment

Micro Orientation: Focus on Individuals and Families
• cognitive theory • ego psychology • crisis theory • knowledge from psychiatry—DSM-IV • knowledge about family issues and processes
Mezzo Orientation: Focus on Groups
• theories about groups
Macro Orientation: Focus on Large Systems
• knowledge about community development • theories underlying the structural approach
Micro to Macro Orientation: Focus on Range of System Sizes and Connections between Systems
• anti-oppressive practice • culture • ecosystems • role theory • labelling theory • strengths perspective • Aboriginal perspectives • feminist perspectives

The remaining areas (cognitive theory, ego psychology, crisis theory, knowledge from psychiatry—DSM-IV, knowledge of family relationships and processes, group theory, community development, role theory, and labelling) represent a reasonable selection of commonly used theories or knowledge perspectives. All of these are important in assessment and intervention but are not viewed as fundamental underpinnings to generalist social work practice. None are covered elsewhere in this book except for labelling, which we view as an important theory in working with involuntary clients and is covered in Chapter 6 on professional relationships. Hence, this chapter devotes more space to these areas than the perspectives covered elsewhere in this book.

Cognitive Theory

Cognitive theory is aimed at individuals (micro systems). As its name implies, cognitive theory emphasizes the thinking process. Central to the theory is the idea that if people can think about their problems in constructive ways then they may be able to do something about them. The theory assumes that behaviour and emotions are products of cognition. Therefore, if people change the way they think, they can also change the way they behave and feel (Goldstein, Hillbert, and Hillbert, 1984; Payne, 1997, pp. 114–36).

Cognitive theory is closely related to behavioural and learning theory. Payne (1997) suggests that in 1977 Albert Bandura, a learning theorist, opened the door to cognitive theory by "arguing that most learning is gained by people's perceptions and thinking about what they experience" (p. 115). Cognitive theorists hold that how people perceive the world around them is instrumental in determining how they feel and behave.

In the past 20 years or so, a number of cognitive approaches have gained importance in social work. Payne (1997) suggests that **cognitive restructuring** is probably the best-known cognitive intervention used in social work. It is assumed that irrational beliefs often dominate the client's thinking. Burns (1990) calls some of this type of thinking "cognitive distortion." For example, a young man who feels discomfort and freezes during social situations, such as parties, likely freezes because of misperceptions about himself, the other people, and the nature of parties, and subsequent distortions of thinking. The task of the social worker is to challenge this thinking and help the young man find ways to structure a new, productive way of thinking. In this example, the hope is that the freezing will end.

Using Cognitive Theory in Focused Assessment

Assessment that uses cognitive theory focuses on the thinking processes, particularly irrational or distorted thinking. General assessment questions that emerge from cognitive theories might be: How does the client perceive the world around him or her? Is part of this perception distorted? Does it lead to irrational thinking? What is the nature of the distorted or irrational thinking? How did distorted learning occur? How does it affect the client? By answering these and other, similar questions, social workers attempt to devise a plan whereby the client learns new ways of perceiving the world and restructuring thinking into productive channels.

Case Example

Kim and Ann

Let's again return to the story of Kim and Ann that was introduced in Chapter 4. Recall that Kim is a family social worker in the Child Protection Agency (CPA). The nightshift worker has placed Ann's three children in temporary custody.

Kim explores with Ann how Ann perceives herself as a parent. Unfortunately, Ann currently thinks that she has very little to offer her children as a mother and gives an example that depicts failure. Kim, however, is convinced that Ann deeply cares for her three children and is really a loving mother with the capacity to develop good parenting skills. Kim has seen evidence of this in a home visit with Ann. Using cognitive theory, Kim could help Ann to identify ways in which Ann has strived to be a good mother and the hopes she has for her kids in the future. Kim counters Ann's view of herself as a poor parent, offering an alternative perspective. In this way, Kim helps Ann restructure her thinking about her capacities as a mother and encourages Ann to recognize that she has the capacity to be a good parent.

Ego Psychology

Ego psychology is really part of a family of theories often called personality theories. The theory assumes that behaviour is a product of both rational and irrational processes. While some behaviours occur because of cognition, others are related to the "irrational" emotional world.

Ego psychology holds that, "The ego is considered to be a mental structure of the personality that is responsible for negotiating between the internal needs [of the person] and the outside world" (Goldstein, 1986, p. 375). "The ego is the part of the personality that contains the basic functions essential to the individual's successful adaptation to the environment. Ego functions are innate and develop through maturation and the interaction along biopsychosocial factors" (Goldstein, 1984, p. 9). While ego psychologists have developed a number of concepts that are useful to social workers, one of the most important of these is the concept of defence mechanisms. A defence is a mechanism that the ego uses to protect itself from anxiety by keeping intolerable threats from conscious awareness (Goldstein, 1986).

Some of the early ego psychologists were Freudian or neo-Freudian psychoanalysts. Erik Erikson is one of the most famous. In his important book *Childhood and Society* (1950), Erikson argued that successful maturation in adulthood depends on mastery of eight stages of child development. Erikson's approach is psychosocial, meaning that he sees both inner forces and the environment shaping child and adult development. (It is recognized that Erikson's framework has its shortcomings because it is based solely on the study of males and a male norm of human development.)

While Freud held that early conscious and unconscious experiences shape almost all of personality, most ego psychologists believe that personality is also determined by interaction with the environment throughout life and that social interaction is crucial. Both Freudians and early ego psychologists thought environment was important, but the latter elevated it to a more prominent position.

White (1963) broke from the Freudian tradition by arguing that along with innate drives such as sex and hunger, people are also driven toward mastery and competence. This need to explore the world, according to White, is a powerful human motivator.

Using Ego Psychology in Focused Assessment

Assessment using principles of ego psychology focuses on understanding the inner person. How does the client protect herself or himself from psychological stress? What defence mechanisms are used? Do the defences lead to pathological behaviour? Can the client learn how to use adaptive defences? How does the client deal with stress? How does the client view herself? What is the client's level of self-esteem? How does the client view her self-competence? How does the client attempt to achieve mastery? What developmental stages have been successfully completed? Were some of the stages incomplete? What effect does this have on the person's current life?

Case Example

Kim and Ann 

Kim recognizes that everyone uses defence mechanisms, but some that Ann uses are counterproductive (some ego psychologists would say pathological). Ann tends to rationalize away her problems. All of us sometimes do this, but Ann tends to deny that she neglects her children's care needs. This denial is one of the reasons why the child protection agency has placed her children in temporary custody.

Kim could explore Ann's childhood using Erikson's framework. The intent would be to determine whether Ann experienced developmental problems at any of Erikson's eight stages. If mastery had not been achieved, the worker (in this case also a therapist) would probably want to engage in therapy to help Ann achieve mastery of the stages in which she experienced difficulty. This might help her understand her children's needs and reduce the neglect.

Workers in child welfare settings might sometimes find ego psychology useful in understanding the problems that Ann faces. However, intervention based on ego psychology often involves long-term therapy and is seldom the preferred choice of action in child protection situations, such as neglect of children and parenting difficulties. A more likely use of ego psychology is in clinical practice in mental health.

Crisis Theory

Unlike most of the theories used by social workers, crisis theory addresses a particular life event. The life event can be traumatic and unexpected (such as a sudden death in the family), or natural events like marriage or the first day of school (Barker, 1987, p. 36).

People in crisis often respond to either a stressful situation they face or some existing condition that appears during a crisis (Zastrow, 1995, pp. 452–53). People who seek help have usually experienced a precipitating event that is often very stressful, such as the loss of a job, a big fight at home, or an accident. Most crises are relatively short term. Pinpointing and understanding the dynamics of the event is often a necessary step in assessment. Crisis theory holds that people who experience a crisis go through a predictable process until the crisis is resolved. The resolution can be either dysfunctional (e.g., grief turns into long-term social and psychological withdrawal) or functional (e.g., grief dissipates and is replaced by a new and strong level of functioning) (Wicks and Parsons, 1984) and can sometimes lead to growth. People who are undergoing a crisis are particularly vulnerable but also are often ready to make constructive use of help. Because of this element of readiness to receive help, crisis theory is very important to social workers in some settings (Germain, 1984; Golan, 1986).

In social work, much can be done during a crisis period to help clients function again in a healthy way. Assisting people to draw on their own capacities and strengths, when possible, is an important part of this work.

Using Crisis Theory in Focused Assessment

Crisis theory focuses attention on a specific life event. Crisis theory holds that people who are experiencing crisis are often in great need of help and are willing to make constructive use of it. Examples of assessment questions that flow from this theory are: What precipitating event led to the problem or crisis? What precipitating event led to seeking help? Were the events the same? What are their dynamics? How did the events affect the client and others close to the client? What immediate steps can be taken to begin resolution?

Case Example

Kim and Ann

Ann is not in a serious state of crisis even though the removal of her children has caused her considerable stress. Suppose, however, that after a few days Ann realizes all of the implications of the recent events and becomes depressed and potentially suicidal as a result. Afraid of what she might do, she calls a crisis hotline. The hotline workers would be responsible for assessing her state of crisis, helping her manage it, and intervening in other ways if needed.

Knowledge about suicide risk is important for all social workers since it can save a person's life. Assessing risk of harm to persons requires considerable preparation and guidance. Social workers assess risk of harm in client situations through (a) the identification of risk (dangers, hazards, and threats to safety); (b) risk prediction (whether the existing risks are likely to lead to danger, based on collected information and professional knowledge); (c) planning for risk management (action to minimize risk of danger, determination of greatest and least risk in possible courses of action, and possible consequences of selected actions); (d) review of the plan for action, and (e) back to other steps as needed (Bailey, 2002, p. 175).

Knowledge from Psychiatry—DSM-IV

This category is different from the others in that it does not reflect knowledge from a theory or perspective but from a type of practice. We include it here because social workers in many fields of practice either work directly with psychiatrists or other mental health professionals, or work indirectly with psychiatrists through referrals, reports, and other connections with the medical system. There is no doubt that psychiatric diagnosis has had a considerable influence on social work assessment, particularly in mental health settings. Psychiatric diagnosis and prognosis of a mental illness often implies levels of social and psychological functioning in a client. In some settings social workers, along with a variety of other professionals, are taught how to formally diagnose mental illness and are expected to do so in their work. This makes it important for social workers to understand the use of the DSM-IV, its interpretation in the workplace, and the implications of a diagnostic label for clients.

The Diagnostic and Statistical Manual of Mental Disorders, 4th edition, or DSM-IV, is the work of the American Psychiatric Association (APA, 1994). It is a standardized source that guides clinical diagnosis of mental illness and other kinds of problems. The first manual appeared in 1952, essentially to help psychiatrists use common names for disorders (Gerhart, 1990, p. 80). The current edition provides not only a detailed description of each category of illness so that illnesses can be readily diagnosed, but also a way to evaluate adaptive functioning and the severity of psychological stressors, and to suggest a prognosis. The manual draws heavily on biological and medical knowledge.

If a correct diagnosis can be made, then a reasonable and effective treatment plan can follow. To much of psychiatry, this means that if the diagnosis is accurate then appropriate chemical treatment can take place; therefore, psychiatry devotes considerable attention to diagnosis. However, in social work—as well as in psychiatry itself—the use of the DSM-IV is controversial.

Sheafor, Horejsi, and Horejsi (2000) summarize much of the most common criticism: "Many social workers question the appropriateness of this diagnostic manual for social work practice. They are bothered by the labelling inherent in the DSM system, by the manual's exclusive focus on pathology, and its lack of attention to environmental context" (p. 375).

Some call diagnosis and the DSM-IV "arbitrary," meaning that the scientific connection between the various diagnostic categories and the reality of symptoms and illness are weak (Chambliss, 2000, pp. 170–74). Hepworth and Larsen (1993, p. 253) see psychiatric diagnosis as having little value to social workers except as it pertains to certain mood disorders, including severe depression and bipolar disorder.

As a response and complement to the DSM-IV, some social workers have developed a "diagnostic" classification system based on person-in-the-environment or ecosystems principles (Kemp, Whittaker, and Tracy, 1997, p. 101). The Person-in-Environment System, or PIE (Karls and Wandrei, 1992), which is in limited use, attempts to "describe, classify and code problems in adult social functioning" (Sheafor, Horejsi, and Horejsi, 2000, p. 372; see also NASW, 1994). PIE recognizes four areas where problems can occur: social functioning, the environment, mental health, and physical health.

Although both emphasize individual problems, the DSM system is unlike the PIE because it draws very heavily on biological and medical knowledge, while the PIE is based on theories that connect individual behaviour with the environment.

While the PIE may be useful to some, it is often difficult to reliably and accurately place people and their behaviours into diagnostic categories, a problem that is shared with the DSM-IV. Further, the complexity of problems and the differences among individuals make it difficult for any diagnostic system based on categorization to meet one of the main goals of such schemes: to prescribe a particular form of treatment. Nevertheless, because of the widespread use of diagnosis, it is important that social workers have a working knowledge of the diagnostic process using systems such as the DSM-IV and the PIE.

Using the DSM-IV in Focused Assessment

Examples of assessment questions that flow from the DSM-IV are: Does the client suffer from a psychiatric illness? If so, what is the nature of the illness? How does it affect the client's ability to function? to work? to form social relationships? What level of social skills does the client have? What medications is the client taking? How do the medications affect the client's behaviour? What is the prognosis?

Case Example

Kim and Ann

As a responsible social worker, Kim needs to be aware of the possibility that Ann could suffer from a mental illness. It could be, for instance, that Ann suffers from chronic and severe depression that affects much of her life, including her parenting abilities. The DSM-IV would give her some indication of how depression comes about and its treatment. If Kim observes such signs, then she should make an appropriate referral. Kim may even have to go further and broker a referral if Ann is reluctant to get help for her depression.

Even if Ann is seriously depressed, Kim's responsibility in her role as a child protection worker is not to diagnose and treat the depression. Instead, it is to broker the referral and to continue to work with Ann, accounting for the fact that she is experiencing depression and that her depression will likely affect the plans for the return of her children.

Knowledge about Family Relationships and Processes

The knowledge that underpins family-focused intervention and family therapy is important to social work, since families are often the focus of practice in numerous settings. The family is an interdependent group in which members' needs and interests are addressed. It can also be the site of many problems (e.g., parenting issues, child maltreatment, substance abuse, illness, and financial strain) (Zastrow, 1995, pp. 220–24) and the context in which members grow, develop, care for one another, and participate in memorable occasions together (e.g., weddings, vacations, births, anniversaries, and funerals).

Systems theory has shaped thinking about family assessment and intervention, in which the family is seen as a system interacting with the environment (Hepworth, Rooney, and Larsen, 1997, p. 277). Family members all interact with one another within the family system, which has effects throughout the family system and beyond it. Helping a person within the family means working with the whole family, since other members are affected by an individual's change efforts and can help by supporting these efforts.

There are many related, specific areas of knowledge, such as **family life cycle** tasks and development, culture, family structure, emotional expression, **family norms** and rules, roles, communication, decision making, strengths and capacities, resilience, power, functions, and boundaries (Hepworth, Rooney, and Larsen, 1997, pp. 278–316).

Exploring knowledge development in family therapy since the 1940s, Becvar and Becvar (2000) include in their review a description of the social construction of meaning and truth, multiple views, the importance of language as a vehicle of power, the use of a story or narrative, and the role of the therapist as impartial actor (see also Freedman and Combs, 1996).

Using Knowledge about Family Relationships and Processes in Focused Assessment

Assessment questions might include: How are individuals' needs for care and attention met in the family, and is this satisfactory? How do family members communicate with one another? How does culture play a role in the family? Are there problems in communication? How is power distributed in the family, and is there conflict about it? How are decisions made? What are the family's strengths? Is the family resilient in the face of problems or change? What rules does the family set (e.g., regarding chores, children's bedtime, and dinner times)? What are individual members' views of the family and its situation?

Case Example

Kim and Ann

After much work, Ann finally has her children returned to her. Kim continues to work with Ann to ensure that she is able to apply the learning from her parenting classes to caring for her three children. In home visits with Ann, Kim sees that Ann's oldest child, Jim, takes on many adult tasks such as cooking and minding the younger children. Ann speaks to this nine-year-old as though he is an adult. Perhaps she copes by relying on him when she feels tired or depressed. However, this is having an impact on Jim, who seems to find it difficult to play with other children his own age and spends much of his time with his mother. Ann feels that Jim is being a really good son and rewards him with special treats from time to time. Ann has few friends from whom she can seek support and companionship, and finds that Jim sometimes offers her these.

In Kim's assessment, there is a problem in the boundary between mother and child. She wants to make a referral to a family therapist in a local family counselling agency because she knows that this kind of problem can create difficulties for everyone in the family. Jim will someday resent not having his own life in activities with his friends. He might also begin to view his mother as weak and without authority. Ann consents to the referral since she wants to help her children and herself. She states that she can see how much she relies on Jim and wants to explore how she can help him while helping herself too.

Theory about Groups

Group work is useful in many social work practice settings, whether it involves clients, coworkers, or others in some collaborative activity. Theory pertaining to groups reflects such areas as group development, tasks and goals, process, growth, dynamics and interaction, cohesion, roles, skills and strengths, power, conflict, norms, and values (Brill, 1998, pp. 182–83; Hepworth, Rooney, and Larsen, 1997, pp. 330–41). A family is a kind of group. So too are groups that have been formed or that come together for therapy, education, self-help, program planning, community projects, or some other reason. Usually a group is formed in response to a need, which shapes its purpose and goals. Social workers, if they are leaders of or consultants to groups, require knowledge of theories about groups in order to be helpful.

In feminist group work, for example, the social worker must understand the interest in affiliation (connection) among women and the importance of emotional maintenance (see Butler and Wintram, 1991).

Using Theory about Groups in Focused Assessment

Assessment questions might include: What is the interest of group members in participating? What is the level of cohesion among the individuals? What roles have individual members taken on, and are these satisfactory? How can the group's development be described? What are the dynamics in the group's relations? How does the group deal with conflict? What skills and strengths exist in the group, and how are they used? Do certain members hold more power than others? If so, how does this affect group maintenance? What norms and values are present in the group?

Case Example

Kim and Ann

Suppose, after the return of her children, Ann loses her new job due to her deteriorating mental health. She also experiences low self-worth and isolation at home with the younger children. Kim, after phoning Ann, is concerned that Ann is not doing well and needs some help. Kim knows of a local community centre that has started groups for women who are raising children on their own. She knows that such a group could enhance Ann's growth and provide her with a supportive environment in which to realize her skills and strengths. Kim also knows that childcare is available and that the centre is close to Ann's home. When told about the resource, Ann agrees to join the group.

In the group, Ann meets other women and takes part in discussions about caring for children, managing on a fixed income, and community organizations that offer resources. At first the group members wait for the facilitator, a social worker with the community centre, to lead discussions, but soon members begin to interact more with one another and set their own agenda for each session. The social worker encourages these efforts and supports the group's development.

Knowledge about Community Development

Community development is focused on work with community groups or voluntary organizations, usually in a small geographic area (community-based). The Internet has broadened this definition through the electronic linkage of people who form communities bound by common interests and goals (e.g., websites and chat rooms set up for environmental, antiwar, and other activists). Community development is difficult to define precisely and may be seen as social work that is community-based, carried out in a community or "street-front" organization, and involves community members or occurs as part of community outreach activities. It is often framed as beneficial or positive (Popple, 2002). However, community organizations are not all good or harmless. Some community development and organizing may, in fact, include activities that are racist and harmful to immigrants, children, or women (e.g., neo-Nazi groups, child pornography rings, and others). In social work, the CASW code of ethics is applied to all practice, and any community organization efforts that contravene professional values, principles, and guidelines cannot be supported.

Some forms of community development may be promoted by the state and conducted in top-down fashion, while other kinds of community development can be termed bottom-up or collective community action. Bottom-up community organizing may represent a direct challenge to the state and some groups in society (Popple, 2002). Some methods used by bottom-up community organizations may be perceived as a threat (e.g., occupation of government buildings or other forms of protest).

Community development has been a part of social work since the settlement house movement and continues to respond to local needs not met by governments or other social service agencies. Community development may be seen as a process involving "the process of establishing, or re-establishing, structures of human community within which new ways of relating, organising social life and meeting human need become possible" (Ife, 2002, p. 2). Community development work can involve a range of projects or initiatives that are aimed to improve community life for members. Examples include a local playground and green space for children to play in, community drop-in centres for youth and older persons, a petition to city government for better policing or street lighting, and others.

In community work, it is important that social workers act as facilitators of community members' efforts, advocating for them and fostering skills in leadership and other capacities among them rather than taking the lead themselves. Without the active participation of community members, there can be little ownership of change efforts by the community. Colleen Lundy (2004) suggests that empowerment occurs through community members' active participation in the decisions that affect them. Their voices and pooled experiences, skills, and knowledge are critical in the process of change.

Using Knowledge about Community Development in Focused Assessment

In community development work, knowledge encompasses perspectives on locality and neighbourhood development and social planning; group work (Rothman, 1996); organizing approaches and methods in mobilization of individuals and groups; running community meetings; collaborating with other staff and volunteers; problem solving; conflict mediation; and, often, grant proposal writing and fund raising (Homan, 1999).

Case Example

Kim and Ann 

Suppose that Ann, with other mothers in her neighbourhood, decides to ask a voluntary organization's social worker to help them establish a play area for young children. Little park or play space is available in the poor inner-city neighbourhood area where they live, and families can not afford the recreation programs available elsewhere. One local home had been gutted by fire and was awaiting demolition by the city. The women thought that the empty lot could be developed into a green space with play equipment for children.

The community social worker, Lilo, was asked to respond to the women's request and began to work with them. He asked about their backgrounds and experiences, finding that some women knew how to write letters and make phone calls to local politicians. Others had organizing skills and connections with local businesses and schools. Lilo wanted Ann and her neighbours to build their capacities and utilize their collective skills to gain the attention of the city council. He advocated for them and supported their efforts. He also acted as a consultant to the women and arranged for meeting space and fax, photocopier, and phone access at the community organization office where he worked. The women needed money to print flyers and Lilo helped them to write proposals for funding.

Theories Underlying the Structural Approach

A structural approach to social work emphasizes inequality and social injustice (Payne, 1997, pp. 214–15; Lundy, 2004). It suggests ways to address these issues in everyday practice with individuals, families, groups, and communities. In structural social work practice, macro analysis is connected to working with individuals.

The goal of structural social work is to help people regain control of their lives (see Chapter 12). The approach makes the assumption that people's problems are often caused by, or at least closely related to, failures in social institutions such as the economy, or, at a lower level, difficulties in understanding a bureaucracy or unfair treatment by an agency such as the court, the police, a child welfare agency, or the mental health system. Such problems are common. The task of the social worker is to help people gain control in their dealings with social institutions.

Using the Structural Approach in Focused Assessment

Assessment that uses a structural approach focuses on the institutions of society, including political institutions. Examples of assessment questions include: Does inequity affect the client's situation? Is injustice evident? How do existing inequities and injustices of programs or institutions affect people whom the programs or institutions are meant to serve? What is their power? How do they use this power? Is this use of power unfair or unjust? What resources exist to address these problems?

If the client is an individual or a family, similar assessment questions can be asked but with the focus on the effect of the institution on the client. For example, how fairly has a social agency dealt with a client? How can the client take charge in dealing with the agency? A social worker might also ask how power relations play a role in family relations (e.g., gender or age) and whether an individual or a family faces social discrimination that impedes access to jobs or housing.

Case Example

Kim and Ann ▼

A week after the court granted temporary custody of her children to foster care, Ann learns that her social assistance payments will stop. While she expected a decrease in the payments, she did not expect complete denial. Both Kim and Ann believe this is very unfair and probably against the policy and related rules of Public Social Services. The lack of assistance is a major problem for Ann and is compounded by her belief that powerful institutions have taken control of her life and that she can do nothing about it. Ann has always deferred to their decisions without questioning them, but often with considerable anger.

With Ann, Kim examined the real power of Public Social Services and the workings of its bureaucracy, as well as Ann's ability to make the bureaucracy work for her. A general goal of this assessment was to help Ann take charge of her relationship with the agency so that she was treated fairly; the specific goal was to have her assistance payments reinstated.

Unlike the other areas that we have covered in this section, which refer to specific theories, perspectives, or approaches, the section that follows refers to a set of principles that shape and help filter assessment.

Anti-Oppressive Practice

The significance of anti-oppressive social work was discussed in some detail in Chapter 7. We noted that this perspective is important when working with clients who have experienced discrimination, marginalization, or oppression and also with everyone we encounter in social work. In recent years, there has been renewed concern with oppression as a fundamental focus of social work practice. Anti-oppressive practice is emerging as an important form of social work intervention that has come to represent good social work.

"Oppression is generally understood as the domination of subordinate groups in society by a powerful (politically, economically, socially, and culturally) group" (Mullaly, 2002, p. 27). Personal oppression occurs when individuals are singled out for oppression by the more powerful. Examples are personal discrimination against an immigrant family in search of adequate housing or attacks on people who are gay. Cultural oppression involves a society's general attitudes, assumptions, and ideas that help to sustain the oppression of a particular group of people; for example, men living on the street. Believing that such people are all addicted to alcohol or drugs, are (or have been) engaged in crime, and have no interest in work represents cultural oppression by our society. Oppression at the structural level is evident when policies and practices create and maintain economic inequality, favouring those who are wealthy and more powerful over those who do not have such resources. For instance, many argue that the large number of the working poor is largely due to our capitalist economic system.

Examples of oppression are numerous. The colonization of Aboriginal peoples, as discussed in Chapter 11, is a prime illustration. Members of nondominant ethnocultural groups are often oppressed through institutional racism and other processes. People who live on the street are oppressed, as are women—who, as a collective, are often dominated by economic and social institutions shaped primarily for male interests. Those who are mentally ill frequently find themselves disenfranchised and dominated by the powerful health and legal systems. Those who are poor generally lack power and are at the mercy of the economic system. The list could go on and on. The key point is that oppression causes social problems (see Mullaly, 2002 for a detailed explanation).

We adopt Ann Bishop's view (2002) that class represents a major structural form of oppression while other sources of oppression, such as sexism, racism, and those based on physical ability, sexual orientation, age, and others, cut across class. As Bishop explains, "on a structural level, class is different from other forms of oppression such as racism, ageism and sexism. Class is not just a factor in inequalities of wealth, privilege, and power; it *is* that inequality. Other forms of oppression help keep the hierarchy of power [class] in place" (p. 82). For example, oppression according to cultural background or skin colour can affect many, but if one has substantial financial resources, these factors may be mitigated to some degree. Those with the lowest income and fewest assets may experience the effects of racism according to cultural background and skin colour more keenly.

Using Anti-Oppressive Practice in Focused Assessment

Anti-oppressive practice is social work practice that challenges oppression and subordination. Leonard (1997) and Mullaly (2002) argue that anti-oppressive practice must take place at both the personal and structural levels and that the interaction between personal and structural oppression is critical in its challenge. An example of personal anti-oppressive practice is to address, through counselling, the harm that oppression has done to a person. Another often cited goal is to help a client become liberated from felt oppression and subordination.

At the structural level, anti-oppressive practice attempts to change the social policies, programs, institutions, and structures that cause oppression. Sometimes clients who experience oppression may find it therapeutic and empowering to engage in social change efforts. For example, this may be the case with Aboriginal persons who as children experienced abuse in foster care. As adults, they attempt to help change the system that caused these problems.

Although we can readily identify groups of people that can be categorized as oppressed (e.g., those who are poor, Aboriginal, addicted to street drugs, etc.), it cannot be assumed that the persons within such groups will themselves feel oppressed. We need to acknowledge that people's own views about whether and how oppression affects them are important. All persons are unique and have the right to interpret for themselves their life experience, rather than having it interpreted for them.

At the heart of anti-oppressive assessment and intervention is the use of reflection and reflexivity by social workers. Understanding the role of class in people's lives and the effects of class with intersecting forms of oppression such as racism, sexism, heterosexism, and ageism is important in all client situations. This is because past experiences and current problems are often related to these effects. It is also possible that people have learned how to overcome or deal with such effects by drawing on supports or strengths. Assessment also needs to consider continuing oppression that is experienced by clients. Critical questions that emerge from a focus on oppression might be: Has the client experienced oppression? What is its nature? Was/is it personal, cultural, and/or structural? How does it affect the client? How does the client perceive the oppression? What can be done about it?

Case Example

Kim and Ann

Not much is known about oppression that Ann has faced, but there are some clues. She has received social assistance for a number of years and has frequent encounters with child welfare agencies. Likely these events need exploration because structural, personal, and perhaps cultural oppression may affect Ann's situation. Kim needs to know the perception Ann has about the effects of oppression in her life situation and make some decisions with Ann regarding what can be done about it.

The view Ann has about herself as a mother, fed for many years by verbal and physical abuse from her husband, represents a form of personal oppression and Kim should explore with Ann the need for counselling to address the hurt that remains from this abusive relationship. Also, Kim needs to explore in some detail with Ann to determine other oppressive situations that continue to affect her life and, if found, determine how to challenge these.

Culture

In Chapter 7, we also discussed the significance of cultural orientation and cultural sensitivity in social work. Cultural factors can strongly affect how clients behave and how they interpret and understand problems, so they are central to social work assessment. Culture is important in all of our lives, not just those of our clients.

Referring to culture, Sheafor, Horejsi, and Horejsi (2000, p. 168) suggest that social workers need to adjust assessment to the culture of the clients with whom they are working. How they see clients depends partly on the worker's culture. Shulman (1999, p. 121) argues that cultural differences can create major barriers between social workers and clients. This is particularly true in assessment.

All interpretations of theory and assessment are culturally dependent. This means that the application of the theory is, at least to some degree, shaped by culture. For instance, in role theory, the definition of deviance or occurrence of role conflicts is different in different cultures. Likewise, what is seen as an appropriate use of power may also depend on cultural factors.

Using Culture in Focused Assessment

It is important for social workers to understand how culture shapes the problems that people present. Questions to consider include: How are the problems interpreted? How do religious or cultural beliefs contribute to or affect the problems? What religious or ethnocultural resources are available that the client might make use of? Are there some cultural beliefs that constrain the client or cause harm? If the social worker comes from a different culture than the client's, the worker must attempt to understand how her or his own culture might cloud or colour personal perceptions. Often social workers, in assessing clients who share the same majority culture, take cultural beliefs for granted and do not explore their effects on clients.

Case Example

Kim and Ann

Kim and Ann are both of Western European decent and are both from blue-collar families. Kim is both English and German, and Ann is second-generation Dutch. Both consider themselves Canadian, not members of an ethnocultural minority group, and generally share the same cultural beliefs.

Ann and her family share a strong work ethic that has deep roots in their Dutch heritage. This has made accepting welfare a bitter pill to swallow for Ann. Kim also wants to explore how Ann's family views child rearing. For example, do they think it is acceptable for small children to be cared for by a nine-year-old sibling? The answer to this question might help Kim understand Ann's decision to leave her children alone.

Ecosystems

The ecosystems perspective was introduced earlier in this chapter. Following are some ideas that are drawn from ecosystems theory (Hepworth, Rooney, and Larsen, 1997; Germain, 1979, 1991; Germain and Gitterman, 1980, 1995) that generate important explanations and principles, many of them testable, and can be used in broad knowledge-based assessment. The first two are derived from a systems perspective and the remainder from ecology.

- *Open systems.* An open system is a functional system, while a closed system is dysfunctional. Change and growth tend not to occur in closed systems.
- *Transactions are reciprocal.* Resources are exchanged among systems, with all systems both receiving and sending resources. This reciprocal exchange is necessary for the well-being and growth of systems.
- *Habitat.* This is a central concept that nicely illustrates the ecological metaphor. As the name implies, it is the place where people (or any biological organisms) live. Habitat must be a place where growth can take place and people feel secure. A good habitat must have productive resources that people can use. When resources are deficient, social, economic, and personal problems often develop.
- *Niche.* This is the position that an organism (in biology, a species) occupies in the environment, including the habitat. For people, it is the position that they occupy in order to experience self-esteem and to feel wanted. A niche is where a person grows and prospers. This concept, which is also very important in the strengths perspective, is developed in more detail in Chapter 10. The ecosystems principle of niche hypothesizes that if people cannot find a good niche, social, economic, and personal problems often emerge.
- *Person/environment fit.* There must be a fit between the person and his or her environment so that both mutually experience benefits and growth. Fit (or the lack of it) occurs through social exchanges. When social exchanges become predominantly negative, development, growth, and general functioning often become impaired.
- *Stress.* Stress in ecosystems theory is similar to the general use of the concept. It is an emotional, personal, or inner response to an internal or environmental stimulus or source and can be either functional or dysfunctional.
- *Coping measures.* These are, in a sense, the ecological equivalents of defence mechanisms in ego psychology. Instead of entirely focusing on internal psychological processes, the ecological view of coping measures is a combination of personal and environmental resources used to deal with life's stressors. A person experiences a stressor, assesses it based on her or his knowledge and experience, and reacts. Stress is normal, and all of us face it in our lives. Sometimes the reaction to a stressful event or situation might put a person into crisis, where emotions cloud clear thinking. The kinds of coping measures used depend on how the person perceives the seriousness of the situation and the resources available to her or him. Some coping measures that people might use to reduce or eradicate stress include seeking information, taking no action at all, drawing on personal resources such as self-esteem, taking time to think things through, denying the problem, and making changes in the environment to deal with the stressor (Germain, 1984).

Using Ecosystems in Focused Assessment

Maybe the most important question that ecosystems poses is: What is the person-in-the-environment fit? Are there problems with this fit? If so, are they sources of the client's problems?

Further examples of questions that flow from this perspective include the following: Does the client experience an open or a closed system? If open, what strengths can the client use? If closed, what factors make it closed? What can be done to help interactions? What is the quality of the client's habitat? What are the most important resources in the habitat? How can the client best use the habitat? What niches does the client find productive? Where are the problems with the niches? What niches might the client like to develop? What are the client's major stressors? Are these stressors internal or environmental? How does the client react to them? What coping measures does the client use? How can they be improved?

Case Example

Kim and Ann

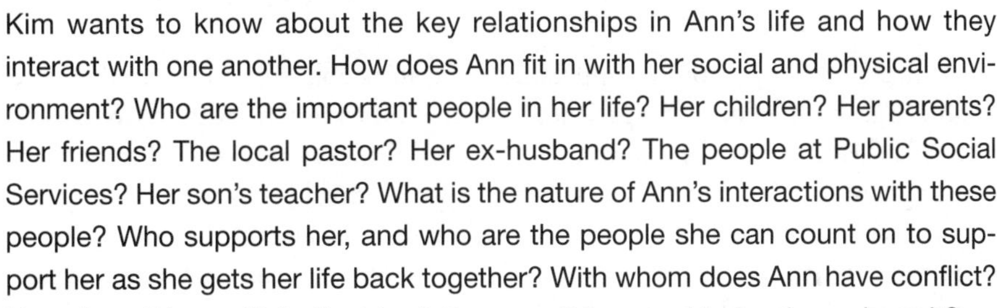

Kim wants to know about the key relationships in Ann's life and how they interact with one another. How does Ann fit in with her social and physical environment? Who are the important people in her life? Her children? Her parents? Her friends? The local pastor? Her ex-husband? The people at Public Social Services? Her son's teacher? What is the nature of Ann's interactions with these people? Who supports her, and who are the people she can count on to support her as she gets her life back together? With whom does Ann have conflict? How does this conflict affect her? Does anything need to be done about it?

Another question that Kim needs to address is whether Ann has a good social niche. The initial assessment has revealed that Ann feels that she does not really fit in anywhere. Ecosystems holds that all people need to feel that they belong. For most, life is empty and lonely if they feel unwanted and that they do not "fit in." Probably one of the most important things Kim needs to help Ann accomplish is to find a comfortable social niche. Carefully exploring Ann's relationships with others may help Ann and Kim develop and use a good social niche for Ann.

Role Theory

Role theory is not an integrated theory but, like many others used by social workers, is a collection of related concepts. Role theory holds that behaviour is a function of social expectations. Groups at all levels of society—from small, primary groups such as families to large groups such as social institutions—set expectations that prescribe the behaviours of people.

These expectations are called norms. Expectations or norms are usually grouped into categories called statuses. When people act in accordance with norms associated with a status, they are conforming to a role.

For example, societies set norms that prescribe what a father is supposed to do. A man's family of origin and current family likely also set norms for the father in a family. This combination of norms defines for that family the status of father. When the father acts in accordance with the prescribed norms, he is carrying out the role of father. Role theorists argue that social norms are powerful determinants of individual behaviour. This is particularly so when clear formal or informal sanctions exist for those who do not act according to these norms. In some societies, people who do not perform well in their roles are shunned by community members or denied certain resources (e.g., loans or social support).

If a person's behaviour violates the norms of a role and there is an attempt to penalize that person, then the behaviour of that person may be seen as deviant. For example, if a father abandons his family, he will likely be defined as deviant, and others, including the legal system, may attempt to force him to conform, at least to the role of provider. Deviance is a behaviour path or trait of an individual that does not conform to the normative expectations of others and toward which others take negative sanctions. Often these sanctions are forms of punishment.

Sometimes norms may conflict and cause strain in people who fill more than one role. Role conflict occurs when people experience incompatible expectations from two or more different sources (Davis, 1986). To illustrate, a teenage father may be expected to be a provider for his young family. His circle of male friends may also want him to continue to participate in their activities. These two different expectations may create conflict within the young father. He may have to choose which expectations to conform to and risk failure in either his role as father or as "one of the guys."

Another problem suggested by role theory is called role ambiguity, which occurs when expectations are unclear. Unclear expectations make it difficult for a person to conform because the norms are unclear. Members of one culture who live in another culture may experience role ambiguity because they have difficulty interpreting the social norms of the new culture.

Using Role Theory in Focused Assessment

Assessment that uses concepts from role theory focuses on the relationship between norms and behaviours. Like ecosystems, the focus is on the person-in-the-environment. Usually the norms expressed by small groups, including primary groups such as the family, are the most relevant. Examples of assessment questions to pursue are: Does the client conform to important norms of relevant others? If not, do others define the client as deviant? If so, how does this affect the client? How does it affect the client's relationships with others? What are the client's most important roles? How well does she or he perform these roles? Does she or he feel comfortable in them? Are they rewarding? Does role conflict occur? If so, how does this affect the client? How can the role conflict be resolved?

Case Example

Kim and Ann 

In some ways a role theory and an ecosystems analysis of Ann's situation are similar. Central to an ecosystems analysis are the questions: What is the nature of key relationships, and how do these affect Ann? Parallel to these queries, role theorists might ask: What are the key expectations of the major actors in Ann's life? Does Ann conform to or deviate from these expectations? Do the expectations cause her role conflict or role strain? Are they ambiguous?

Kim's initial assessment suggests that Ann may frequently feel role conflict in her role as mother and as sole provider. The only jobs that she has been able to find that pay reasonable wages require considerable evening work. This is also the time during which she feels she should be with her children. Ann's solution to this problem has been to seek public assistance. As a result, the family barely has sufficient income to survive, causing additional strain for Ann.

Labelling Theory

Labelling theory, which is closely related to role theory, was introduced in Chapter 6. A person is seen as deviant when she or he breaks social rules. Usually this occurs when a person does not conform to role expectations. Sometimes the rules that are broken are formal ones, such as laws, but more often rules are informal. For example, we all have an expressed or implied understanding of how we are supposed to behave in a wide variety of social situations. If we break these codes, we may be perceived as deviant by others.

Labelling is the process that others use to help define behaviours as deviant. To labelling theorists it is not the tag or label—such as homosexual, schizophrenic, delinquent, and so on—that is important but the implications and consequences of the tag. For example, the damage occurs when a person who is tagged "schizophrenic" is ostracized, discriminated against, degraded, segregated, or otherwise treated in a negative manner and faces forms of social control because of the schizophrenia. Labelling theory suggests that these consequences can be devastating for individuals who are defined as deviant.

Using Labelling Theory in Focused Assessment

Most perspectives and theories that social workers use are micro-oriented or, like role and ecosystems theory, centre on the person-in-the-environment. The primary unit of analysis in the first instance is the individual, and the second is the relationship between the environment and individual. Labelling shifts the focus of assessment to the analysis of groups and the larger social system. While intervention might be intended to help clients adapt to situations that label, the real intervention should be with those who do the labelling. Thus, the target of intervention is often not the client. To illustrate, suppose Ibrahim is having trouble in school and has been referred to the school social worker. The worker discovers that Ibrahim's teacher is treating him differently because he is a recent immigrant. The fact that the teacher has very low expectations of immigrants has contributed to Ibrahim's difficulty in learning at school. In this case scenario, the social worker should target for intervention the teacher's labelling and her views of immigrants.

Examples of general assessment questions that arise from labelling theory include the following: Is the client perceived by others as breaking a social code or rule? Is the client defined as deviant, at least by some? If so, what are the labelling processes? How do these affect the client? What are the social and psychological consequences of the labelling for the client?

Case Example

Kim and Ann ▼

Ann's Dutch background has reinforced a strong work ethic. As far as her parents and siblings are concerned, Ann has failed in her efforts to provide for her family. An implied but clear expectation was that Ann would marry, have children, and be supported by a responsible husband. The marriage failed, and hence so did her main means of support. Ann's family also expected, after the marriage failure, that Ann would be able to manage both employment and parenting. These are the same roles in which Ann experiences major role conflict. Again, in the eyes of her parents and siblings, she is a failure. Her family's disapproval has contributed to the erosion of Ann's self-confidence and self-esteem.

Kim wants to help Ann find ways to rationally and emotionally handle and defend against the labelling. Even as it occurs, Ann might find ways to mitigate its effects. Kim also, with Ann's permission, wants to target some members of her family for intervention, hoping to stem the labelling and improve family relationships.

Strengths Perspective

The strengths perspective will be discussed in detail in Chapter 10. A strengths approach capitalizes on people's capacities, vitality, abilities, strong points, talents, courage, and power. The approach uses people's own resources to help them grow as human beings, improve their quality of life, and develop their own problem-solving skills. It is a developmental process that assumes that, if growth and quality of life improve, improved problem-solving skills will follow. This approach incorporates ideas such as wellness, support, empowerment, and wholeness. It also assumes that improving a person's quality of life will often contribute to other gains.

There is a connection between the ecosystems and strengths approaches. For example, finding good habitats and niches are both strengths and ecosystems principles. Like the ecosystems approach, the strengths perspective emphasizes the connections that people have with their environment. Both perspectives view the relationship between the person and the environment as an inseparable, integrated whole. Both approaches also emphasize empowerment.

Using the Strengths Perspective in Focused Assessment

Assessment principles that flow from the strengths perspective, as one would anticipate, focus on understanding strengths. What are the client's strengths? How does the client use his or her strengths? Does the client perceive that he or she has strengths? How does the client typically handle problems? Can the client muster sufficient inner or environmental resources to solve his or her own problems? Does the client have the capacity to solve these problems?

How can the social worker help the client develop his or her own problem-solving skills? How does the client empower himself or herself? What can the social worker do to help the client empower himself or herself? To what extent is the client resilient?

Some of the questions that flow from this perspective are similar to those from the ecosystems perspective. For example, what is the client's niche? Is the niche functional or dysfunctional? Might the client find self-help groups helpful? Can a self-help group become a comfortable niche for the client?

Case Example

Kim and Ann

A central function of Kim's assessment should be a good understanding of Ann's strengths. Reference to some of the previous analysis may help illustrate.

For example, from role theory, what roles does Ann find important? Which roles make her feel that she has or can gain control over her life? Ecosystems suggests that finding a productive niche is important. Who in Ann's life can and will be able to provide important social supports as she engages in the process of regaining custody of her children? If she succeeds in overturning the decision to cut off her social assistance, this should help her gain not only new skills in dealing with bureaucracies but also the realization that she has some ability to influence powerful social institutions.

In the past, Ann's parents have been important to her and have been good social supports. It is only after they began to define her as a failure that their positive relationships began to break down. Kim needs to explore in some detail the nature of these family relationships, particularly why the relationships were important to all family members and how to rebuild them. This rebuilt support system could be one of the most important resources that Ann can draw on.

Aboriginal Perspective

Chapter 11 describes an Aboriginal perspective of social work based on the views and culture of the northern Plains peoples. The perspective emphasizes the importance of wholeness, harmony, balance, and the interconnectedness of all things. The goal of practice can be seen as the achievement of *mino-pimatasiwin,* roughly translated as "the good life."

Healing is an important process in Aboriginal perspectives, and while the concept is similar to social work's use of helping and treatment, it is also very different. Aboriginal healing includes restoration—fixing, reconciling, or resolving something that is perceived to be wrong. However, the goal of healing is *mino-pimatasiwin.* Thus, healing is really a developmental concept—a lifelong journey that is the responsibility of all people, not just clients. As achievement of *mino-pimatasiwin* gets closer, the person is better able to fix and resolve problems.

More so than in the ecosystems perspective, the Aboriginal view emphasizes the interconnectedness of all things, including people, the environment, the land, and all parts of nature. Nature is seen as part of the inseparable whole.

Using an Aboriginal Perspective in Focused Assessment

An Aboriginal perspective helps assessment in two different ways. First, it helps social workers understand clients who are Aboriginal, particularly those who adhere to traditional ways. Second, the perspective helps with focused assessment of all clients.

For example, what is the journey that the client is using to reach *mino-pimatasiwin*? Is the journey of healing taking place? To what extent does the client perceive her or his life to be in balance? How does the client connect (or not) with all aspects of her or his environment? What appears to be out of balance? Are some of these connections problematic?

Case Example

Kim and Ann ▼

Neither Ann nor Kim is Aboriginal. However, an Aboriginal perspective is relevant to Ann's situation because it can place the process that Ann will pursue in context. Ann needs to heal. Her ultimate goal is very much like the achievement of *mino-pimatasiwin,* the good life. Translated, this might mean establishment of a healthy social niche and caring relationships. Achievement of these goals might be seen as a step toward *mino-pimatasiwin.*

Further, the process necessary to meet these goals is healing. Healing is not a short process but a lifelong journey. Neither the main goal of *mino-pimatasiwin* nor Ann's immediate goals will be achieved easily, nor will she find complete success in the short term. An important step in the healing process is for Ann to understand the interconnections between all parts of her life and her environment.

▲

Feminist Perspective

Feminist social work is consistent with structural social work in many respects. Much of the feminist focus is on issues of inequality and social injustice. Feminist social work is described in detail in Chapter 13 of this book. This approach is concerned with eliminating domination, subordination, exploitation, and oppression. In working with women, a belief in their innate health and ability to "identify and mobilize inherent individual and collective capacities for healing, growth, and personal/political transformation" (Bricker-Jenkins, 1991, p. 277) is important. Women's strengths must be acknowledged, applied, and built on in a context that stresses equality in the relationship between clients and social workers.

Feminist social work is as much at ease with micro practice as it is with large macro and political systems. Attempts have been made to apply structural social work principles to micro-level practice; however, feminist social work has seen greater development of its principles in micro practice applications. Feminist social workers also hold (as do structural social workers) that personal and political issues cannot be separated.

Two concepts that are very important to feminist social work practice are empowerment and validation. Empowerment refers to people being able to take control and ownership of their lives. This instils a sense of self-esteem and accomplishment that is necessary for personal growth. Validation is seen as a step toward empowerment. It is a feeling that the client is heard, understood, and listened to, and a belief by the client that her experiences and views are important and respected.

Using a Feminist Perspective in Focused Assessment

Assessment that uses feminist principles focuses on understanding processes such as empowerment, validation, oppression, and human capacity for growth. Empowerment and capacity for growth are as important to feminist assessment as they are when using the strengths approach.

Questions that may be used in assessment include the following: Have exploitation and oppression taken place? If so, what are the dynamics? Does the client feel exploited or oppressed? If so, how does this affect the client's personal life and psychological functioning? Does the client understand the political forces that lead to oppression and exploitation? What does the client think can and should be done—if anything—about these inequities?

What are the client's strengths? How can she mobilize her capacity for growth? How can she empower herself? What does she need to feel validated? What helps her to feel that she has an important and respected place in her world?

Case Example

Kim and Ann

Ann's ex-husband Jack has been refusing to pay child support even though the family court has ordered him to do so. A feminist analysis might suggest that this may be due to social policies that do not respond adequately to the realities of many women who are single parents. While the order for child support is on paper, neither the courts nor the enforcement authorities have chosen to ensure that Jack pays.

Kim wants to find a way to ensure that Jack resumes his child support—a feminist worker would search for ways to take necessary action so that payments are made. However, Kim also discovers that Ann feels the lack of child support is partly her own fault. Since she thinks she has failed as a mother, she feels that to some degree she does not deserve the payments. This view does not surprise Kim, but she holds a very different position. She believes that a major part of Ann's parenting problems are the result of the payments having stopped. Kim will tell Ann this but knows that simply telling her so will have little impact.

Thus, Kim decides on a different tactic. She is aware of a small group of women who are experiencing similar problems and have had one meeting to discuss whether they can take some collective action. They are being guided and assisted by a competent activist and feminist. Kim tells Ann about the group, and Ann decides that she will attend their next meeting. Kim has several goals in mind. (Note that structural analysis as well as other perspectives could also lead to the same or similar goals.) The first and obvious goal is to give Ann a way to regain the child support payments. Kim believes that this group has a good chance of succeeding. Second, and probably more important, the group provides a situation in which Ann might be validated. If she sees that others face the same problem she does, she may come to believe that she is not the cause of the problem. The women have a legal right to child support. This message, coming from peers who are experiencing the same problems, is likely to be much more powerful than anything Kim might say. Third, Kim strongly believes that Ann needs to empower herself. Both the validation process and the collective action to regain child support should go a long way in Ann's empowerment.

CONNECTING KNOWLEDGE WITH FOCUSED ASSESSMENT: AN EXAMPLE

The above discussion has shown how a variety of views, perspectives, and theories can be used. We have also shown how each casts the assessment of Kim and Ann, some being more pertinent to the case example than others. Now we will show how focused assessment might be used in "real life." Jacob is a social worker at Community Mental Health Centre. His primary responsibility is to provide community mental health services to a wide variety of people, termed "patients" in the agency setting.

The Employing Agency

The employing agency influences the social work assessment. Jacob works in a medical setting but, as is typical, the staff understands the importance of social and psychological factors in mental illnesses. The centre has two functions. One is to treat mental illnesses, often using medications, while the other is to help patients learn to live quality lives even with the illness. Agency purpose and mandate are significant factors in assessments. It is also important that Jacob, as well as all other staff, learn how to access risk of harm to self or others with particular understanding of how to assess risk of suicide. Further, Jacob's social work assessment is likely to be influenced by the psychiatric diagnosis.

If Jacob, like Kim, were employed by a child welfare agency, the influence of the agency would be different. The policies and mandates are different. Understanding risk of abuse would be central.

Worker Orientation

Most social workers develop their own orientation to practice. As discussed earlier, this orientation becomes a lens that affects and influences assessment and intervention. Jacob is very much influenced by the strengths perspective. He also has a rather strong commitment to cognitive theories, believing that he can teach people how to maximize their strengths in order to address mental health problems. This fits nicely with the second function of the agency: "to help people to live quality lives even with their illness." Successful practice in a social agency depends upon the worker's ability to merge or marry his or her orientation with the purpose and mandate of the employing agency. This is an absolutely necessary (but not sufficient) condition of successful agency practice.

Further, Jacob is committed to anti-oppressive practice. He needs to ensure that his and his colleagues' assessments and actions not only do not oppress the patients of the mental health centre, but also help to reduce any oppression faced by the patients.

Application to Clients: Focused Assessment and Use of a Broad Knowledge Base

Jacob is routinely assigned patients who are being treated by a psychiatrist. His responsibilities include helping them with marriage or family problems, assisting them to seek and maintain employment, and dealing with a variety of their personal and relationship problems. Some of his patients (clients) are experiencing depression, while others have an anxiety disorder. Still others may have been given a diagnosis of bipolar disorder or schizophrenia. Regardless of the problems and illness, Jacob understands his role in the agency and is keenly aware of his orientation. As he gathers information about the patients with whom he works, he focuses on asking questions about their strengths. His assessment will likely emphasize the strengths of the patients and how they can use these to recover from their illness.

Since Jacob is influenced by cognitive theory, he will likely look for distorted thinking and try to understand how it occurred and how it influences the life of the patient. During Jacob's assessment, he will search for strengths that will help him discover a way to assist the patient learn how to overcome this distorted thinking.

Jacob also understands the importance of relationships and connections and how ecosystems can be used to assess relationships. Almost all who have a mental illness have, in one way or another, been labelled. His assessments usually include the effects of the labelling process on the client and a search for how he can use the patient's strengths to counter the effects of labelling. Not only must assessment be focused, but also the knowledge used needs to be broad based. In Jacob's work at the Community Mental Health Centre, he selects knowledge that is useful for the particular circumstances of the client. Selection from the knowledge base depends upon the approach or perspective of the social worker, the agency's orientation and mandate, and particular client situations.

CHAPTER SUMMARY

This chapter has two major themes: broad knowledge-based and focused assessment. Broad knowledge-based assessment uses combinations of perspectives, approaches, or theories to focus assessment. Certain perspectives or theories are better suited to some situations than others. An important skill of social workers is to be able to selectively use these perspectives and theories with particular clients and situations. This is a skill that must be learned over time and honed throughout one's professional life.

There are four major sources of knowledge: life experience, culture and tradition, authority, and observation and testing. Social workers must use all of these sources in assessment.

The broad base of knowledge should be cast within an ecosystems framework, which focuses assessment on the person in her or his environment. The areas of knowledge cover the micro to macro continuum. The chapter described 16 areas of knowledge that are important in broad knowledge-based assessment. Importantly, many of these complement one another, and they all add different dimensions to assessment. One might say that this is an eclectic approach to assessment, and we agree if an eclectic approach also means a focused one.

Focusing assessment by using perspectives, approaches, and theories to help pose important and meaningful questions helps social workers understand clients and their situations. A scattered approach without a framework is not a good way to conduct assessment. To arrive at solutions to problems and answers to important questions we must first ask the right questions. Each of the broad areas of knowledge outlined in this chapter can be used to focus assessment on areas that the social worker might explore with clients.

NOTE

1 Unfortunately, the use of the terms "ecosystems," "systems," and "ecology" varies. For example, different scholars see the connection between systems and ecology differently. Some, such as Compton and Galaway (1999, p. 34), equate ecosystems with the ecological and person-in-the-environment perspectives. Others, including Skidmore et al. (2000, p. 48), see ecology as a subset of the systems perspective. Dubois and Miley (1992, p. 60), with a still different view, argue that ecology and general systems theory form a *unifying* perspective for social work practice.

The Strengths Approach as a Development Process

Chapter Goal

To explain how the strengths approach is fundamental to social work practice.

This Chapter

- stresses that helping should emphasize strengths and development rather than people's deficits and problems
- shows how the strengths approach emphasizes client growth, development, and quality of life
- emphasizes empowerment as a major goal of social work practice
- develops the concept of a consumer-driven approach
- connects the strengths approach to the ecosystems perspective
- suggests that one of the most important resources for helping people is self-help groups
- shows that one of the most important attributes of people is resilience and that social workers often underestimate resilience
- argues that all relationships, including professional helping relationships, are reciprocal and that in good helping relationships both client and worker should be seen as partners who both contribute and receive rewards

INTRODUCTION

This chapter and the next three conclude a major theme of this book: that generalist social work practice needs to be based on a variety of perspectives, approaches, and theories that cover the micro to macro range. This chapter is the first to present an approach that goes beyond problem solving. While the previous chapter developed a broad knowledge base for assessment, the remaining chapters, while not neglecting assessment, also focus on approaches to intervention.

STRENGTHS, DEFICITS, AND PROBLEM SOLVING

The idea of focusing on strengths is not new. Since the time of early casework, practitioners have focused on working with clients' strengths, and there is widespread agreement in social work, regardless of the approach, that this is an important part of practice. Compton and Galaway (1999), in the context of problem solving, write, "Developing a solution to [the] problem will call upon strengths brought by the client, you, and the environment. Thus, the problem solving model is strengths focussed" (p. 7). Johnson, McClelland, and Austin (2000) seem to agree with Compton and Galaway but add that the strengths perspective "refocuses the traditional problem solving process by emphasizing the involvement of the client in a solution-focussed process that builds on client strengths" (p. 75). However, the strengths perspective goes beyond problem solving.

Until very recently, the use of the strengths approach has generally been poorly articulated and without strong supportive research. Recent important work has changed this, most notably the work of Saleebey (1992, 1997c, 2000, 2002), who has clearly articulated a strengths approach and helped to separate it from problem solving.

Social workers, like most helping professionals, tend to focus on problems. This was clearly articulated in Chapter 8. Problem-oriented practice by definition centres on the dynamics of the problem, including the causes, the context, and how the problem affects the individual (if the problem is of the individual) and others in the person's life. The strengths perspective holds that the lexicon, underpinnings, and indeed the focus of the problem-solving process is on deficits of clients (see Goldstein, 2002; Saleebey, 2002; and Cowger and Snively, 2002). Far too often practice centres on deficits.

Emphasis upon deficits means that the worker attempts to understand problems by looking for and understanding "weaknesses" or "limitations." The focus is on "What went wrong?" Once the deficits (what went wrong) are understood, the worker can then begin to take steps toward problem solution, often by some correction of the deficit (Spearman, in press).

The strengths perspective forcefully argues that social work practice is bad practice if clients are viewed in terms of their deficits. Such practice that uses a deficit model not only is inconsistent with the ideology and values of social work but also is sometimes counterproductive.

Social workers following a strengths approach usually engage clients with the intent to help them solve problems. However, instead of working directly with client problems—or even balancing work between client problems and strengths—the strengths approach dramatically shifts the balance to strongly emphasize people's strengths. This approach enhances the problem-solving model by providing both a constructive critique of and a way to rethink traditional practice. Further, and importantly, the strengths approach is a direct, frontal attack on efforts to treat personal and social problems as pathologies or deficits.

The strengths approach is not a unified theory. It is instead a collection of many concepts, ideas, and notions of practice based on the fundamental principle that helping can best take place if its focus is on strengths. Some of the most important principles are described in this chapter.

PROMOTION OF PERSONAL GROWTH AND QUALITY OF LIFE

All of the approaches that we cover in this book share the idea that working with strengths is important, but each comes at it a little differently. (Chapter 14 compares the various approaches with one another.) This chapter focuses on the strengths of individuals. Feminist and structural approaches tend to assume that people's problems are often not the result of individuals' shortcomings but are due to difficulties, including inequities and injustices, in our social institutions. The emphasis of practice in these approaches is often to mobilize individuals' strengths, sometimes in the form of collective action, to address these inequities and injustices and in turn help individuals. The Aboriginal concept of healing is like a journey whose goal is to find "the good life." It is like the strengths approach in that people mobilize themselves to reach their full potential.

The strengths approach is really about personal growth, development, and quality of life. The central propositions of a strengths approach are clear and straightforward. The strengths approach uses people's own resources to help them meet four goals: (1) to grow as human beings, (2) to improve their quality of life, (3) to develop their own problem-solving skills, and (4) to deal with their stress and adversity. To meet these goals, the approach capitalizes on people's capacities, vitality, abilities, talents, courage, and power. Compared with problem solving, the strengths approach is **developmental**—focused on growth—instead of restorative, focused on correcting an existing problem. It incorporates ideas such as wellness, support, wholeness, growth, development, and quality of life. Growth and development, the approach asserts, will lead to increased problem-solving skills.

The action stage in the problem-solving approach is intervention to help people solve problems. The counterpart in the strengths perspective is to help people solve problems themselves. While by definition the problem-solving approach is problem-based, the strengths perspective may completely avoid *direct* efforts to problem solve.

To illustrate, imagine a rosebush that is about to burst into full bloom. Over the past few days, Sam the gardener has noticed that the bush is not progressing as he had hoped. On one of his daily inspections, Sam's sharp eyes notice that the edges of a few leaves are brown, dry, and curled. He turns a leaf over and, as he suspected, discovers dreaded aphids. Sam hurries to his garden shed, grabs the pesticide can, and sprays the plant with a white powder. He has used a problem-solving approach to attack the aphids. His approach is really analogous to the medical model: he examined the rosebush (inspected the leaves), diagnosed the problem (figured out there were aphids), and prescribed a treatment (applied the pesticide).

Let's assume that instead of using environmentally unfriendly pesticides Sam released a large number of ladybugs in his garden. Within a couple of days, the friendly bugs have accomplished the same task as the pesticide by eating the aphids. However, the process is still one of problem solving, and the medical model was used. The only difference is the acceptability and ethics of the mode of intervention.

Now Sam, being the excellent gardener that he is, increases the loving care of his rosebush. He prunes some overhanging branches of a large tree to give the roses more sunlight. He adds a special blend of nutrients to the soil and gives the bush exactly the correct amount of water. Sam takes all the steps necessary to promote the growth of the plant. The promotion of growth helps the sick plant become healthy again so it can resist aphids. Sam is using a developmental approach: he draws on the strengths inherent in the plant to grow, bloom, and survive given support. Of course, engaging in solving its own problems is impossible for a rosebush. At this point the analogy breaks down.

Sam used only part of the strengths equation. A strengths perspective really focuses on helping people solve their own problems. To complete the equation, a social worker operating from a strengths perspective promotes growth and development through engaging clients to take charge of their own lives, which includes problem solving. The process is one of empowerment; the goal, one of development and growth. Unlike the means Sam used in the garden, the strengths approach is a very human process.

To illustrate, when Manitoba experienced the makings of a disaster during the Flood of the Century, thousands of workers and volunteers helped build sandbag dikes to hold back the flow of the Red River. From a problem-solving perspective, the sandbagging effort was clearly an attempt to solve the problem of the flooding river. However, there was a positive side to the situation. People felt good because neighbours were helping neighbours. People working together to prevent a disaster kindled a sense of neighbourhood and community. Working together to prevent flood damage may have improved their perceived quality of life, perhaps in the way they felt about living in their neighbourhood. From a strengths perspective, people's response to the crisis made for a better quality of life.

The garden and flood examples illustrate the problem-solving and strengths perspectives. Most would agree that the problem of the aphid infestation needed direct, frontal intervention. Without the pesticide or ladybugs the problem would have been difficult to solve. Likewise, no one would argue against the attempt to hold back the water of the Red River. However, a rose cannot grow and flourish without the enhancement of sun, water, and nutrients. A city or neighbourhood without a sense of community does not make for a good quality of life. The case example presents another illustration of the problem-solving and strengths perspectives.

In day-to-day social work practice, workers draw on both problem-solving and strengths approaches. Certainly a major function of social work is to help people solve problems. The way to help people problem solve is to use their own strengths. The following discussion and related examples of the strengths perspective develop this important point.

Case Example

Linda and Mac

Mac MacGregor is a 36-year-old man who was diagnosed as having schizophrenia at age 21. During the past 15 years he has been hospitalized six times for his schizophrenia, for a total of 4.5 years. Mac's life skills are limited. Particularly when under stress or excited, he puffs his cheeks in and out when he breathes. This is an annoying habit that draws negative attention from others. He is shy to the point of being withdrawn and has never held a job for more than four months.

Linda Whitefeather is a community mental health worker assigned to Mac. Linda began working with Mac before his discharge. She quickly discovered that Mac has been on medications for a number of years. The hospital staff believed that Mac triggered his last hospitalization by refusing to take his medication. All concerned, including Linda, believe that monitoring Mac's medication is an important part of discharge, at least initially, but Linda wants to go further.

Among other things, Linda believes that the quality of Mac's living arrangements is very important. She weighs a couple of options. The first possibility is to discuss with Mac his needs and wants regarding housing. She would try very hard to understand his needs and then make arrangements with the local housing authority. Her second option is to not only engage Mac in a process that would identify his needs and wants, but also help him make his own arrangements.

In the case example, monitoring Mac's medication is clearly a problem-solving issue. So is finding him suitable housing. However, the strengths perspective adds a new dimension. Linda understands that if Mac is to survive outside an institution, he needs to be able to make life decisions himself. She wants to use the experience of finding housing to help Mac learn how to make decisions. The intent is to help Mac grow in his decision-making capacities. The use of decision making to promote growth is similar to the use of enhancers to encourage the growth of the rose. Empowering Mac is more important than finding him housing, because encouraging his growth and development offers him the potential for an enhanced quality of life.

Empowerment

The concept of empowerment has attracted considerable attention in the past number of years. Social work has embraced the idea to such an extent that it is a core of most practice that deals with individuals to communities (Simon, 1994). Empowerment began as an idea with a specific, almost technical, meaning but that was then adopted into everyday language. The concept now has numerous uses and connotations. It captures important ideas but has taken on such a broad meaning that its usefulness is at considerable risk. Empowerment is now a murky concept.

For example, the political left coined the term in the 1960s, and it became a feminist cornerstone. Feminists argue that empowerment is a way for women to counter oppression. In this context it often has a gender-specific connotation (Yoder and Kahn, 1992). In contrast, conservative politicians have used the term when arguing that reducing income taxes will empower people and corporations to have more control of their income and finances. In the United States, there is a conservative cable station called National Empowerment TV. The same word thus has very different meanings and conceptualizations (Fisher and Karger, 1997, p. 48).

The strengths approach sees empowerment as a process. People use their own resources, abilities, and power to take charge of their own lives. Empowerment applies to individuals, families, groups, organizations, and communities (Saleebey, 1997a).

To illustrate, often social workers are faced with a decision between doing something for a client or supporting the client in her or his own initiative. Usually, if the worker decides to support the client's initiative, a goal is to help the client empower herself or himself. This is important whether the task at hand is simple or complex.

For example, a group of people in an inner-city community may feel overwhelmed and frightened by the number of deliberately set fires in their area. They have little sense of community spirit. A social worker employed by a neighbourhood organization hears their concerns and encourages them to come to a local meeting. The residents tell him that they are worried for their families and afraid that an arsonist could target one of their homes next. Many are afraid to speak out publicly until they are at the meeting. They feel powerless to do anything and want to move to another part of the city. If people come together to protect their neighbourhood by speaking out, raising people's awareness about the problem, and seeking support from other community members and the municipality, they are doing something. They also feel less fearful, more in control, and thus empowered as a group. In this case, the social worker encouraged the residents to participate in the meeting in the hope that they would become empowered through joining forces with others to seek solutions. Had he tried to direct the group's actions, they would likely not have found their common voice, nor would they have attempted to take on neighbourhood change.

The strengths view of empowerment also holds that the act of intervention can be and often is a way of disempowering people. Social workers who make decisions for clients reduce the ability of clients to make their own decisions. Intervention itself implies a power differential between social worker and client. Too often, social workers use this power differential to expedite treatment without considering the need to let people take charge of their own lives.

In the case example, Linda would find it easier to find an apartment for Mac. All she has to do is locate a real estate broker and let the broker do the legwork. Mac may even be appreciative of and very comfortable in his new home. Or Linda can decide that Mac needs a group home and can arrange accommodation for him. Either action is acceptable using a traditional problem-solving approach. However, the strengths approach would concentrate on Mac taking charge of his own life to the extent of his abilities.

Helpers cannot empower others—empowerment is not something someone can give. It is, however, something that everyone can strive for. In this sense, empowerment is like human dignity and self-worth. Children, adults, and people who are mentally ill, homeless, and disenfranchised all have inside them the power to take charge of their own lives, but to varying degrees. The role of the social worker is to encourage and support the inner strengths of clients so that, to the best of their ability, they take control of their own lives. While few would disagree with the importance of empowerment, the strengths approach makes this idea central to work practice.

Professional Relationships and the Strengths Approach

Increasingly, scholars and social workers alike are raising questions about approaches that place the helper (therapist, counsellor, etc.) in control of the helping process. The traditional problem-solving model tends to view the social worker as the expert in charge of the helping process and generally assumes that it is up to the worker to act in the best interest of the client (see Chapter 8). Even though the social worker–client relationship is a partnership, it is a partnership of unequal power. In involuntary relationships the worker may have varying degrees of absolute power over the client. In voluntary relationships, the worker is generally viewed as an expert with helping skills.

A Consumer-Driven Approach

A consumer-driven model of practice (see Anthony, 1993) suggests a significantly different emphasis. A consumer-driven approach starts with the deeply held value, closely related to self-determination, that adults have the capacity and strength to make life decisions by themselves without interference from professional helpers. This is so even if the worker believes that the client is making the wrong decisions. Among other things, this means that clients can choose whether they need help, who is to provide the help, and how it is to be provided. The worker, while still an expert, acts more as an adviser or consultant. A similar principle is articulated in both Aboriginal (Chapter 11) and feminist (Chapter 13) approaches. A consumer-driven approach implies that the nature of the helping process should be client oriented rather than worker directed. While the approach still advocates a partnership, there is an active effort to reduce the power differential. The client is seen as in charge of the helping process. In a sense, this approach tips the emphasis of control in the partnership from that of the worker to that of the client. The worker's roles often become that of adviser and consultant. Other roles such as counsellor, enabler, or advocate may be offered, but the choice for their use is solely that of the client.

Unfortunately, the consumer-driven approach is not absolute, particularly when clients are involuntary or the function of the worker is mandated, such as in the criminal justice system. The section "Involuntary Problem-Solving Relationships and the Principle of Best Interest" in Chapter 8 presents guidelines for situations that require social workers to act in the best interest of clients even without their consent. Consumer-driven approaches have emerged primarily in such fields as physical disabilities and mental illness.

Sometimes conflicts between a best-interest approach and a consumer-driven one have important consequences for a client. See the case example for an illustration.

Case Example

Linda and Mac ▼

It has been eight months since Mac was discharged from the hospital. He is beginning to complain that his medication is causing him to feel "dragged out," and he cannot think clearly. He reports this to both his psychiatrist and Linda. The psychiatrist cannot find a reason to change the medication and leaves the dosage and type unchanged. Linda suspects that Mac might be trying to find an excuse to stop taking his medication. But she has also previously thought that maybe Mac does not really need it, and together with the medical team and Mac they should begin to plan to reduce or even eliminate his medication.

Linda expresses her suspicions about Mac avoiding his medication, and he vehemently denies doing so. He counters with a request for a second opinion from another psychiatrist. Even though Linda is beginning to question the medication, she is reluctant to help Mac with his request because her agency has a good relationship with the psychiatrist and does not want to upset her. However, Linda also feels that Mac has the right to make such decisions by himself and this takes priority over her reluctance.

Following the principles of a consumer-driven approach, Linda would agree without qualification that Mac has the right to a second medical opinion. Mac has the power to make this decision. To thwart this request would be completely counterproductive in empowering Mac to make his own life decisions. This is so even though Linda may feel that Mac is really looking for an excuse not to take his medication.

In a best-interest approach, Linda might resist helping Mac in his request. Her reasoning may be that consistent use of medication is necessary to prevent hospitalization. Surely a trained psychiatrist knows what is best for Mac, a chronically ill, withdrawn, sometimes paranoid man with schizophrenia. It is in Mac's best interest to abide by the expert's decisions.

Now assume that Mac threatened to stop taking his medication if he did not get it changed. A consumer-driven approach would still assume that he has the right to make this decision even though Linda feels it is the wrong one. Further, Linda should continue to help

Mac despite his decision, respecting Mac's judgment. The best-interest model, on the other hand, might lead Linda to take action to prevent Mac from stopping his medication. She might, for instance, refuse to provide her services (a common practice in some mental health centres) or might even warn him that he might be re-admitted to the hospital if he refuses his medication.

Note that both approaches would agree that direct protective action must be taken if the professional staff believes that Mac is at risk to himself or others by not taking the medication. Again, the social work codes of ethics help address this issue.

(Although not explored here, if Mac decided to go off his medication on his own, Linda could explore with him ways that he could do so safely.)

Case Example

Linda and Mac

After a couple of months Linda and Mac are at ease with each other. They have met half a dozen times, and Mac has found reasonably good living accommodations even though he is paying more than Linda likes. Both of them have discussed Linda's commitment to empowerment (of course, using different words than those used in this book). Mac has expressed, in his own abrupt way, appreciation that Linda truly encourages him to make his own decisions, and he likes her position of noninterference.

Linda decides that they are ready to talk about how Mac's Scottish upbringing might have an influence on his life. Earlier she had thought this might be important when he spoke briefly about what he wanted from life.

At first Mac has a hard time responding. He is not used to discussing his background and does not really like talking to anyone unless he has to. Linda knows that people who experience schizophrenia and paranoia can sometimes be very sensitive to overtures from others. Mac could easily misinterpret her questions as prying. Mac begins by describing his parents, children of immigrants, as hard-working, poor, Presbyterian farmers. Soon, as Linda listens carefully, he begins to describe their strict discipline and puritanical beliefs.

Then, out of the blue, Mac blurts, "How can you help me explore my background? You're Indian. I'm not anything like you!" Linda is taken aback a bit but not surprised. She could, as some might do, attempt to turn the question back to Mac by asking, "Why is this important to you?" If she does this, Mac will likely become defensive and withdraw from her question. This response would be a conversation stopper.

Linda takes a few minutes to describe her urban Aboriginal background and her decision about 10 years ago to learn much more about her Ojibwa culture. At that time, she was also engaged in her social work education. She describes her deep commitment to the Aboriginal value of noninterference in the lives of others. Linda relates how this position is similar to the strengths perspective views of empowerment and self-determination. Linda tells Mac that this approach allows her to work with people from many cultures even though she does not fully understand each person's culture. Mac likes this response.

The client–social worker relationship is shared or reciprocal. Human relationships that are rewarding are usually reciprocal. In a professional social work relationship, there may be rewards for both client and worker. Mac is rewarded by knowing that he has met some success in his own problem solving, and Linda feels good because Mac acknowledges that her approach has contributed to his successes. Note that in many client–social worker relationships, success or failure may not be evident during the course of intervention.

The example illustrates another principle of reciprocal relationships. When Linda chooses to tell Mac something about her Aboriginal background and culture, she is sharing experiences with Mac. Mac is rewarded in at least two ways. First, Linda is giving Mac more information so that he can better understand her background. This implies trust and openness, important ingredients in human relationships. Second, and maybe unrecognized by Mac, he is learning something new about a culture that is perhaps foreign to him.

Linda is also rewarded. She likes the fact that Mac was open enough to talk about his background. She knows this is difficult because it probably hurt and he has fears associated with his illness. She also learns a little more about Scottish culture.

In summary,

- Successful human relationships, including professional relationships, are reciprocal and shared experiences.
- One way to encourage reciprocal relationships is for social worker and client to share stories related to their own lives and culture, as appropriate. Exchanging selected information can be useful to both parties.
- The strengths approach is compatible with cross-cultural practice.

Membership and Belonging

The principle that everyone must have a sense of belonging and membership is also central to the strengths perspective. The approach assumes that people are social beings and therefore need to feel that they are an integral part of a family, a culture, a society, and relevant groups. A number of related concepts emerge from this belief.

The problem-solving approach may address issues of membership by focusing on alienation. Alienation occurs when people feel dispossessed and not part of essential elements of society. The problem-solving approach tends to view alienation as a deficit or pathology and a problem that needs a solution.

While the strengths approach does not deny the importance of alienation, the focus of practice can be radically different. Instead of emphasizing what is wrong with the client, this approach shifts the focus to enhancing the client's sense of membership and belonging. In other words, practice that uses the strengths approach may never deal directly with or focus on the problem itself.

Case Example

Linda and Mac

Several weeks after his hospital discharge, Linda notices that Mac seems a little down. After exploring his feelings with him, Linda realizes that when Mac was in the hospital he actually had a sense of belonging. She discovers that Mac took some pride in keeping his part of the ward tidy and enjoyed compliments that others gave him for his efforts. He also spent time watering plants in a small greenhouse and cleaning the day room connected to "his" ward. The hospital staff told Linda that Mac considered the day room his own space. Mac had created a personal niche, a place that was his.

Since his discharge, Mac no longer has a niche. He also does not receive compliments from others that are uplifting. He feels he is not contributing anything and even feels alienated.

A **personal niche** is an area in the environment that a person carves out that gives him or her a sense of belonging and ownership. In the case example, in order for Mac to remain outside the hospital, he needs to find a new personal niche. Part of Linda's job could be to help him find this niche.

The example also raises another important membership issue. By taking care of the ward and day room, Mac, in his own way, was contributing something to the hospital, to something bigger than himself. The appreciation shown by others and Mac's own sense of contribution raised his self-esteem. Belonging is a perceptual and reciprocal process. It is perceptual because what really counts for Mac is how he feels about doing his part. His contribution (input) brings him a feeling of self-satisfaction. To him it signifies a job well done. The process is reciprocal because for Mac to feel good about himself, he had to both give and receive. By contributing, Mac received cues from others that they appreciated his efforts. His perception that others liked what he was doing gave him some sense of satisfaction. The contribution (tidying), no matter how small it appears, became for Mac as important as the reward (praise from others) itself.

Now Mac feels that he is doing nothing that others consider constructive, so he does not consider himself useful. Linda has her work cut out for her. How can she help Mac engage in activities that he considers productive and useful? This is so important that Mac will likely need to return to the hospital if he cannot re-establish a sense of belonging and membership outside the institution.

A Social Niche and a Macro Connection

The ecosystems perspective (see Chapter 9) is compatible with the strengths approach. Recall that ecology, a major contributor to the ecosystems perspective, is a biological concept. Biologists have recognized that studying individual species alone is not adequate to understand life. To fully understand life, we must comprehend how each life form relates to others and to its environment. Biologists are particularly interested in the interdependence of species. The study of ecology thus includes the interactions among and dependence of different plants and animals (for example, see Strickberger, 1990).

A biological niche is a position that a species holds in relationship to other plants and animals in its environment. It is the place in the environment that a species has carved out for itself (Germain and Gitterman, 1995, p. 818). Understanding niches includes knowing what the species can contribute to the ecology and what the species requires from the ecology in order to prosper.

Taylor (1997) has suggested an analogous concept, the social niche. A social niche, unlike a personal niche, applies to a category of people. Taylor defines a social niche as "the environmental habitat of a category of persons, including the resources that they utilize and the other categories of persons they associate with" (p. 219). For example, academics establish a social niche. They contribute to society through their research and scholarship, often funded by granting agencies; they work in universities; they relate to others, often those in the same or similar fields outside the university, by sharing their work; and so on. A social niche, according to Taylor, is conceptually more similar to a biological niche than a personal niche because, like a biological niche, the reference is to the environment of a grouping (of academics) rather than of individuals (individual professors). A biological niche refers to a species, while a social niche refers to a particular category of people. The social niches that people belong to can be functional and empowering or dysfunctional and oppressive.

Another way of putting this is that niches can be enabling or entrapping. An entrapping niche is a dysfunctional niche in which one gets caught and there seems no way out. In our case example, Mac is in an entrapping niche that is largely defined by his schizophrenia and lack of social skills. This type of niche is shared by many others who suffer from schizophrenia.

Mac has been and is labelled both schizophrenic and mentally ill. He is not personable and has an annoying puffing habit. He has been categorized and negatively labelled. Partly because of the label and associated stigma and partly because of his limited social skills, he cannot find a job, his financial resources from social assistance payments are very limited, and others in his community do not like to associate with him. All of these factors serve to further bury him in his entrapping niche. He feels that he does not belong and is not wanted. Mac has found himself in an entrapping niche that is very difficult to escape, prohibits his growth, and reduces his quality of life. Mac's habits exacerbate his problems, but his problems are also due to the wider social system, which has defined the entrapping niche for people who are labelled mentally ill or schizophrenic. Mac and most others who are defined as mentally ill are often powerless to escape their entrapment.

An enabling niche (Taylor, 1997), on the other hand, is one that fosters personal development and quality of life. A goal of intervention in the strengths perspective is to help clients find or develop enabling niches, and to target entrapping niches for change.

Self-Help: An Enabling Niche

Finding an enabling niche can be difficult. It must be one in which the person is accepted and where the person is seen for who she or he is rather than as representative of a category. The person must perceive this niche as rewarding and providing opportunities to grow and learn skills (Taylor, 1997, p. 223). One possible enabling niche that might be overlooked by practitioners operating out of an expert, best-interest model is the self-help group.

The self-help movement is at least 60 years old. Probably the most well-known self-help group is Alcoholics Anonymous. In recent years, self-help groups have flourished and include cancer support groups, survivors of abuse groups, anxiety and depression groups, to name only a few.

Self-help groups can be empowering because they help people address their own problems in the company of others who have had or are having similar experiences. Members empathize with and understand the fears, emotions, difficulties, experiences of stigma, and disabilities that others in similar situations face. Probably most importantly, self-help groups can be enabling social niches. People who suffer from the same kinds of problems often find a safe, comfortable, rewarding, and respectful environment in such groups (of course, not everyone feels comfortable sharing their problems in a group setting).

Case Example

Linda and Mac

Linda realizes that Mac will likely have to return to the hospital if he cannot find a comfortable social niche. She mentions to Mac that she knows a member of the local schizophrenia association, a self-help group. She recounts what she knows about the group and asks his permission to contact her friend. Linda will ask her friend to speak to Mac about the association and the possibility of his joining. Mac likes the idea.

Linda is sure the association will help Mac feel wanted and respected, even with his quirky habits. She hopes that this will be an enabling social niche that may even help Mac open doors to other enabling niches.

Resilience

Resilience is another important concept in the strengths approach. Resilience is the ability to bounce back from traumatic and difficult life experiences. Far too often, social workers believe that their clients do not have the capacity to recover on their own from these experiences. Recent literature (e.g., Masten, 1994; Saleebey, 1997b; Shulman, 1999, pp. 67–73; Wolin, 1993) suggests that professionals generally underestimate people's ability to cope with adversity.

It is easy to explain after the fact why some people exposed to risk factors react with deviant and antisocial behaviours. For example, we may explain why James is a drug addict by understanding James's background of poverty and physical and sexual abuse as a child. Explaining why people become deviant has been the preoccupation of many scholars and researchers. However, now researchers and others are turning the question on its head: Why do many people who are exposed, for example, to poverty and physical and sexual abuse go on to lead productive and fulfilling lives? While the answers to this question are far from complete, what we do know is that resilience seems to be a very widespread and important human trait, and it is present in children right up to elderly people (Shulman, 1999).

Another implication of resilience can be understood by using major disasters as an example. During disasters like serious hurricanes or chemical spills, many people experience psychological trauma. Some respond to the crisis with symptoms of depression, anxiety, nightmares, and the like. We can attempt to understand these as pathologies, but we can also take a different viewpoint—why do the great majority of people who experience such events respond with resilience and strength? Unfortunately, this question is seldom asked.

Case Example

Linda and Mac

Every day, Mac is reminded of his seemingly uncontrollable habit of puffing his cheeks out when he breathes. People sometimes stare; others refuse to make eye contact with him. Mac is very sensitive to such responses. One day when he is walking to a shopping centre, a group of teenagers jeers at and taunts him. Two of them mimic him. Mac is devastated.

Linda thinks this experience will be a big setback for him, and that he is too fragile to handle the humiliation. However, the next morning Mac appears to be himself again.

Frequently, we expect clients to be frail and unable to handle adversity. The strengths perspective holds that we underestimate our clients. Sometimes our expectations for such underachieving lead to a self-fulfilling prophecy, because people tend to live up to others' expectations.

In retrospect, Linda realizes that she needs to understand and appreciate the resilience that Mac has demonstrated in response to the disrespect that others have shown him and to the stigma he has experienced. Despite his illness and symptoms, Mac still lives his own life. He continues to go for strolls even though he knows others will look at him in odd ways. He enjoys his coffee at the local café, although he sits in a corner where he cannot readily be observed by others. Rather than doubting his capacities, Linda should have expected that Mac would react with resilience. The strengths view promotes those activities that will improve Mac's resilience and coping capacities.

Evaluation

Chapter 8 explains how the problem-solving approach requires social workers and clients to articulate problems, goals, and interventions in measurable terms.

Generally, evaluation in the strengths approach is less clear. For instance, how would Sam the gardener ever really know that trimming branches of the tree would help the growth of his roses? Can Linda and Mac ever be sure that the skills Mac learns from house-hunting result in his learning more generalized decision-making skills? Such connections are difficult to make without sophisticated, time-consuming, and costly research.

This observation can have important funding implications for various programs. No one questioned the importance of sandbags when the Red River waters rose. The flood-fighting effort had a ready supply of cash, mostly from governments. The residents fighting arson in their neighbourhood are also concerned about their homes and community safety. This is important to the basic survival of families in the area. However, if one wants to establish a community program with the explicit purpose of improving the sense of community (continuing from the flood-fighting effort), one would likely find that money is very scarce. Part of the reason is that community solidarity is an abstract idea. How can a funder be sure that the community program actually leads to solidarity? How can community solidarity even be explained as a desirable goal? Generally, programs that have developmental goals are more difficult to sell than those intended to solve specific problems.

CULTURALLY SENSITIVE SOCIAL WORK PRACTICE AND THE STRENGTHS APPROACH

The strengths approach has embedded in it a number of principles that are useful in working with people of diverse cultures. Chapter 7 suggested that in order to be part of a culture one has to be an insider, to live as a member of that culture. An outsider can learn, appreciate, and understand much about a culture but cannot become part of it unless he or she becomes an insider. In cross-cultural social work practice, the worker, by definition, is an outsider to the client's culture. The strengths approach offers some principles that help a social worker who is not part of the same culture work with members of that culture in a productive and sensitive manner. Several of the ideas from the strengths perspective can be adapted and blended into some important practice foundations for work with people of different cultures.

Reciprocal Relationships

One of the reasons the strengths perspective is particularly useful in cross-cultural social work, as discussed earlier in this chapter, is because the approach, like a feminist view, is built on a partnership of reciprocal relationship in which the client directs the action. If the client wants to use the social worker as an expert (e.g., counsellor, advocate, enabler, mediator/negotiator, or other roles), the choice is that of the client, as long as the client is aware of and can make such choices. It may be necessary to first discuss the purpose and role of social work services with clients since these may not be familiar to them. This approach shows respect and acceptance of the client's culture; it does not imply that the worker's culture is somehow superior.

Part of reciprocity is that both client and social worker gain from the relationship. This involves give and take from both parties. One thing a client can offer the social worker is a better understanding of the client's culture. This benefits the worker not only in that more about the client is understood, but also in that she or he should develop a deeper and better understanding of the other's culture. Taking the time to learn about another's culture is also a way to show respect and appreciation of that other culture and its customs.

The Client's Story

The social worker must listen to the client's story very carefully. It will be cast in the context of his or her culture, not the worker's. Fully understanding it may be difficult.

The social worker's understanding of the story will be filtered by the worker's culture. As we have argued previously, if the worker does not understand her or his own culture the worker will have even more difficulty in understanding that of another person. Assessment must be based on understanding the client in the context of a client's own culture.

The strengths approach holds that the client's own description and interpretation of his or her problems are the most important of all the sources of information. Part of this story is the client's aspirations and goals. We not only must take these very seriously, but also must understand that these goals are cast in terms of the client's cultural orientation and probably her or his understanding of the dominant culture.

Cultural Support

An important intervention that flows from the strengths perspective is *support.* Clients need to live their own life, a life that is not controlled by professionals. Often, however, clients' growth and capacity for problem solving can benefit considerably from formal support, such as that of a professional helper, and informal support, such as that of family. Supporting people's desires and goals is enabling and not intrusive. This includes supporting another's cultural expression. It is a way to build strengths.

While support is important in all of social work, it is particularly necessary in cross-cultural work. Direct intervention by the worker may be not only ineffective but also inappropriate because of her or his lack of understanding and because the worker is an outsider. Furthermore, people generally accomplish more if they are in charge. For example, during the U.S. civil rights movement of the 1950s and 1960s, non–Afro-Americans could effectively support the movement by such activities as attending rallies and doing behind-the-scenes work, but the important work and leadership needed to come from Afro-Americans themselves. Similarly, non-Aboriginal social workers can support such issues as self-government and an Aboriginal justice system. They can even act as advisers. But, negotiating, designing, and implementing such new programs are best done by Aboriginal people themselves and within the context of Aboriginal cultures.

Social workers and clients may be able to access important cultural resources. For example, suppose a social worker is helping an Aboriginal family prepare for the return of their recently disabled father. As part of the helping process, the father has shown that he wants to return to his cultural roots and live life in a more traditional manner. By doing so, he uses traditional Aboriginal practices to enhance well-being and seek spiritual fulfilment. Elders from the family's community may be able to assume the responsibility of helping the family prepare for the father's return home. In such cases, a social worker must be prepared to support a client's use of cultural resources even if this means relinquishing what were formerly the worker's responsibilities.

As another example, consider a Chinese teenager who speaks little English who has been convicted of shoplifting and put on probation. The probation officer is a middle-aged man of Ukrainian descent with little knowledge of Chinese culture. However, the officer does understand that the boy has had a tough time adjusting in Canada and that he will need support if he is to develop a productive adult life. Instead of the probation officer taking direct action by himself, he helps the boy find resources in the Chinese community. Through a program that uses volunteers, they find a young Chinese man who will act as a role model—something like a "big brother" for the client. The probation officer is still responsible for establishing the rules of the probation and monitoring progress, but he has turned much of the helping role over to a cultural resource.

Cultural Membership and Belonging

"Membership" can mean belonging to a family, a group of friends, and so on, but cultural membership may be equally important. Individuals who belong to minority cultures frequently feel that they do not belong in the dominant culture. They may even feel that their culture does not belong in the larger, dominant culture. Practitioners working with members of diverse cultures need to be aware that clients may lack a sense of belonging because of cultural factors.

Case Example

Linda and Mac

The fact that Linda chooses to use a strengths approach is not an accident. She traces her background and culture to the Ojibwa First Nations. Over the years Linda has achieved a good sense of understanding of who she is, her Ojibwa culture, and her connections with the pluralistic society in which she lives. Her culture emphasizes principles that are consistent with a strengths approach. Therefore, she naturally gravitated toward practice strategies that fit her values.

Linda knows that Mac's Scottish heritage has been an important part of his life. She does not yet know how it influences his current life.

However, Linda knows enough about the Scots to assume that, for many, a strong sense of personal independence was likely very important, and Mac probably felt he did not live up to this standard. Further, many cultures value an ability to take charge of one's own life and prize discovering ways to increase the quality of life. Linda also knew that in some other cultures, an individual's independence was second to family well-being and community harmony. Generally, the principles of the strengths approach can apply across cultures with differing values and practices.

Note that social workers should use practices that are consistent with their own culture, beliefs, and values. If they use a therapy or intervention that their cultural and personal values do not support, social workers tend to be ineffective. This is because they experience conflict between what they believe and how they behave.

Social workers must also be sure that whatever approach they use is consistent with the cultural values and traditions of clients. Because the strengths perspective focuses on principles accepted by many cultures, it is an important approach in cross-cultural social work practice.

CHAPTER SUMMARY

The strengths approach uses people's own resources to meet four goals: (1) to grow as human beings, (2) to improve their quality of life, (3) to develop their problem-solving skills, and (4) to deal with stress and adversity. The approach capitalizes on people's own capacities, vitality, abilities, strong points, talents, courage, and power. Compared with problem solving, the strengths approach is developmental instead of restorative and does not focus on deficits. It incorporates ideas such as wellness, support, wholeness, growth, development, and quality of life instead of focusing on problems. The approach asserts that growth and development lead to increased problem-solving skills.

The strengths approach is particularly consistent with the ideology and values of social work (see Chapter 3). It is an approach that maximizes client self-determination and helps achieve the twin ideas of equity and social justice. In traditional social work practice, the importance of values and principles such as self-determination, acceptance of all people and belief in their intrinsic worth, empowerment, and commitment to self-realization, growth, and healing is mitigated by the view that the worker is an expert who is in charge of the helping process.

With the strengths perspective, the focus shifts from the best interest of the client to a consumer-driven approach. The social worker acts more as a consultant whose expertise the client can access. The client is in control of the process and decides whether help is necessary, who should provide it, and what kind of help is needed. The relationship is still a partnership, but with a different emphasis in roles. The professional helping relationship is seen as reciprocal, meaning that all parties must perceive the relationship as productive and beneficial. In good helping relationships, both client and social worker are partners who contribute and receive rewards.

Too often, social workers think that the people whom they serve are completely consumed by their problems. In reality, clients have many dimensions to their lives. The strengths approach emphasizes the development of the quality of people's lives, particularly in non-problem areas. This is particularly true in areas such as mental health, where the problem may be chronic. The strengths approach helps people build lives around long-standing problems.

Similarly, social workers often underestimate the capacity of clients. We tend to assume that because people are clients their capacities are limited. The strengths approach strongly challenges this assumption and argues that most people are remarkably resilient.

An ecosystems view of practice is often consistent with the strengths approach. For example, an important goal of intervention can be to help people find enabling niches, an ecological concept. A self-help group might, for some, be an enabling niche. One of the ways that workers can help some people find enabling niches is to connect them with self-help groups.

Finally, in the strengths approach the primary emphasis should be on helping people to empower themselves. A helper cannot empower someone else but can help others find ways to empower themselves.

chapter 11

An Aboriginal Approach to Social Work Practice

by Michael Anthony Hart

Chapter Goal

To summarize an Aboriginal approach to social work practice, with an emphasis on how such an approach can inform, enrich, and enhance generalist social work practice.

This Chapter ▼

- shows how an Aboriginal approach incorporates historical factors, particularly the social and psychological effects of colonization on the person
- explains the medicine wheel as one of the models that guides an Aboriginal approach and describes some of the teachings that flow from it
- suggests that the concept of *mino-pimatisiwin,* roughly translated as "the good life," is both a life goal of all and the highest-level goal of the helping process set by client and social worker
- explicates a set of key concepts and values that guide an Aboriginal approach
- describes the healing and helping process and the helping relationships of an Aboriginal approach
- compares an Aboriginal approach with conventional social work

MAKING CONNECTIONS

Many Aboriginal people[1] utilize the services provided by social workers. Although there are an increasing number of Aboriginal social workers, most social workers tend to be from dominant North American cultures. Earlier in this book we introduced two concepts, both connected to an Aboriginal approach: the use of strengths in helping (Chapter 10), and the emic perspective of cross-cultural social work (Chapter 7). In this chapter, we show how Aboriginal concepts and practices can inform helping, offering possibilities for all social workers to enrich practice in unique and culturally supportive ways.

The position taken here explicitly avoids imposing specific treatments and cultural values—including professional social work values and beliefs—on clients. Helping takes place within the culture of the client and in the context of the client's own background. People are supported to use the capacities and strengths that flow from their own culture and life experience. Helping and healing take place in the context of one's community. For an Aboriginal client (or any client), helping occurs within that person's own culture, according to the needs and wishes of the client. This perspective contributes to the whole of social work practice.

At the same time, helping takes place in a political and historical context. What has occurred in the past in the name of helping cannot be changed today, but it can provide rich teaching material and lessons to use today. It is not easy for those who have experienced difficulties as a result of events related to colonization to recall memories that create distress and alienation. By studying the process of European colonization and the policies and practices that resulted, we can better understand the impact of structures and events that work to oppress people (see Bishop, 1994, 2002). We can also benefit by understanding our own and others' feelings, ideas, and experiences of oppression so that in our work we strive for relationships that are supportive, caring, and mutually respectful.

UNDERSTANDING ABORIGINAL PEOPLES' HISTORICAL CONTEXT

To be prepared to work with Aboriginal peoples, a social worker needs to understand the history of colonization that the peoples have faced. Since this history is well outlined by several authors (Dickason, 2002; Miller, 2000; Mawhiney, 1995), a few points are highlighted here to demonstrate the experiences that have led to the destruction of Aboriginal peoples' social institutions and internalized oppression.

Among the first dynamics that led to the oppression of Aboriginal peoples were the changes to their economic systems. At one time, all Aboriginal nations were self-sustaining while actively trading with one another. They brought their economic skills and abilities into the Euro-Canadian fur trade economy. However, when the fur trade collapsed and European wars in North America ended, they found the settlers treating them as hindrances instead of economic partners and military allies. Laws were passed by the settlers that outlawed fundamental aspects of Aboriginal peoples' economies, such those banning the potlatch and the give-away ceremonies. Even when Aboriginal nations attempted to adopt the imposed system and made further alterations to their economic systems, new laws were introduced to keep them from fully participating. This is readily seen by reviewing the law that stopped Aboriginal farmers and ranchers from selling their produce for anything more than subsistence (Carter, 1990).

Oppression also occurred on a political level when the Canadian government imposed systems for Aboriginal peoples to govern themselves. For status First Nations peoples, this meant the oppression of their traditional forms of governance and the imposition of the *Indian Act* Chief and Council system. It is important to realize that this imposed system did not allow for a truly representative government that could address a wide spectrum of concerns. Instead, under the *Indian Act* system all matters to be discussed had to be approved first by the government-appointed Indian agent before a Chief and Council could address the matter. Once matters were discussed, any resolution had to be agreed upon by the appropriate federal minister before being enacted. When people attempted to address grievances they had with the government and the *Indian Act* system, laws were passed to stop them from organizing and effectively dealing with the issues brought forward. These laws included one that would fine and/or imprison anyone receiving monies for the prosecution of claims on behalf of a First Nations band—in other words, a person could not legally represent a First Nation and receive payment for services rendered (Canada, 1927). Another law fined and/or imprisoned any person who attempted to organize three or more First Nations people to make any request or demand of any agent or servant of the government in a riotous, disorderly, or threatening manner or in a manner calculated to cause a breach of the peace (Canada, 1884). Other barriers were also in place to stop people from organizing, such as the need for a pass from the Indian agent to leave a reserve (Miller, 2000).

These types of laws have also carried into other matters. There were attempts to directly attack the cultures of various Aboriginal peoples. Laws were passed that outlawed some of the peoples' spiritual ceremonies, such as the piercing and give-away ceremonies, without the non-Aboriginal peoples' understanding of the significance and role of these ceremonies. By encouraging and enforcing the pass system, Indian agents, priests, ministers, and law enforcement officials also attempted to stop the people from gathering to fulfill their spiritual obligations vis-à-vis the ceremonies. Indeed, aspects of Aboriginal peoples' cultures were deemed as evil, barbaric, and uncivilized. As a result of this view, many non-Aboriginal people—including government officials such as Deputy Superintendent General of the Federal Government Duncan Campbell Scott—took significant steps to eliminate Aboriginal cultures and control the activities of Aboriginal people (Titley, 1986). One example was banning a First Nations person from public poolrooms by fining and/or imprisoning the Aboriginal person and/or the poolroom owner (Leslie and Maguire, 1978).

Aboriginal social institutions were also attacked. Aboriginal peoples had well-organized means to address such matters as education, medicine, justice, and family issues. However, the people's ways of addressing each of these areas were suppressed and denied for many decades. Multiple generations of Aboriginal children were forcefully removed from their families to attend residential schools. Access to lands that held key medicinal plants used for healing and ceremonies was hindered, if not stopped. The communities' ability to deal with justice issues was undermined as a foreign justice system was imposed with laws and consequences that followed non-Aboriginal peoples' perceptions of justice and met their needs.

Families that had been able to deal with issues such as adoption and security through their extended kinship and community were torn apart and restructured through government laws, policies, and practices.

THE PRESENT CONTEXT

The examples above reflect the overall attack Aboriginal peoples have faced. However, we must recognize that while these examples are historical, many similar events continue to occur today. For example, the Canadian government has recently attempted to introduce the *Governance Act* without the proper and full participation and consultation of First Nations peoples (Boisard, 2002; Southern Chiefs' Organization, 2002). From the perspective of the First Nations leadership, the *Governance Act* served to meet the needs of the government rather than the people it affected. Aboriginal peoples continue the struggle to exercise their Aboriginal and treaty rights. Among these are First Nations peoples' treaty land entitlements. Land rights could provide a resource for First Nations to develop their much-needed economic base (Wien, 1999). However, the federal government continues a lengthy negotiation process to settle some claims, while others are not addressed at all (Assembly of First Nations, 2004a). It is important to note that the Canadian government determines which settlements will be considered. At the individual level, Aboriginal people continue to face acts of racism, whether it is from police officers callously leaving individual Aboriginal people at the outskirts of a city in severe winter weather, or whether it is a court that objectifies an Aboriginal woman who has been killed but that views her killers in a sympathetic light (Brass and Abbott, n.d.; Razack, 2000).

As a result of social inequity and continuing discrimination, Aboriginal peoples remain the poorest group of people in Canada and often face the worst social conditions. For example, off-reserve First Nation and Métis peoples have attained lower levels of education, lower average household incomes, and are less likely to have worked the entire year when compared to non-Aboriginal populations in Canada (Statistics Canada, 2003). They also have a higher incidence of chronic health conditions, particularly diabetes, arthritis, long-term activity restrictions, and major depressive episodes. They are more likely to smoke, be obese, and drink heavily than non-Aboriginal people (Statistics Canada, 2003). Further, the proportion of Aboriginal individuals with AIDS has been rapidly rising (Indian and Northern Affairs Canada, December 2002).

Similar conditions are reported for the on-reserve First Nations population (Sibbald, 2002; Indian and Northern Affairs Canada, 2002). In addition, it is reported that status First Nations peoples have higher rates of suicide. In particular, the suicide rate for First Nations male youths is five times greater and for female youths is eight times greater than the rate of their non-Aboriginal counterparts. When compared to the general Canadian population, First Nations individuals experience tuberculosis at a rate 6.6 times greater, are three times as likely to have diabetes, and are twice as likely to report a long-term disability. Most Aboriginal people live at or below the poverty line, and 62 percent of First Nations people over the age of 15 consider alcohol abuse a problem in their community (Sibbald, 2002).

Aboriginal people are incarcerated at a rate five to six times greater than the non-Aboriginal population (Indian and Northern Affairs Canada, 2002). The adult prison population is as high as 76 and 59 percent Aboriginal in Saskatchewan and Manitoba, respectively (Statistics Canada, 2001). The number of Aboriginal women who have been incarcerated has been increasing, while those for Black and Caucasian women have decreased (Correctional Services Canada, 2002). When compared to non-Aboriginal women, Aboriginal women are more likely to experience all forms of violence at the hands of their current partners, especially some of the most severe forms (Brownridge, 2003).

SOCIAL WORK'S PARTICIPATION IN THE OPPRESSION PROCESSES

The social work profession has not been an innocent bystander to the colonization of Aboriginal peoples in North America. For example, in the 1960s child welfare workers began entering Aboriginal communities in significant numbers. In following their own white, middle-class values and child-rearing practices they did not consider the colonial context and the significance of Aboriginal values and life practices. As a result, Aboriginal children were apprehended from their families and communities and adopted out to distant places, including countries abroad. While this event is referred to in Canada as the "sixties scoop" (Johnston, 1983), it continued into the 1980s and resulted in the loss of thousands of Aboriginal children from their home communities.

When conventional social work was practised, it often took the form of authoritarian control and regulation by external agents who had little understanding or appreciation of Aboriginal cultures and realities. As Collier (1993) states, "[T]he social worker was sent in with a job defined in an urban agency bureaucracy, not one defined or even informed by the needs or interests of the community in which the work was done. As a result, the social worker may have actively helped to dislocate people due to her/his adherence to policies and regulations which negated the unique situation of the community" (p. 44).

The social work profession has also contributed to the oppression of Aboriginal peoples through the reliance on theories, approaches, and practices based on and developed from non-Aboriginal perspectives. Privileging these perspectives, social work practice has often ignored the significance of Aboriginal peoples' historical and present colonial context in the situations they face. Without a critical historical and social analysis, the application of such theories and approaches tends to lay responsibility for the effects of the colonial oppression squarely on Aboriginal individuals. It also leads to the trivialization of Aboriginal perspectives and practices, the continued use of non-Aboriginal ways of helping by ill-prepared social workers, and a continued distancing between social work and Aboriginal people. Nor do cross-cultural practice concepts and practice methods help when it is assumed that social workers are white non-Aboriginal people and those they help are not.

Given the history of Aboriginal peoples in North America, the impact of colonization on individuals and communities, and the limited manner in which social work has addressed Aboriginal perspectives, we can understand why social workers usually employed by urban government departments have problems in being accepted by the communities. The authority that a social worker is given by her or his urban employer to carry out certain work (e.g., child protection) may pose a threat. Thus, social workers are viewed as oppressors, or agents of social control sent by an agency that does not appear to represent the Aboriginal community's interests. According to this view, social workers' primary obligation and loyalty is to the agency, a holdover from the colonization that they represent, rather than to a caring, helping process. The social worker may have never intended to affect community members in such a way. Whatever the reason, there is no doubt that this common perception of social workers is absolutely the polar opposite of the values and principles of social work practice.

AN ABORIGINAL APPROACH

Aboriginal peoples have been utilizing their own approaches to helping one another for centuries. Many Aboriginal social workers have incorporated these approaches or aspects of them in their professional practice. However, such approaches have not always been respected on their own merits by the social work profession. In recognition of this concern, the Canadian Association of Social Workers (1994b) has acknowledged the need for greater understanding and respect of Aboriginal practices. In order to contribute to the development of this understanding and, in turn, respect for these approaches, one approach is outlined here.

It is important to note that Aboriginal peoples vary extensively in their worldviews. This becomes readily apparent when you consider the diversity of Aboriginal peoples throughout the territory now called Canada. There are more than 50 nations, including the Innu, Mikmaq, Maliseet, Odawa, Kanien'kehaka, Anishinaabe, Cree, Dakota, Blackfoot, Salish, Haida, Tutchone, Dene, Inuit, and Métis nations. There are over 630 First Nations throughout Canada (Assembly of First Nations, 2004b), more than 50 Inuit communities (Inuit Tapiriit Kanatami, 2004), and numerous Métis communities and settlements. Aboriginal people live on reserves, in settlements, small rural communities, remote isolated locations, and large urban centres. Further, the cultures of the many peoples are a direct reflection of their traditional lands and environments. The diversity of the peoples is considerable given the great diversity in the land and environment throughout Turtle Island.[2] From this great diversity it is easy to understand that there is also a variety of Aboriginal helping approaches (for examples, see Duran and Duran, 1995; Morrisseau, 1998). The approach in this chapter is based on Aboriginal helping practices with a focus on Aboriginal peoples in Canada, particularly the Prairie provinces. With these points in mind, this is *an* Aboriginal approach, not *the* approach.

Background of the Approach

One of the models that guides this approach and that is frequently mentioned in the literature is the medicine wheel (Absolon, 1993; Bopp et al., 1985; Garrett and Myers, 1996; Regnier, 1994; Young, Ingram, and Swartz, 1989). The medicine wheel is an ancient symbol of the universe used to help people understand things or ideas we often cannot physically see. It reflects the cosmic order and the unity of all things in the universe (Regnier, 1994), but it can be expressed in many different ways as there is no absolute version of the wheel (Bopp et al., 1985; Calliou, 1995). Indeed, many Aboriginal peoples, such as the Anishinabe, Cree, and Dakota, have utilized the medicine wheel and given it their interpretations (Regnier, 1994). As a central symbol used for understanding various issues and perspectives, the medicine wheel reflects several key and interrelated concepts that are common to many Aboriginal approaches to helping. Many of the following concepts help explain the medicine wheel. These concepts are outlined here as the foundation to this Aboriginal approach. They are wholeness, balance, relationships, harmony, growth, healing, and *mino-pimatisiwin.*

Key Concepts

Wholeness

In order to understand the concept of wholeness it is important to recognize that the medicine wheel (see Exhibit 11.1) has been used to illustrate many teachings that can be expressed in sets of four and represented in the four cardinal directions, east, south, west, and north (Bopp et al., 1985; Calliou, 1995). For example, the medicine wheel has been used to explain the four aspects of humanness. According to this teaching, every individual comprises four key aspects, namely the emotional, physical, mental, and spiritual. Individuals are not whole unless they recognize and actively develop each aspect of their humanness. Other teachings

Exhibit 11.1 ▼ **Common Structure of the Medicine Wheel**

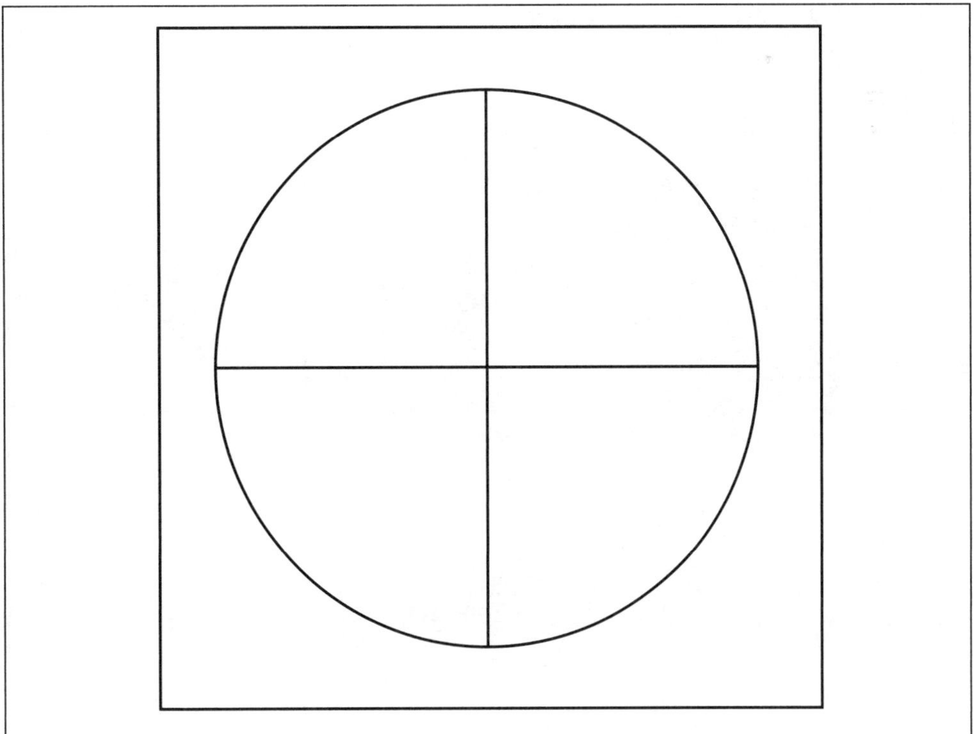

that are addressed through the medicine wheel include the people of the four directions (identified as the red peoples, yellow peoples, black peoples, and white peoples), the four cycles of life (birth/infancy, youth, adulthood, and Elder/death), elements (fire, water, wind, and earth), and the four seasons (spring, summer, fall, and winter) (Bopp et al., 1985; Hart, 1992; Regnier, 1994) (see Exhibit 11.2). Wholeness is directly related to these and other teachings. Each of these teachings is part of a single whole. We can come to fully understand one teaching only if we can understand how it is connected to all other parts and teachings reflected in the medicine wheel.

Exhibit 11.2 ▼ Examples of Teachings of the Medicine Wheel

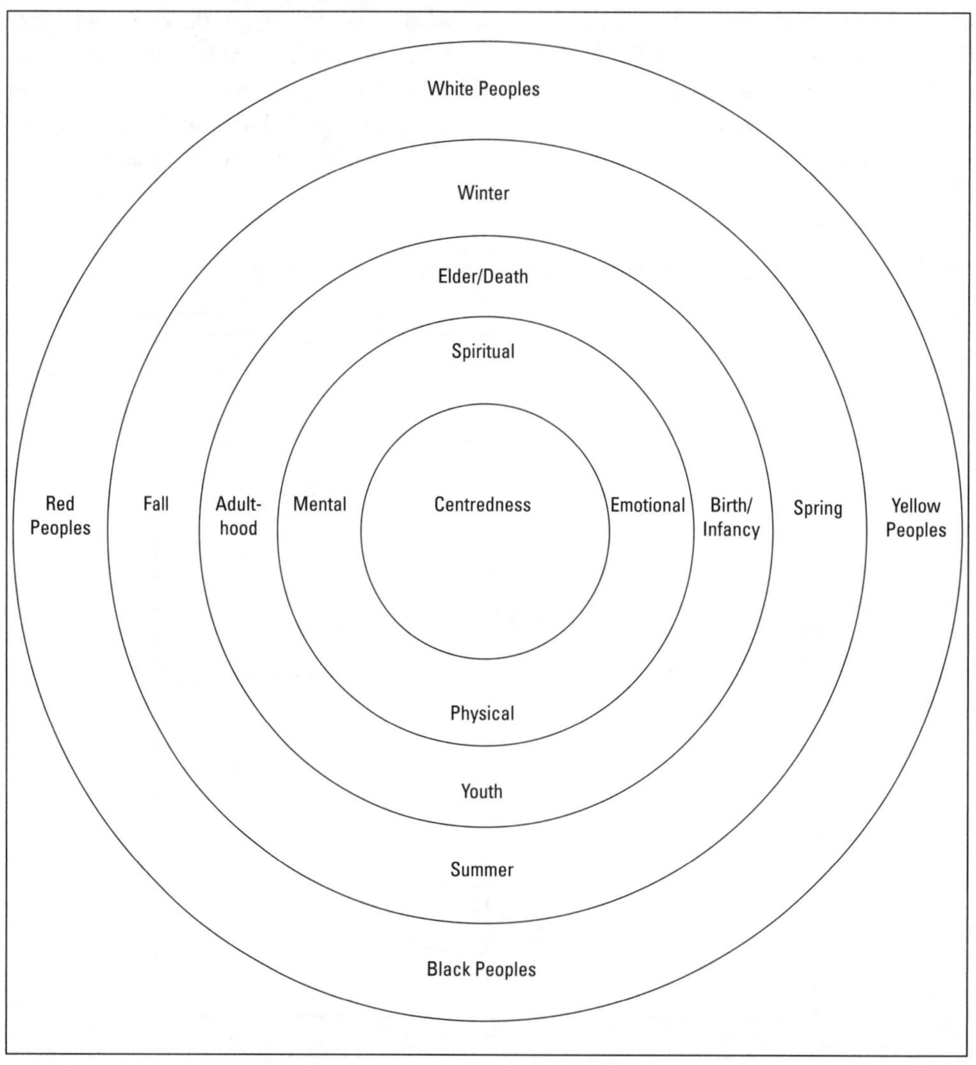

Wholeness in the cycle of the year requires movement through all seasons, wholeness in life requires movement through the phases of a human life, and wholeness in human growth requires the development of all aspects. The year life [all the cycles that evolve during one year of life] and human growth can come to completion through this movement to wholeness. This movement is natural and fundamental to all living things (Regnier, 1994, pp. 132–33).

Thus, wholeness is the incorporation of all aspects of life. In order to focus upon the whole it becomes necessary to give attention to each part. This attention is reflected in the next key concept.

Balance

The concept of balance implies that each part of the whole requires attention in a manner where one part is not focused upon to the detriment of the other parts (Clarkson, Morrissette, and Regallet, 1992). Balance occurs when a person is at peace and harmony within and with all other living things, including the earth and natural world (Longclaws, 1994). It also includes paying attention to both positive and negative aspects of people (Absolon, 1993; Nabigon and Mawhiney, 1996). While balance is periodically achieved, it is never truly achieved for an indefinite period of time. As in all living systems, it has to be strived for continuously. When there is an unequal focus on one part of the medicine wheel there is an imbalance. Such imbalance is considered the source of a person's disease or problems (Canda, 1983; Malloch, 1989). A person who does not strive for balance will not be able to develop his or her full potential. In order to restore balance, each part of the medicine wheel must be addressed in relation to all of the other parts (Peat, 1994).

Relationships

Balance involves more than just paying attention to each and every part of the medicine wheel. If it did, one could take a reductionistic view of only giving equal time to each part so that balance could be achieved. Balance includes giving attention to what connects each part of the medicine wheel; in other words, the relationships among all the parts.

Relationships between people characterize human life and are essential to people's well-being. Attention must also be given to the relationships within a person. Dion Buffalo (1990) states that "the traditional Cree approach is also holistic, concerned with and giving equal consideration to an individual's mental, physical, emotional, and spiritual well-being within the Sacred Circle of the universe" (pp. 118–19). People also are in relationship with entities surrounding them, including the earth, plants, animals, and the universe as a whole. Thus, in order to achieve balance people need to constantly foster the relationships between entities outside, as well as within, themselves. It is this fostering of relationships that is central to the next key concept.

Harmony

Harmony is frequently mentioned as a state to be sought after, whether it is harmony within oneself (Odjig White, 1996), with others (Brant, 1990), in the world (Canda, 1983), or in the universe (Regnier, 1994; Johnston, 1976). The concept of harmony not only is a state of being, but also leads to a good life (Dion Buffalo, 1990; Longclaws, 1994). Harmony involves the relationships of all the various powers, energies, and beings of the cosmos; when everyone—human, animal, plant, and planet—fulfills their obligations and goes about their proper business, then they are in harmony (Peat, 1994). There is also the notion that harmony includes respect for our relationships with others, within oneself, and in the give and take between entities (Nabigon, n.d.). Overall, harmony requires finding a good fit between the components of life through collaboration, sharing what is available, and cooperation and respect. It involves peace, respect, and establishing connections. Through this harmonizing process one fosters the next key concept, growth.

Growth

Growth and learning involve developing the body, mind, heart, and spirit in a harmonious manner. People have the capacity to grow and change, and their growth is dependent upon using their volition to develop their physical, emotional, spiritual, and mental aspects (Bopp et al., 1985). Thus, growth is viewed as a lifelong process that leads people to their true selves. Growth can be seen as movement through life cycles toward wholeness, balance, interdependence or connectedness, and harmony within oneself and with other living things; it is the movement toward the centre of the wheel (Longclaws, 1994; Nabigon and Mawhiney, 1996; Regnier, 1994). The centre is the place of optimum growth and healing.

Healing

Within an Aboriginal perspective, healing is not defined as something that is done when an illness or a problem is present. Instead, healing is viewed as a journey; it is something that is practised daily throughout our lives (Absolon, 1993; Ross, 1996). Illness and problems are viewed as disconnections, imbalances, and disharmony (Malloch, 1989). Thus, "healing is the transition that restores the person, community, and nation to wholeness, connectedness, and balance" (Regnier, 1994, p. 135). In this sense, healing is developing centredness.

From this perspective, an individual's healing not only is necessary for that individual, but also is important for all people around that person since they are all interconnected (Longclaws, 1994, p. 32). However, healing for an individual begins with that individual. As such, healing involves individual responsibility for one's own well-being and growth.

Mino-pimatisiwin

It is through the taking of responsibility for their own personal healing and growth that individuals will be able to attain ***mino-pimatisiwin*** (in Cree, pronounced me-no-pi-maa-ti-si-win)—the good life.

The good life is the goal of living life fully, learning, and healing. This growth and attempt to reach the good life is not just an individual focus—it also involves the family and community. Herring (1996) speaks of self-actualization in a manner that reflects the idea of reaching *mino-pimatisiwin*. He suggests that "Native cultures emphasize cooperation, harmony, interdependence, the achievement of socially oriented and group goals, and collective responsibility. Thus the goal [of self-actualization] is more akin to family and tribal self-actualization" (p. 74).

Key Values

To reach *mino-pimatisiwin,* particular values have been emphasized.

Sharing

Among the values emphasized, sharing takes a central place. The many things shared among people include practical and sacred knowledge, life experiences, and food (O'Meara, 1996). Sharing with others tends to be a natural way of developing human relationships. Sharing promotes equality and democracy in that everyone is considered as valuable as any other person and treated accordingly (Brant, 1990). It also reduces feelings such as greed, envy, and arrogance that may cause conflict within the group. It is believed to be so fundamentally important that any breach would result in sickness (Zieba, 1990).

Respect

Another value that is extensively emphasized and believed to be one of the foundations of many Aboriginal cultures is respect (Briks, 1983). Calliou (1995), providing a First Nations explanation, states that "we unconditionally respect all beings because we all begin as seeds from the same materials of this Mother Earth. In the circle no one individual (two-legged, four-legged, mineral, or plant, etc.) is deemed 'more than' or 'less than' another, so that treatment which elevates or denigrates one or the other is ruled out" (p. 67). Respect means to treat someone or something with consideration; to show honour, esteem, deference, and courtesy; and sometimes to yield to another's wishes out of politeness. It is a central responsibility in all relationships, including spiritual relationships (Hampton et al., 1995).

Spirituality

Many Aboriginal people hold a deep sense of spirituality. It is a core characteristic of many Aboriginal cultures and is evident in many aspects of Aboriginal helping practices. Even though you will find individual Aboriginal people who do not demonstrate such a sense of spirituality, to ignore their sense of spirituality is to deny a part of them as Aboriginal peoples.

Concepts Related to the Perception of Person

View of Human Nature and Activity Orientation

Human nature in an Aboriginal approach is seen as good, although the existence and expression of bad attributes by people are also recognized (Absolon, 1993; Waldram, 1997). According to Longclaws (1994), "it was believed that people were born good but that throughout life the teachings of the medicine wheel provided guidance and therefore protection from evil forces present in the universe that could lead people astray and off the good, or red, road" (p. 26). Further, while everyone has a direction and purpose in life, they have to actively strive to develop themselves positively toward *mino-pimatisiwin* (Bopp et al., 1985; Longclaws, 1994; Regnier, 1994). At the same time, "while people develop to come to know their true nature, the traditional Native also nurtures the experience of being alive"

(Hampton et al., 1995, p. 259). Thus, while an Aboriginal approach mainly views people in a state of being (Nelson, Kelley, and McPherson, 1985), it also includes them in a state of being-in-becoming (Regnier, 1994).

View of Individuals, Time Orientation, and Relationships

As previously noted, all people have a purpose and are active as they strive to grow toward *mino-pimatisiwin.* This growth and development take place through people's own actions in life. This does not mean that they are oriented only to the future. In fact, as Brant (1990) states, "the Native person has an intuitive, personal and flexible concept of time" (p. 536). Life experiences and events that take place in the past and in the present time are all important, especially in terms of how future generations will be affected. Indeed, past personal and generational experiences are important to the present time, as well as how present events will affect future generations (Benton-Banai, 1988; Clarkson, Morrissette, and Regallet, 1992). For example, when considering the effects of a child being removed from a family, they will reflect on the aspirations of past generations and how such a move will affect future generations, as well as how the future generations will be able to carry on the past generations' aspirations.

Relationships are central to each person's well-being and life goals, and in each person's life relationships are made and remade. Individuals are deeply influenced by and influence the relationships in their lives, including relationships between and within entities (people, spirits, and things). To "try to accommodate those relationships instead of dominating the things within them—seems to lie at the heart of a great many Aboriginal approaches to life" (Ross, 1996, p. 63).

Relationships are guided by good conduct, since good conduct leads to *mino-pimatisiwin* (Hallowell, 1992). Good conduct in relationships involves not interfering in and not judging the affairs of others, since interference and judgments limit a person's self-determination (Janzen, Skakum, and Lightning, 1994; Good Tracks, 1989). Relationships that enhance harmony and avoid coercively directing others' behaviour are promoted. Overall, positive relationships are central to an Aboriginal approach.

Among the many relationships that are present, the relationship between women and men is key. Within this approach it is recognized that both genders have purposes as part of the whole of life. There has to be balance between women and men. One cannot be focused upon to the detriment of the other. Instead, both have to harmoniously support one another as they strive for *mino-pimatisiwin.* This support is enhanced through the sharing between genders, not the domination and/oppression of one over the other.

Concepts Related to Functioning

Role of History

The process and effects of colonization have to be understood, not only as a structured relationship, but also as a personal experience (McKenzie and Morrissette, 2003; Morrissette, McKenzie, and Morrissette, 1993). The spiritual aspect of Aboriginal peoples has suffered great stress due to colonization, and this aspect requires special attention. The human service professions, such as social work, come face to face with the current problems stemming from harmful past events and practices. Duran and Duran (1995) discuss colonization in relation to psychology. Their statement applies equally to social work:

> The past five hundred years have been devastating to our communities; the effects of this systematic genocide are currently being felt by our people. The effects of the genocide are quite personalized and pathologized by our profession via the diagnosing and labelling tools designed for this purpose. If the labelling and diagnosing process is to have any historical truth, it should incorporate a diagnostic category that reflects the effects of genocide. Such a diagnosis would be 'acute and/or chronic reaction to colonialism.' (p. 6)

This quotation emphasizes that human service professions need to seriously consider impacts of the politics of colonization in North American history. Thus, an Aboriginal approach incorporates historical factors such as the effects of colonization on the person, family, and community. This makes real the popular social work slogan, "The personal is political," often attributed to feminist social work practice (see Chapter 13).

Individual Development: The Cycle of Life

Equally important as the effects of colonization on people's functioning is the cyclical nature of life. This cycle has been viewed in relation to the medicine wheel, where life is seen as having four key phases; within each phase tasks are developed, but not necessarily in consecutive order (Bopp et al., 1985; Calliou, 1995). These four phases are often referred to as the birth/infant phase, the child/youth phase, the adult phase, and the Elder/death phase. Thus, while it is possible to describe particular developments and achievements in relation to particular life phases (Longclaws, 1994), these phases are significant to people as individuals so that they can best understand their own development.

Importance of Consciousness and Unconsciousness

Dion Buffalo (1990), in identifying the importance of the unconscious, stated that the Plains Cree heal individuals by bringing the unconscious conflict and resistance to a conscious level where issues can be worked on. Often this process incorporates spiritual dimensions that are reached through dreams and visions. Among the traditional Plains peoples, dreams are held in high regard and are seen as a source of knowledge and power (Irwin, 1994). It is believed that spiritual beings—*pawaganak* in Cree—can offer guidance to people. They are contacted through dreams, and it is these contacts that enhance a person's ability to reach *mino-pimatisiwin* (Dunsenberry, 1962).

Ermine (1995) reviewed this process of learning, securing power, enhancement, and help through such events as dreams and visions. He stated,

> In their quest to find meaning in the outer space, Aboriginal people turned to the inner space. This inner space is the universe of being within each person that is synonymous with the soul, the spirit, the self, or the being. The priceless core within each of us and the process of touching that essence is what Kierkegaard called inwardness [1846]. ... Aboriginal people found a wholeness that permeated inwardness and that extended into the outer space. Their

> fundamental insight was that all existence was connected and that the whole enmeshed the being in its inclusiveness. In the Aboriginal mind, therefore, an immanence is present that gives meaning to existence and forms the starting point for Aboriginal epistemology. (p. 103)

In this activity it is essential to note that this inward-looking process is important not only for individuals, but for the community as well. Overall, Aboriginal philosophy is a spiritual philosophy that strongly incorporates the unconscious and the conscious (Aitken, 1990).

Nature of Change and the Role of Motivation

Change in an Aboriginal approach is tied to balance, relationships, and harmony. Aboriginal peoples see the universe in a constant state of movement in which there is an order of alliances, compacts, and relationships among the energies and spirits of the world (Peat, 1994). This order, being in continuous motion, is always in a state of transition between order and chaos. As such, balance in the universe occurs in an environment of movement, transition, and change. Another way to view change, according to Chief Simon Baker, is to see it in terms of cycles (Baker and Kirkness, 1994). To illustrate, people are always involved in transitional processes, either directly or indirectly. Change occurs due to actions that occur outside an individual—say, when a winter storm strikes or a family member moves away. Such occurrences are part of the cycle of life. Change can also happen as a result of inner processes, such as feelings of fear, or a new understanding of oneself after a meaningful experience. When individuals are not balanced within, are disconnected in their relationships, or are in disharmony with their environment, then change is required. It is necessary to regain one's balance. At other times, when individuals feel they have achieved balance and attempt to remain "stuck" in that particular state, their growth is hindered since the world around them continues to change. Therefore, the nature of change is that it is an ongoing transitional process of balancing and connecting relationships within the individual, between individuals, and between individuals and their environment (Longclaws, 1994; Regnier, 1994). This process is not limited to the individual, but also involves relationships at a familial, communal, and tribal or national level (Briks, 1983; LaDue, 1994).

The primary motivation for growth and change lies in the desire to reach *mino-pimatisiwin* (Aitken 1990; Hallowell, 1992); therefore, the onus is on the individual to pursue change in her or his life. Emphasizing this personal responsibility for change, Ross (1996) stated,

> Only you can find the will to take those first steps towards trusting others, towards taking hold of the hands that reach down to help you. The healers can show you how they trust each other, how they don't let go of each other, but they can't force you to reach out yourself. They can only demonstrate, teach, encourage and receive. Everything else must come from the individual who needs the healing (p. 190).

Power

Power exists in all living entities. For people it is tied to their ability to imagine something or to make a choice and then implement actions so that the imagined something or the choice becomes a reality. Ideally, power should be used to help oneself and others to strive for *mino-pimatisiwin*. It is used to help people learn, heal, and grow, which in turn can lead to greater access to power. People's access to power is not evenly distributed throughout any society. What becomes highly significant is how the power that is available to an individual, group of individuals, or part of a society is used by them. A variation in the distribution of power may be acceptable as long as the power is used to contribute to the creation and maintenance of balance, relationships, and harmony for all individuals and entities. Therefore, the more power a person or group has access to, the greater the responsibility that person or group has to contribute to the well-being of others.

Power is abused when an individual, a group, a society, or an entity, for its own gain, hinders or attempts to hinder another person, group, society, or entity's learning, healing, or growth. Abuses of power result in imbalances, broken relationships, and disharmony. While it may appear in this situation that the individual or group with the power is growing stronger, in the larger picture there is little growth, and the likelihood of deterioration is great. As in trickster stories of various indigenous nations, this deteriorating state is unlikely to remain as a change will likely come either from within those abusing their power or by force from an external resource that will result in a redistribution of the power to a more balanced state.

The Helping Process

Focus of Helping

In an Aboriginal approach to helping, emphasis is given to the relationships held by the people being helped. It is especially essential to nurture the relationship between a client and worker and to enhance its development and growth as a part of helping.

The focus of the helping process is restoring relationships that have become out of balance (Ross, 1996; Malloch, 1989). From a holistic perspective, it could be said that "an intervention will need to restore physical well-being to the body and harmony to the damaged social and spiritual relationships" (Ellison and Ellison, 1996, p. 148). As in all social work practice, work with clients can be focused at the individual, family, community, or broader level of relationships. In addition, the level of relationships can be further extended to include people's relationships with the Creator and Mother Earth (Clarkson, Morrissette, and Regallet, 1992). In an Aboriginal social work approach, those providing assistance to clients are required to focus on maintaining their own balance, connectedness, and harmony—in other words, centredness—since they are in relationship with the people receiving help (Nabigon and Mawhiney, 1996; Nelson, Kelley, and McPherson, 1985). Indeed, it is emphasized that "before you can reach out to help the people around you, you must first understand how to help yourself" (Antone and Hill, 1990, p. 7).

The Helping Relationship and Specific Techniques

The helping relationship is one in which the helper and the person receiving the support are involved in a shared experience of learning and growing. There is no distinction in terms of status or position. In this shared experience the helper is fundamentally a supporter involved in an interdependent relationship with the person receiving the help (Nelson, Kelley, and McPherson, 1985). In order to respect individual autonomy, those offering help are required to be indirect, nonjudgmental, and noncoercive in their methods of practice (Longclaws, 1994; Nabigon and Mawhiney, 1996). As Boldt and Long (1984) point out, no human being has control over another's life. In the end, it is up to the individual what direction she or he takes. While some healers have been noted to be very direct and have used direct interventions (Malloch, 1989; Young, Ingram, and Swartz, 1989), most interventions that are parallel with social work practice involve a relationship of interdependence and support, and tend to remain fairly indirect. For example, when working with people, Aboriginal helpers do not direct action. Instead, they may share their own or others' experiences in the same or a similar situation. The person listening to what was said would be free to use the information in the manner he or she wishes to use it, including not at all. Of course, when the safety of another is at risk direct intervention may be required, such as in situations where someone is physically abusing another or attempting suicide.

Specific techniques reflect this relationship. In an Aboriginal approach, storytelling is frequently used as a method of addressing issues (Bruchac, 1992; Dion Buffalo, 1990; O'Meara, 1996). Some situations may call for the helper to share experiences that directly relate to the situation being addressed. Other situations may call for the sharing of stories in a general manner, thus allowing individuals to personally discover the meaning in the story that relates to them.

The use of humour is another important technique. According to Aitken (1990), "humour to our people is probably one of the greatest medicinal strengths" (p. 29). He considered it as an indirect nurturing approach that is both nonconfrontational and noninterfering. For example, the use of humour can help individuals to see the situations they are experiencing from a new perspective, and perhaps a lighter point of view.

Role modelling is another technique that can be indirect, nonconfrontational, and supportive (Brant, 1990; McCormick, 1995). The role-modelling process, or "teacher as healer," requires that a person live life as it is to be taught and wait for the student to come seeking knowledge (Katz and St. Denis, 1991, p. 31).

In an Aboriginal social work approach, the referral to or support of Elders is often highlighted. Significantly, Elders are often seen as people who have learned from life and are able to transmit the culture (Malloch, 1989; Stiegelbauer, 1996; Waldram, 1997). Transmitting the culture is considered a key aspect of the healing process for Aboriginal peoples (LaDue, 1994; McKenzie and Morrissette, 2003). Elders also provide counselling, offer spiritual guidance, and conduct ceremonies (Couture, 1996; Stiegelbauer, 1996; Waldram, 1997).

Conducting ceremonies and following rituals are significant techniques utilized in an Aboriginal approach. There are many ceremonies, and these are carried out in varying ways depending upon the practices of the First Nations peoples involved. They include smudging, prayer, naming ceremonies, pipe ceremonies, sweat lodges, feasts, and fasting. Despite the variability, "[C]eremonies assist individuals in centring themselves and give them strength to participate in a lifelong learning process" (Longclaws, 1994, p. 26). Ceremonies are not referred to as rights to be exercised, but as obligations to be fulfilled for one's renewal in the life cycle. They are ways to facilitate healing and to discharge emotions through crying, yelling, talking, swearing, singing, dancing, and praying (Ross, 1996). The discharge of emotion in and of itself is in fact seen as a healing method (McCormick, 1995).

Specific Knowledge and Skills of the Helper

One reason Elders are respected as sources of help is because of their experiences and how they have learned from those experiences (Couture, 1996; Stiegelbauer, 1996). They have reached the point of living the life they wish to teach. People who conduct healing ceremonies go through a learning process that incorporates years of intense study, acquiring the knowledge needed to fully work as an Aboriginal healer (LaDue, 1994). Utilizing an Aboriginal approach in the helping process at least requires the ability to appropriately use the basic knowledge and skills that reflect and respect Aboriginal worldviews and the ways of life that stem from these views. These include eliminating the expert role, maintaining humility, demonstrating centredness, acknowledging the spiritual, listening, being patient, using silence, and speaking from the heart.

People offering help cannot see themselves as experts in the healing process since "there is no inherent distinction between the helper and the helped" (Nelson, Kelley, and McPherson, 1985, p. 241). Humility, not judgment, needs to be emphasized (Nabigon and Mawhiney, 1996; Ross, 1996). Helpers need to incorporate personal experience to demonstrate alternatives for healing and therefore should be active in developing their own centredness (Nelson, Kelley, and McPherson, 1985; Ross, 1996).

Since centredness involves the spiritual aspect of people, and since the helper role includes acting as a mediator between the physical and spiritual aspects of creation, helpers need to acknowledge the spiritual (Absolon, 1993; Malloch, 1989). The need to be patient and a good listener are also necessary, since nondirective approaches take time. "The professional may need to alter his or her communication style, learning to sit patiently through long pauses and to listen rather than to be directive or to interrupt the speaker" (Broken Nose, 1992, p. 384). Related to listening and patience is the use of silence. Peat (1994) states that "coming-to-know arises out of silence. It is this same quality of silence that strikes so forcefully when you meet with a Native person" (p. 75). Silence is related to another skill that should be developed—the art of speaking from the heart:

> Out of this power of silence great oratory is born. When Native people speak they are not talking from the head, relating some theory, mentioning what they have read in some book, or what someone else has told them. Rather, they are speaking from the heart, from the traditions of their people, and from the knowledge of their land; they speak of what they have seen and heard and touched, and of what has been passed on to them by the traditions of their people. (Peat, 1994, p. 75)

Speaking from the heart also includes the attempt to reach and touch the listener's heart. This process is important because such actions honour the listener by having the speaker share something that is truly meaningful, and not just information. Thus, it is by reaching inward and speaking from their own heart that people are able to reach others. In social work, speaking from the heart shows genuineness, empathy, and concern. It brings worker and client together in their common humanity.

Goal Setting

Since the Aboriginal approach outlined here espouses personal responsibility, goal setting is to be determined by the person being helped (Aitken, 1990; Nelson, Kelley, and McPherson, 1985). Unless the person has approached a traditional healer or Elder asking for a particular problem to be cured, the assessment of what goals are to be sought is also determined by the person being helped (Nabigon and Mawhiney, 1996; Nelson, Kelley, and McPherson, 1985). Due to the fact that for many people following an Aboriginal approach the central goal is to achieve *mino-pimatisiwin,* the good life, goal setting is a personal responsibility. Helpers utilizing an Aboriginal approach can only act to support the person being helped to develop her or his goals. In this way, the people seeking help direct their own actions and take responsibility for reaching their own goals.

Application

In utilizing an Aboriginal approach in practice, social work helpers begin with themselves. They need to prepare themselves by being aware of their own emotional, mental, spiritual, and physical well-being, how these aspects are balanced and connected, and how they move to establish harmonious relationships within themselves and with others. Social work helpers then need to recognize that they are role models of positive growth and well-being, and as such are required to demonstrate respect and be prepared and willing to share their experiences of growth. Those who take on the job of social worker begin on a kind of journey, one in which they learn about themselves as people and as participants in a relationship with people seeking help. They will see the difficult situations, problems, and pain created by the structures in our society and by people in distress. They will also see the beauty of discovery, healing, and growth within themselves and in the universe around them. In this way, it is important for social workers to be centred themselves and to maintain their well-being and balance as they take up this challenging and rewarding work.

In working with people seeking help and/or support, social work helpers need to develop understandings of each person's personal, family, community, and national histories and how these histories may be brought into play in the present, including how they may relate to the colonial oppression Aboriginal peoples face. To develop this understanding, the helpers need to listen to the life stories that people share. They are required to hear about and support the people seeking help to consider all the relationships they have. Awareness of each internal component of the people seeking help should be developed by the helper and the people themselves. There must be consideration of questions such as: Is the person able to express a full range of emotions appropriately, to take physical care of himself or herself, to meet cognitive challenges and actively learn, and to feel and express his or her sense of spirituality? There must also be awareness of the external factors influencing this person, in particular the oppression she or he has experienced and the strength that can be derived from her or his identity and culture. Some questions that should be considered are as follows: How may this person's life experience be an individual reflection of the oppression Aboriginal peoples have faced? Are the actions of this person a consequence of internalized oppression? What aspects of his or her culture can be tapped into as a source of support and growth for the individual? The relationships between internal and external elements should be considered in relation to each other—in other words, holistically.

The positive growth of these components and relationships should be focused upon as the helper supports the individuals to develop her or his own goals. An outline of how centredness can be achieved should be shared between the helper and the person seeking help. There may be use of ceremonies within some sessions. For example, a smudging ceremony in which cleansing plant medicines are burnt and the smoke is used to wash oneself may be conducted. Alternatively, there may be ceremonies conducted outside the sessions that may become part of the healing journey. People seeking help and possibly the helper may participate in ceremonies, such as sweats or sharing circles, carried out by healers or Elders.

Finally, and importantly, the social work helper and the person seeking help will have to decide on how to best utilize the support of Elders. Elders may be sought by the helper to give advice and direction on how to proceed or points to consider. Alternatively, the person seeking help may wish to be referred to an Elder for support. The case example describes the situation of Aboriginal clients seeking help for their problems. Consider the details given and, applying an Aboriginal approach, reflect on how you would try to help.

Case Example

Joan and Don

Joan is a 24-year-old single mother of three children: Adam, 5; Ariel, 4; and Neepin, 1. Adam and Ariel were taken into care by Child and Family Services soon after Joan and her former partner, Stan, moved to the city from their community. Joan and Stan, the father of Adam and Ariel, were together for four years. While their relationship began without serious concerns, it developed into one where Stan was physically abusive toward Joan, particularly when they were on drinking binges that lasted for a few days. Stan left Joan soon after the apprehension of Adam and Ariel. They were taken during one of the binges. Stan left on the pretence that "she was obviously wasn't worth it since she couldn't even keep the kids." Since that time three years ago, he has never had contact with Joan or the kids. Joan has attempted to have her kids returned, but she had agreed that they remain in the care of her mother and father until she could "straighten out her life." Her parents, Moses, 62, and Marie, 59, live in their home community. They have had nine children, of which Joan is the youngest. The oldest five of Joan's siblings live in the same community, while another resides in a neighbouring reserve and the remaining three live in the same city as Joan. Joan has not made any efforts to stay connected with her siblings because "they think they are so good since they've stopped drinking."

Just over a year ago, Joan met Don, the father of Neepin. Don is also 24 years of age. He has been trying to break away from a gang in which he was a member. He had been hanging out with the gang for six years before he was arrested for participating in beating a man. He was sentenced to two years minus a day three years ago, when he was 20. While imprisoned, Don met and spent time with an Elder who came to the prison on a weekly basis. His experience with the Elder influenced him considerably, and he reached out to an employment preparation program for help. While he tries to keep away from the gang lifestyle, other members come around periodically to get him to "go for a ride." Fortunately, Don has a good relationship with the members at the top of the gang hierarchy, who are willing to allow Don to go in light of his efforts to reconnect with his cultural traditions.

It was soon after he was released that he met Joan, and within two months they were expecting Neepin. Joan was impressed with Don's gang lifestyle, but she was also impressed with his beginning-level knowledge of their traditions. She had not heard of these cultural traditions since she was a small girl living in her community.

You are a social worker who has recently been employed in the same social service organization that runs the employment program in which Don participates. You work in a group-format program that supports young parents in developing general life skills with a focus on the skills of caring for their children. As part of the program, you also provide personal counselling to the participants. Upon the recommendation of the worker with the other program in which Don participates, Don and Joan signed up for your program. You have been directed by your supervisor to work with Joan and Don individually and as a couple in addition to your group facilitator duties. How will you, as a recently educated social worker, approach a couple who have a desire to live in traditional Aboriginal ways but are still connected to the challenges that have brought them to your program?

In reading the case example about Joan and Don, think about the values, concepts, and principles you have read about in this chapter. How might you incorporate the historical and present colonial reality that influences them? How might the concepts of wholeness, harmony, and balance be important to Don and Joan? How might these concepts relate to you in this situation? What might you be bringing into the relationships that you will be trying to establish with Joan and Don? What role could relationships, growth, and healing play in Joan's life? What role could relationships, growth, and healing play in Don's life? What might *mino-pimatisiwin* look like for each of them individually and as a couple? How might you find out? If Joan or Don spoke to you of dreams or visions, what importance do you think these might have for them? If either spoke of a relationship to the spirits and to the universe as a whole, how might you understand these? What techniques in helping could be useful (e.g., social worker–client relationship, use of Elders, ceremonies and rituals, setting goals)? How might you raise their consciousness of the colonization Aboriginal peoples face so that it relates to both Joan and Don?

Some might say that you must be a member of Joan and Don's culture (Innu, Cree, Anishinabe, Dakota, Haida, or other Nation) to help them. While it could be an asset, we do not limit the potential of others from being able to help them. We recognize that there are resources within their culture that might be very important to them and that a non-Aboriginal social worker (or an Aboriginal social worker who does not identify with traditional culture) may not be able to make use of. These include ceremonies and practices such as sweat lodges, traditional healing circles, and use of Elders. While you may not be able to gain access to these resources, you could support the couple's use of them. In learning about Don and Joan's culture from them, you may be indirectly supporting them in their growth and healing.

The overarching principles of relationship and helping through support are important. As shown in earlier chapters, support has many dimensions. Besides the support you can offer, there may be some support in the city and their home community that can be utilized. When you begin to work with Joan and Don, you can support them first by listening and being patient. You might then be able to help them in learning to relate to their families and community again or support them to discover what it means to be a couple from their cultural perspective. But these possibilities must be client directed. Joan or Don may ask your advice, but that may come after they are ready to trust you. This may take time considering their past history with social workers. The challenges they are facing, such as gang members wanting Don to join them, may cause them to move away from the changes they are making. They will need to know whom to contact should any problems arise. Sharing such information with each of them as needed will likely be necessary. On another level, you may be able to utilize their past experiences with the child welfare and justice systems as a means to introduce concepts of colonization, systemic and internalized oppression, and the need for oppressed peoples to connect with others at a community level. You may also consider incorporating these concepts in the group you facilitate and in which Don and Joan are members.

Both Don and Joan may want information from you about what you know about them and their problems. In promoting a relationship that is egalitarian, you would likely want to tell them what you know. If this is not admissible by your employer, how would you deal with the situation without losing your new job?

You cannot force either Joan or Don to take a course of action that they are not ready for or do not want at all. The support you provide must demonstrate respect for their own search for healing and growth. Unless you are able to build mutual respect in your relationship with them, it will be nearly impossible to engage in an effective helping process. Once you have developed a sense of mutual respect, you will be able to utilize your power as a social worker to support them in their growth and healing. In this situation, support will mean allowing them to identify how you can best help from the information you share about yourself, your role, your abilities, and your connections.

The well-known social work slogan "Start where the client is" comes to mind. It is best not to impose your understanding of Joan's and Don's problems on them, but to find out what they think they need. Some of this may be specific to their cultural orientation or other features of their lives (such as their desire to reconnect to their culture). Listening for awhile before speaking is a good idea. Try to understand their life experiences from an emic (insider's) perspective. Your cultural background may or may not be different from theirs, so you will filter what you learn through your own culture and background. This is true for any helping encounter. Joan and Don can tell you about their lives, their home, and their community, and this will give you a good sense of what it is like to live in their world. You must be prepared to share aspects of yourself to facilitate this exchange, if that is what is wanted by Joan and Don. The information will also be useful to you as their social worker. Once you have developed a connection with the couple, you do not want to avoid talking to them about their experiences with the child welfare and criminal justice systems; however, you will need to learn how to comfortably address these with Joan and Don. Until trust is developed in the relationship, this approach is likely the best.

From an alternative perspective, what if you were a child and family services worker responsible for ensuring the safety of Neepin? How would you work with Joan and Don in light of your mandate? How would you incorporate an Aboriginal approach when you are required to ensure certain goals are met? A key to answering this question is to remember whose goals are whose, and how power is to be used. Try to remember each of the points outlined in the previous scenario.

AN ABORIGINAL APPROACH AND CONVENTIONAL SOCIAL WORK

This book has explained that conventional social work is formulated around the problem-solving process. An Aboriginal approach, as described in this chapter, is one of four approaches that this book argues informs, critiques, and enriches conventional practice. While an Aboriginal approach is particularly suited to working with Aboriginal peoples, its concepts and ideas enrich all of social work.

Conventional social work is organized around a problem-solving process. An Aboriginal approach is not. Instead, an Aboriginal approach centres around the abstract goal of *mino-pimatisiwin*—a good life and the lifelong journey of growth and healing. Problem solving is but one part of this journey. The emphasis on this journey is on wholeness, balance, connectedness/relationships, and harmony. Like the strengths approach (Chapter 10), an Aboriginal approach emphasizes people's vitality and capacities. In an Aboriginal approach people need to be able to solve their own problems, and as the journey toward *mino-pimatisiwin* continues, problem-solving capacity increases and improves.

In an Aboriginal view, helping and healing are connected but are not the same thing. Healing is viewed as a journey and something that is practised daily throughout everyone's life. Illness and problems are viewed as disconnections, imbalances, and disharmony. Healing is the journey to *mino-pimatisiwin,* which is achieved through maintaining centredness. As such, healing involves individual responsibility for one's own well-being and growth.

As stated earlier, the focus of the helping process is on restoring relationships that have become out of balance. From a holistic perspective, it could be said that "an intervention will need to restore physical well-being to the body and harmony to the damaged social and spiritual relationships" (Ellison and Ellison, 1996, p. 148).

Helping is not seen as a direct solution of specific problems as in problem-solving processes. Instead, helping is often viewed as but one part of the healing process. Helping, in this sense, is assisting another in his or her process of healing.

The helping relationship is one in which the helper and the person receiving the support are involved in a shared experience of learning and growing. Both conventional social work and an Aboriginal approach see the helping relationship as central to helping. They also view the relationship between social worker and client as a mutual partnership. However, an Aboriginal approach carries this view further in that the helper and the person being helped are in an interdependent relationship where they can both learn and grow. Ideally, a helper using an Aboriginal approach is to have experiential knowledge of centredness and the issues she or he is addressing. Goals are determined by the person being helped in an Aboriginal approach and connect to lifelong processes of healing. In the ecosystems approach, as in problem-solving processes, goals are specifically related to the problem and are usually determined mutually between the helper and the person being helped.

An Aboriginal Approach and Ecosystems

Ecosystems was introduced in Chapter 9 as a person-in-the-environment perspective. Central to an ecosystems approach is the interaction and connections between the person and the environment. It is not much of a stretch to suggest, as some do (see Longclaws, 1994), that an Aboriginal approach bears some resemblance to a person-in-the-environment perspective and to an ecosystems view. It is true that an Aboriginal approach focuses heavily on relationships, including the relationship between people and their environments. In this sense, it is a person-in-the-environment perspective. Further Aboriginal concepts such as balance and disharmony share similarities with the ecosystems principles, like equilibrium and disequilibrium. However, as was shown throughout this chapter, the Aboriginal perspective is both much broader and more inclusive.

Neither ecosystems nor an Aboriginal approach is, as such, a theory. Instead, both are used in social work as perspectives and approaches and provide frameworks for practice. Ecosystems is drawn from biological ecology. There is no social ecological theory, although many testable hypotheses can be drawn from ecosystems. An Aboriginal approach has been developed over many centuries by North American Aboriginal cultures and represents a worldview that has only some similarities to ecological ideas. In this context, an Aboriginal perspective and ecosystems are not of the same order; ecosystems is a framework borrowed from biology. An Aboriginal perspective is a broader worldview with a very wide range of principles and teachings.

Central concepts in ecosystems are transaction and interface. Transaction generally refers to the interactions and connections between systems including a person and the person's environment. Ecosystems holds that all systems have abstract boundaries or, metaphorically speaking, edges that distinguish and separate a given system from other systems. Often, however, systems connect with one another and overlap. The interface is the point at which systems come into contact with one another. An ecosystems approach holds that social work assessment and intervention should focus on these twin concepts of transaction and interface. In the ecosystems approach, social workers seek to restore the fit between the person and the environment (Sheafor, Horejsi, and Horejsi, 2000, p. 92).

An Aboriginal approach is similar but also very different. In an Aboriginal approach, as in ecosystems, the connections between parts are emphasized. Similar to the ecosystems concentration on fit between person and environment, an Aboriginal approach focuses on restoring relationships that have become out of balance. However, an Aboriginal approach goes much further in that it also centres on the wholeness of everything, including the person, the environment, the spiritual and physical worlds, the universe, and the connections among all of these parts. Thus, wholeness is the incorporation of *all* aspects of life. To focus on the whole, it becomes necessary to give attention to each part.

Further, an Aboriginal approach includes understanding the conscious and unconscious, with an emphasis on spirituality. Spirituality is vitally important as the basis of all connections and beings. As such, healing involves the spiritual aspect of people.

The focus of ecosystems is narrower and centres on maximizing individual growth and development through people's transactions and fit with the environment. Mutual causality between environment and person, stress, adaptation, and goodness of fit between person and environment are emphasized. The ecosystems approach avoids inner-self factors such as the unconscious and spirituality, and if addressed at all they remain at the periphery of the approach.

In summary, it is important that social workers not confuse an Aboriginal approach with ecosystems even though they have some important similarities.

CHAPTER SUMMARY

This chapter has articulated a range of ideas and concepts that together make up an Aboriginal approach to social work. This approach is based on a broad worldview that has important implications for all of social work. As an approach to social work, it both challenges and informs conventional ideas and practices. In many respects, an Aboriginal perspective is the product of adapting a centuries-old helping and healing process to modern society and conditions.

The history of Aboriginal peoples in North America is one of colonialism, involving a process of attempted cultural assimilation, subordination, and economic exploitation. Conventional social work is often seen as part of the colonization of Aboriginal peoples, as in the past it took the form of authoritarian control and regulation by external agents who had little understanding or appreciation of Aboriginal cultures. The healing and helping process with Aboriginal peoples must often address the personal and social wounds of colonization.

Aboriginal peoples vary extensively in their worldviews. The approach developed here is based on a few of these Aboriginal worldviews, thus it is *an* Aboriginal approach, not *the* approach. One of the models that guides this approach and that is frequently mentioned in the literature is the medicine wheel. As a central symbol used for understanding various issues and perspectives, the medicine wheel reflects several key and interrelated concepts and teachings that are common to many Aboriginal approaches to helping and may be seen as the foundation to the Aboriginal approach described in this chapter. These concepts are wholeness, balance, relationships, harmony, growth, healing, and the important goal of *mino-pimatisiwin*—the good life.

The Aboriginal approach described in this chapter is one of many that are being used in various helping professions, including social work. Its focus is on relationships within and between beings, with the ultimate goal of growing toward *mino-pimatisiwin.*

NOTES

1 A legal term used to refer to First Nations, Métis, and Inuit people. In this chapter, "Aboriginal peoples" refers to people who have family connections to First Nations ancestry, including individuals referred to as American Indians. "Aboriginal people" has been used to refer to individuals, and "Aboriginal peoples" to groups.

2 Turtle Island is the name used by some Aboriginal peoples to refer to North America.

Structural Social Work and Social Change

Chapter Goal

To describe the structural approach and demonstrate how structural social work can effectively be used in everyday direct social work practice to effect social change.

This Chapter ▼

- connects structural social work with radical social work and anti-oppressive social work
- presents a social work approach that directly confronts all forms of discrimination, oppression, repression, and subjugation
- stresses the need for reflection and reflexivity in social work
- identifies and describes some of the practice applications of structural social work
- describes and discusses the importance of collective action
- shows that structural social work, unlike person-in-the-environment approaches, centres on the environment itself
- connects social work practice with the socioeconomic and political environments
- identifies and articulates a number of useful roles in structural social work
- demonstrates how a structural analysis and intervention can be used in everyday practice

FOUNDATIONS OF STRUCTURAL SOCIAL WORK

Structural social work has its roots in a radical perspective of practice. **Radical social work** focuses heavily on a **conflict perspective** and analysis of the existing social order. The worldview of radical social workers is based on eliminating injustice and inequality, redistributing economic resources, analyzing power, and working toward a society that is based on cooperation and sharing (Burghardt, 1986, pp. 590–617; Payne, 1997, 214–37). This approach to social work focuses on a socialist analysis of state control and oppression, and advocates changing the existing social order and related structures that oppress people. Traditional social work is seen as a form of social control that maintains social problems. Classism, patriarchy, racism, ageism, sexism, heterosexism, imperialism, and ableism are seen as oppressive forces (Davis, 1991; Mullaly, 1997, pp. 108–10). Radical social work has also been characterized by its flexibility and openness in responding to the demands and issues of various groups that experience discrimination and oppression (Langan and Lee, 1989).

CONNECTION BETWEEN RADICAL AND STRUCTURAL SOCIAL WORK

Radical social work theory, in the past, has not offered much to frontline practitioners working with clients (Mullaly, 1997). Structural social work, a perspective articulated in Canada by Moreau (1979) and later championed by Mullaly, offers a direct practice application of radical social work that leads to social change.

There are, however, other examples of attempts to link radical thinking to practice. Janis Fook, in her book *Radical Casework: A Theory of Practice* (1993), provides examples comparing how client situations are approached from conventional and radical social work orientations. Her book illustrates how radical casework is essentially good social work practice.

Structural social work tends to focus on applications at the level of frontline practice. It is not only concerned with the oppressive features of social structures, but also responds to those who are oppressed. This chapter articulates ways to understand and apply structural social work.

ANTI-OPPRESSIVE SOCIAL WORK

In Chapter 9 we introduced oppression and anti-oppressive practice. According to Mullaly (2002), oppression is dynamic, affecting differently social relationships between individuals and groups, at different times and in different situations. As evident in the story of Tom (Chapter 6), a boy who experienced labelling and discrimination, oppression may also be internalized by those who feel its effects. It is not simply a matter of one group oppressing another. Also, people or groups who see themselves as oppressed often attempt to fight against oppressive practices by taking action (e.g., letter writing, lobbying politicians, organizing marches, and performing street theatre). As discussed in Chapter 7, social work seeks ways to eradicate discrimination, subjugation, and oppression of individuals and groups. Anti-oppressive social work practice counters the effects of these processes through intervention at individual, group, and community levels, recognizing that diverse forms of oppression have always existed and continue to exist in our society.

Anti-oppressive social work should form a backdrop or frame for all of social work. Social workers as part of good daily practice need to help clients handle oppression they have experienced and, in Mullaly's (2002) words, challenge personal, cultural, and structural issues that promote and cause oppression. Anti-oppressive social work is particularly congruent with structural social work because both acknowledge and work to counter oppression based on class, race, sex, physical ability, sexual orientation, age, and others.

Background

In the 1960s and 1970s, the feminist, civil rights, and peace movements, among other **social movements,** introduced critiques of social work practice as it existed at the time in North America and Britain. Criticism was levelled at many professions that were seen as maintaining social inequality and protecting the existing relations of power by a few over many others. Professional helpers, working on behalf of the state, were viewed as perpetuating injustice by not initiating change to benefit those who were most disadvantaged or oppressed in society. Social work that was involved in service delivery under these conditions was regarded as supporting the status quo (Galper, 1975) and the continued oppression of clients. Social work was—and continues to be—caught in a contradiction because it served to control clients on the one hand while trying to help them on the other.

Social workers as a group daily face the difficulties of people who are poor, ill, lonely, in conflict with the law, or otherwise troubled. Sometimes the differences between people who are in difficulty and those whose job it is to help them are not very large. "Social workers, *unlike other workers,* confront daily, as their job, the victims of an economic and political structure that creates poverty and humiliation" (Bailey and Brake, 1980, p. 8). As social workers, we are subject to the same conditions and structures as our clients, but unlike many clients, we have acquired a professional education and other privileges that provide advantages.

Radical social work ideas disagree with a singular focus on the individual as an architect of his or her situation, and stress how problems are caused by or related to social factors and events that are beyond individuals' direct control. However, without a social revolution it would be difficult to implement all of the goals of radical social work. Some suggest that social workers join with workers in labour unions and get involved in political parties to work for change outside their profession (Fook, 1993, p. 6). Few guidelines are available, however, for social workers to practise using a radical approach. Everyday social work practice, involving large caseloads and complex human problems, takes up much time and energy, leaving little for social action. How can social workers realistically combine the two?

Colleen Lundy (2004, pp. 63–67) identifies five goals of structural social work. The following activities are involved: (1) acting as allies of clients to promote their rights and advocate for their interests; (2) bringing people together to solve problems and effect social change; (3) analyzing the effects of poverty and unequal distribution of wealth to avoid blaming individuals; (4) working to enhance the power of clients in relation to social workers in practice situations; and (5) promoting and supporting clients' personal change goals. As Lundy describes, the goals and practices of structural social work in Canada have been advanced by an extensive study by Moreau and Frosst (1993) at Carleton University.

A Conflict Perspective

Structural and radical social work, based on the notion that society is characterized by conflict between groups of people, acknowledges differences in power, influence, and access to the good things in life. Traditional social work is based on an order perspective.

Simply put, the **order perspective** sees society as holding common values and sharing a similar culture. This view holds that, in general, people in our society have similar chances to succeed in life. However, some are better at succeeding, or are luckier, than others. This perspective also assumes a consensus among the majority of people regarding how social institutions function in society.

The conflict perspective rejects such a view, claiming that society consists of people with opposing views and interests who are continuously trying to have their ideas and wishes recognized. Society is not seen as held together by consensus but by "differential control of resources and political power" (Mullaly, 1997, p. 119). A critique of the present social order and capitalism is central to structural social work: "Social work is seen as both reproducing and able to undermine patriarchy, racism and class society" (Moreau with Leonard, 1989, p. 10). Agreement among people cannot be assumed, since diverse groups of people with varying views and interests constantly struggle to have their needs met through public channels. In addition, the interpretation of needs often differs among groups (Fraser, 1989). For example, publicly provided health care may be seen as covering a wide range of curative and preventive health care services by some people, but can also be viewed as limited to more narrow physician-provided care by others.

Framing

Wharf and McKenzie (1998) state that how a problem is framed suggests the range of solutions being considered: "[Framing] sets out preferences and prescribes limits based on ideologies and experiences, but refrains from the explicitness expected of a definition [of a social problem]" (p. 41). They describe how the problem of poverty, as an example, could be framed either as people's lack of desire to work hard, or as too few available jobs, or as complex factors related to broader social trends. The prevailing viewpoint on the problem (usually put forward by the current government) shapes the strategies and methods that are developed to deal with it. Pointing to possible outcomes of different framings of the problem, Wharf and McKenzie suggest that there could be increased incentives (or penalties) for not working, job creation measures, or broader policy initiatives.

The way in which these outcomes are created is complex and depends on many factors. Nancy Fraser (1989) explains how public debate about people's needs (needs talk) and how these needs are interpreted constantly shift. She refers to childcare, once considered a private, domestic issue but one that has now become the subject of public debate as governments and various groups strive to put forward their vision of what is needed. A perspective that acknowledges the influence of different voices (e.g., parents, childcare providers, the state, workplaces) in the public forum of policymaking can help us understand how alternate views or "framings" take hold at different times and in different places, affecting how problems are seen and resolved. Drawing attention to the experiences and voices of individuals who have not always been heard and who have knowledge to share can be useful.

The Place of Structural Social Work in Practice

By the late 1970s, structural social work was being taught in a number of North American and European social work schools, including Carleton University in Ottawa. Maurice Moreau was a strong proponent of structural social work (Bailey and Brake, 1980). He saw this work as addressing various intersecting forms of oppression, not only the class structure (Mullaly, 1997). His book *Empowerment through a Structural Approach to Social Work* (Moreau with Leonard, 1989) is a report of research on how social workers applied principles of structural social work and dealt with barriers and opportunities in their day-to-day practice. The social workers who took part in the study had graduated from Carleton University and had been exposed to structural social work, emphasizing an "analysis of power at all levels, a community approach and client empowerment" (Moreau with Leonard, 1989, p. viii). Findings from the study suggest that social workers worked within their organizations and with their clients for change, but faced considerable difficulty in becoming involved in broader-level change, which was often seen as problematic for their organizations. The less autonomy and workplace support for social change that workers had, the more difficult it was to fully apply a structural approach. The results of the research point out that social workers felt that they could not act independently without risking the well-being of their clients or their job security. Although they strove to apply structural social work principles, they faced some limitations due to their professional and workplace environments. The study concludes that social work

> operates in a wider social context which delimits the possibilities open to its workers or to clients. In order both to understand and take effective action, structural social workers have to perceive and act outside the social framework *as well as within* it. To do so, they must protect themselves both within social agencies in which they work and outside their confines. (Moreau with Leonard, 1989, p. 277)

What this means is that structural social workers find spaces and opportunities for change in their own agencies and organizations as well as in the broader social environment, but do not do so without care and without weighing the consequences of their actions.

People's personal problems are seen as primarily caused by unequal socioeconomic (also referred to as "class") features, which control and exploit individuals in society. Material (food, clothing, and shelter) and personal needs must be separated in order to avoid "blaming the victim" so that clients are not held wholly responsible, for example, for their situation of poverty. As discussed earlier, it is necessary to look beyond the individual person or family to address the source of problems. Social workers must examine the social, economic, and political conditions that lead to or create poverty for some and wealth for others, rather than the reasons individuals and families fail to maintain themselves. Collective action (e.g., advocating for better wages in an industry, organizing a media campaign or rally) is seen as a particularly effective means of addressing people's needs from a macro level (Payne, 1991, p. 205).

STRUCTURAL SOCIAL WORK AND DIRECT PRACTICE

Most social workers are employed in **direct practice** positions. Only a few find jobs in which the primary function is based on collective action and activism. However, direct practice workers should still engage in efforts to bring about social change in their own work and take part in collective action.

Often, direct practice workers acknowledge the importance of social change but go about their daily work without a hint of social change activity. A comment by Laurence Shulman (1999) typifies this position. In his widely read and respected book *The Skills of Helping*, on social work practice with individuals, families, groups, and communities, Shulman acknowledges, in reference to radical social work practice, the importance of the need to "modify institutionalized oppression." He then asserts,

> The client cannot wait for the major changes in our society that will be needed to modify institutionalized oppression. Thus, while we need a conceptualization of practice which reframes our way of viewing client troubles and requires us to act on injustices in our society (and agencies), we simultaneously must provide services to the victims of these injustices. (p. 27)

Most of direct social work practice is concerned with how to help clients adjust, adapt to, and make use of the resources of a system that we acknowledge as unjust. This is the nature of the problem-solving approach. As is common among social work practitioners, practice theorists frequently acknowledge the importance of social change and then dismiss it as something for someone else or another branch of social work to deal with.

Direct service practitioners are primarily responsible for providing services to clients even if the system is unjust. But this does not relieve these same practitioners of the responsibility to engage in social change, because social change is at the root of social work. The CASW's code of ethics emphasizes the importance of eliminating oppression and injustice and enhancing humanitarian and egalitarian ideals. All social workers have the responsibility to work toward these ends.

This task is not easy. Frontline workers cannot suddenly become agents of social change, but in almost all direct practice there is room to work toward social justice and equality. Much of the balance of this chapter addresses this type of work.

REFLECTION AND REFLEXIVITY IN SOCIAL WORK

A number of authors point out that social workers must critically reflect on their practice, which means unpacking its underlying ideology, assumptions, and values. Reflection requires a willingness to examine oneself and a desire to learn about alternative views on client situations and worker interventions. Reflection advances to reflexivity when insights are integrated into subsequent social work practice. As Payne, Adams, and Dominelli (2002) assert, "*Reflexivity* means being in a circular process where social workers 'put themselves into the picture' by thinking and acting with the people they are serving, so that their understandings and actions inevitably are changed by their experiences with others" (p. 3).

We believe that reflection and reflexivity help social workers to practise critically. The understanding acquired when these processes are part of everyday practice can lead to improved client assessment and intervention skills and greater satisfaction among social workers in the work they perform.

APPLYING THE STRUCTURAL APPROACH IN PRACTICE

Overview

Mullaly (1997) suggests that structural social work practice can take place inside and outside the sociopolitical system. However, he emphasizes that, in both instances, the goal of working for social change works against the system.

Working outside the system is essentially a political activity. It entails social activism related to social movements and building coalitions to challenge established institutions. Union organizations and professional associations can be used as vehicles for social change. Frequently, working outside the system involves electoral politics, often at the local level (see Mullaly, 1997, Chapter 10). Relatively few social workers find paid employment in positions where the intent is to work outside the system.

In this chapter, we focus on how generalist social workers can use structural social work principles in their regular practice. In Mullaly's words, this is work within but against the system. As you will recall, social workers who use the problem-solving approach work with clients on problems within their environment, rather than on problems in the environment itself that negatively affect people. For example, think of the situation of a family living solely on social assistance benefits. They may come to see a social worker because they are not able to stretch the money they receive to pay for rent, groceries, and other needs. The family may be facing some crisis that creates additional financial strain, say the illness of one member.

A social worker who applies the problem-solving framework will explore the situation of the client and how the family has been managing up until now. She or he will usually ask about supportive and stressful relationships within the family and with systems outside it, and about the family's coping strategies and how they have managed problems before. Once the need for help is clear, the social worker and clients plan what work needs to be done and agree on the goals and actions to meet these needs. One strategy might be to increase the resources of the family so they will have enough to eat. People differ in terms of their access to resources, backup systems, or supports that can be drawn on for help during tough times, and this capacity will also be a part of assessment. Based on mutual planning and goals, the social worker might then refer the family to a food bank, offer help in planning nutritious and economical meals, and suggest shopping strategies. She or he might also advocate on behalf of the family by contacting the social welfare department and asking whether the family's benefits can be increased. Essentially, the social worker does not initiate change beyond the clients and their current relationship with the social welfare department.

Collective Action

Structural social work challenges the above approach through its focus on **collective action**—working together for change—beyond the client–agency boundary at the levels of community and society. Although the strategy of increasing people's resources so that they can meet their basic needs is an important one, other strategies aimed at broader changes must also be used. Making connections between the individual or family situation and the social, economic, and political context in which they are embedded is necessary. "No matter how well meaning a social worker, a criticism is justified if, as a result of dealing with a client, that client remains unaware of the public dimension of his or her problems" (Bailey and Brake, 1980, p. 8).

For example, the social worker, aware that social assistance benefits, like many other social programs, are being steadily decreased by the government, might want to work alongside clients with a local antipoverty or welfare rights group to lobby the government, help organize a rally to oppose social assistance reductions, or write letters to government leaders. A structural social worker might also work in a local community to initiate projects to increase resources at the community level, such as community vegetable gardens or food co-ops.

A structural approach must include at its centre the active search for and identification and use of people's individual and collective strengths. Coming together with others who face similar circumstances or problems can increase the pool of strengths, adding to its power and diversity. In community organizing, the need for representation from all groups makes for a richer breadth of ideas and talents that can be used in local planning and action. When common goals and working relationships are established in a group, a sense of direction and energy results. The stress on collectivities in structural social work makes it especially useful in social work in community organizations, or as Carniol (1995) terms it, in "alternative social services" (p. 123), where collaborative and cooperative work characterizes the relationships between social workers and community residents who want to improve their lives. Some of the roles of such social workers have been discussed in Chapter 4.

One problem with the structural approach is that sometimes collective action will not, at least in the short run, actually help the individual client. How can one work in an agency that provides a mandated social service (e.g., child welfare, public welfare, or corrections) and still attempt to change the social structure so that the changes actually help individual clients? There are many ways to make this possible. For example, suppose you are working as a counsellor in a public welfare agency in the inner city. All of your clients are on social assistance. You and some of your coworkers recognize that food takes up a large proportion of benefits they receive. Your group considers and then quickly rejects the idea of organizing public demonstrations and actively lobbying for an increase in welfare payments. You are civil servants and you could risk losing your jobs. Further, you recognize that, given the current government emphasis on reducing deficits and cutting taxes, increases are unlikely.

One of your colleagues has heard of community kitchens (adapted from a Latin American model), where food is purchased at low cost and cooked and eaten communally or stored for the use of local families. This is really a kind of co-op that has worked well in many other Canadian cities. Why not help your clients organize a community kitchen? This sort of action is not only good structural social work, it is also simply good social work. This kind of project might also lead to other collective activities at the local community level or beyond.

There are some similarities between how the problem-solving framework and structural social work are applied. Both address and attempt to solve problems. However, in structural social work the emphasis is on collective change and social action, while in the problem-solving approach the client is expected to have her or his needs met within the boundaries of the existing social structure.

Structural features in society may be experienced negatively, contributing to or creating problems for people. Discrimination and oppression adversely affect many people's lives. Consider a young boy who is often teased by his classmates because he has a hearing impairment, or a Muslim woman whose style of dress is met with disdain at work. Bishop (1994) explains that there are many forms of oppression besides that related to socioeconomic class. Racism, sexism, and heterosexism, as well as discrimination due to disability, national origin, religion, age, and others, can oppress people whether they are rich, middle class, or poor. Discrimination cuts across classes, but people who have more money and other resources are better able to protect themselves from it or to confront it directly. With reference to disability, for example, Bishop states,

> You will find more people with disabilities the lower you go in the class strata, because discrimination based on disability affects the education and employment opportunities of people with disabilities. Also, a disability limits the life of a person in a lower class more than it does someone who has wealth and power. (p. 65)

From the quotation above, it is possible to understand that being poor and living with a disability may mean fewer opportunities to succeed in education or work. The accommodations that help to reduce barriers (e.g., computer technology, mobility devices, etc.) can be costly to purchase.

A social worker is concerned with the structures in society and how they act to oppress people (Mullaly, 1997). These structural features are significant in clients' life situations.

Structural Social Work and the Environment

Social work practice tends to focus mainly on interpersonal relationship issues rather than on the social environment itself. The ecosystems approach (see Chapter 9), currently in widespread use in social work practice, emphasizes people's capacity for coping and adapting as well as reaching out to resources in the surrounding environment when help is needed. Germain and Gitterman maintain that when such resources are not available or are denied, "the professional function is to influence those structures and processes to be more responsive to client need" (cited in Wharf, 1990, p. 23). This principle of the ecosystems approach, which encourages social workers to work toward changing structures and processes to respond better to client needs, resembles the ideals of structural social work. In reality, the approaches are quite different.

In ecosystems, the focus is squarely on the connections between the person and the environment and not, as in a structural view, on the environment itself. Another way of putting it is that in ecosystems the unit of analysis is the connection between the person and the environment, whereas in structural social work it is the environment. In practice, most social work is conducted with individuals and families and is not aimed at broader-level change. Improving the environment so that people can obtain material and other resources to improve their lives (e.g., jobs, financial help, housing, counselling, etc.) is often difficult.

Although they have the greatest stake in changing their situation, people who are most affected by structural problems often have the fewest resources and least influence in speaking out for change (Wharf, 1990, p. 23). Most social workers, due to agency mandates and resource constraints, tend to focus more on working with people's personal or interpersonal problems and far less on environmental or structural ones. Psychosocial aspects are only one part of a person's life, however, and the influence of social structures must be seen to be connected to them (Fook, 1993, pp. 43–44).

Case Example

Maria and the Low Family ▼

Kai Low is a 30-year-old man who took a construction job upon completing high school. He married at a young age and, with his wife, Linh, a newcomer to Canada, spent many difficult years trying to make ends meet. They have an eight-year-old son, Kevin, a quiet boy who is doing relatively well in the third grade at a nearby school. Last year, Kai injured his lower body while working on a nonunion, private job when he was unable to find other work. He was not covered by workers' compensation or any other insurance. Kai decided not to sue because the company moved out of town and he did not know where it had gone. Besides, he had no money to pay a lawyer. He was hospitalized for a month, discharged home, and then referred for regular physiotherapy. Kai has had a long rehabilitation period as he has struggled to regain strength in his legs and back. He has been receiving some financial support from social assistance since his employment insurance benefits ran out a few months ago.

Linh works as a seamstress in her own home. The piecework wages she earns are too low to maintain the family. As a result, the family has had to move to a cheaper apartment and borrow money from relatives to make ends meet. Kai is upset and angry about his situation. He has begun to argue with his wife about money. He is also worried about how he can find a job again once he is well enough. He knows that he can't physically handle construction work again. Feelings of failure dominate his thoughts. He feels ashamed when his parents visit because he thinks they are disappointed by his inability to work and his need to accept help from the government. He was raised to believe that providing financially for his family was his primary responsibility.

Linh has phoned Maria, a social worker whose agency is listed in the phone book. Maria's agency offers job training and work placement for people who are unemployed. Linh tells Maria about the family's situation. Maria can clearly hear the stress and concern in Linh's voice. She asks Linh to talk to her husband, who is willing to meet with Maria provided she can help him get a job.

In thinking about the family's difficulties, Maria knows she'll want to help Kai with his personal concerns, but she also wants to consider his social situation—how he and his family have been affected by inequitable social arrangements (e.g., lack of workplace protection, low wages, and exploitive piecework). Maria reflects on her ideas about this couple's problems. She wants to carefully consider how her own assumptions about their relationship might influence her actions.

After she spends time learning from the couple about their situation, Maria changes the way she planned to work with the couple, because she realized that her assumptions were incorrect. Maria also acknowledges the couple's strengths as they struggle to maintain their family with little support and few rewards. She recognizes how distress and hardship can occur when people are not blessed with health and wealth. In this case, the family's coping capacity is seriously affected.

Consider the case example of Maria and the Low family. A problem-solving or strengths approach would frame this situation using an ecosystems, role theory, or another person-in-the-environment conceptualization that explains individual behaviours in an environmental context. The family's problems, while not their or the system's fault, are their responsibility. It is up to them to do something about the problems. The system will help them, within its capabilities, but in the end it is up to the Lows to make the best use of available resources.

A structural analysis takes a very different perspective. While Kai still needs to recuperate from his accident, the family's main problems are seen as structural rather than individual (see Payne, 1997, p. 214). The Lows' problems need to be understood in a political and economic context (see Fisher and Karger, 1997, pp. 43–64, for a discussion of the context of social work practice). The Lows are victims of a social system that does not effectively meet the needs of people who experience difficulties in life or who are disadvantaged in some way. The economic system, based on industrial capitalism, works against people like Kai and Linh who are unable to take advantage of the system (Burghardt, 1986).

The social safety net has failed the Lows. Their income, after Kai's accident, is too low to meet their needs. There is no built-in program or appropriate follow-up for him to begin preparing for a return to the job market or job retraining while he is receiving physiotherapy. The reasons for the limited programs are both political and economic.

Kai and Linh also have immediate needs that must be met. Although a structural analysis sheds an important and different light on the family's problems, any social change will likely be too late for them. Maria clearly has a responsibility to respond to Linh's request for help concerning job training and placement for her husband. Maria probably has two immediate priorities: to ensure that the Lows are not going hungry and that their basic needs are being met, and to involve Kai in a helping process. From this point on, Maria and the Lows will need to negotiate the goals and next steps.

Nevertheless, Maria may still try to use this situation to engage in social change. In Kai's case, she may offer to look into regulations and standards of safety for short-term contract work. Kai may not have known that the company's lack of insurance coverage for injuries would mean that he would have no protection if something happened to him. It might be determined that the company was operating illegally and could be held liable for the accident. Social workers might advocate for better working conditions and benefits so people don't "fall through the cracks." Letters could be written on Kai's behalf to government representatives, unions, or occupational health organizations. If he is agreeable to this, Maria could also help to bring people with similar experiences together to discuss the issues so they can consider taking action.

Maria would likely want to discuss Linh's situation as it seems that her job is unsatisfactory. Perhaps the experience she has in sewing would help her to find a better job that includes employee benefits.

It is possible that the Lows may decide not to participate in these initiatives. Perhaps they do not want to "make waves" or they justifiably feel vulnerable in their current situation. Structural social workers take care not to coerce clients into becoming involved, do not reveal clients' identity without their permission, and do not put their own desire to correct an injustice or change policies above the needs of the client. Although difficult decisions must be made in taking client situations to a higher level, the social work codes of ethics give workers a mandate to promote social change to better people's lives.

It is much easier to work with people at the individual or interpersonal level and aim for small changes in behaviour than to strive to change features or institutions of society. In carrying out any change effort, it is essential for social workers to carefully consider the risks and potential consequences for clients and themselves, asking questions such as: What effects might there be for the social worker, the client, and the worker's organization? What does the client have to gain or lose? Is the client prepared and able to take the risks that are involved?

Roles in Structural Social Work

Chapter 4 outlined a number of roles in generalist social work. Of these, at least three roles can also be used in structural social work: advocate (particularly class advocacy), enabler, and educator. Two others—social policy analyst and policy activist—might be applied to effect system change.

Maybe the most frequent role that direct practice workers fill in using a structural perspective is advocacy. Sometimes the reason a social worker advocates on behalf of a client is because the worker's skills in accessing an important resource or influencing a decision are simply better than the client's, so the chances of success are better. At other times, the need for advocacy results when a client or group of clients wants to change an oppressive, discriminatory, or unjust policy. Most workers will, from time to time, face the need to address such a structural issue.

Usually advocacy is not thought of as collective action because it is the social worker who advocates. However, a structural approach particularly emphasizes class advocacy—action that is taken on behalf of a group of clients. The group, for example, must inform the worker and negotiate with him or her to ensure that the worker clearly understands the issues and can address the different views among group members. While the collective action is not a direct social change attempt, class advocacy does require collective group participation.

The enabler role can be used to facilitate collective action. In a sense, it is the opposite of advocacy by a social worker in that the attempt at social change is made by a collective of others. Sometimes a direct practice worker faces a situation in which a solution to a problem requires the worker to mobilize clients in order to deal with an injustice that unfairly affects them. At other times a social worker may be approached by a group of clients with a request for action.

Often, enabling requires that the social worker be an educator. In order for clients to engage in social action, including collective action, they need to be informed. The social worker may be in a position to provide clients with important information or to help them search out, find, and use such information.

Ben Carniol (1995) suggests several ways that social workers can apply structural principles. The first of these he calls reconstructed social work counselling. The heart of this process is to view counselling as a shared experience between worker and client, with the client in charge and in control. This view of counselling is quite different from that of problem solving (Chapter 8) but very similar to the consumer-driven approach of the strengths perspective (Chapter 10), an Aboriginal approach (Chapter 11), and feminist practice (Chapter 13).

In some ways Carniol's second proposal is an extension of his first. In most social service programs, the government (in public agencies) or the board of directors (in private organizations) controls policy and determines programs. Alternative social services are a plan in which the users control the provision of services.

> Alternative services usually spring from the work of a specific oppressed community or movement: First Nations people, ethnic and visible minorities, lesbians and gay men, local tenants' groups, the disabled, or ex-psychiatric patients, with women being worse off in each of these groups, which is why women are the majority of users of social services. (Carniol, 1995, p. 123)

Social action is the mobilization of people to put pressure on established institutions, using nonviolent protests and demonstrations, to change programs or policy. Carniol argues that social workers can use labour unions to help establish equity and mitigate against injustices. Finally, he also argues that **coalitions** are powerful ways to initiate social change and start a social movement, or broad-based organized effort to create change. Coalitions bring together different people from different constituencies to work on a common problem, greatly increasing their resources and ability to bring pressure for change. For example, immigrant or Aboriginal women may need to organize in order to resolve an injustice. If both groups can form alliances with, say, each other or with labour unions, church groups, or women's organizations, then the likelihood of success is considerably greater.

Carniol (1995) argues that these strategies are not without pitfalls. For example, social movements and social action groups tend to have a short lifespan. Some of the strategies are very difficult for social workers employed in mandated agencies, such as corrections or child welfare, to carry out. However, user- or consumer-driven approaches are becoming more common in Canada. First Nations and Métis people, for example, are beginning to establish their own social agencies and programs. While structural social work supports such moves, Carniol warns that care must be taken to avoid the problems experienced by older, more conventional approaches.

EXAMPLE OF STRUCTURAL SOCIAL WORK AND DIRECT PRACTICE

Some may think that the principles of structural social work are too esoteric and removed from daily life to be useful in generalist social work practice. They argue that it is difficult to put the principles into practice. To counter this criticism, the Low family case example illustrates the importance of understanding the socioeconomic environment of clients and how clients might engage in social change that benefits themselves as well as other members of society. This section uses the case of Kenny to further articulate a number of principles of and approaches to social change that can be implemented by generalist social workers in their regular practice. This case example also demonstrates how the structural approach can be used in direct practice and complements other interventions, including the problem-solving and strengths approaches. The intent is to clearly demonstrate that frontline, generalist social workers cannot afford to ignore structural and social change skills.

In the case of Kenny and the boarding homes of Martins Grove, it will be seen that not only was it good social work practice for the case manager to help individual clients select a social change strategy over restorative intervention, but also that the social change strategy was easier and more efficient.

Case Example

Kenny and the Boarding Homes of Martins Grove

Kenny was first admitted to the mental health centre 14 years ago. At the time, he was 27 years old. He had previously held a number of unskilled jobs and had never married. One day, when walking to work at a car wash, Kenny began to hear voices. These voices were sometimes loud but were usually just mutterings. The voices bothered Kenny, but he did not tell anyone about them.

At the same time, Kenny began to develop a deep fear of "catfish." Catfish are ugly, slimy fish with long whiskers that are often found on the bottom of muddy rivers. Kenny began to believe that there were huge catfish lurking at the bottom of nearby rivers, and he became obsessed with the fish.

One day a particularly loud voice told him that the owner of the car he was cleaning was evil and that Kenny must destroy the inside of the car. If Kenny did not, catfish would rise from the rivers. Before anyone could stop him, Kenny ripped the car seats with a screwdriver, broke the windows, and destroyed the dashboard. The police were called, and Kenny was arrested and taken to the hospital for assessment. Shortly after being admitted, he began to ramble about the huge catfish and how ugly and fearful they were. Kenny was diagnosed with schizophrenia.

For the next seven years after Kenny's first admission to hospital, he had periods of symptom remission followed by stays at the centre for up to six months. When out of the hospital, he would become lonely and stop taking his medication. Nightmares about the catfish would return.

Kenny felt safe in the mental health centre, mostly because of the routine. He particularly enjoyed his work in the garden and, during winter, in a small greenhouse. Generally Kenny could avoid the severe episodes if he took his antipsychotic medication. Both Kenny and the staff at the centre knew that he needed a supportive living arrangement, maybe for the rest of his life.

Danielle, Kenny's new case manager, learned that he liked the cottage and lake country and that there were some small, marginal farms that boarded mental health clients near several lakes in an area called Martins Grove. The farm that was selected for Kenny offered an opportunity for him to putter in a garden much as he did at the centre. Danielle suggested to Kenny that they take a drive to see one of the farms.

Kenny moved to the farm and was there, without incident, for eight months. He formed reasonably good relationships with the other boarders, and he liked Anna and Josef, the owners. His symptoms reappeared only once: Anna reported one day that when fishing, she happened to catch a catfish. This set Kenny off and the old fears returned. He began to babble almost incoherently. Luckily, however, Anna was able to calm him down. Kenny, amazingly, understood that catfish were commonly caught in the nearby rivers and that they were harmless even though very strange looking. Kenny seemed to have taken a very small step toward recovery.

Anna and Josef were also pleased. They were gratified that Kenny seemed to fit in, and the room and board fees from Kenny and the other clients provided the couple with much-needed income.

The community mental health workers were impressed by the environment that the farm couple provided. Over a few years, the number of residents had risen from two to four. Also, because of the success that Anna and Josef were having, 11 other families in the community began to house people who suffered from a serious mental illness. In total, 29 residents were boarded in affordable and supportive housing. The boarding-home program at Martins Grove not only had become an excellent resource for the mental health centre, but also was beginning to nicely contribute to the local economy. In a way it was a cottage industry. Then two events occurred at almost the same time, both of which could have spelled disaster for the program.

Kenny relied on social assistance to pay for his board. At first, the local welfare department agreed that Kenny was eligible for the boarding home. The total cost was far less than that of keeping Kenny in the hospital. The money he received was sufficient to cover the cost of his board, buy a few clothes, and give him about $35 pocket money per month. Since Kenny had few expenses, he usually managed to save a part of his pocket money.

The Martins Grove welfare department had a policy of requiring annual medical reports, including diagnosis and prognosis. From the report at the end of Kenny's first year at the boarding home, it was clear that Kenny was adjusting quite well. The welfare department had just introduced a workfare program that required able-bodied recipients to find work to cover at least part of their livelihood. If recipients could not find work in the competitive job market, they were required to work at a job to be determined by the department. Otherwise, their welfare benefits would be cut off. Since Kenny seemed to be improving, the local welfare department felt that he was now able-bodied and could work.

Kenny, Danielle, Anna, and Josef were stunned when they found out about these plans. Kenny was improving because he was in a safe environment. He was now 41 years old, and his last and highest-paying job had been washing cars over 14 years ago. The puttering he did in the garden and greenhouse could hardly be counted as real work. Kenny, in the opinion of Danielle, Anna, Josef, and his psychiatrist, did not have the work or social skills required for competitive employment. It was likely that if Kenny was required to find employment, the mere mention of it could cause the terrible catfish to resurrect themselves in his mind. He would probably require rehospitalization.

The second event was potentially even worse. Some of the neighbours had become alarmed at the growing number of boarding homes in the area. They formed an action group that called for a municipal bylaw restricting boarders to one per household. The effect of the bylaw would be to shut down the boarding homes. The rationale given was that the area was a quiet, rural neighbourhood and that allowing boarding homes to spring up would change the nature of the community for the worse. The action group was able to solicit support from two of the six municipal councillors. They tabled the bylaw before the Martins Grove Municipal Council.

For Anna and Josef and the other boarding-home operators, this was alarming. Taking in boarders had improved their standard of living and had allowed them to remain on their small, marginal farms. To all of them, operating a boarding home had become a small cottage industry that gave them a reasonable standard of living. If the number of boarders was cut to one, their future would be very uncertain.

Danielle and the boarding-home operators suspected that the action group actually had motives other than those stated. Many of the boarding-home residents looked “odd,” and some had an “institutional shuffle.” Others could be seen talking to themselves in public. Almost none had found work, and most did not participate in local events. When they did take part, it was almost always as a group and as onlookers rather than as participants. A good example was at the local fastball games. The boarders would often come as a group and sit together in the bleachers. They kept to themselves. It annoyed the community residents that some of the boarders would sometimes cheer for the visitors.

None of the boarders is violent, yet many in the community seem to fear them. Danielle and others believe that the real motive behind limiting the boarding homes is to rid the community of perceived “undesirables” and “deviants.”

Direct Service or Social Change?

Danielle is a direct service, generalist social worker employed by a community mental health centre as a case manager. She is not a social activist, nor does she consider herself “political.” In the example, not only is the hard work of Danielle and others at risk of collapsing, but, more important, the gains that many residents have made over the last three or four years are also in serious jeopardy. Danielle and her colleagues have two choices. One is to concede that their work as case managers has encountered a wall, and that the social workers and their clients will need to start over. The other choice is to become “political,” to use their social action and social change skills.

Both options are considered. If the professional staff retreats, years of hard work will be lost. Clients who are doing fine in their boarding homes will likely experience major setbacks. A few may never again be able to make a satisfactory recovery. Further, the task of finding new boarding homes in another location is formidable. No one is sure that the homes can really be replicated.

The social change option is much more attractive. If successful, then the boarding-home program in Martins Grove could continue. Further, after careful analysis, the case managers actually think not only that there is a better chance for the success of social change than for the direct service option, but also that the social change option would be easier and more efficient. This is so because of the enormous amount of work that would be required to rebuild the program somewhere else. Further, if they fail, plan B—the direct service choice—would still be available.

Strategies of Action

A structural analysis holds that both events in the case example are forms of oppression. The first, the loss of social assistance, is a structural problem with a social institution—the welfare department. The second is oppression in the form of discrimination that is sometimes deep seated in communities, often unspoken until a situation like the one at Martins Grove arises. People fear those who seem different from them. If Danielle began all over again to find Kenny a new home, according to a structural analysis she would become part of the oppression.

The Proposed Workfare Program

To ensure that Kenny and others do not lose their source of social assistance income because of a forced work scheme, the local welfare policy needs to be changed. A structural view would also contend that the entire social welfare system is oppressive and unjust. All people have a right to a decent standard of living. The means test, part of social assistance programs, is grossly unfair, as is the requirement to work (workfare) in order to receive welfare. (According to the National Anti-Poverty Association [1995] in Canada, workfare jobs are menial, wages are very low, and few, if any, employment benefits are included.)

The mental health professionals at Martins Grove understood all this but, rightly, focused on only a very small part of the social welfare policy: the injustice of a policy that would require people who suffer from long-term mental illness and are placed in boarding homes to work in order to receive welfare. This suggests an important principle of social change for direct service workers: target something that is reasonable and that has the potential to be successfully resolved and managed given the skills and resources of the workers. In the case example, it would not have been wise for this group to attempt to change the overall policy on workfare. However, it is entirely possible if they are successful at a more limited level that this could open the door to reform of the entire system of workfare.

After some preliminary work, Danielle and her colleagues agreed that their target was clear—the Martins Grove Welfare Board. The board had the power to change the workfare policy. Two strategies were considered. One was for one or more of the professional staff to advocate on behalf of the group or for a professional advocate, possibly a lawyer, to be hired to do so. The group would need to build an argument based on the benefits that the boarding homes brought to the community of Martins Grove.

The second strategy was to enable the group of clients to collectively act on their own behalf. Several were quite capable of doing so. This strategy had the benefit of engaging and investing the clients in their own lives, a form of empowerment (Mullaly, 1997, pp. 167–70). Further, if the clients were visible, the chance of influencing the Welfare Board was increased. The clients' personal lives would take on political meaning.

As part of the empowerment process, the workers acted as educators to help the clients understand the social welfare policies that affected their lives, a process called **consciousness-raising.** This included helping them understand and reflect on the dehumanizing influences of the policies.

Consciousness-raising, used by structural theorists but borrowed from feminist theory and adult education, is further discussed in Chapter 13 on feminist social work. As used here in a structural context, it has two parts:

First, consciousness-raising is reflection in search of understanding dehumanizing social structures. Second, consciousness-raising is action aimed at altering societal conditions. The two must go hand in hand; action without reflection is as unjustifiable as reflection without action. (Longres and McLeod, 1970, p. 268, cited in Mullaly, 1997, p. 170)

In the end, the clients as a group understood the issues and selected two of their members to act on their behalf.

Outcomes Both strategies were implemented. Two case managers and two clients negotiated with the Welfare Board. The advocates persuaded the board that most of the boarders would not be able to work. However, they agreed that some could and would gain satisfaction if the work was consistent with their skills. While this was officially a compromise solution, the case managers considered that all of their clients were winners because they had, in the end, opened some community doors for clients who had work potential and wanted jobs.

The Ban-the-Boarding-Homes Movement

The second problem, the anti-boarding-homes movement, was very different because it reflected negative, discriminatory attitudes and an unreasonable view of the boarding-home residents. The case managers also thought the movement posed considerable risk to the boarding homes because they suspected that the discriminatory values were shared by some vocal people in the rural community and the "ban-the-boarding-home" movement might be able to generate wider support.

The case managers had two targets. The first was the anti-boarding-home movement itself. The ultimate goal was to get the members of the movement to reconsider their attempt to eliminate the homes. However, prejudices are hard to change. Therefore, a more realistic goal was to limit and reduce local support for this movement.

The second target was the Martins Grove Municipal Council. The professional staff was more optimistic about influencing the council than they were about the grassroots movement. They reasoned that the council was less interested in oppressing a harmless and benign community group and more interested in maintaining the economic benefits that such a group might bring to Martins Grove. The case managers believed the old cliché "Money talks." Thus, instead of making oppression their primary focus of argument, their main position was that the boarding homes were an important economic asset for the community. As such, why should the council discriminate against them and the clients they served?

Unlike the strategy of advocacy with the Martins Grove Welfare Board, the professional helpers believed that they needed a coalition (Mullaly, 1997) of boarding-home residents and operators. They thought that action needed to be taken by a collective rather than by individuals, and that the collective needed to include residents of Martins Grove, not the professional case managers. They needed to take the issue to the public.

Implied in this strategy is that success in maintaining the boarding homes, will, in the end, be determined by powerful interests. A structural view holds that societies, including communities, are made up of conflicting interests. If the ban-the-boarding-homes movement gains too much support, the balance of power might be tipped in their favour. On the other hand, if the residents and boarding-home operators developed a strong power base, then they could gain the upper hand, at least while their case was being heard. The strategy was to use the coalition in order to gain the needed power and, hence, the upper hand.

As a first step, Danielle called a meeting of boarding-home clients and operators. She used consciousness-raising tactics to help these groups not only to understand the problem and begin identifying how the coalition might operate, but also to understand the problem from the point of view of the anti-boarding-home supporters. During the meeting, one of the operators said that he knew two church groups that might join them. The coalition quickly expanded, gaining more support and power.

During the next meeting, which included members from the two church groups, two people, one from a church group and one boarding-home operator, were selected as spokespeople for the coalition. The church group representative, Ellen, had a little political campaign experience, and the boarding-home operator, Yves, was known as a good organizer. Danielle was pleased to see the coalition use its collective strengths. From this point on, the coalition operated on its own. Danielle and her colleagues worked behind the scenes doing tasks that enabled the coalition.

The coalition agreed that one important task was community education. They asked Henry, one of the case managers, to assume this role. His task was to provide information about mental illness in as many ways as possible, and in particular to attempt to allay the fears local residents had about the boarding-home residents. One of Henry's tasks was to frame (see Wharf and McKenzie, 1998) the problem to show that the boarding-home residents not only were harmless but also in fact contributed to the community, particularly economically.

Despite the importance of keeping the power base of the anti-boarding-homes movement small, the coalition's major focus was on influencing the Municipal Council. Only two counsellors had been swayed by the movement. The coalition believed that all of them were primarily interested in economic matters. The council really did not care whether the boarders were people with a mental illness as long as they were harmless and brought money into Martins Grove. The coalition decided to attack on three fronts. First, they circulated a petition supporting the homes. Second, Ellen and Yves prepared a written brief and submission for the council. The thrust of the brief was based on research undertaken by two of the case managers (information gained from mental health financial records and the tax returns of boarding homes and residents) that showed the homes were making a major financial contribution to the community. Third, Ellen, Yves, and another resident, Matthew, lobbied each councillor on an individual basis.

Outcome The result of all this effort was that the anti-boarding-homes movement remained small. The economic agreement won the day with the Municipal Council. The proposed bylaw failed in a four-to-nothing vote, with two councillors abstaining.

Note that throughout this scenario there should have been no risk to the social workers' employment. What they did was just good social work. However, in order to be successful they needed the support of their mental health centre. In this and similar situations, it is important that workers seek and gain the support of their superiors.

CRITIQUE OF STRUCTURAL SOCIAL WORK

Structural social work is concerned with how the social work profession, which trains and rewards practitioners for work at the personal and interpersonal level, offers fewer opportunities for practitioners to form alliances with oppressed people, their clients, through political and community action (Payne, 1991, p. 205). On the other hand, structural social work theorists have been criticized for promoting consciousness-raising and collective action—the political—at the expense of people's immediate individual issues—the personal (Langan and Lee, 1989). Some authors, however, suggest ways to bridge the political and personal features of social work practice with clients (Fook, 1993). The case example in this chapter shows how Kenny's needs were met within the larger collective action.

Critics point out that structural social work offers a means of understanding, but little guidance about what to do. Like traditional social work, it relies on people gaining insight into the structural roots of their problems and then making changes as needed. However, people do not necessarily change even when they understand the roots of problems. For example, a young man with an addiction to alcohol may know that he cannot secure long-term work because employers do not want to hire someone with an addiction, but this does not necessarily mean he will stop drinking.

According to some, radical theory sets out a narrow view of power without really exploring the complex nature of power relations, especially at the interpersonal level (Payne, 1991, p. 215). Radical theory has tended to view power as static, as available to some but not to others. The dynamic nature of power can be seen when one political party in an election loses its following to another, only to rise again during a subsequent election campaign. Some writers (e.g., Bishop, 1994) have asserted that power needs to be seen not simply as a resource that is owned and used by those who have it over those who do not. Certainly, some have more claim to power than others due to their position, wealth, or kinship. Power can be given or taken. At the same time, power can be shared among people, and it can shift from one person to another at different times and in different places (Bishop, 1994).

CHAPTER SUMMARY

Structural social work is based on radical social work theory. The structural approach is an effort to put into practice the tenets of radical thinking. Collective action is central to this approach.

Collective action is a powerful political tool that can initiate change, often at the grass-roots level. Social workers can often help clients work collectively. The collective as a whole can benefit, as well as the individuals, often clients, who initiate the action. Collective action can also be empowering when it gives people a sense of being in control of their lives.

Social workers must not confuse the structural approach with a person-in-the-environment perspective. Person-in-the-environment perspectives, including ecosystems and role theory, and even an Aboriginal approach, focus on the transaction or connection between people and the environment. The structural approach focuses on the environment itself, defined as the social structure, and attempts to initiate social change. The ultimate goal is for individuals to benefit, but analysis and intervention are directed toward changing the social structure.

The socioeconomic environment is very important to structural analysis. For social workers this means having a basic understanding of the economic system, particularly as it affects and shapes the circumstances of clients.

The important goal of structural social work—to eliminate the social oppression of people—is not easily attained. Achieving social change is usually difficult and takes considerable time and energy. Influential groups in society will likely not give or share power and resources easily. Many social workers are unable or unwilling to risk frustration and failure given the odds against them. It is often easier to turn a blind eye to inequality and injustice. Nevertheless, even small-scale successes are important first steps toward a more just and caring society.

There are certainly situations where people have worked to change oppressive social conditions or structures and met with success—for example, the work done by women's groups and committed individuals in calling attention to domestic violence. These efforts have led to changes in laws, changes in social and agency policies and practices, and an increase in services.

A major part of this chapter has centred on explicating a number of roles of social work that make use of structural analysis and intervention, but social workers in all settings need to consciously consider principles of structural social work in their everyday practice.

chapter 13

A Feminist Approach to Social Work

Chapter Goal

To discuss the nature and significance of feminism in social work and the practice principles that form a feminist approach to social work.

This Chapter ▼

- questions why women, rather than men, are most often social work clients and social workers
- defines feminist social work from the perspective of women scholars who first brought it to the attention of the profession
- describes three main orientations in feminism that can be applied to social work
- presents the views of diverse groups of women regarding the relevance of feminism to them
- sets out key principles for a feminist approach to social work practice

INTRODUCTION

This chapter promotes an approach to feminist social work that appreciates and affirms the diversity and commonality among women. The range of women's strengths, knowledge, and lived experience is acknowledged and highlighted. The core values, principles, and practice methods of feminist social work can be applied in generalist practice in various fields.

The principles of feminist social work practice have been developed over several decades. Social workers have increasingly applied feminist principles to practice. While there is no single theory of feminist social work practice, a collection of powerful social work practice principles, values, and interventions have emerged from feminist thinking and ideology (see Dominelli and McLeod, 1989; Dominelli, 2002). For example, feminists have contributed to social work's understanding of the importance of power and empowerment in assessment and intervention (Yoder and Kahn, 1992).

It is also important to note that not only men and/or male-influenced institutions oppress women. Women can oppress and mistreat other women. Women are part of the same society with men, and are affected by the same structures. The divisions between women related, for example, to class, cultural background, sexual orientation, age, and physical ability can be factors that lead to marginalization and oppression of some women by other women and by society in general (see Dominelli, 2002, p. 23). Feminist social work principles that address intersecting oppressions are, thus, important.

Many feminist principles are consistent with the strengths and structural social work approaches, and present some challenges to more conventional practice, particularly problem solving. However, feminist social work differs from these due to its creation by women social workers and its focus on women and their concerns.

Few social agencies—aside from those that provide services solely or primarily to women—adopt, as policy, a feminist approach. In this sense, feminist practice is not mainstream social work. However, most of the feminist ideas of practice can be integrated by many individual social workers in day-to-day social work. For example, the feminist practice principle of validation of a client's experience can also occur in other practice approaches. There is no question that feminist principles, and new applications and strands of feminist theory, will continue to influence social work. At the same time, feminism may have little currency with women social work clients who have found their own strategies to survive (Lundy, 2004, p. 51) and give voice to their struggles, without identifying as feminists. For others to use the word "feminist" to refer to them would not be appropriate.

WOMEN AND SOCIAL WORK

Why is it that most social work clients tend to be women? And why are most social workers, especially at the front line, women? Lawrence (1992) points out that, "By understanding that women share a common developmental experience, as social workers we have to contend with the fact that we are very much like our clients" (p. 40). This may be so, but social workers have usually had the benefit of a university education and a professional income, which many social work clients have not.

An examination of the construction of social work practice and social policies, including the underlying assumptions about, and expectations for, women and men is helpful for all reflexive social workers. Exploring the importance of gender both in the client–social worker relationship and as a feature that shapes a person's experience is critical for enhancing practice. It is also important to examine the roots of assumptions, ideas, and perspectives we take for granted about the social roles and responsibilities of women and men, and how these contribute to the way we view clients and their situations. It is our responsibility to carefully reflect on our position in relation to assumptions and viewpoints in social work and to practise reflexivity in our work.

In social work, just as in society, women tend to be responsible for childcare and health. Women take responsibility for the care and nurturing of others, especially family members and friends. Many women also face considerable stress at various times in their lives when they need to earn an income and at the same time ensure the well-being of children, spouses, parents, and others. Daughters or daughters-in-law, often with their own families to care for and other work to do, come to mind. Why? Day-to-day caring for the sick is the sort of work that is divided according to gender, and always has been. What is different about providing caring work now, if anything? If your answer is that nowadays many women hold down jobs outside the home (or work in their homes) and have other responsibilities, you have identified a key problem that places substantial pressure on many women. Yet, as a society, these issues have not been adequately recognized or dealt with (see Baines, Evans, and Neysmith, 1998).

Women who wish to stay in the home to care for children and/or family members while their spouses earn an income to support the household are poorly supported by social policies. These women receive no compensation for performing important caring labour and are disadvantaged in their old age due to reduced pension benefits. Some Nordic countries, on the other hand, have paid attention to the important role of care provision and have made provisions for those who take time away from paid work to raise children or care for other family members.

Social workers might find themselves offering support and other resources to help women who face difficult caregiving responsibilities. The goal may be to try to alleviate some of the stress, arrange for respite care, or explore other sources and types of care. For example, when a hospital patient is due to be discharged after surgery, often a social worker is given the task of ensuring that a care provider will be available at home to assist with changing dressings, monitoring medication, preparing meals, and other work. More often than not, the person performing this work is a woman, whether a paid homecare nurse or homemaker, or an unpaid family member or friend. Sometimes a combination of paid and unpaid services is used. Increasingly, the health care system demands and relies on informal help as shorter hospital stays and more complex care needs become more common (Simmons, 1994). Some women may have developed intricate networks of help and support in their communities to draw upon when a crisis or other need arises (see, for example, Migliardi, Blum, and Heinonen, 2004).

FEMINISM AND SOCIAL WORK

Background and Context

A feminist approach is not only for women, but also for all people in society. Referring to Charlotte Bunch (1983), Van Den Bergh and Cooper (1986) in their important early work point out that feminism "is a vision born of women, but it addresses the future of the planet with implications accruing for males as well as females" (p. 2). This statement suggests that feminism should be seen as holding promise for a better society that benefits everyone.

Current forms of feminism began in North America during the 1960s along with radical student and civil rights movements. As a relatively new movement, feminism continues to undergo challenges and changes. The social work profession has been slow to incorporate feminist principles, although Canadian scholars, such as Mary Valentich and Helen Levine, and American scholars, including Mary Bricker-Jenkins, Nan Van Den Bergh, and Lynn Cooper, pointed out in the 1970s and 1980s how feminism can be used to critique, enrich, and transform social work (Valentich, 1986). Feminism has played an important role in establishing the need for women's shelters, alternative health programs, and counselling services focused on women's needs. Feminist ideals influence social work practice with women who are facing abusive relationships, poverty, problems in providing care to others, concerns arising from life transitions, a need for reproductive health care, body image problems, and other issues (Russell, 1989; Hanmer and Statham, 1988; Dominelli, 2002).

In some organizations, such as women's health centres and feminist counselling agencies, programs are aimed specifically at women, and policies and mandates based on feminist principles guide workers' practices (Van Den Bergh and Cooper, 1986; Russell, 1989). However, in the organizations in which most social workers are employed (e.g., child protection), a feminist approach tends to be less evident. Hanmer and Statham (1999) point out that in child protection situations where social workers assess children's care, mothers are scrutinized, even if there is a father present, and often without due consideration of the considerable demands on their time, energy, finances, and other resources. Individual practitioners, however, may abide by and apply feminist principles in their work by striving to avoid mother blaming, and acknowledging and fostering women's resilience and strengths in difficult circumstances.

Hanmer and Statham (1999, pp. 141–42) also stress that it is important for social workers to prepare themselves to be woman-centred practitioners. Methods include gaining clarity on our work; contributing to ongoing examination of emerging issues of concern to women as part of practice; ensuring accuracy of facts in research we use; continuing to enhance our practice skills to challenge sexism in society's institutions; requesting supervision and training to assist us in becoming better practitioners; bringing to light policies and practices that do not include voices and experiences of women and/or do not help them; and maintaining records of current and helpful resources for women.

Generally, key feminist principles include linking the personal to the political through consciousness-raising, validating women's strengths and experiences, reducing power differences, promoting self-disclosure and sharing of knowledge, and creating supportive environments (Russell, 1989; Van Den Bergh and Cooper, 1986). Feminist principles are not necessarily in conflict with other practice approaches. Some concepts appear similar to an ecosystems perspective, such as seeing people as situated within their broader social contexts, or person-in-environment (Germain, 1979), and recognizing people's strengths as assets and resources in the client–social worker relationship (Saleebey, 1997c). There are, however, some key differences. These ideas will be taken up later.

Feminist Research

Feminism has also challenged established conventions in research design and methods, the roles of the researcher and those studied, and the nature of knowledge (see Fonow and Cook, 1991). Feminist perspectives have promoted ethical practices that respect participant needs, demystify and share the research process, and make improving women's lives a goal of the research (see Stanley and Wise, 1993; Fonow and Cook, 1991; Naples with Clark, 1996; Eichler, 1997). Feminist researchers have pointed out that social research is not a neutral process, nor can it claim to be objective. Research that is conducted by a female researcher may differ from research that is carried out by a male researcher (Smith, 1990). Methods and processes in research using feminist viewpoints often see those researched as active participants in the study rather than as passive subjects responding to a researcher's questions (see Ristock and Pennell, 1996).

Let us illustrate some of the above concepts with an example drawn from research conducted on women who have experienced physical violence at the hands of their spouses. First, a feminist researcher would consider where she stands in relation to the research topic and the participants. The life experiences and understanding that bring her to study women survivors of violence would likely inform her position as researcher in the context of the topic and the research process. She would also want to reduce the power difference between herself and the research participants. One way to do this would be to acknowledge that many women experience violence in the home, whether they are professional women with a university education, refugees fleeing war, lesbian women, single mothers on welfare, or women living with disabilities. Other ways would be to participate in common activities together such as sharing food (e.g., during discussion about the research), and involving the research respondents in data analysis, in validation of findings, and in writing about the research findings.

A feminist researcher would want to make sure that in conducting the research, the participants are treated with respect, care, and concern. The ethics of such research would need to be well considered beforehand so that the women participants are given the information they need to make an informed choice, are provided with opportunities to ask questions, and are given access to counselling services if they experience distress as a result of the research process. This distress could occur, say, when the researcher conducts face-to-face interviews with women who have lived through violence. The feminist researcher takes responsibility for the participants' well-being in the research and must ensure that any difficulties they experience are addressed. The researcher would be also interested in the ways she could help to promote the empowerment of women—for example, through bringing to light not only problems women have had but also the resources they found and used to survive. Research methods might be designed to validate the women's experiences and uncover strategies for improving policies or services that could benefit women experiencing violence in the home. This would be an example of making the personal political. When the findings are written up in a report, the researcher would offer participants an opportunity to comment on them.

Liberal, Radical, and Socialist Orientations

Although there are many common threads among feminist perspectives and practice, there is no single perspective or practice that is used in social work. Instead, there are three main orientations: liberal, radical, and socialist (Nes and Iadicola, 1989; Saulnier, 1996). There are also challenges to these feminist orientations that have emerged from Black and minority ethnic women, disabled women (Hanmer and Statham, 1999), and Aboriginal women. Each orientation offers its own perspective on human nature, society, causes of inequality, and how relations between women and men need to change. The orientation adopted by a feminist social worker influences how a client's issues or problems are identified, assessed, and treated. There are differences across the orientations, but also some core principles common to all.

Liberal Orientation

Liberal feminists stress the need for women to have equal rights with men. They point to the inequality of opportunities available to women, and call on them to become more competitive and assertive in meeting their own needs. The aim is not to challenge the nature of society but to remove the barriers that stand in women's way. In the liberal feminist orientation, the public sphere is the focus rather than the private domain (Saulnier, 1996). Individual choice and self-determination are valued as the means for women to improve their lives and reach their full potential. Social work intervention is geared toward helping people with individual solutions, facilitating support groups (e.g., for assertiveness training), and advocating for women to gain equal access to programs and services. A social worker guided by liberal feminist ideals advocates or lobbies for change at the societal level where she sees obstacles to women's equal access to social services, employment, or education (Nes and Iadicola, 1989). Liberal feminists have been active mainly in childcare and pay equity issues (Dominelli, 1997).

Notably, according to Code (1993), liberal feminists do not acknowledge that if equal opportunity for women in society is actually achieved it will not be enough to create true equality. She maintains that existing rules, structures, and institutions in society, built primarily by men and according to their worldviews and interests, cannot be easily changed to accommodate women. Without these broader changes, women's social inequality will continue, supported by current legislation, employment practices, and welfare programs that inadequately consider many women's experiences, interests, and needs. Instead, injustice toward women will continue (Code, 1993; Saulnier, 1996, p. 20).

Radical Orientation

A practitioner applying a radical feminist approach views society, which is largely shaped and ruled by men (patriarchy), as the root cause of women's oppression. Drawing from radical feminist writings, Nye (1988) points out that these authors view the power of men over women as always having been present in human history. Acts such as rape and wife beating are seen as evidence of abusive male power. Relationships between women and men are affected by sex-role socialization; for example, boys generally learn more about how to compete and be assertive while girls learn more about developing relationships and caring about others. Institutions are seen as dominated by male-centred viewpoints, and decision-making responsibility is accorded to males over females in such areas as the legal system, politics, the economy, and so on.

As an illustration, consider how violence against women was once viewed. Spousal abuse was seen as an individual act that took place in the privacy of the family home. In effect, the notion "A man's home is his castle" was accepted. This meant that it was difficult for abused women to obtain help. Only recently has the issue come to be treated as a crime and raised to the public level (Hoff, 1990).

The power differential between women and men in many relationships and in most societies has consequences that, in the extreme, can lead to violence against women. Women who experience abuse in the home may not feel that it is unusual, especially if they have lived in violent homes throughout childhood (see, for example, *In Search of April Raintree* by Beatrice Culleton). In many cases, it may be difficult for a woman to leave a violent home if she has no economic resources, has nowhere else to go, or hopes that things will get better. Hearing from abused women about their particular experiences is necessary to understand how they view and cope with their lives. By doing so, social workers can better understand the effects of the abusive relationship on the woman client's self-esteem and her capacity to act in her own interest.

Radical feminists believe that biological reproduction and the institution of motherhood have been cast to reflect men's interests; women, therefore, need to resist male control and focus on "moving toward a full affirmation of woman-centred values. It is a voyage toward a separate and self-affirming women's culture" (Code, 1993, p. 42). The chosen methods of intervention are consciousness-raising for women and men—increasing their awareness of structural and social realities and the effects of these on their personal lives—self-help groups, and women-only group initiatives and activities (Nes and Iadicola, 1989). The aims of such methods are to raise awareness of how personal problems are rooted in the patriarchal nature of society, which affects us all, and to transform people and society itself to become more caring and nurturing, qualities seen as common among women (Saulnier, 1996).

To help women who have experienced oppression in our male-dominated society, alternative ways of living in communities with other women is encouraged. The role of a radical feminist social worker is to promote individual and political change with the goal of eliminating patriarchy and its oppressive effects on everyone (Nes and Iadicola, 1989).

A problem with radical feminism is its view that male dominance has always existed and is expressed in similar ways around the world. This assertion has been questioned by Black and Third World feminists, who disagree that there is a universal kind of patriarchy that affects all women in the same ways (Dominelli, 1997, p. 35). In fact, racism, rather than sexism, may be a more prevalent form of oppression experienced by women who are immigrants, refugees, and members of visible minorities (Bannerji, 1995). Structural issues, besides sexism, affecting women are poorly addressed by radical feminism (Dominelli, 2002). One could also question the radical feminist notion that women possess particular female qualities—for example, caring and nurturing capacities—that men do not, at least not to the same degree. The extent to which women's and men's behaviour is determined by biology or social learning is not known.

Socialist Orientation

Socialist feminism has some features in common with a radical feminist perspective. However, it focuses on an analysis of the forms of work done by women and men, and it recognizes that capitalism oppresses both sexes (Dominelli, 1997). Men are, however, seen to gain from women's labour in the home through the relegation of childcare, household chores, and other service work to women. This household labour is not paid for, nor is it included in national calculations of the gross domestic product (Waring, 1996). At the same time, women are treated as a reserve pool of labour available at lower wages for part-time employment that offers few employment benefits (Saulnier, 1996). Even when women are employed full time in the labour force (productive work), they are still expected to take primary responsibility for maintaining households and children (reproductive work). There is a need to compensate caring work in the household, whether the care is provided to children and/or other family members, so that women outside the wage work system are also seen as economically productive.

Socialist feminists acknowledge that the effects of oppression based on sex and class reduce the choices people have about how they can solve problems and live their lives. Some of the contradictions in capitalist economic systems (e.g., accepting some level of unemployment in order to guarantee a reserve supply of workers) are seen as contributing to individual and family problems, especially when a family member is unemployed (Nes and Iadicola, 1989). Socialist feminists emphasize the use of consciousness-raising activities and coalition building to eradicate all forms of oppression and injustice in society. Dominelli (2002) explains that some men have used a pro-feminist analysis to create facilities for men. These kinds of facilities may be helpful to groups of men who wish to examine and counter abusive behaviours they have used, discuss their concerns about child rearing, and many other topics.

Both the radical and socialist views focus social work intervention on structural and institutional change over individual change, although problems of an individual nature are not ignored. In this sense, feminist social work practice shares commonalities with structural social work. Stressing that the personal is also political and that individual problems and situations are connected to or created by societal structures and institutions are common themes. Another feature that runs across feminist and structural approaches is the need to do more than work with individual clients. Social workers can help by bringing women together, promoting community and collective action (Van Den Bergh and Cooper, 1986) and woman-centred community services (Hanmer and Statham, 1999, pp. 153–57).

Illustration of Differences in Orientation

To illustrate the differences in orientation, suppose a social worker is employed in a women's centre in a middle-class neighbourhood. Semareh, a client, approaches the worker and relates how she has worked in a large, nonunionized company for more than 15 years as a junior accountant. At any one time, the company employs 30 to 40 people in similar positions. For the past several years, Semareh had been raising two children, liked her job, and was content not to seek advancement to senior levels.

A few years ago Semareh found out that her male colleagues who were doing exactly the same job were consistently paid higher wages than she was. When Semareh first noticed this differential, she did not think too much of it. Then she began to see younger, more recently hired, men being paid substantially more. Semareh did not want to make waves and possibly jeopardize her job. However, a week ago she got up enough nerve to approach her supervisor about the discrepancies and was told that the new men were hired under a different job title and at the "going rate" for new accountants. The company could not afford to pay anyone else more. Semareh was angry—very angry! She had worked there for 15 years, was a highly competent and skilled worker, and for 15 years had been rewarded with low pay. Now she asks the social worker what she should do.

Probably, feminist workers of any orientation would attempt to at least help Semareh find ways to establish pay equity. They would attempt to support her views and feelings, possibly through validation. Certainly they would help her define alternative courses of action and then select from them.

Semareh would learn from the social worker that what the company was doing was illegal. With support from the social worker, she could engage a lawyer to begin legal action against the employer. This is an individual-focused problem-solving approach cast in a liberal feminist perspective. The liberal feminist approach would also be to help Semareh break down the barriers that prevent fair wages. Her individual situation could be brought to the attention of a lawyer and conflict resolution with the company may be sought. Although more likely from a radical or socialist feminist perspective, the social worker might even explore the possibility of helping Semareh take the first steps toward organizing other women workers in the company and elsewhere who have been similarly treated. This, of course, would entail risk for Semareh. However, if pay equity is achieved, a liberal feminist would consider her work completed.

Both a socialist and a radical feminist would be more likely to advocate further action. They would view Semareh's situation not only as discrimination by the company but also as a reflection of the values of society, including workplaces, about the value of women workers. The socialist feminist would emphasize the problems with capitalism and acknowledge how capitalism uses women as cheap sources of labour. Unionization, with a focus on ensuring women's representation and rights, and other public action would be potential strategies. The radical feminist would tend to see the problem as a reflection of male social domination and patriarchy. She might attempt to help by involving Semareh in a women's consciousness-raising group to explore the ways that patriarchy affects women in the workplace and to collectively advocate and rally for justice for women employees.

Socialist feminist workers might set up a program of class advocacy in the women's centre to advocate on behalf of groups of women who experience pay inequity and are not aware of their legal right to equal pay for work of equal value. Or they may begin some other form of social action, such as taking steps to assert women workers' rights in the company or the accounting profession and demanding that women be better supported to participate in workplace hiring decisions. Semareh might want to hear from other women in her line of work to see whether they too have experienced discrimination in the form of lower pay. Socialist feminists might work to enable Semareh to identify and organize other women workers to take action against companies where women accounting staff face direct or indirect discrimination. Or they could consider the issue from a broader perspective and organize protests to ensure women workers' rights and involve women workers from all walks of life.

A radical feminist orientation might involve advocating for fair pay on behalf of Semareh and other female employees whose jobs have been reclassified, but underlying any social work practice strategy would be the idea that the sexist society and all its institutions need to be transformed to eliminate male domination and hierarchies. This is clearly a fundamental and long-term goal. Radical feminist social work would then focus on raising consciousness and supporting women through creating alternative, female-organized groups and institutions (Nes and Iadicola, 1989; Dominelli, 2002). Unfortunately, this may not be a suitable personal solution for Semareh.

The socialist feminist might use coalition building as a strategy to change the workplace practices that foster pay inequity. However, both a socialist and a radical social worker would address and attempt to change the unjust policies and practices that allow pay inequity between women and men to occur. This strategy would involve fundamental and long-term change efforts, requiring significant resources and commitment to sustain them.

Divergent Meanings and Significance of Feminism

Feminist models that are based on the experiences of white, upper- or middle-class women have been countered by writers who stress that sexism and racism both oppress women (Anthias and Yuval-Davis, 1992). Writers speaking about women of Asian background (e.g., George and Ramkissoon, 1998; Bannerji, 1995; Ng, 1993) also provide compelling arguments against universalizing women's social subordination. The effects of race and class, difficult and often significant parts of life experience, are reflected in feminist social work (e.g., Guttiérez, 1991). Studies that focus on the experiences and views of immigrant women help to enrich social work literature, bringing out the effects of "interlocking relationships between race-ethnicity, class and gender" (George and Ramkissoon, 1998, p. 103). Language and other barriers exist for immigrant and refugee women in seeking help for problems related to unemployment, stress, housing, health care, and physical abuse. Such barriers may also keep them away from social workers. Therefore, it is especially important to recognize that simply approaching a social worker may be a very difficult and major step for some women. The worker who has some understanding of ethnoculturally competent practice and settlement issues of immigrants may be better prepared to provide help (George and Ramkissoon, 1998, p. 116). Further, alternative ways of responding to difficulties by women within cultural communities need to be explored because they add much to social workers' knowledge about the range of interventions useful in a situation (Migliardi, Blum, and Heinonen, 2004). The effects of race, ethnocultural identity, and class, as daily features of many women's lives, might be seen not as individual problems but as issues needing wider attention.

Aboriginal women have questioned how the term "feminism" fits their lives. Some believe that feminism does not fit with Aboriginal women's vision of a society in which women's place is at the centre of the community, as it was in the past (Osennontion and Skonaganleh:rá, 1989). They point out that the feminist movement was primarily developed by white women to respond to their realities and needs, excluding the voices and ideas of those women whose lives had been more significantly affected by other forms of oppression. The North American feminist movement has been criticized for not considering the adverse effects of a history of racism and European colonization on Aboriginal women (Osennontion and Skonaganleh:rá, 1989; Monture, 1993). Lucille Bruce (1998) describes how Aboriginal women leaving abusive relationships in isolated communities where English is not widely spoken and Native tradition and culture are practised face numerous barriers to getting help. Unless culturally sensitive and appropriate assistance is available and accessible, Aboriginal women trying to leave abusive situations will not find the help they need (CCSD and NWAC, 1991). Aboriginal women social workers, like social workers from other backgrounds, differ in their acceptance and use of feminist social work practice principles.

Women who live in rural areas, particularly on farms, have not been given adequate consideration in social policies that often affect them differently from urban women. For example, in the calculation of women's contributions to family farms, women often do not receive their fair share of income or benefits (Waring, 1996). The image of a male farmer sitting astride his tractor takes centre stage, hiding the female partner in "women's work," such as raising the chickens and tending the family garden. Lack of access to childcare, women's shelters, counselling services, and other help is often a problem. In addition, the possibility of taking part in local and higher-level policy processes and decision making can be an obstacle for rural women with primary child- or elder-care responsibilities.

Women with disabilities have brought attention to the particular challenges of living in a society that discriminates against females and those who have a disability. The different realities of women with disabilities, which may involve greater potential for being poor, abused, or receiving insensitive treatment by health care practitioners, and negative social attitudes about physical or developmental differences, have only recently been described (Asch and Fine, 1988). Wendell (1993) points to the need for a feminist theory of disability that acknowledges diversity among women: "[W]e will need to know how experiences of disability and the social oppression of the disabled interact with sexism, racism and class oppression" (p. 225). The issues facing women living with disabilities have not been adequately integrated into feminism, and there is room for further work. For their voices to be central, research studies that will shed light on the experiences and views of women with disabilities need to involve study participants as visible partners who design research questions and methods, analyze data, and interpret findings.

According to Diane Driedger (1993), women who have disabilities face obstacles in participating with men in groups for people with disabilities and in women's organizations. Driedger describes how she was unable to attend meetings of well-known Canadian women's groups due to the lack of accessibility. She was told that there were stairs to climb, an impossibility for a person in a wheelchair. To counter these barriers, women with disabilities formed their own organization, the DisAbled Women's Network (DAWN) (Driedger, 1993). There are, of course, variations among women with disabilities in terms of the type of disability and how it shapes quality of life, the availability and success of accommodations such as adaptive technology, and other features of daily life, including income and employment, access to a supportive social network, and satisfactory care provision. Women living with disabilities have formed groups to advocate for themselves and to raise awareness of the effects of various forms of oppression in their lives. The need to break stereotypes and promote understanding of women with many kinds of disabilities is a central concern (Williams, 1992; Wendell, 1993; Asch and Fine, 1988).

With increased interest in women's aging, and the impact of chronic and disabling conditions, more attention will likely be given to disability as a feminist issue.

> Most of us will live part of our lives with bodies that hurt, that move with difficulty or not at all, that deprive us of activities we once took for granted or that others take for granted, bodies that make daily life a physical struggle. ... Encouraging everyone to acknowledge, accommodate and identify with a range of physical conditions is the road to self-acceptance as well as the road to liberating those who are disabled now. (Wendell, 1993, p. 227)

The concerns of lesbian women are beginning to emerge in social work (see, for example, the *Journal of Gay & Lesbian Social Services*). The heterosexist basis of social policy and social work practice can be seen, for example, in assumptions about the composition of families, the gender of parents, health care directives, pensions, and the capacity of lesbian couples to raise children. Difficulties in gaining acceptance from parents and other family members who may not recognize the legitimacy of same-sex co-parents can create problems in families (Epstein, 1993, p. 21). Issues affecting lesbians as they age, such as care preferences in old age and advanced directives (instructions for care in case of imminent death), are also of concern (Healey, 1994). When a lesbian is in need of a personal care home due to increasing frailness, her partner can advocate on her behalf to ensure that a bed at the desired facility is secured. In the event of an accident or serious illness, a lesbian woman's partner can make health care staff aware of the patient's wishes regarding efforts to sustain her life artificially.

As social work clients, lesbians no doubt receive a great deal of inappropriate help, whether or not practitioners know about the women's orientation. As Brown (1992) states, "In practice, social agencies tend to deal with lesbians in one of two ways. Either the woman's specific needs as a lesbian remain unrecognized and ignored, or her lesbianism becomes the central preoccupation, the prism through which her every word and action is interpreted" (p. 201). The kind of help that responds to the specific needs of an individual is required. It must not focus solely on sexual orientation, because there is a danger that this will be accompanied by intervention based on assumptions and prejudice. A social work response that includes a broader and richer understanding of women's—including lesbian women's—health, parenting, individual life transitions, and family life cycle issues would be most helpful (Brown, 1992, p. 205).

As women age, the issues they face often involve the legacy of discrimination experienced in earlier years. Poor pension benefits, for example, are a direct result of low pay, inadequate workplace policies for women employees, part-time employment benefit limitations, and lack of pension programs for women who perform unpaid work at home (Leonard and Nichols, 1994). Women, who tend to live longer than men, also face fewer state supports in health care and social services due to the continuing trend to cut costs and limit services (Cox, 1998). Poor housing and health care and limited access to transportation may await many. Until recently, most feminist writing made little mention of older women or the issues that affect and interest them. Feminist social work literature also reflected this gap, focusing instead on women prior to mid-life (Hughes and Mtezuka, 1992). The growing numbers of people living to an advanced age means that more attention now needs to be given to protecting health and well-being and to ensuring that support is available to all of us as we age.

Various forms of oppression, such as those based on sex, disability, sexual orientation, age, ethnoculture, and class, can operate at the same time and intersect at different times and in different places (Bishop, 1994). Think of how being an immigrant and an older woman with a disability, for example, might present barriers in seeking housing and social services. Of course, it cannot be assumed that being oppressed means that women are always victims. It is evident that when difficult situations arise, women use whatever resources they have to deal with them. A feminist social work approach that attempts to understand these intersections and their effects is needed. So too is an approach that builds on individual and collective capacity and resilience. Such developments hold the promise of a richer, more inclusive feminist approach to social work.

Applying Feminist Principles in Practice

Feminist social work practice, based on a core of principles, is concerned with eliminating domination, subordination, exploitation, and oppression of women. In working with women, a belief in their innate health and ability to "identify and mobilize inherent individual and collective capacities for healing, growth, and personal/political transformation" (Bricker-Jenkins, 1991, p. 277) is important. Such an approach would also be applied in feminist social work with men, especially to help them gain awareness of the effects of constraining gender role ideals on men and women. Women's and men's strengths are to be acknowledged, applied, and built on in a social work relationship that aims to reduce the difference in power between clients and social workers. Some ways that feminist social workers establish more egalitarian relationships with clients include discussing with them the practice approach and methods, sharing client records when possible, promoting nonhierarchical relationships, building connections among women, encouraging women's overall development, and self-disclosing in appropriate ways (Van Den Bergh and Cooper, 1986; Russell, 1989).

Situations can arise in which it may be inappropriate to apply some feminist methods. For example, you would likely not choose to use consciousness-raising about women's oppression as a method with a woman who is in deep mourning over the sudden death of her husband. The most important intervention is listening to and supporting the woman in her grief, and validating her experiences and feelings. Social workers must exercise judgment to select the practice methods that best suit the situation and time. This is true for any social work model or approach.

Validation

Practice principles help to anchor feminist social work with clients and provide a framework to guide activities. Bricker-Jenkins (1991) refers to these as methods for personal and political transformation, stating that women need validation of their experiences to feel that they have been believed and heard. This validation enables women to make sense of what has happened to them and tell about it in their own way. For example, reflect on the experience of an Aboriginal woman who was sent to an Indian residential school in childhood:

> The effects of children being forced into residential/mission schools is still being felt today. Generations of aboriginal people had their lives and culture disrupted, which resulted in a people growing up with no parents, no home life, no language of their own and not much in the way of love, comfort or security. These displaced children were unable to grow, unable to parent. (CCSD and NWAC, 1991, p. 2)

No one except a woman who has experienced it can really know what it was like to have lived and been educated in a residential school. The memory and perception of the experience may change over time but it still needs to be understood as coming from the individual's unique experience. The significance of these events becomes more clear to the client as she tells her story to the social worker. The process of listening and validating to make sense of what happened may be far more important than any actions taken to resolve a specific problem. As Saleebey (1997a) writes, "[O]ur voices may have to be quieted so that we can give voice to our clients" (p. 10).

Clients need to be seen as resilient and possessing the capacity to make changes in their lives. Enabling them to give voice to their own experiences and views can begin the process of consciousness-raising for growth and healing. Validation honours clients' stories of their life experiences and is especially helpful when clients disclose traumatic experiences such as abuse. Feminist group work can help women face what happened to them and reconstruct their experience and their lives differently (Butler and Wintram, 1991). Further, when a group shifts "from individualist explanations to social, structural, and political analyses, they find that personal as well as collective empowerment ensues" (Naples with Clark, 1996, p. 179).

Consciousness-Raising

Social analysis, according to Russell (1989), involves making connections between the personal and the political and exploring how individual distress or problems have roots in unequal access to the resources that improve people's quality of life in society (p. 73). This process of analysis can also take place through consciousness-raising activities. For example, a woman trying to raise three children alone may experience personal feelings of failure and be given a prescription for antidepressants. Her situation is not an uncommon one. Could it be rooted in the current expectations that society has of women as mothers? Perhaps knowing that public assistance is deliberately kept low, that childcare is expensive and often inadequate, and that good jobs are scarce might help in explaining how this woman's individual situation is not of her own making. An acknowledgment that the personal is political—that individual failings or problems have social causes and connections—can help to free her from feeling personal blame. Of course, such acknowledgment is not enough. Further action is needed to address and improve the situation. What would you suggest that might help?

Consider the situation of a woman living with a physical disability who faces certain barriers in trying to secure a job. She may feel distress and frustration and be referred to a social worker to help her deal with her feelings, but it is also evident that she lives in a society where there are prejudices against people with disabilities, and many workplaces are not accessible or accommodating. The social worker would want to know about the individual woman's feelings and experiences to help her strengthen her self-esteem and confidence to approach potential employers. Although this might be helpful, it would also be necessary to offer the client a way to understand the bigger picture to see that she is not to blame for her situation. The woman living with a disability needs to know that the social and physical environments are disabling due to obstacles that are yet to be dismantled. By joining with others who face or have faced similar problems in trying to live independently, she might feel more empowered personally. In a group, she can work collectively with others in identifying ways to eliminate social and physical workplace barriers that block women with disabilities from finding employment. While the example illustrates principles of the feminist perspective, the focus, as in the strengths approach (see Chapter 10), is on helping the client to use her own resources and abilities. Like the structural approach (see Chapter 12), the intervention includes addressing structural problems, the broader social barriers that hinder women with disabilities in meeting needs that are required for a good quality of life.

The views of the client and social worker may be far apart with regard to the impact of gender on their circumstances and life chances. Perspectives can be shared, however, for mutual learning. It is not the job of the feminist social worker to change clients' thinking to conform to feminist principles when these are not accepted by clients, or when it is inappropriate in a situation. Feminist social workers interpret and use feminist principles in helping clients to work toward the goals they have set. This does not mean that only by convincing a woman that she has been socially oppressed because she is female will there be any chance that she can deal with her situation or problems. Clients must be free to choose their own perspective and make their own decisions, not forced to adopt those of the social worker. If a feminist social worker cannot work with a client whose views she sees as an obstacle to change, it would be best to locate another social worker with a different practice orientation for the client.

Transformative Action

Moving from consciousness-raising to action that is transformative beyond the individual level is a key concern in feminist social work (Levine, 1989; Bricker-Jenkins, 1991). As an example of transformative action, women who have experienced discrimination in pay due to their gender may move from an individual counselling situation to work together as a group where they can publicly demand compensation. As a result of their actions, it will be more difficult for employers to pay women less than men for the same type of work. Again, believing that the personal is political is a central principle in feminist social work; there is a recognition that individual problems are often connected to broader social structures and the limitations these impose (Van Den Bergh and Cooper, 1986).

Affirmation

Russell (1989) includes as a principle of feminist social work practice the affirmation of the worth of traditionally female characteristics and work. This affirmation is necessary in countering past discrediting of women and the work women have traditionally carried out in caring for children, cooking, and doing other domestic tasks and the perspective that household work is not important work. This, as in the strengths approach, also means that a woman's strengths and resilience in difficult situations need to be recognized (Saleebey, 1997c).

One effect of oppression is that those who experience it may internalize beliefs that contribute to maintaining the oppression. For example, a woman who is repeatedly told by an abusive partner that she cannot perform adequately in any job may soon come to believe it and to doubt herself (Bishop, 1994). Self-esteem and confidence are often affected, and self-determination is undermined when women are undervalued. Thus, feminist practice includes affirming the worth of the individual in the context of the larger society.

Development of the Whole Person

The need to ensure that basic needs such as food, safety, and security are taken care of is highlighted in feminist social work practice (Bricker-Jenkins, 1991), as in all social work practice. Abraham Maslow's (1970) hierarchy of needs, illustrating that basic survival needs must be addressed before higher-level needs, directs the social worker to make fulfilling basic needs the first priority. A client who has not had a meal in two days needs to be nourished, and a client who fears that her partner will kill her needs to feel safe before any other work can begin.

Encouraging total development, including personal growth and exploring and integrating new behaviours that are free of gender stereotypes (Russell, 1989, p. 75), can also enhance feminist practice. This might occur when a male client chooses to leave a highly paid professional job to concentrate on childcare. More generally, promoting caring and respectful relations that support an environment that allows this kind of personal change is a feature of feminist social work. The man who makes the choice to stay at home with his children while his partner works should be supported in his aims. Loosening the bonds of rigid gender expectations helps to create flexible and more humane social environments.

In Chapter 7, the situation of Lola, an immigrant from a South American city, was described. Below we discuss a similar situation: that of Belita, someone Lola came to know through taking the course on family violence. We use Belita's situation to illustrate how feminist principles apply to a group situation addressing partner abuse and how Belita's life was changed as a result of her participation in the course.

Case Example

Belita

Belita, a 43-year-old woman who had emigrated two years ago to join her husband in Canada, was six months pregnant. She had a few female friends who had left the same South American country some years ago due to civil war. Belita was fearful, distressed, and ashamed to let these friends know that her husband had been beating her regularly. Sometimes it happened after a night spent drinking with his friends. At other times, it occurred because he was unhappy with her cooking or cleaning. She worried about what would happen when the baby came.

Belita was taking an English as a Second Language course at a local community centre. There were many other immigrant women and men in the classes and she enjoyed her time with them and looked forward to the day she could speak, read, and write well enough in English to be a travel agent. She had been a travel agent for five years before she came to Canada. Other class members provided her with baby clothes and information about hospital birthing and breastfeeding. Some offered to babysit when she needed respite time. In the class, a special training program was to be given to all women. These would be in separate classes and in English. The course instructor said that it would help develop their English vocabulary and provide some important information to them. There would be 10 classes given on violence in the family, with guest speakers, videos, and discussions. Belita was very curious about what would be presented, but also did not want people to know what was happening to her. She hoped that she could learn from the sessions.

In the family violence sessions, Belita learned that she was not alone. Many women in the class had similar experiences, even those who had lived in Canada longer. Some of them talked about how their in-laws in Canada abused them verbally or forced them to work in their businesses. Others told about brothers or partners who physically and psychologically abused them, sometimes with such force that they had to go to a walk-in clinic or emergency department. During all these incidents, the women claimed they had fallen or had an accident. They were terrified of speaking up about what had really happened, because most thought they would be deported.

Belita was profoundly affected by what she learned in the sessions. She cried, told her story, and was comforted and supported by the women in the class. She learned about her rights, about laws, about the cycle of violence, and about immigration policy. Belita found the courage to tell her woman friends about the abuse, now that she knew there was help in the community for her.

Her friends, at first hesitant to believe her, admitted that they had heard about what her husband had done from their own partners. Theirs was a tight-knit community, one where men and women had many separate social activities.

After the next beating, Belita ran from the house and went to stay with a woman she had met in the course. One of the instructors also provided information about resources and helped Belita to lay charges. Although it was difficult, Belita's move had opened up new opportunities to her. She realized, importantly, that she was not alone, that she had help and support from friends, and that she could help others in similar situations too.

The case situation above demonstrates feminist principles in a group setting. Validation of Belita's experience by other women helped her to feel acknowledged, believed, and heard. The affirmation that she received helped her feel supported and valued. Consciousness-raising helped Belita learn that the violence was not her fault and that she had a right to be safe in her home. She also understood how the cycle of violence had been a factor in her situation. From consciousness-raising, Belita was determined to use her new learning to educate and help other women in her cultural community who were being abused. This resulted in transformative action, moving Belita to take action for change. During her time in the course, Belita felt that she developed as a person in other ways, not just in terms of the content she learned. She experienced a sense of empowerment, agency, self-fulfillment, and accomplishment as a result.

The Role of Power

Power in feminism is seen as a flexible resource that enables people's empowerment, and it can be extended and shared. The focus is on power within a person and power in collaborative relations with others rather than on power over people (Bishop, 1994). This concept challenges the definition of power as a purposeful method or outcome of domination and control. The need to give value to process, not only to product or result, is important in feminist social work (Van Den Bergh and Cooper, 1986). How people conduct their work and build relationships with others requires just as much attention as the result of their efforts. This idea fits well with social work in general, where there is a focus on building caring, respectful relationships with clients as a necessary part of practice.

Working with Men

Feminist social work is not only for women (Bricker-Jenkins and Hooyman, 1983)—men, families, groups, and communities can also be helped by an application of these principles. Clearly, a central idea in feminist social work is that the effects of male privilege and female subordination must be critically examined and challenged. Such analyses necessarily involve both the client and the social worker. A client shares her or his perspective, meaning, and understanding with the worker, and the worker in turn offers her view of the situation. Using good communication skills, the social worker presents information and ideas with care and concern for the client's well-being, paying attention to the process in the relationship and moving toward specific goals. These goals are established as much as possible through mutual discussion and consensus. A social worker cannot impose her or his own ideas on the client, but can explore these with him or her.

Whether men can or should refer to themselves as feminist or pro-feminist has also been a subject of discussion (Schact and Ewing, 1997). Many women who are feminist social workers prefer that men who ascribe to feminist ideals and apply feminist principles in their work use the term *pro-feminist,* reserving feminist practice for women alone (Valentich, 1986). In this way, men are identified as supporters of feminism at a time when feminist social work practice still needs to be developed further by women, who bring to it their gender-specific practice experience and knowledge. Mary Valentich (1986) has pointed out that there is clearly a need in social work for men who practise using feminist approaches. In working with men who abuse women, or even with women who are lone parents, for example, male practitioners will find that feminism can offer valuable resources. There are, however, some circumstances in which a male social worker, pro-feminist or not, may be unacceptable. Likely many women clients who have survived sexual abuse or rape by male perpetrators wish to work with a female practitioner. Thus almost all—if not all—workers in women's shelters and rape crisis centres are women.

Early family therapy models have been criticized for their assumptions about families and ideas about what a family ought to be, ignoring the many forms and variations that exist. Feminists have observed the inequality between men and women in families, seeing how idealized family roles trap women. The systems-based explanations of families as interacting parts divert attention away from power differences and their effects on male and female relationships in families (Laird, 1995), effectively minimizing responsibility in situations where a woman is abused, and blaming mothers when children exhibit problems (Hare-Mustin, 1978). Feminist family therapy, drawing on core principles of feminist practice, can be used in work with families to promote egalitarian gender relations and problem solving that avoids blaming women and assuming acceptance of traditional gender roles and tasks.

Recognizing Diversity

The diversity among women is highlighted in current feminist writing thanks to critiques by women who questioned why their lives were not reflected in earlier feminist works. In practice, women's unique histories, including the strengths they have developed and drawn upon in their lives, need to be "discovered and engaged by practitioners" (Bricker-Jenkins, 1991, p. 283). This means beginning where each woman is and assisting her in identifying where she wants to be and how she might get there.

CHAPTER SUMMARY

This chapter has discussed why the majority of clients and social workers are women, not only today, but also from the early days of social work.

Feminist social work focuses on critically evaluating the individual and collective choices that shape women's lives. It also seeks to challenge barriers that block women and others who are oppressed from realizing their full potential (Bricker-Jenkins, 1991, p. 285). Emphasizing strengths, rather than focusing on weakness or pathology, is important when working with clients. These features are not unique to feminist social work; the strengths perspective in social work (Saleebey, 1992, 1997c), for example, also stresses client strengths as resources for dealing with current problems. A feminist social worker needs to be prepared to reflect on her practice, creating safe spaces and supportive environments for clients. She is also required to provide women with resources that will help them and challenge sexist policies and practices in her workplace (Hanmer and Statham, 1999). The fact that feminist social work centres on women's experiences and realities, linking the personal to the political, makes this approach relevant and necessary for social work and is also consistent with the structural approach.

The various forms of feminism shape ideas about the causes of women's problems, what needs to be done about them, and what practice methods might be used. Although the major orientations in feminist social work are liberal, radical, and socialist, there are a number of other views about the place of feminism and its relevance for particular groups of women. Essentially, it has been argued that feminism needs to acknowledge and include diverse groups of women, such as older women, Aboriginal women, women with disabilities, lesbians, and women from nondominant ethnocultural groups. The impact of different, intersecting forms of oppression, not only those based on gender, also needs to be understood.

Feminist principles in social work practice include valuing client strengths and resilience; emphasizing process, even over outcome; reducing power differences and sharing knowledge for empowerment; recognizing that the personal is political; creating nurturing and caring environments; valuing diversity; and using consciousness-raising for personal and collective empowerment (Van Den Bergh and Cooper, 1986; Russell, 1989; Bricker-Jenkins, 1991). These principles echo some similar ideas in the strengths (Chapter 10) and structural (Chapter 12) approaches.

In choosing to practise according to feminist principles, a social worker may be challenging conventional practice. The organizations in which social workers are employed have their own culture, which may present challenges for feminist practice (Hooyman, 1991). There may be disagreements between social workers and their colleagues or employers, for example. There are, of course, many variations in how feminist principles and practice methods are applied. Depending on the workplace environment and culture, the degree of support for feminist social work will vary. This doesn't necessarily mean that social work agencies and organizations discourage practice that uses feminist principles. Even when they do, there may be room for change.

chapter 14

Putting It All Together: Problem Solving and Beyond

Chapter Goal

To bring together the various approaches and perspectives discussed in this book and show how they compare with and enhance the problem-solving process.

This Chapter ▼

- provides an overview of social work approaches and perspectives
- explains how these approaches and perspectives inform and enhance problem solving
- reiterates the basic principles that form the foundation of all social work practice
- summarizes approaches to practice for comparison

INTRODUCTION

Good generalist social work practice is based on the fundamental ideals of promotion of social justice and equality, and a commitment to people's self-realization, growth, healing, and well-being. To reach these ideals, generalist social workers must apply a variety of approaches and perspectives that range from direct micro and mezzo practice to social change at the macro level. Problem solving is a foundation of generalist social work, but practitioners must learn and use it flexibly in conjunction with a variety of approaches and practice orientations. Whether a social worker's practice orientation is Aboriginal, structural, or feminist, the problem-solving process can be integrated or adapted to meet the needs of different client situations.

There is no single or unique approach to social work practice. While many principles of practice are foundational to all of social work (e.g., values, importance of helping relationships, contract with clients, and so forth), social workers must be able to use a variety of approaches and perspectives depending on many factors, including the current situation, nature of the problem, culture, and agency setting. The central theme of this book is that social workers not only must clearly understand the traditional problem-solving approach to social work practice, but also must be able to extend practice depending on the situation, and move beyond by using other approaches and perspectives, including strengths, Aboriginal, structural, and feminist. At the same time, social workers must critically reflect and be reflexive, learning from their work with clients and always striving to enhance their practice with new insights. This is particularly important in advancing anti-oppressive and antiracist social work practice.

On the one hand, these approaches and perspectives enhance, enrich, and adapt problem solving. On the other hand, we have also shown how these same approaches critically address shortcomings and gaps in conventional practice.

EXTENDING PROBLEM SOLVING

People in all cultures develop a process for solving problems, although methods and problem situations may differ across cultures. In most Western cultures problem solving is at the heart of how we think. Science and research make use of forms of problem solving that we come to know and understand. (For example, see Grinnell, 1993, and Rubin and Babbie, 1997, for a discussion of the research process in social work.) The medical model, discussed in Chapter 8 of this book, is a problem-solving method of practice. Western cultures emphasize problem solving; it is a process cast in the context of a technological society that stresses advancement and discovery in industry, medicine, engineering, and many other fields.

Due to its use in Western countries, it is not surprising that social work developed a problem-solving orientation. Richmond (1917) first articulated a framework much like the medical model, and Perlman (1957) refined, modernized, and broadened it. Compton and Galaway (1999) cast the problem-solving process in a person-in-the-environment context, bringing it up to date and identifying its features. This model in social work and in our society works when social work is defined as a restorative process—one that takes action to solve a problem after the problem is identified. Social work probably cannot develop a model of practice that does not include a problem-solving component. Yet the problem-solving process or approach often does not fit neatly into the delivery of human services.

In the problem-solving process defining the problem is often a professionally dominated activity, supported by referral information and existing records stating what client problems exist. The client's view of what happened, how she or he got into this situation, and what issues are of most importance to her or him at this time may not be fully considered. The context of the person and her or his capacities and resources may be overlooked or may be perceived as important only for the purpose of solving the problem. Using problem solving as the overriding framework in social work limits the possibilities for seeing people as actively engaged in growth, healing, and change in their own ways and with the resources they have available. By beginning with an assessment of client strengths, abilities, capacities, and means, we can widen our understanding of human functioning and resilience in difficult periods and in happier times. So, in the strengths perspective, the problem-solving process should not frame helping, but instead be used as a tool when appropriate.

The strengths perspective (Chapter 10) both compares and challenges the problem-solving process, particularly in the sections on resilience, self-help, and the central role of the consumer, and holds that helping can take place without focusing on the problem but by complementing problem solving. This perspective stresses that client strengths need to be at the heart of the helping activity. It is a holistic approach that focuses on the well-being, vitality, and resilience of clients.

In an Aboriginal approach to social work (Chapter 11), it is important to spend time listening to a client's story and developing mutual respect and trust, selecting the best time and circumstances to initiate problem solving—say, when a client requests guidance in implementing a change in his or her life. This is one way to adapt problem solving to an Aboriginal approach to social work. Problem solving in this approach remains mostly client directed, with the social worker offering guidance and support as needed. It may also be possible that the problem-solving process is not used at all if it is not suited to the situation (e.g., where the helper acts as a cultural guide or support by listening and responding to the client's story).

Structural social work (Chapter 12) and feminist social work (Chapter 13) approaches emphasize the connection between the personal and the political or an individual's situation and its social roots. In both of these approaches the macro, or societal, level is central. We can illustrate using a feminist social worker's view of a couple facing financial strain due to expensive childcare arrangements. The social worker recognizes that our society and government expect women to provide childcare while men work outside the home. Although this notion is premised on traditional gender roles and an adequate income by one income earner, generally a man, today many women need and want to participate in the labour force. Despite the fact that most parents need to earn an income, existing social policies and service provisions to support families requiring daily childcare are less than adequate. Nor are there adequate provisions in cases where one spouse wishes to provide full-time childcare at home. As a result, families must seek out suitable and affordable services from a patchwork of facilities and providers. For parents whose incomes are low, childcare costs can be high in relation to income (see Ferguson, 1998, for a useful analysis of this issue). A feminist social worker would understand this dilemma and the stress it creates for parents, especially for women who feel pulled in several directions. The worker would help the couple see that the situation is not their personal failing but a failure of the current social welfare system. At the micro level, the social worker would listen to the couple's account, affirming and supporting their resolve to do what they feel is best for their children. In addition, some new strategies or resources might be suggested, and a problem-solving process might be used as a framework. In using problem solving, the couple, with the worker, could explore options, plan and contract, take action, and evaluate the outcome. If a solution to the problem of high-cost childcare is found, then the client–social worker relationship may come to an end.

Macro-level work might involve a broader strategy for social change, one that addresses the gap in social policy. The social worker could support the couple in joining with a parents' group committed to changing current childcare provisioning, conduct research on the issue, and provide information about what has been initiated or is being suggested by governments. If appropriate, the social worker could join the clients in trying to improve current childcare provisions through community organizations or the social worker's professional association. In taking such action a feminist social worker connects the personal to the political, helping to bring what is seen as a private issue to public attention.

A structural social worker would likely behave in a similar way in the same situation. Both a feminist and a structural approach acknowledge the need to see individual problems as having social roots, and both emphasize action at the macro level as an integral part of social work practice, however challenging this may be. Structural and feminist approaches also stress connections between individual empowerment and collective fulfillment. By joining with others who have similar interests and ideals, strength and commitment can often be enhanced and relationships become richer. (One must be prepared that collective efforts may not always be successful, however.) Addressing social change is highlighted in both the structural and feminist approaches. Social workers are obligated to support social change that is aimed at eliminating discrimination, oppression, and other injustices.

CONTEXT AND FOUNDATIONS OF SOCIAL WORK PRACTICE

Traditional problem solving and the emerging approaches developed due to many historical events. Social work, as explained in Chapter 2, developed as a result of a number of social forces that began about 200 years ago and accelerated near the end of the 19th century. The most important of these forces, industrialization and urbanization, are still changing and affect all our lives. Social workers continue to practise in the context of ever-changing social and economic systems.

The beginnings of a problem-solving approach are rooted in the medical model and honed, adapted, and expanded to emphasize people in their environment. Systems and ecological perspectives have had a strong influence on modern problem solving. However, many recognize the shortcomings of a problem-solving approach and have developed and articulated alternative perspectives and methods such as those in the strengths, Aboriginal, structural, and feminist approaches.

In our view, today's social work cannot be understood unless we also understand how the profession emerged. Social work has an exciting history and was in the forefront of social change that has led to our modern health and social programs, including health care and social insurance.

A central theme of ours is that social work's view (image) of the world is filtered by an ideological lens that most members of the profession share. This ideology shapes the way that clients are viewed and social policies are conceptualized, developed, and implemented, and it shapes the nature of practice, including assessment and intervention. A major part of social work ideology is a set of values based on humanitarian and egalitarian ideals and reflected in the Canadian Association of Social Workers' code of ethics. Within the frame of these two fundamental ideals, social work emphasizes and is characterized by the following values that are applied to practice:

- the right of every person to be safe from harmful and abusive environments
- the importance of the acceptance and intrinsic worth, integrity, respect, and dignity of every human being
- the right to self-determination
- the right to social justice, which includes the elimination of oppression, domination, subordination, and exploitation
- individual and collective empowerment of people who are vulnerable, oppressed, and/or living in poverty
- commitment to individuality, self-realization, growth, healing, and well-being of people
- the belief that all people have the responsibility, individually and collectively, to provide resources, services, and opportunities for the benefit of one other and humanity
- the belief that a person's cultural background is to be respected

USE OF A RANGE OF APPROACHES AND KNOWLEDGE

Social workers who embrace different orientations emphasize different values. For example, the strengths perspective is organized around the importance of the values of self-determination, empowerment, and commitment to self-realization, growth, and healing. This is not to say that the other values are unimportant to this approach. Structural and feminist social work practice also regard these values as very important but centre on collective empowerment, the right to social justice, and the elimination of oppression, domination, subordination, and exploitation.

Social work practice takes place in the context of social policy. We hold that all social workers need to understand social policy. The processes of policymaking involve social workers not only because they come to know the impacts on their clients, but also because they interpret policy every day in the work they do. Social workers also have opportunities to participate in policymaking through the activities of their professional associations, workplaces, public meetings, and through research and writing.

In social work, a good relationship and formation of a mutual, working contract between clients and workers is essential. This does not mean that a client has to like a social worker or that a social worker has to like a client. Effective practice depends on a helping, mutual relationship between client and worker. In many situations, clients are not interested in building a relationship with a social worker. The practitioner must work hard to establish communication and reach out to such clients. All social workers must develop ways of working with clients who are unwilling to work with social workers.

Relationship is central to all social work approaches. The importance of building a respectful and trusting relationship is fundamental, for example, in an Aboriginal approach to helping, described in Chapter 11. The Aboriginal helper's aim is often not to be directive, but to offer support and help within a relationship that reflects culturally specific practices. The helper acknowledges the help seeker's own resources and views in the context of Aboriginal culture and the broader universe. Feminist social work practice emphasizes the need for reducing power and for mutual sharing in the relationship between worker and client. In a feminist approach, the relationship can be a means for mutual learning and support.

Social work practice is a personal endeavour. What is appropriate and workable for one worker may not be for the next. How the range of approaches and perspectives is used depends on the practitioner's personality, culture, ideology, experience, and education. This position does not mean that social workers have the right to impose their values, beliefs, and ideologies on clients—quite the contrary. The essence of this principle is that the social worker's primary helping tool is her or his "self"—a self that includes sensitivity, capacity to build helping relationships, personality, practice style, and beliefs. The worker must learn to use these qualities of self in helping others.

A social worker needs to work effectively across cultures since practice is culturally based. This means that practice, regardless of approach, must be both culturally competent and consistent with the culture of people served. Techniques, skills, and knowledge differ depending on the cultural context. (See the discussion of ethnic competence in Chapter 7.) For example, an Aboriginal social worker might feel competent in making use of the medicine wheel as a means of helping Aboriginal youth in trouble. However a worker of non-Aboriginal background may not share the same competence. Yet, he or she can learn about the medicine wheel's significance in Aboriginal culture and for clients. The knowledge and skills of a non-Aboriginal worker may not allow him or her to use culturally specific methods, but would enable a worker to be sensitive to cultural beliefs and practices that are important to clients. Such openness and understanding can build relations in cross-cultural helping.

In our multicultural society, social workers and clients often work across cultures, including the workers' own professional culture and ethnocultural orientations. Being open to diverse ways of seeing and dealing with troubling issues and situations, respecting culturally specific beliefs and practices that are beneficial to clients and that differ from one's own, and appropriately using cultural resources to help clients are of critical importance. These features of good cross-cultural social work do not come easily to most, but need to be learned and nurtured. Sometimes the practice of social work itself is foreign to clients and we must explain what we do, how, and why.

Another important lens that filters practice is the selection and use of knowledge upon which we base assessment and intervention. Certainly the knowledge that is emphasized depends, in part, on the approaches used by the worker. Social work practice uses multiple approaches and multiple theories. Our profession has drawn from numerous disciplines and bodies of theory to define and shape social work practice. A theme of this book is that knowledge used by social workers needs to be broad based yet focused. By broad based, we mean that social workers need to be able to selectively draw on a wide range of knowledge to engage in effective practice. By focused, we mean that social workers must be able to use their broad knowledge base to focus or "zoom in" on assessment in different contexts and situations. A scattered approach without a framework is not a good way to conduct assessment.

Social work practice also needs to be able to draw from many sources as society, people's issues, and resources change. The ability to respond to change is crucial to our profession. Without such a capacity, we are poorly equipped to address current concerns such as occupational stress, issues in same-sex relationships, isolation of older people living alone, inner-city transitions, and many others. Our profession also aims to build theory through research and writing, especially theory about practice. Social work research extends our knowledge of diverse aspects of social problems, policies, services, and practice methods.

Social work's history of direct practice and service to individuals, families, and groups is a cornerstone in our profession and continues to be at the core of social workers' daily activities. We believe that it is not enough to focus on micro and mezzo practice, important as they are; social workers must also confront the context in which we practise.

Further, as we have discussed in various parts of this book, social work as a profession is faced with a contradiction. On the one hand, social workers try to promote clients' well-being and help them care about themselves and others. On the other, we control clients by monitoring their behaviour to ensure that they are following laws and rules, and if they are not, we take appropriate action or report this to the courts or other authorities. Our professional education and training emphasize these functions in our work—for example, in corrections, social assistance (welfare), and child protection. The work we do in ensuring that clients follow stipulated rules aims to protect society and to help clients meet some of their own needs.

Our society is characterized by inequality and numerous social problems, some of which are addressed in varying degrees, while others are poorly addressed. The character of our society's policies and social provisions reflects how people's needs are seen and publicly provided for at the level of the state. In Canada, our health care system has, at least until recently, met people's needs for primary health services and hospital and physician-provided care relatively well. On the other hand, our society is able to accept poverty among lone-parent families in which the parents (usually mothers) have few good job prospects or affordable childcare. The social safety net we have had is increasingly threatened by budget cuts and gaps in social provisioning.

It can be argued that social spending has to be contained even if this means greater inequality in society. While budgets do indeed have to be effectively managed, there is no guarantee that our society will be better off in the future if we focus on reducing spending on social programs today. Social workers can help in observing and documenting the barriers and unmet needs faced by hard-pressed groups in society—for example, those who are elderly, disabled, jobless, ill, young, and others. This would represent a contribution to social change.

COMPARATIVE SUMMARY OF FIVE APPROACHES TO SOCIAL WORK PRACTICE

Exhibit 14.1 sets out some key elements of the problem-solving process, the strengths perspective, and the Aboriginal, structural, and feminist approaches. For each, the elements that we have highlighted are as follows:

- overview
- problem definition
- assessment
- goals
- intervention
- self-determination
- involuntary clients
- role of the client
- nature of the process
- role of self-help groups
- problem ownership
- resilience
- contract
- client–social worker relationship
- cross-cultural social work

Summarizing these features helps to highlight key similarities and differences across the approaches. The table also ties together ideas that have been discussed earlier, some of which have been illustrated by examples from practice. It is important to note that this table presents an ideal or common situation, but in the real world not all situations are ideal, and there may be overlap between one approach or perspective and another in some features. For example, the role of the client in the problem-solving process is seen as relatively passive; however, this role may be active depending on the situation. The strengths perspective stresses active participation of the client in the helping relationship, but this may change if the client's life or someone else's is endangered. In such a situation, the social worker must take action to prevent harm to the client or another person.

CHAPTER SUMMARY

The nontraditional strengths perspective and Aboriginal, structural, and feminist approaches can be used to critique, inform, enrich, and enhance problem solving and, when used in combination, can meet the goals of generalist practice that range from direct practice to social change. These nontraditional or alternative approaches go beyond problem solving. As such, they expand social work in directions that help us meet our humanitarian ideals through interpersonal helping and achieving social justice.

Exhibit 14.1 ▼ Social Work Approaches at a Glance

OVERVIEW	Problem Solving	Strengths Perspective
	Helps people find solutions to personal and social problems. The steps are (1) problem articulation, (2) assessment, (3) goal setting, (4) intervention, and (5) ending, with evaluation occurring at each step.	Helps people find solutions to problems but emphasizes personal growth and development so that people are able to do their own problem solving.
Aboriginal Approach	**Structural Approach**	**Feminist Approach**
A general approach focusing on developing centredness and growth through the concepts of wholeness, balance, connectedness/relationships, and harmony.	Identifies the roots of people's problems primarily in the unequal distribution of resources, especially wealth, in society. Social change and collective empowerment are goals. Structures that create oppression of poor people, people who are disabled, old people, women, homosexuals, and others need to be eliminated.	Stresses connecting the personal to the political, empowering women, validating women's experience, and affirmation and transformative action to enhance women's lives.
PROBLEM DEFINITION	**Problem Solving**	**Strengths Perspective**
	The process by which client and social worker identify and clarify the types and the nature of problems. The focus is on clarifying the problems to be worked on. Problems are often defined as individual limitations or deficits.	Part of a wider process that includes clarifying and identifying all relevant facts of a client's life. The focus is on client strengths rather than deficits.

Aboriginal Approach	Structural Approach	Feminist Approach
Part of the process of establishing wholeness, relationships, harmony, and centredness in the lifelong journey of healing and growth toward *mino-pimatasiwin*—the good life. The focus is thus on the relationships within and between individuals and entities.	Occurs within a context of work with clients in which the roots of individual problems are traced to social causes—especially, but not solely, class. Social workers advocate for clients, working collectively to identify problems and striving to resolve them.	Forms part of the process of consciousness-raising for women, in which the personal is made political and problems are named. Gender oppression, patriarchal relations, and confining social expectations create problems for women, men, and families.
ASSESSMENT	**Problem Solving**	**Strengths Perspective**
	The analysis of a problem in the context of relevant systems so that goals can be set and a treatment or preventive strategy can be developed. Emphasis is on understanding the nature of problems in the context of people's environments and interactions within them.	Focuses on people's capacities, vitality, abilities, strong points, talents, courage, and power, which help them grow as human beings, improve their quality of life, and develop their own problem-solving skills. Understanding the nature of problems and their effects is secondary to analyzing strengths.
Aboriginal Approach	**Structural Approach**	**Feminist Approach**
Focuses on the whole person and whether and how the relationships between individuals and other entities are connected, balanced, growing, and in harmony, and what is needed for individuals, families, communities, and the surrounding world to move toward centredness and *mino-pimatasiwin*. Assessment is directed by the person seeking help.	Takes place as the client's situation unfolds. The social worker does not play an expert role, but learns from the client about his or her experiences and understanding of his or her situation and how it came about. Mutual respect and reduction of power differences are important, as is fighting "victim blaming."	Centres on the client as the expert of her experience. Assessment is conducted with the client's safety and needs in mind. Mutuality in the client–social worker relationship is important, as is the reduction of power differences between the client and practitioner. A feminist social worker does not impose her views on a client but may explore with the client to offer alternative explanations.

GOALS	Problem Solving	Strengths Perspective
	Solving, in partnership with the client, identified problems.	Helping people harness their own resources to solve problems while promoting their growth, development, and quality of life.
Aboriginal Approach	**Structural Approach**	**Feminist Approach**
Oriented toward seeking *pimatasiwin*. Specific goals are determined by the individuals seeking help with the support of the helper.	Assisting individuals who experience the effects of social injustice and eliminating social inequality and structural oppression due to class, gender, age, sexual orientation, disability, and other forms.	Supporting the empowerment and fulfillment of women individually and collectively and eliminating gender oppression in society.

INTERVENTION	Problem Solving	Strengths Perspective
	The action that a social worker and/or client take toward problem solution. Generally intervention flows from the assessment and from goals that have been established. Intervention emphasizes treatment—direct action by a social worker to alleviate a problem.	Promotes growth and/or quality of life. Empowerment is emphasized so that people can take control of their own lives and successfully do their own problem solving.
Aboriginal Approach	**Structural Approach**	**Feminist Approach**
Focuses on supporting individuals to maintain, or regain, balance and spiritual connection in life so that they become more centred and in harmony with themselves and their surroundings. In other words, interventions promote growth toward *mino-pimatasiwin* and are not necessarily problem focused.	Stresses the partnership between client and social worker. Advocacy and social action may be used, in addition to micro and mezzo interventions, when client situations require it. The social worker helps the client deal with the effects of problems attributed to social causes such as oppression.	Based on the goals and needs of the client, and aimed at validating experience and knowledge, building self-esteem, and individual and collective empowerment. The centrality of feminist ideals and a supportive relationship enhance intervention. Client and social worker are allies in effective change.

SELF-DETERMINATION	Problem Solving	Strengths Perspective
	Best interest of the client is key. The social worker is the expert and in a clear position of power over the client. Accepts the principle of self-determination within limits, such as those spelled out by the code of ethics. Empowerment is in the context of best interest.	A consumer/client-driven approach with a very strong emphasis on a client's right to self-determination. The focus is on empowering clients and de-emphasizing client–social worker power differentials. Both of these are circumscribed in agency policy and social work mandates.
Aboriginal Approach	**Structural Approach**	**Feminist Approach**
Self-determination in a manner that positively supports individuals' relationships is primary. In the helping relationship, both the individuals receiving help and the helpers are self-determining while respecting others in the relationship. Thus the focus is on the well-being of all involved.	An important concept that reflects strength and direction in life. For people who are oppressed, being self-determining is powerful, building a sense of entitlement to the resources in society. Collectively, the self-determination of like-minded persons can lead to action against social injustice.	Viewed as essential for clients as a means to build personal strength and empowerment. It is also recognized that self-determination can enpower women to collectively act at the macro level to improve the economic, legal, and social position of women.

INVOLUNTARY CLIENTS	Problem Solving	Strengths Perspective
	Best-interest principle permits work with involuntary clients; that is, if "worker knows best" is assumed, then work with involuntary clients can be justified.	Using a consumer/client-driven approach the consumer maintains control. Using this approach, as far as the legal mandate will permit, often assists in forming relationships with involuntary clients because the clients maintain control.

Aboriginal Approach	Structural Approach	Feminist Approach
Involuntary clients are given control over the parameters of the relationship so that the balance between their needs and those around them are maintained. In other words, the general goal of *mino-pimatasiwin* holds not only for individuals but also for their families and communities.	Involuntary clients, survivors in a society characterized by injustice and inequality, are treated in a respectful and nonjudgmental manner. It is important to be open and clear about the involuntary nature of the relationship, and to recognize that client situations are often linked to events or circumstances beyond their control.	Seen in the context of a patriarchal society characterized by unjust gender relations. The client is given a full opportunity to be heard and her or his experiences and feelings are validated. The power difference between social worker and client is discussed openly and reduced as much as possible.
ROLE OF THE CLIENT	**Problem Solving**	**Strengths Perspective**
	Relatively passive. While the client is expected to engage in solving his or her own problems, the social worker acts as the primary change agent.	Relatively active. The client is expected to solve her or his own problems. The social worker attempts to help the client maximize personal strengths to promote growth and enhance general problem-solving skills.
Aboriginal Approach	**Structural Approach**	**Feminist Approach**
Active in that the client is expected to determine his or her own path and make his or her own movements toward healing and growth. The helpers are supports and models on the journey.	Needs to be active to ensure that she or he will be able to determine her or his own needs and what changes must occur. The social worker helps in supporting and affirming the client, possibly joining with her or him in broader-level social change.	Active in that the client offers his or her account of the situation that is troubling, determines what he or she would like to see change, and works with the social worker to achieve his or her goals. The worker supports and guides the client in an egalitarian relationship.

NATURE OF THE PROCESS	Problem Solving	Strengths Perspective
	Restorative. Social worker action takes place only after the problem has been identified. Prevention relates to preventing future problems.	Promotional. Social worker action helps promote general growth and development. A strong preventive component is stressed that is not necessarily problem focused.
Aboriginal Approach	**Structural Approach**	**Feminist Approach**
Promotional in that the individual focuses on striving toward healing, growth, centredness, and *mino-pimatasiwin*.	Empowering in that individual empowerment is connected to broader-level empowerment of oppressed groups in society.	Empowering not only for individual empowerment of the client but also for the collective empowerment of women.
ROLE OF SELF-HELP GROUPS	**Problem Solving**	**Strengths Perspective**
	Marginally supported and sometimes seen as a hindrance to effective therapy.	Strongly supported and encouraged to form. They are seen as a step toward individual empowerment.
Aboriginal Approach	**Structural Approach**	**Feminist Approach**
Likely taking the form of talking, sharing, healing, or spiritual circles. Are methods or processes that directly reflect an Aboriginal approach. As such, they are supported.	Seen as potentially useful for individuals to gain strength to change their situations and act to better their own lives and those of others with whom they share issues and challenges.	Seen as helpful resources for clients who have common experiences and problems, and can promote sharing and mutual help for growth, healing, and empowerment.
PROBLEM OWNERSHIP	**Problem Solving**	**Strengths Perspective**
	The problem/deficit belongs primarily to the individual. Generally, the individual must adjust and adapt to the larger system and use the system to her or his advantage.	The individual owns the problem and has the responsibility to solve it. A problem is not defined as a deficit.

Aboriginal Approach	Structural Approach	Feminist Approach
Problems are those events/issues that move people away from centredness. Thus, problems may be viewed on an individual, family, or community level, particularly in the relationships within and between people. Responsibilities for problems lie at the level most directly affected by the movement away from centredness, since all are part of a whole.	Problems are experienced and felt by individuals, families, groups, and communities, but are seen as rooted in an unequal society in which some groups experience adversity and oppression. Individuals must actively participate in advocating for themselves and for others who face similar circumstances.	Although experiences and events can create problems that affect individuals, families, and groups and are owned by them, the roots of such problems can be located in patriarchal society and unequal gender relations. An individual needs to be able to name the problem and take steps to change its impact on him or her.

RESILIENCE	**Problem Solving**	**Strengths Perspective**
	Seen as an asset that all people have to help them through life.	Clients, like all people, are presumed to be highly resilient and possessing an inherent power and capacity for growth.
Aboriginal Approach	**Structural Approach**	**Feminist Approach**
Seen as lying not only within individuals but also throughout the universe. While people look within themselves for the strength to address those events/issues causing movement away from centredness, they can also use others for support, including those within the spiritual realm.	Seen as a resource used by all people in facing adverse situations in life. It helps those who are poor, ill, old, or otherwise challenged or oppressed, in a society that does not adequately care for all, to harness the resources and strengths to live.	Seen as a human quality that is available to all people in many difficult situations. For women, it is used to survive violence, for example. Resilience is a strength that helps women to heal and make changes for themselves and others.

CONTRACT	Problem Solving	Strengths Perspective
	The process of agreeing on problems, assessment, goals, and intervention strategies, which is seen as essential. It is also an outcome. The contract may be in principle or in writing. The client is assumed to want help.	Seen as essential. While not different in substance from that used in problem solving, its importance is elevated. The contract may be in principle or in writing. The client is assumed to want help.
Aboriginal Approach	**Structural Approach**	**Feminist Approach**
Based on what individuals present and seek, and the individual's and helper's understanding of balance, relatedness, harmony, and centredness. Contracts may or may not be formalized, depending on the desires of the individuals involved.	Enables the social worker and client to be clear and directed in their work together. It is a mutual agreement, formal or informal, that can be changed as needed and offers a guide as to what is to come for both the client and worker.	Important because it represents an understanding that is accepted by both social worker and client. The process of contracting is open, mutual, respectful, and flexible, promoting sharing and support. The contract can take a verbal or written form.

CLIENT–SOCIAL WORKER RELATIONSHIP	Problem Solving	Strengths Perspective
	Tends to be more reciprocal than not, but the social worker is seen as both the person in charge and as an expert.	A successful relationship is reciprocal and involves shared experiences. The client is an expert on her or his own life experience.
Aboriginal Approach	**Structural Approach**	**Feminist Approach**
A positive relationship is paramount to the process. The relationship is reciprocal and interdependent.	By its very nature, structural social work strives for partnership in the relationship. The worker aims not only to engage the client in a mutual relationship, but also to bring people together for social action. The client is an expert on his or her own life.	A mutual and respectful relationship is highlighted. Sharing and reducing power differences promotes reciprocity between client and worker. The client is an expert on her or his own life.

CROSS-CULTURAL SOCIAL WORK	Problem Solving	Strengths Perspective
	Not specifically addressed, but the social worker must have some knowledge of the client's ethnocultural background and the significance of his or her own.	This approach is useful in cross-cultural social work, particularly when one lacks knowledge of a client's culture. The client is an expert on her or his experience, including the significance and meaning of her or his ethnocultural background.
Aboriginal Approach	**Structural Approach**	**Feminist Approach**
An Aboriginal approach is compatible with cross-cultural social work practice, as it is a broad-based perspective that incorporates individual mental, physical, emotional, and spiritual aspects of life.	Structural social work acknowledges forms of oppression related to race and cultural background. Culture is also seen as a potential resource for clients.	A feminist social work approach addresses the diversity of women, including, but not limited to, ethnocultural background. In cross-cultural social work relationships, as in all others, clients are viewed as unique individuals with diverse experiences and histories, including oppression due to culture or race.

In this chapter, we have examined similarities and differences across a range of approaches to provide a synopsis of some of the important features of social work practice. We have also summarized how the problem-solving process can be used within various approaches and perspectives and how, in some, the process may be less important than in others. Although there are tensions between problem solving and the strengths perspective and Aboriginal, structural, and feminist approaches, it is possible to adapt a problem-solving process to situational needs and social worker orientations.

It is the hope of the authors that this book has presented possibilities that can be further explored in practice. It is in the work of each social worker with his or her clients that practice is shaped and reshaped reflexively to meet the needs of the workplace, the profession, and our society.

Glossary

Agency: (1) a common name given to an organization, private or public, that provides social services to people; (2) the capacity to act or to exert power.

Boundaries: an invisible line separating people's psychological, physical, and/or social space that, if crossed, can create discomfort. Boundaries can be permeable, allowing some movement across them, or rigid, not allowing others to cross. A person's culture, relationship with another, and situation can affect the setting of boundaries between her or him and others. Professional boundaries, family boundaries, subsystem boundaries, and personal boundaries are some applications of the concept.

Clinical evaluation: a type of research that monitors or assesses the effectiveness of direct (clinical) social work practice.

Coalition: a broad-based alliance or group of people or organizations that have similar aims or ideologies and that usually engage in social change.

Cognitive restructuring: a set of techniques, drawn from cognitive theory—a cluster of theories that emphasize the rational or "thinking" abilities of people—that attempts to change distorted or dysfunctional thinking into constructive patterns.

Collective action: political action carried out by a group working together for change.

Conflict perspective: a view that assumes divergent and competing interests in society, based on differences in power and influence.

Consciousness-raising: a process of educating people about the political and social policies that affect their lives. The term comes from the work of Paulo Freire (1970), a Brazilian educator, and involves increasing the awareness of people as active and knowing agents in deepening their understanding about the social and structural realities of their lives, and searching for a way to transform their lives through active participation in social change.

Construction: an interpretation of meaning about some phenomenon in society, for example, what is a "typical family" or a "problem child." A social construction refers to a shared meaning or truth as formed by people in a certain place, time, and context.

Consumer: sometimes used to replace the word "client," usually by agencies or social workers who view the person being helped as being in charge of the helping process. Another connotation is that the consumer is a user of selected services.

Developmental (theories): a broad class of theories that focus on the growth processes of people.

Direct practice (or services): sometimes called clinical practice, work that usually involves direct micro intervention with clients in a process of helping or therapy. Direct practice can be contrasted with policy practice, or macro-level intervention, in which broader systems, policies, or services are the focus of action. Direct practice might also be accompanied by intervention beyond the individual client or clients when change at other levels is sought on behalf of a client.

Discharge planning: often refers to work done by a hospital social worker in helping a client to prepare and plan for departure to home from hospital. The social worker might assist by assessing the person's needs prior to discharge and after, and arrange for needed social services in the community.

Domain (of social work): usually means the realm of social work that includes ideology, values, knowledge, and so on. In some instances, there is a more narrow usage, which refers to system size. For example, the domain of casework is usually seen as work with individuals and sometimes families, while the domain of group work is usually small groups.

Empowerment: enabling people to use their own resources, abilities, and power to take charge of their own lives.

Family life cycle: the stages or phases a family moves through over the life course (for example, becoming a couple, having children, raising children, launching children, retirement and old age, and death). The diversity in family forms contributes to variations in family life cycles.

Family norms: unwritten rules about what is acceptable and expected behaviour for people holding particular roles in a family. Family norms refer to standard patterns (e.g., Sunday visits, decision making about major expenditures).

Family therapies: forms of intervention that focus on the family and include a range of traditions and methods developed over time, such as strategic family therapy and structural family therapy.

Feedback loop: in the problem-solving process, the transmission of evaluative information to one or more of the earlier stages of the process so that, if necessary, new action or correction can take place.

Feedback mechanism: in the problem-solving process, the means of evaluation that helps to ensure that the evaluation is continuous and ongoing.

Fields of practice: various broad areas in which social workers are employed—for example, child welfare, health, criminal justice, mental health, family services, social assistance (welfare), and so on.

Framework: an overall structure that holds different but related parts together. A framework can be composed of theories and concepts that fit together (e.g., a feminist framework can integrate theories about gender roles and concepts such as validation and empowerment).

Freudian theory: psychoanalytic theory as first postulated at the turn of the 20th century by Sigmund Freud. Psychoanalytic theory is a complicated theory of personality based on psychic determinism (mental functioning does not happen by chance) and holds that much of personality is motivated by unconscious forces.

Goal attainment scaling: a type of evaluation in which prespecified concrete and measurable outcomes (goals) are measured against actual or attained outcomes. Goal attainment scaling is a specific form of goal attainment evaluation in which the goals are tailored to meet the needs of individual situations—that is, to measure the extent to which the specific goals of a particular intervention have been met.

Human service: a service provided for people for their welfare (education, nursing, social work, psychology, etc.). Social work is a human service profession.

Hypothesis: an assertion that is presumed to be true and can be tested using scientific methods.

Institution: (1) an abstract and often vague term used for a custom, principle, group, or element of a society that has a set of common characteristics. For example, the family is sometimes considered a social institution and consists of elements like mother, father, and children. The social welfare institution (or system) consists of such elements as child welfare, public assistance, and old age assistance. (2) A physical plant or building that is used to provide a social service or health program—for example, a hospital, a mental hospital, and a prison. See also **social institution**.

Intra-psychic: psychological dynamics and forces that are internal to the person.

Licensing: regulation of the practice of social work through legislation by professional organizations applies only in some jurisdictions.

Life model of social work: articulated by Carel Germain and Alex Gitterman in 1980, this model is based on the ecological approach. It stresses the transactions between people and their environments over the course of their lives.

Likert categories (scale): a type of question often used in social research that orders responses—for example, strongly agree, agree, disagree, strongly disagree.

Macro system: a community or neighbourhood. Macro social work practice deals with such large groups of people.

Managed health care: in the United States, refers to a system of services that are organized and provided by a cluster of health care practitioners and facilities (a health maintenance organization, or HMO) for clients who are registered to receive services.

Mandated organization: an agency that has the responsibility to carry out a legislated function. For example, child welfare agencies often are mandated to carry out child protection functions.

Mezzo system: a small group of people. Mezzo social work practice deals with such groups of people.

Micro system: an individual or an intimate small group, such as a family. Micro social work practice deals with individuals and families.

Mino-pimatisiwin: ongoing striving to live a good life by being a good person according to traditional teachings.

Narrative: a story told (orally or in writing) by a person or people. Narrative therapy refers to the use of stories as a means of helping.

Neo-Freudian theory: revisions of psychoanalysis that have been postulated by a variety of personality theorists. For example, ego psychology theorists are often considered neo-Freudian.

Order perspective: a perspective that sees society as holding common values and sharing a similar culture, thus giving people similar chances to succeed in life.

Organizational policy: can be written or inferred. The policies of an organization provide standards and guidelines for practice with clients. Often some flexibility is possible in day-to-day practice.

Paradigm: a fundamental framework that organizes a view of something. A paradigm in social work might be the view and theories that hold that helping is a restorative process.

Personal niche: an environment or place in which a person feels comfortable or fulfilled.

Philanthropy: the practice of charitable giving or helping—for example, by donating money annually to a community service organization.

Postmodernism: a broad collection of ideas and positions that continue to be debated by social scientists. In general, postmodernism resists single explanations of truth, acknowledges that people construct what they see and experience in their own way, and rejects the notion that the application of science and reason will improve the world. For further study on this complex topic in relation to social work, see the work of Pease and Fook (1999) and Chambon and Irving (1994).

Practice approach: a perspective that is applied to a social work intervention. See also **practice perspective**.

Practice perspective: a broad framework, based on ideology and knowledge, that guides social work. While a theory is a tight network of concepts, a perspective consists of a set of ideas, values, and knowledge that are loosely connected. Often a perspective incorporates several similar theories. For example, a person-in-the-environment perspective usually includes, among others, the use of systems theory, ecological theory, and role theory. See also **practice approach**.

Private practice: social work practice in which the worker receives a fee for service; it often takes place in a for-profit clinic or counselling group. Most private practitioners provide therapeutic or counselling services to individuals or families.

Process evaluation: a form of evaluation in which the methods or means of intervention are assessed and monitored.

Program evaluation: a kind of research that assesses or monitors the processes and outcomes of social service programs.

Psychoanalysis: a type of psychotherapy based on a complicated theory of personality grounded in psychic determinism (mental functioning does not happen by chance) that holds that personality is presumed to be motivated by unconscious forces. Sigmund Freud was the founder of psychoanalyis, which is still practised today by some psychotherapists.

Psychodynamic: the interactions of and relationships among the complex, active, and continuously changing psychological forces (e.g., behaviour, cognition, motivation, drives, self, etc.) of individuals.

Psychosocial (and biopsychosocial): in social work, reflects the combination of psychological and social aspects of the person. The term "biopsychosocial" also includes biological aspects.

Psychotherapies: a very broad term used to describe a psychological treatment or intervention (therapy) that focuses on such factors as personality, cognition, behaviour, learning, and emotions.

Qualitative evaluation: broadly, involves research methods in which the data are words, not numbers. There are a variety of traditions in qualitative research, each with different roots and methods. Qualitative methods can include participant observation, individual interviews, focus group discussions, archival research, and images.

Quantitative designs: research designs that involve the use of numerical data and statistical methods in data analysis. Quantitative designs might use surveys and experimental or quasi-experimental research.

Radical social work: a perspective of social work practice that focuses heavily on conflict ideology and analysis of the existing social order.

Rating scale: a means used to order or rank a set of questions used in a questionnaire. For example, a rating scale might be used to evaluate and order a consumer's view of the effectiveness of a social program.

Research methods: include participant observation, interviews, and mailed surveys that are used to collect information about research questions that are of interest.

Restorative approach: as opposed to preventive, developmental, or promotional, an approach in social work that attempts to help correct or treat an existing problem, and restore the client to a prior state.

Single-subject design: a research design commonly used by social workers in direct (clinical) practice that applies the reasoning used in the quasi-experimental design, called time series (repeated measures over time), to evaluate the effectiveness, impact, or outcome of interventions of single cases. Sometimes single-subject designs are used to evaluate programs.

Social control: the outcome or action of a professional worker, agency, representative of a court, or other legally mandated organization that is intended to regulate, govern, or restrict the activities and behaviour of a client. Usually the action is taken to protect a third party, such as children in abuse cases or the public when the client has been convicted of a crime.

Social institution: a collection of interrelationships among organizations and entities that serve a particular social purpose. One can refer to the social institution of marriage, the legal system, and education, for example. See also **institution**.

Social justice: an abstract and strongly held social work ideal that all people should have equal rights to the resources of a society and should expect and receive fair and equal treatment.

Social movement: a broad-based organized effort to create change. The women's movement, disability rights movement, and the lesbian and gay rights movement are examples.

Social (welfare) policies: guidelines, rules, and practices usually formed by governments to arrange or direct individuals in their interactions with other people, organizations, and society. Often social policy reflects a prevailing set of values and assumptions present in society, but these and the social policies on which they are based may be contested by different groups. Some social policies relevant to social work are those on child protection, health care, and social assistance (welfare).

Social safety net: the net or protective cushion consisting of programs, services, and allocations usually provided for by governments, but also by voluntary organizations, that ensure people's well-being. In recent years, the social safety net has been torn due to budget cuts and other factors.

Social welfare: the well-being of all people in a society. Social welfare also refers to the set of publicly provided programs, services, and delivery systems in fields such as health, education, housing, child care, and income security that contribute to a better society.

Solution-focused approach: a practice method involving brief therapy stressing client achievements and strengths. The solution-focused approach highlights positive growth by drawing on what has been helpful to the client in the past (Saleebey, 1997c).

Theoretical framework: the basic conceptual structure of a theory. Usually, when used in social work, the term refers to knowledge that is organized according to the structure of a given theory.

Theory: a network of concepts that are either logically or empirically related to one another. A theory either explains part of the world or predicts events. A practice theory helps social workers intervene with clients. A theory about human behaviour usually explains behaviour and sometimes attempts to predict behaviour.

Therapy: in generic use, refers to a remedial and directed process, usually the cure or treatment of an illness or disease. In social work, therapy generally has a somewhat broader meaning and includes the treatment of a problem. Some see therapy as interchangeable with counselling.

References

Absolon, K. (1993). Healing as practice: Teachings from the medicine wheel. A commissioned paper for the WUNSKA network. Unpublished manuscript, Canadian Schools of Social Work, Ottawa, Ontario.

Addams, J. (1910). *Twenty years at Hull House, with autobiographical notes.* New York: MacMillan.

———. (1930). *The second twenty years at Hull House, September 1909 to September 1929, with a record of a growing world consciousness.* New York: MacMillan.

Assembly of First Nations. (2004a). *Fact sheet: First Nations & specific claims.* Retrieved June 28, 2004, from http://afn.ca/Programs/Treaties%20Lands/factsheets/specific_claims_fact.htm.

———. (2004b). *Description of the AFN.* Retrieved December 9, 2004, from http://www.afn.ca/About%20AFN/description_of_the_assembly_of_f.htm

Aitken, L. (1990). The cultural basis for Indian medicine. In L. Aitken and E. Haller, eds., *Two cultures meet: Pathways for American Indians to medicine*, pp. 15–40. Duluth, MN: University of Minnesota–Duluth.

Akman, D. (1972). *Policy statements and public positions of the Canadian Association of Social Workers.* St. John's, NF: Memorial University.

American Psychiatric Association (APA). (1994). *Diagnostic and statistical manual of mental disorders*, 4th ed. Washington, DC: APA.

Anthias, F., and Yuval-Davis, N., with Cain, H. (1992). *Racialized boundaries: Race, nation, gender, colour, and class and the anti-racist struggle.* London: Routledge.

Anthony, W. (1993). Recovery from mental illness: The guiding vision of the mental health system in the 1990s. *Psychosocial Rehabilitation Journal 16*(4): 11–23.

Antone, B., and Hill, D. (1990). *Traditional healing: Helping our people lift their burdens.* London, ON: Tribal Sovereign Associates.

Armitage, A. (1993). The policy and legislative context. In B. Wharf, ed., *Rethinking child welfare in Canada*, pp. 37–63. Toronto: McClelland and Stewart.

———. (1996). *Social welfare in Canada revisited: Facing up to the future,* 3rd ed. Don Mills, ON: Oxford University Press.

Armstrong, P., and Armstrong, H., eds. (1996). *Wasting away: The undermining of Canadian health care.* Toronto: Oxford University Press.

Armstrong, P., Armstrong, H., Choiniere, J., Fieldberg, G., and White, J. (1994). *Take care: Warning signals for Canada's health system.* Toronto: Garamond Press.

Armstrong, P., Armstrong, H., Choiniere, J., Mykhalovskiy, E., and White, J. (1997). *Medical alert: New work organizations in health care.* Toronto: Garamond Press.

Asch, A., and Fine, M. (1988). Introduction: Beyond pedestals. In M. Fine and A. Asch, eds., *Women with disabilities: Psychology, culture and politics*, pp. 1–37. Philadelphia: Temple University Press.

Bailey, D. (2002). Mental health. In R. Adams, L. Dominelli, and M. Payne, eds. *Critical practice in social work* (pp. 169–80). Houndmills, UK: Palgrave.

Bailey, R., and Brake, M., eds. (1980). *Radical social work and practice.* London: Sage.

Baines, C., Evans, P., and Neysmith, S., eds. (1998). *Women's caring.* Toronto: Oxford University Press.

Baker, S., and Kirkness, V. J. (1994). *Khot-la-cha: The autobiography of Chief Simon Baker.* Vancouver: Douglas & McIntyre.

Bandura, A. (1977). *Social learning theory.* Englewood Cliffs, NJ: Prentice-Hall.

Bannerji, H. (1995). *Thinking through: Essays on feminism, Marxism, and anti-racism.* Toronto: Women's Press.

Barker, R. (1987). *The social work dictionary.* Silver Springs, MD: NASW.

Barker, R. (1991). *The social work dictionary*, 2nd ed. Silver Springs, MD: NASW.

Barnett, H. (1950). The beginning of Toynbee Hall. In Lorne Pacey, ed., *Readings in the development of settlement work.* New York: Association Press.

Barnlund, D. (1988). Communication in a global village. In L. Samovar and R. Porter, eds., *Intercultural communication: A reader*, pp. 5–14. Belmont, CA: Wadsworth.

Bartlett, H. (1961). *Analysing social work practice by fields.* New York: NASW.

———. (1970). *The common base of social work practice.* New York: NASW.

Becker, H. (1963). *Outsiders: Studies in the sociology of deviance.* New York: The Free Press.

Becvar, D., and Becvar, R. (2000). *Family therapy: A systemic integration*, 4th ed. Boston: Allyn and Bacon.

Beers, C. (1908). *The mind that found itself.* New York: Longmans, Green.

Bellamy, D., and Irving, A. (1986). Pioneers. In J. Turner and F. Turner, eds., *Canadian Social Welfare,* 2nd ed., pp. 29–50. Don Mills, ON: Collier Macmillan.

Benton-Banai, E. (1988). *The mishomis book.* St. Paul, MN: Red School House.

Berkowitz, N. (1996). Social work practice in hospital settings: A bio-psychosocial perspective. In N. Berkowitz, ed., *Humanistic approaches to health care,* pp. 33–48. Birmingham, UK: British Association of Social Workers/Venture Press.

Berkowitz, N., and Jenkins, L. (1996). Social work practice in the health care arena. In N. Berkowitz, ed., *Humanistic approaches in health care: Focus on social work,* pp. 1–12. Birmingham, UK: Venture Press.

Bidgood, B., Krzyzanowski, S., Taylor, L., and Smilek, S. (in press). Food-banks: Food insecurity in a land of plenty? In T. Heinonen and A. Metteri, eds., *Social work in health and mental health: Emerging developments and international perspectives.* Toronto: Canadian Scholars' Press.

Biestek, F. (1957). *The casework relationship*. Chicago: Loyola University Press.

Bishop, A. (1994). *Becoming an ally: Breaking the cycle of oppression*. Halifax: Fernwood.

———. (2002). *Becoming an ally: Breaking the cycle of oppression in people,* 2nd ed. Halifax: Fernwood Publishing.

Blum, E., and Heinonen, T. (2001). Achieving educational equity in social work through participatory action research. *Canadian Social Work Review 18*(2): 249–66.

Boisard, S. (2002). Why First Nations people cannot accept Robert Nault's initiative. *Canadian Dimension 36*(4): 33–36.

Boldt, M., and Long, J. A. (1984). Tribal traditions and European–Western political ideologies: The dilemma of Canada's Native Indians. *Canadian Journal of Political Science 17*(3): 537–53.

Bond, T. (1993). *Standards and ethics for counseling in action*. London: Sage.

Bopp, J., Bopp, M., Brown, L., and Lane, P. (1985). *The sacred tree*, 2nd ed. Lethbridge, AB: Four Worlds Development Press.

Brammer, L., and MacDonald, G. (1996). *The helping relationship: Process and skills.* Boston: Allyn and Bacon.

Brant, C. (1990). Native ethics and rules of behaviour. *Canadian Journal of Psychiatry 35*: 534–39.

Brass, M. (Reporter), and Abbott, H. (Producer) (n.d.). Starlight tours. *The National Magazine.* Retrieved January 11, 2004, from http://www.cbc.ca/news/indepth/firstnations/starlighttours.html.

Bricker-Jenkins, M. (1991). The propositions and assumptions of feminist social work practice. In M. Bricker-Jenkins, N. Hooyman, and N. Gottlieb, eds., *Feminist social work practice in clinical settings*, pp. 271–303. Newbury Park, CA: Sage.

Bricker-Jenkins, M., and Hooyman, N. (1983). A feminist world view: Ideological themes from the feminist movement. In M. Bricker-Jenkins and N. Hooyman, eds., *Not for women only: Social work practice for a feminist future*, pp. 7–22. Silver Springs, MD: NASW.

Brieland, D. (1995). Social work practice: History and evolution. In *Encyclopaedia of social work*, 9th ed., vol. 3, pp. 2247–57. Washington, DC: NASW Press.

Briks, M. (1983). "I have the power within to heal myself and to find truth": Tumak's cousin (fifty-five minutes with a Native Elder). *The Social Worker/Le Travailleur Social 51*(2): 47–48.

Brill, N. (1998). *Working with people: The helping process*, 6th ed. New York: Longman.

Broad, D., and Anthony, W. (1999). *Citizens or consumers? Social policy in a market society.* Halifax: Fernwood.

Broken Nose, M. A. (1992). Working with the Oglala Lakota: An outsider's perspective. *Families in Society: The Journal of Contemporary Human Services 73*(6): 380–84.

Brown, H. C. (1992). Lesbians, the state and social work practice. In M. Langan and L. Day, eds., *Women, oppression and social work: Issues in anti-discriminatory practice*, pp. 201–19. London: Routledge.

Brown, R. (1991). Legal issues and health care social work. In P. Taylor and J. Devereux, eds., *Social administrative practice in health care settings*, pp. 73–85. Toronto: Canadian Scholars' Press.

Brownridge, D. A. (2003). Male partner violence against Aboriginal women in Canada. *Journal of Interpersonal Violence 18*(1): 65–83.

Bruce, L. (1998). A culturally sensitive approach to working with Aboriginal women. *Manitoba Social Worker 30*(2): 1–10.

Bruchac, J. (1992). Storytelling and the sacred: On the use of Native American stories. In B. Slapin and D. Seale, eds., *Through Indian eyes: The Native experience in books for children*, pp. 91–97. Gabriola Island, BC: New Society.

Buchanan. (in press). Problem drug use in the 21st century: A social model of intervention. In T. Heinonen and A. Metteri, *Social work in health and mental health: Emerging developments and international perspectives*. Toronto: Canadian Scholars' Press.

Bunch, C. (1983). *Going public with our vision.* Denver, CO: Antelope.

Burghardt, S. (1986). Marxist theory and social work. In F. Turner, ed., *Social work treatment: Interlocking theoretical approaches*, 3rd ed., pp. 590–617. New York: Free Press.

Burke, M., and Stevenson, H. M. (1994). Fiscal crisis and restructuring in medicare: The politics and political science of health. *Canada. Health and Canadian Society 1*(1): 51–80.

Burns, D. (1990). *The feeling good handbook.* New York: Penguin.

Butler, S., and Wintram, C. (1991). *Feminist groupwork*. London: Sage.

Callahan, M. (1993). The administrative and practice context: Perspectives from the front line. In B. Wharf, ed., *Rethinking child welfare in Canada*, pp. 64–97. Toronto: McClelland and Stewart.

Calliou, S. (1995). Peacekeeping actions at home: A medicine wheel model for a peacekeeping pedagogy. In M. Battiste and J. Barman, eds., *First Nations education in Canada: The circle unfolds*, pp. 47–72. Vancouver: University of British Columbia Press.

Camilleri, P. (1996). *(Re)Constructing social work*. Aldershot, UK: Avebury.

Campfens, H. (1997). *Community development around the world: Practice, theory, research, training*. Toronto: University of Toronto Press.

Canada, Dominion of. (1884). *Statutes of Canada, 47 Victoria: Volumes I–II*. Ottawa: Drow Chamberlin, Law Printers to the Queen's Most Excellent Majesty.

———. (1927). *Revised statutes of Canada, 1927: Volume II*. Ottawa: Frederick Albert Acland, Law Printer to the King's Most Excellent Majesty.

Canadian Association of Schools of Social Work. (2001). *In critical demand: Social work in Canada, final report*. Ottawa. Retrieved June 2004 from www.cassw-acess.ca. Also available at www.socialworkincanada.org.

———. (2003). *Standards for accreditation*. Ottawa. Retrieved June 2004 from www.cassw-acess.ca.

Canadian Association of Social Workers (CASW). (1994a). *Code of ethics*. Ottawa: CASW. (Also available online at www.casw-acts.ca/Ethics.htm.)

———. (1994b). The social work profession and Aboriginal peoples: CASW presentation to the Royal Commission on Aboriginal Peoples. *The Social Worker 62*(4): 158.

Canadian Community Health Survey. (2002). Ottawa: Statistics Canada.

Canadian Council on Social Development (CCSD) and Native Women's Association of Canada (NWAC). (1991). *Voices of Aboriginal women: Aboriginal women speak out about violence*. Ottawa: CCSD.

Canda, E. R. (1983). General implications of shamanism for clinical social work. *International Social Work 26*(4), 14–22.

Carniol, B. (1995). *Case critical: Challenging social services in Canada*, 3rd ed. Toronto: Between the Lines Press.

Carter, S. (1990). *Lost harvests: Prairie Indian reserve farmers and government policy*. Montreal: McGill–Queen's University Press.

Chambers, C. (1963). *Seedtime of reform: American social service and social action 1918–1933*. Minneapolis: University of Minnesota Press.

———. (1986, March). Women in the creation of the profession of social work. *Social Services Review*, 1–33.

Chambliss, C. (2000). *Psychotherapy and managed care: Reconciling research and reality.* Needham Heights, MA: Allyn and Bacon.

Chambon, A., and Irving, A., eds. (1994). *Essays on postmodernism and social work.* Toronto: Canadian Scholars' Press.

Chambon, A., Irving, A., and Epstein, L., eds. (1999). *Reading Foucault for social work.* New York: Columbia University Press.

Chandler, R. (1986). *The profession of social work.* In J. Turner and F. Turner, eds., *Canadian Social Welfare*, 2nd ed., pp. 331–44. Don Mills, ON: Collier Macmillan.

Chavis, D., and Wandersman, A. (1990). Sense of community in the urban environment: A catalyst for participation and community development. *American Journal of Community Psychology 18*(1): 55–81.

Clarke, J. N. (1996). *Health, illness and medicine in Canada*, 2nd ed. Toronto: Oxford University Press.

Clarkson, L., Morrissette, V., and Regallet, G. (1992). *Our responsibility to the seventh generation: Indigenous peoples and sustainable development.* Winnipeg: International Institute for Sustainable Development.

Cloward, R. (1994). Should charismatic leaders be recruited by grassroots organizations to promote social change? Yes. In M. Austin and J. Lowe, eds., *Controversial issues in communities and organizations*, pp. 23–27. Boston: Allyn and Bacon.

Code, L. (1993). Feminist theory. In S. Burt, L. Code, and L. Dorney, eds., *Changing patterns: Women in Canada*, pp. 19–57. Toronto: McClelland and Stewart.

Collier, K. (1993). *Social work with rural peoples.* Vancouver: New Star Books.

Compton, B., and Galaway, B. (1994). *Social work processes*, 5th ed. Pacific Grove, CA: Brooks/Cole.

———. (1999). *Social work processes*, 6th ed. Pacific Grove, CA: Brooks/Cole.

Connaway, R., and Gentry, M. (1988). *Social work practice.* Englewood Cliffs, NJ: Prentice-Hall.

Conrad, P., and Schneider, J. (1980). *Deviance and medicalization: From badness to sickness.* St. Louis, MO: C. V. Mosby.

Correctional Services Canada. (2002). *Race profile population trends.* Retrieved January 13, 2004, from http://www.csc-scc.gc.ca/text/prgrm/fsw/statistical/stat_e-12_e.shtml.

Couture, J. E. (1996). The role of Native Elders: Emergent issues. In D. A. Long and O. P. Dickason, eds., *Vision of the heart: Canadian Aboriginal issues.* Toronto: Harcourt Brace.

Cowger, C. (1997). Assessing client strengths: Assessment for client empowerment. In D. Saleebey, *The strengths perspective in social work practice*, pp. 59–76. White Plains, NY: Longman.

Cowger, D., and Snively, C. (2002). Assessing client strengths: Individual, family and community empowerment. In D. Saleebey, *The strengths perspective in social work practice,* pp. 106–23. Boston: Allyn and Bacon.

Cox, R. (1998). The consequences of welfare reform: How conceptions of social rights are changing. *Journal of Social Policy 27*(1): 1–16.

Culleton, B. (1992). *In search of April Raintree*. Winnipeg: Peguis.

The Daily. (2003, Sept. 3). Statistics Canada. Accessed on June 13, 2004, from http://www.statcan.ca:80/Daily/English/030903/d030903a.htm.

Daly, C. (1995). An historical perspective on women's role in social work in Canada. In P. Taylor and C. Daly, eds., *Gender dilemmas in social work: Issues affecting women in the profession*. Toronto: Canadian Scholars' Press.

Davis, A. (1991). A structural approach to social work. In J. Lishman, ed., *Handbook of theory for practice teachers in social work*. London: Jessica Kingsley.

Davis, L. (1986). Role theory. In F. Turner, ed., *Social work treatment: Interlocking theoretical approaches*, 3rd ed., pp. 541–63. New York: Free Press.

Dei, G. J. S. (1996). *Anti-racism education: Theory and practice*. Halifax: Fernwood.

Dei, G. J. S., and Calliste, A., eds. (2000). *Power, knowledge and anti-racism education: A critical reader*. Halifax: Fernwood Publishing.

Devore, W., and Schlesinger, G. (1991). *Ethnic-sensitive social work practice*, 3rd ed. New York: Merrill.

Dickason, O. P. (2002). *Canada's First Nations: A history of founding peoples from earliest times,* 3rd ed. Toronto: Oxford University Press.

Dickinson, H. (1994). Mental health policy in Canada: What's the problem? In B. S. Bolaria and H. Dickinson, eds., *Health, illness, and health care in Canada*, 2nd ed., pp. 466–81. Toronto: Harcourt Brace & Company.

Dion Buffalo, Y. R. (1990). Seeds of thought, arrows of change: Native storytelling as metaphor. In T. A. Laidlaw, C. Malmo, and Associates, eds., *Healing voices: Feminist approaches to therapy with women*, pp. 118–42. San Francisco: Jossey-Bass.

Dominelli, L. (1997). *Sociology for social work*. London: Macmillan.

———. (2002). *Feminist social work theory and practice*. Houndmills, UK: Palgrave.

Dominelli, L., and McLeod, E., eds. (1989). *Feminist social work*. London: Macmillan Education.

Draucker, C. B. (1993). *Counseling survivors of childhood sexual abuse.* London: Sage.

Driedger, D. (1993). Women with disabilities: Naming oppression. *Resources for Feminist Research/Documentation sur Recherche Feministe 20*(1–2): 5–9.

Driedger, L. (1996). *Multi-ethnic Canada: Identities and inequalities.* Toronto: Oxford University Press.

———, ed. (1987). *Ethnic Canada: Identities and inequalities.* Toronto: Copp Clark Pitman.

DuBois, B., and Miley, K. (1992). *Social work: An empowering profession.* Boston: Allyn and Bacon.

Dunsenberry, V. (1962). *Montana Cree: A study in religious persistence.* Stockholm: Almquist and Wicksell.

Duran, E., and Duran, B. (1995). *Native American postcolonial psychology.* Albany, NY: State University of New York Press.

Eichler, M. (1997). Feminist methodology. *Current Sociology 45*(2): 9–36.

Ellison Williams, E., and Ellison, F. (1996). Culturally informed social work practice with American Indian clients: Guidelines for non-Indian social workers. *Social Work 41*(2): 14–151.

Epstein, L. (1985). *Talking and listening: A guide to the helping interview.* St. Louis, MO: Times Mirror/Mosby.

Epstein, R. (1993, Summer/Fall). Breaking with tradition. *Healthsharing*: 18–22.

Erikson, E. (1950). *Childhood and society.* New York: Norton.

Ermine, W. (1995). Aboriginal epistemology. In M. Battiste and J. Barman, eds., *First Nations education in Canada: The circle unfolds*, pp. 101–12. Vancouver: University of British Columbia Press.

Evans, P., and Wekerle, G., eds. (1997). *Women and the Canadian welfare state: Challenges and change.* Toronto: University of Toronto Press.

Falk, J. H. T. (1928). Social work in Canada. In International Conference of Social Work, *1st Conference report*, pp. 223–47. Paris: International Conference of Social Work.

Fellin, P. (1996). *Mental health and mental illness: Policies, programs, and services.* Itasca, IL: Peacock.

Ferguson, E. (1998). The child care debate: Fading hopes and shifting sands. In C. Baines, P. Evans, and S. Neysmith, eds., *Women's caring*, pp. 191–217. Toronto: Oxford University Press.

Figueira-McDonough, J. (1993). Policy practice: The neglected side of social work intervention. *Social Work 38*(2): 179–88.

Fischer, J., and Corcoran, K. (1994). *Measure for clinical practice: A sourcebook.* New York: Free Press.

Fisher, R., and Karger, H. (1997). *Social work and community in a private world.* New York: Longman.

Fleras, A., and Elliott, J. L. (1999). *Unequal relations: An introduction to race, ethnic, and Aboriginal dynamics in Canada*. Scarborough, ON: Prentice Hall/Allyn and Bacon.

Flexner, A. (1915). Is social work a profession? In *Proceedings of the National Conference of Charities and Corrections*, pp. 576–90. New York: The Conference.

Fonow, M., and Cook, J. (1991). *Beyond methodology: Feminist scholarship as lived research.* Bloomington, IN: Indiana University Press.

Fook, J. (1993). *Radical casework: A theory of practice*. St. Leonard's, Australia: Allen & Unwin.

Fraser, N. (1989). Struggle over needs: Outline of a socialist–feminist critical theory of late-capitalist political culture. In N. Fraser, ed., *Unruly practices: Power, discourse and gender in contemporary social theory*, pp. 161–87. Minneapolis: University of Minnesota Press.

Freedman, J., and Combs, G. (1996). *Narrative therapy: The social construction of preferred realities*. New York: W. W. Norton & Company.

Freeman, S. (2000). *Ethics: An introduction to philosophy & practice*. Belmont, CA: Wadsworth/Thompson Learning.

Frumkin, M., and Lloyd, G. (1995). Social work education. In *Encyclopaedia of Social Work*, 19th ed., vol. 3, pp. 2238–46. Washington, DC: NASW Press.

Fusco, L. (1999). The techniques of intervention. In F. Turner, ed., *Social work practice: A Canadian perspective*, pp. 48–57. Scarborough, ON: Prentice Hall Allyn and Bacon Canada.

Galper, J. (1975). *The politics of the social services.* Englewood Cliffs, NJ: Prentice-Hall.

Garrett, M. T., and Myers, J. E. (1996). The rule of opposites: A paradigm for counseling Native Americans. *Journal of Multicultural Counseling and Development 24*(2): 82–88.

Garvin, D., and Tropman, J. (1992). *Social work in contemporary society*. Englewood Cliffs, NJ: Prentice-Hall.

George, U., and Ramkissoon, S. (1998). Race, gender, and class: Interlocking oppressions in the lives of South Asian women in Canada. *Affilia 13*(1): 102–19.

Gerhart, Ursula C. (1990). *Caring for the chronic mentally ill.* Itasca, IL: Peacock.

Germain, C. (1979). *Social work practice: People and environments*. New York: Columbia University Press.

———. (1984). *Social work practice in health care: An ecological perspective*. New York: The Free Press.

———. (1991). *Human behavior in the social environment: An ecological view.* New York: Columbia University Press.

Germain, C., and Gitterman, A. (1980). *The life model of social work practice.* New York: Columbia University Press.

———. (1995). Ecological perspective. In *Encyclopaedia of Social Work,* 19th ed., vol. 2, pp. 816–24. Washington, DC: NASW Press.

Gitterman, A. (1996). Ecological perspective: Response of professor Jerry Wakefield. *Social Service Review 70*(3): 472–75.

Goffman, E. (1961). *Asylums.* New York: Doubleday.

Golan, N. (1986). Crises theory. In F. Turner, ed., *Social work treatment: Interlocking theoretical approaches,* 3rd ed., pp. 296–340. New York: Free Press.

Gold, N. (2002). The nature and function of assessment. In F. Turner, ed., *Social work practice: A Canadian perspective,* pp. 143–54. Toronto: Pearson Education Canada.

Goldstein, E. (1984). *Ego psychology and social work practice.* New York: Free Press.

———. (1986). Ego psychology. In F. Turner, ed., *Social work treatment: Interlocking theoretical approaches,* 3rd ed., pp. 514–40. New York: Free Press.

Goldstein, H. (1992). Victors or victims: Contrasting views of clients in social work practice. In D. Saleebey, *The strengths perspective in social work practice,* pp. 27–38. White Plains, NY: Longman.

———. (2002). The literary and moral foundations of the strengths perspective. In D. Saleebey, *The strengths perspective in social work practice,* pp. 23–46. Boston: Allyn and Bacon.

Goldstein, H., Hillbert, H., and Hillbert, J. (1984). *Creative change: A cognitive-humanistic approach to social work practice.* London: Tavistock.

Good Tracks, J. G. (1989). Native American noninterference. In D. R. Burgest, ed., *Social work practice with minorities,* 2nd ed., pp. 273–81. Metuchen, NJ: Scarecrow Press.

Gordon, W. (1962). A critique of the working definition. *Social Work 7*(4): 3–13.

———. (1969). Basic constructs for an integrative and generative conception of social work. In G. Hearn, ed., *The general systems approach: Contributions toward a holistic conception of social work,* pp. 5–12. New York: Council on Social Work Education.

Government of Manitoba. (2003). Manitoba freedom of information and protection of privacy (FIPPA). Retrieved June 13, 2004, from http://www.gov.mb.ca/chc/fippa/introduction/privacyprotection.html.

Graham, J., Swift, K., and Delaney, R. (2000). *Canadian social policy: An introduction.* Scarborough, ON: Prentice Hall Allyn and Bacon Canada.

———. (2003). *Canadian social policy: An introduction.* Toronto: Prentice Hall.

Gray, J. (2001). Clinically significant differences among Canadian mental health acts. *Canadian Journal of Psychiatry 46*(4): 315–22.

Gray, J., Shone, M., and Liddle, P. (2000). *Canadian mental health law and policy.* Markham, ON: Butterworths Canada.

Green, J. (1995). *Cultural awareness in the human services: A multi-ethnic approach.* Needham Heights, MA: Allyn and Bacon.

Green, J., and Thorogood, N. (1998). *Analyzing health policy: A sociological approach.* London: Longman.

Greenwood, E. (1957). Attributes of a profession. *Social Work 2*(3): 45–55.

Grinnell, R. (1993). *Social work research and evaluation,* 4th ed. Itasca, IL: F. E. Peacock.

Grob, G. (1991). *From asylum to community.* Princeton, NJ: Princeton University Press.

Guttiérez, L. (1991). Empowering women of color: A feminist model. In M. Bricker-Jenkins, N. Hooyman, and N. Gottlieb, eds., *Feminist social work practice in clinical settings,* pp. 199–214. Newbury Park, CA: Sage.

Halli, S., and Driedger, L., eds. (1999). *Immigrant Canada: Demographic, economic and social challenges.* Toronto: University of Toronto Press.

Halli, S., Trovato, F., and Driedger, L., eds. (1990). *Ethnic demography: Canadian immigrant, racial and cultural variations.* Ottawa: Carleton University Press

Hallowell, A. (1992). *The Ojibwa of Berens River, Manitoba: Ethnography into history.* Edited with preface and afterword by J. Brown. Fort Worth, TX: Harcourt Brace Jovanovich College.

Halpern, J., Sackett, K., Binner, P., and Mohr, C. (1980). *The myths of de-institutionalization: Policies for the mentally disabled.* Boulder, CO: Westview Press.

Ham, C., ed. (1997). *Health care reform: Learning from international experience.* Buckingham, UK: Open University Press.

Hampton, M., Hampton, E., Kinunwa, G., and Kinunwa, L. (1995). Alaska recovery and spirit camps: First Nations community development. *Community Development Journal 30*(3): 257–64.

Hanmer, J., and Statham, D. (1988). *Women and social work: Towards a woman-centred practice.* London: Macmillan Educational.

———. (1999). *Women and social work: Towards a woman-centred practice,* 2nd ed. Houndmills, UK: British Association of Social Workers/Macmillan Press.

Hardcastle, D., Wenocur, S., and Powers, P. (1997). *Community practice: Theories and skills for social workers.* Oxford: Oxford University Press.

Hare-Mustin, R. (1978). A feminist approach to family therapy. *Family Process 17*: 181–94.

Hart, M. (1992). The Nelson House medicine lodge: Two cultures combined. In M. Tobin and C. Walmsley, eds., *Northern perspectives: Practice and education in social work*, pp. 61–66. Winnipeg: Manitoba Association of Social Workers and University of Manitoba Faculty of Social Work.

Healey, S. (1994). Diversity with a difference: On being old and lesbian. *Journal of Gay & Lesbian Social Services 1*(1): 109–17.

Health and Welfare Canada. (1986). *Ottawa charter for health promotion.* First International WHO Conference on Health Promotion. Ottawa: Health and Welfare Canada.

Health Canada. (1998). Health promotion in Canada—A case study. *Health Promotion International 13*(1): 7–26.

Heinonen, T., and Metteri, A., eds. (in press). *Social work in health and mental health: Emerging developments and international perspectives.* Toronto: Canadian Scholars' Press.

Hepworth, D., and Larsen, J. (1993). *Direct social work practice: Theory and skills.* Pacific Grove, CA: Brooks/Cole.

Hepworth, D., Rooney, R., and Larsen, J. (1997). *Direct social work practice: Theory and skills*, 5th ed. Pacific Grove, CA: Brooks/Cole.

Herberg, D. (1993). *Frameworks for cultural and racial diversity: Teaching and learning for practitioners.* Toronto: Canadian Scholars' Press.

Herring, R. D. (1996). Synergetic counseling and Native American Indian students. *Journal of Counseling and Development 74*(6): 542–47.

Hick, S. (2002). *Advocacy, activism, and the Internet: Community organization and social policy.* Chicago: Lyceum Books.

———. (2004). *Social welfare in Canada: Understanding income security.* Toronto: Thompson Educational Publishing.

Hoff, L. (1990). *Battered women as survivors.* London: Routledge.

Holmes, G. (1997). The strengths perspective and the politics of clienthood. In D. Saleebey, ed., *The strengths perspective in social work practice*, 2nd ed., pp. 151–64. White Plains, NY: Longman.

Holosko, M., and Taylor, P. (1992). *Social work practice in health care settings.* Toronto: Canadian Scholars' Press.

Homan, M. (1999). *Promoting community change: Making it happen in the real world.* Pacific Grove, CA: Brooks/Cole Publishing.

Hooyman, N. (1991). Supporting practice in large-scale bureaucracies. In M. Bricker-Jenkins, N. Hooyman, and N. Gottlieb, eds., *Feminist social work practice in clinical settings*, pp. 251–70. Newbury Park, CA: Sage.

Hughes, B., and Mtezuka, M. (1992). Social work and older women: Where have the older women gone? In M. Langan and L. Day, eds., *Women, oppression and social work*, pp. 220–41. London: Routledge.

Ife, J. (2002). *Community development: Community-based alternatives in an age of globalisation.* Frenchs Forest, NSW, AU: Pearson Education Australia.

Indian and Northern Affairs Canada. (2002, December). *Social development—Health and social indicators.* Retrieved January 13, 2004, from http://www.ainc-inac.gc.ca/gs/soci_e.html.

Inuit Tapiriit Kanatami. (2004). *Backgrounder: Inuit Tapiriit Kanatami.* Retrieved December 9, 2004, from http://www.itk.ca/media/backgrounder-itk.php.

Irving, A. (1994). From image to simulacra: The modern/postmodern divide and social work. In A. Chambon and A. Irving, eds., *Essays on postmodernism and social work*, pp. 19–32. Toronto: Canadian Scholars' Press.

Irving, A., Parsons, H., and Bellamy, D. (1995). *Neighbors: Three social settlements in downtown Toronto.* Toronto: Canadian Scholars' Press.

Irwin, L. (1994). Dreams, theory, and culture: The Plains vision quest paradigm. *American Indian Quarterly 18*(2): 229–45.

Ivanoff, A., Blythe, B., and Tripodi, T. (1994). *Involuntary clients in social work practice: A research-based approach.* New York: Aldine deGruyter.

James, C. (1995). *Seeing ourselves: Exploring race, ethnicity and culture.* Toronto: Thompson Educational.

James, C., and Shadd, A., eds. (2001). *Talking about identity: Encounters in race, ethnicity and language.* Toronto: Between the Lines Publishing.

Janzen, H. L., Skakum, S., and Lightning, W. (1994). Professional services in a Cree Native community. *Canadian Journal of School Psychology 10*(1): 88–102.

Johnson, D. W., and Johnson, F. (2003). *Joining together: Group theory and group skills.* Boston: Allyn and Bacon.

Johnson, L. (1995). *Social work practice: A generalist approach*, 5th ed. Needham Heights, MA: Allyn and Bacon.

Johnson, L., McClelland, R., and Austin, C. (2000). *Social work practice: A generalist approach*, Canadian ed. Scarborough, ON: Prentice Hall Allyn and Bacon Canada.

Johnston, B. (1976). *Ojibway heritage.* Toronto: McClelland and Stewart.

Johnston, P. (1983). *Native children and the child welfare system.* Toronto: Canadian Council on Social Development in association with James Lorimer and Co.

Kaminski, L., and Walmsley, C. (1995). The advocacy brief: A guide for social workers. *The Social Worker 63*(2): 53–58.

Karls, J., and Wandrei, K. (1992). PIE: A new language for social work. *Social Work 37*: 80–85.

Katz, R., and St. Denis, V. (1991). Teachers as healers. *Journal of Indigenous Studies 2*(2): 23–36.

Kemp, S., Whittaker, J., and Tracy, E. (1997). *Person–environment practice: The social ecology of interpersonal helping.* New York: Aldine de Gruyter.

Kidneigh, J. (1965). History of American social work. In *Encyclopaedia of social work*, 15th ed., pp. 3–18. New York: NASW.

Kiresuk, T., Smith, A., and Cardillo, J. (1994). *Goal attainment scaling: Application, theory and measurement.* Hillsdale, NJ: L. Earlbaum Associates.

Kirst-Ashman, K., and Hull, G. (1993). *Understanding generalist practice.* Chicago: Nelson Hall.

———. (1999). *Understanding generalist practice*, 2nd ed. Chicago: Nelson Hall.

Kirwin, B. (1996). *Ideology, development and social welfare: Canadian perspectives.* Toronto: Canadian Scholars' Press.

Kitsuse, J. (1962). Societal reaction to deviant behaviour. *Social Problems 9*(3): 247–56.

Konopka, G. (1983). *Social group work: A helping process*, 3rd ed. Englewood Cliffs, NJ: Prentice-Hall.

Kufeldt, K., and McKenzie, B., eds. (2003). *Child welfare: Connecting research, policy and practice.* Waterloo, ON: Wilfrid Laurier University Press.

LaDue, R. A. (1994). Coyote returns: Twenty sweats does not an Indian expert make. *Women and Therapy 15*(1): 93–111.

Laird, J. (1995). Family-centred practice: Feminist, constructionist, and cultural perspectives. In N. Van Den Bergh, ed., *Feminist practice in the 21st century*, pp. 20–40. Washington, DC: NASW Press.

Langan, M., and Lee, P. (1989). Whatever happened to radical social work? In M. Langan and P. Lee, eds., *Radical social work today*, pp. 1–18. London: Unwin Hyman.

Lawrence, M. (1992). Women's psychology and feminist social work practice. In M. Langan and L. Day, eds., *Women, oppression and social work*, pp. 32–47. London: Routledge.

Leah, R. (1995). Anti-racism studies: An integrative perspective. *Race, Gender and Class 2*(3): 105–22.

Leighninger, L. (1987). *Social work search for identity.* New York: Greenwood Press.

Lemert, E. (1951). *Social pathology.* New York: McGraw-Hill.

Leonard, P. (1997). *Post modern welfare: Reconstructing an emancipatory project.* London: Sage.

Leonard, P., and Nichols, B. (1994). Introduction: The theory and the politics of aging. In P. Leonard and B. Nichols, eds., *Gender, aging and the state*, pp. 1–16. Montreal: Black Rose Books.

Lésemann, F. (1984). *Services and circuses: Community and the welfare state.* Montreal: Black Rose Books.

Leslie, J., and Maguire, R. (1978). *The historical development of the Indian Act,* 2nd ed. Ottawa: Treaties and Historical Research Centre, Indian and Northern Affairs Canada.

Levine, H. (1989). Feminist counseling: Approach or technique? In J. Turner and L. Emery, eds., *Perspectives on women in the 1980s*, pp. 74–98. Winnipeg: University of Manitoba Press.

Li, P. (1999). *Race and ethnic relations in Canada.* Don Mills, ON: Oxford University Press.

———. (2003). *Destination Canada: Immigration debates and issues.* Don Mills, ON: Oxford University Press.

Lieby, J. (1978). *A history of social welfare and social work in the United States.* New York: Columbia University Press.

Locke, B., Garrison, R., and Winship, J. (1998). *Generalist social work practice: Context, story and partnerships.* Pacific Grove, CA: Brooks/Cole.

Loewenberg, F. M., and Dolgoff, R. (1985). *Ethical decisions for social work practice.* Itasca, IL: F. E. Peacock Publishers.

Longclaws, L. (1994). Social work and the medicine wheel framework. In B. Compton and B. Galaway, eds., *Social work processes*, 5th ed., pp. 24–33. Pacific Grove, CA: Brooks/Cole.

Lundy, C. (2004). *Social work and social justice: A structural approach to practice.* Peterborough, ON: Broadview Press.

MacInnis, G. (1953). *J. S. Woodsworth: A man to remember.* Toronto: Macmillan.

MacKay, I. (1993). Historical perspective of social work in health care. *Manitoba Social Worker 26*(3): 5–6.

Mackintosh, M. (1992). Questioning the state. In M. Wuyts, M. Mackintosh, and T. Hewitt, eds., *Development policy and public action*, pp. 61–89. Oxford: Oxford University Press and The Open University.

Malloch, L. (1989). Indian medicine, Indian health: Study between red and white medicine. *Canadian Women Studies 10*(2/3): 105–12.

Mann, H. (1968). *Notes for a history: School of Social Work, University of Manitoba.* Winnipeg: University of Manitoba.

Maslow, A. (1970). *Motivation and personality*, 2nd ed. New York: Harper and Row.

Masten, A. (1994). Resilience in individual development: Successful adaptation despite risk and adversity. In M. Wang and E. Gordon, eds., *Educational resilience in inner city America: Challenges and prospects.* Hillsdale, NJ: Erlbaum.

Mawhiney, A. M. (1995). The First Nations in Canada. In J. C. Turner and F. J. Turner, eds., *Canadian social welfare,* 3rd ed., pp. 213–30. Scarborough, ON: Allyn and Bacon.

McCormick, R. (1995). The facilitation of healing for the First Nations people of British Columbia. *Canadian Journal of Native Education 21*(2): 251–322.

McIntosh, P. (1989, July/August). White privilege: Unpacking the invisible knapsack. *Peace and Freedom*, 10–12.

McKenzie, B., and Morrissette, V. (2003). Social work practice with Canadians of Aboriginal background: Guidelines of respectful social work. *Envision: The Manitoba Journal of Child Welfare 2*(1): 1–39.

McKnight, J. (1998). Turning communities around. *Canadian Housing 15*(1): 9–12.

McMahon, M. (1994). *Advanced generalist practice with an international perspective.* Englewood Cliffs, NJ: Prentice-Hall.

Meyer, C. (1970). *Social work practice: A response to the urban crisis.* New York: Free Press.

———. (1983). *Clinical social work in an eco-systems perspective.* New York: Columbia University Press.

———. (1988). The eco-systems perspective. In R. Dorfman, ed., *Paradigms of clinical social work*, pp. 275–94. New York: Brunner/Mazel.

Migliardi, P., Blum, E., and Heinonen, T. (2004). Immigrant and refugee women's action against violence: A prevention strategy. In C. Ateah and J. Mirwaldt, eds., *Within our reach: Preventing abuse across the lifespan,* pp. 76–89. Halifax: Fernwood Publishing.

Miley, K., O'Melia, M., and DuBois, B. (1998). *Generalist work practice: An empowering approach*, 2nd ed. Boston: Allyn and Bacon.

Miller, J. R. (2000). *Skyscrapers hide the heavens,* 3rd ed. Toronto: University of Toronto Press.

Milloy, J. (1999). *A national crime: The Canadian government and the residential school system, 1879 to 1986.* Winnipeg: University of Manitoba Press.

Montigny, E.-A. (1997). Been there, done that: 1890s precedents to 1990s social policies affecting the aged and their families. In R. Blake, P. Bryden, and J. Strain, eds., *The welfare state in Canada: Past, present and future*, pp. 125–37. Concord, ON: Irwin.

Moreau, M. (1979). A structural approach to social work practice. *Canadian Journal of Social Work Education 5*(1): 78–94.

Moreau, M., and Frosst, S. (1993). *Empowerment II: Snapshots of the structural approach in action.* Ottawa: Carleton University Press.

Moreau, M., with Leonard, L. (1989). *Empowerment through a structural approach to social work: A report from practice.* Montreal: École de service social.

Morrisseau, C. (1998). *Into the daylight: A wholistic approach to healing.* Toronto: University of Toronto Press.

Morrissette, V., McKenzie, B., and Morrissette, L. (1993). Towards an Aboriginal model of social work practice. *Canadian Social Work Review 10*(10): 91–108.

Morrissey, M. (1997). The uses of culture. *Journal of Intercultural Studies 18*(2): 93–107.

Moxley, D. (1989). *The practice of case management.* Newbury Park, CA: Sage.

Mullaly, R. (1993). *Structural social work.* Toronto: McClelland and Stewart.

———. (1997). *Structural social work: Ideology, theory, practice*, 2nd ed. Toronto: Oxford University Press.

———. (2002). *Challenging oppression: A critical social work approach.* Don Mills, ON: Oxford University Press.

Nabigon, H., and Mawhiney, A. (1996). Aboriginal theory: A Cree medicine wheel guide for healing First Nations. In F. J. Turner, ed., *Social work treatment: Interlocking theoretical approaches,* 4th ed., pp. 18–38. Toronto: The Free Press.

Naples, N., with Clark, E. (1996). Feminist participatory research and empowerment: Going public as survivors of childhood sexual abuse. In H. Gottfried, ed., *Feminism and social change: Building theory and practice*, pp. 160–83. Chicago: University of Illinois Press.

National Association of Social Workers (NASW). (1994). *Person-in-the-environment system.* Washington, DC: NASW.

———. (1997). *Code of ethics.* Washington, DC: NASW. (Also available at www.naswdc.org/code.htm.)

National Forum on Health. (1994). *The future of our health and health system.* Ottawa: Health Canada. (Videotape.)

Nelson, C. H., Kelley, M. L., and McPherson, D. H. (1985). Rediscovering support in social work practice: Lessons from Indian Indigenous human service workers. *Canadian Social Work Review 2*: 231–48.

Nes, J., and Iadicola, P. (1989). Toward a definition of feminist social work: A comparison of liberal, radical, and socialist models. *Social Work 34*(1): 12–21.

Ng, R. (1993). Racism, sexism, and immigrant women. In S. Burt, L. Code, and L. Dorney, eds., *Changing patterns: Women in Canada*, pp. 279–307. Toronto: McClelland and Stewart.

Northcott, A. (1994). Threats to medicare: The financing, allocation, and utilization of health care in Canada. In B. S. Bolaria and H. Dickinson, eds., *Health, illness, and health care in Canada*, 2nd ed., pp. 65–82. Toronto: Harcourt Brace & Company.

Nye, A. (1988). *Feminist theory and the philosophies of man.* New York: Routledge.

O'Connor, I., Wilson, J., and Setterlund, D. (1995). *Social work and welfare practice.* Melbourne, Australia: Longman.

O'Connor, P. J. (1986). *The story of St. Christopher's House 1912–1984.* Toronto: Toronto Association of Neighbourhood Services.

O'Meara, S. (1996). Epilogue. In S. O'Meara and D.A. West, eds., *From our eyes*, pp. 123–41. Toronto: Garamond Press.

O'Reilly, M. (1999). Hunger strikers protest First Nations health care. *Canadian Medical Association Journal 160*(11): 1547–48.

Odjig White, L. (1996). Medicine wheel teaching in Native language education. In S. O'Meara and D. A. West, eds., *From our eyes*, pp. 107–22. Toronto: Garamond Press.

Osennontion and Skonaganleh:rá. (1989). Our world. *Canadian Woman Studies 10*(2/3): 7–19.

Padilla, Y. (1997). Immigrant policy: Issues for social work practice. *Social Work 42*(6): 595–606.

Parsons R., Jorgensen, J., and Hernández, S. (1994). *The integration of social work practice.* Pacific Grove, CA: Brooks/Cole.

Payne, M. (1991). *Modern social work theory: A critical introduction.* London: Macmillan Press.

———. (1997). *Modern social work theory*, 2nd ed. Chicago: Lyceum Books.

Payne, M., Adams, R., and Dominelli, L. (2002). On being critical in social work. In M. Payne, R. Adams, and L. Dominelli, eds., pp. 1–12. *Critical practice in social work.* Houndmills, UK: Palgrave.

Pearson, G. (1975). *The deviant imagination: Psychiatry, social work, and social change.* New York: Holmes & Meier.

Pease, B., and Fook, J. (1999). *Transforming social work practice: Postmodern and critical perspectives.* London: Routledge.

Peat, F. D. (1994). *Lighting the seventh fire: The spiritual ways, healing, and science of the Native American.* Toronto: Canadian Manda Group.

Pecnik, N., and Miskulin, M. (1996). Psychosocial assistance to refugees and displaced women in Croatia. *Groupwork 9*(3): 328–51.

Peile, C., and McCouat, M. (1997). The rise of relativism: The future of theory and knowledge development in social work. *British Journal of Social Work 27*: 343–60.

Perlman, H. (1957). *Social casework: A problem solving process.* Chicago: University of Chicago Press.

Pincus, A., and Minahan, A. (1973). *Social work practice: Model and method.* Itasca, IL: Peacock.

Ponting, R. (1994). Turning the heat up. In D. Glenday and A. Duffy, eds., *Canadian society: Understanding and surviving in the 1990s*, pp. 86–116. Toronto: McClelland and Stewart.

Popple, K. (2002). Community work. In R. Adams, L. Dominelli, and M. Payne, eds. *Critical practice in social work,* pp. 149–58. Houndmills, UK: Palgrave.

Postl, B. (1997). It's time for action. *Canadian Medical Association Journal 12*(157): 1655–56.

Pumphrey, R., and Pumphrey, M. (1961). *The heritage of American social work.* New York: Columbia University Press.

Rachlis, M., and Kushner, C. (1994). *Strong medicine: How to save Canada's health care system.* Toronto: HarperCollins.

Ramsey, R. (1984). Snapshots of practice in the twentieth century. *The Social Worker 52*(1): 11–15.

Razack, S. H. (2000). Gendered racial violence and specialized justice. The murder of Pamela George. *Canadian Journal of Law and Society 15*(2): 91–130.

Reamer, F. (1995). *Social work values and ethics.* New York: Columbia University Press.

Regnier, R. (1994). The sacred circle: A process pedagogy of healing. *Interchange 25*(2): 129–44.

Rehr, H. (1998). Health care and the social work connection. In H. Rehr, G. Rosenberg, and S. Blumenfield, eds., *Creative social work in health care: Clients, the community, and your organization*, pp. 7–19. New York: Springer.

Rehr, H., Rosenberg, G., Walther, V., Showers, N., and Young, A. (1998). Educating for social-health care: Social work practitioners, students, and other health care professionals. In H. Rehr, G. Rosenberg, and S. Blumenfield, eds., *Creative social work in health care: Clients, the community, and your organization*, pp. 129–52. New York: Springer.

Rein, M. (1974, Sept.). Social policy analysis and the interpretation of beliefs. *The American Institute for Planners Journal*, 297–310.

Rice, J., and Prince, M., eds. (2000). *Changing politics of Canadian social policies.* Toronto: University of Toronto Press.

Riches, G. (1985). The rise of the food banks and the collapse of the public safety net. *Social-Worker-Travailleur-Social 53*(1): 5–6.

———. (1986). *Food banks and the welfare crisis.* Ottawa: Canadian Council on Social Development.

———. (1997). *First World hunger: Food security and welfare politics.* New York: St. Martin's Press.

Richmond, M. (1917). *Social diagnosis.* New York: Russell Sage Foundation.

Ristock, J., and Pennell, J. (1996). *Community research as empowerment: Feminist links, postmodern interruptions.* Toronto: Oxford University Press.

Robison, W., and Reeser, L. C. (2000). *Ethical decision making in social work.* Boston: Allyn and Bacon.

Rochefort, D. (1993). *From poorhouses to homelessness: Policy analysis and mental health care.* Westport, CT: Auburn House (Greenwood).

Rodway, M. (1986). Systems theory. In F. Turner, ed., *Social work treatment: Interlocking theoretical approaches,* 3rd ed., pp. 514–40. New York: Free Press.

Romanow, R. (2002). *Final report: Building on values—The future of health care in Canada.* Ottawa: Commission on the Future of Health Care in Canada, Government of Canada.

Rooney, R. (1992). *Strategies for work with involuntary clients.* New York: Columbia University Press.

Ross, R. (1992). *Dancing with a ghost: Exploring Indian reality.* Markham, ON: Octopus Books.

———. (1996). *Returning to the teachings: Exploring aboriginal justice.* Toronto: Penguin Books.

Rothman, J. (1994). *Practice with highly vulnerable clients: Case management and community-based services.* Englewood Cliffs, NJ: Prentice-Hall.

———. (1996). The interweaving of community intervention approaches. *Journal of Community Practice 3*(3/4): 69–99.

Rothman, J., and Sager, J. (1998). *Case management: Integrating individual and community practice,* 2nd ed. Boston: Allyn and Bacon.

Rothman, J., and Tropman, J. (1987). Models of community organization and macro practice perspectives: Their mixing and phasing. In F. Cox, J. Ehrlich, J. Rothman, and J. Tropman, eds., *Strategies of community organization: Macro practice,* 4th ed., pp. 3–20. Itasca, IL: Peacock.

Rubin, A., and Babbie, E. (1997). *Research methods for social work*, 3rd ed. Pacific Grove, CA: Brooks/Cole.

Russell, M. N. (1989). Feminist social work skills. *Canadian Social Work Review 6*(1): 69–81.

Saleebey, D. (1992). *The strengths perspective in social work practice.* White Plains, NY: Longman.

———. (1997a). Introduction: Power in the people. In D. Saleebey, ed., *The strengths perspective in social work practice*, 2nd ed., pp. 3–20. White Plains, NY: Longman.

———. (1997b). Community development and individual resilience. In D. Saleebey, ed., *The strengths perspective in social work practice*, 2nd ed., pp. 199–216. White Plains, NY: Longman.

———. (1997c). *The strengths perspective in social work practice*, 2nd ed. White Plains, NY: Longman.

———. (2002). *The strengths perspective in social work practice,* 3rd ed. Boston: Allyn and Bacon.

Sands, R., and Nuccio, K. (1992). Postmodern feminist theory and social work. *Social Work 37*(6): 489–94.

Saulnier, C. (1996). *Feminist theories and social work: Approaches and applications.* New York: The Haworth Press.

Schact, S., and Ewing, D. (1997). The many paths of feminism: Can men travel any of them? *Journal of Gender Studies 6*(2): 159–76.

Schneider, L., and Streuning, E. (1983). SLOF: A behavioural rating scale for assessing the mentally ill. *Social Work Research and Abstracts 19*: 9–21.

Schram, B., and Mandell, B. (2000). *An introduction to human services: Policy and practice.* Needham Heights, MA: Allyn and Bacon.

Schur, E. (1971). *Labeling deviant behavior*. New York: Harper and Row.

Sears, A. (1995). Before the welfare state: Public health and social policy. *Canadian Review of Sociology and Anthropology/Revue Canadien de sociologie et anthropologie 32*(2): 169–88.

Shah, B., Gunraj, N., and Hux, J. (2003). Markers of access to and quality of primary health care for Aboriginal people in Ontario. *American Journal of Public Health 93*(5): 798–802.

Sheafor, B., Horejsi, C., and Horejsi, G. (1997). *Techniques and guidelines for social work practice*, 4th ed. Needham Heights, MA: Allyn and Bacon.

———. (2000). *Techniques and guidelines for social work practice*, 5th ed. Needham Heights, MA: Allyn and Bacon.

Shebib, B. (2003). *Choices: Interviewing and counselling skills for Canadians.* Toronto: Prentice Hall.

Shulman, L. (1984). *The skills of helping: Individuals and groups*, 2nd ed. Itasca, IL: Peacock.

———. (1999). *The skills of helping: Individuals, families, groups and communities*, 4th ed. Itasca, IL: Peacock.

Sibbald, B. (2002). Off-reserve Aboriginal people face daunting health problems: StatsCan. *Canadian Medical Association Journal 167*(8): 912.

Siegel, E. (1994). Social policy for advanced generalist practice. In M. McMahon, ed., *Advanced generalist practice with an international perspective*, pp. 184–204. Englewood Cliffs, NJ: Prentice-Hall.

Simmons, J. (1994). Community-based care: The new health social work paradigm. *Social Work in Health Care 20*(1): 35–46.

Simon, B. (1994). *The empowerment tradition in American social work: A history.* New York: Columbia University Press.

Skidmore, R., Thackeray, M., Farley, O., Smith, L., and Boyle, S. (2000). *Introduction to social work*, 8th ed. Needham Heights, MA: Allyn and Bacon.

Smith, C., and White, S. (1997). Parton, Howe and postmodernity: A critical comment on mistaken identity. *British Journal of Social Work 27*: 275–95.

Smith, D. (1990). *The conceptual practices of power: A feminist sociology of knowledge.* Toronto: University of Toronto Press.

Sommer, R., and Osmond, H. (1961). Symptoms of institutional care. *Social Problems 8*(3): 254–63.

Southern Chiefs' Organization. (2002, Winter). Why SCO rejects the First Nations Governance Act. *South Wind: The Quarterly Newsletter of the Southern Chiefs' Organization Inc. 1*(3): 3.

Spearman, L. (1971). Conformity of mental hospital patients to staff's behavioural expectations. Unpublished doctoral dissertation, George Warren Brown School of Social Work, Washington University, St. Louis, MO.

———. (2004). Ten-year employment trends of graduates of the University of Manitoba Faculty of Social Work: 1990–2000. Paper presented at the CASSW 2004 Conference, Winnipeg.

———. (in press). A developmental approach to social work practice in mental health: Building on strengths. In T. Heinonen and A. Metteri, eds. *Social work in health and mental health: Emerging developments and international perspectives.* Toronto: Canadian Scholars' Press.

Specht, H. (1988). *New directions for social work practice.* Englewood Cliffs, NJ: Prentice-Hall.

Specht, H., and Courtney, M. (1994). *Unfaithful angels: How social work abandoned its mission.* New York: Free Press.

Specht, H., and Specht, R. (1986). Social work assessment: Route to clienthood (part I). *Social Casework 67*: 525–32.

Spitzer, W., and Nash, K. (1996). Educational preparation for contemporary health care social work practice. In M. Mailick and P. Caroff, eds., *Professional social work education and health care: Challenges for the future*, pp. 9–34. New York: The Haworth Press.

Stanley, L., and Wise, S. (1993). *Breaking out again: Feminist ontology and epistemology.* London: Routledge.

Statistics Canada. (2001). *Aboriginal peoples in Canada.* Ottawa: Statistics Canada.

———. (2003). *Aboriginal peoples survey 2001: Initial findings—Well-being of the non-reserve Aboriginal population.* Ottawa: Statistics Canada.

Stiegelbauer, S. M. (1996). What is an Elder? What do Elders do? First Nations Elders as teachers in culture-based urban organizations. *The Canadian Journal of Native Studies 16*(1): 37–66.

Strickberger, M. (1990). *Evolution.* Boston: Jones and Bartlett.

Suchar, C. (1978). *Social deviance: Perspectives and prospects.* New York: Holt, Rinehart, and Winston.

Sullivan, N., Mesbur, E. S., Lang, N., Goodman, D., and Mitchell, L., eds. (2003). *Social work with groups: Social justice through personal, community and societal change.* Binghamton, NY: The Haworth Press.

Sullivan, P. (1994). A long and winding road: The process of recovery from mental illness. *Innovations and Research 3*(3): 20.

Sullivan, T., and Baranek, P. M. (2002). *First do no harm: Making sense of Canadian health reform.* Vancouver: UBC Press.

Sulman, J., Savage, D., and Way, S. (2001). Retooling social work practice for high volume, short stay. *Social Work in Health Care 34*(3/4): 315–332.

Taylor, J. (1997). Niches and practice: Extending the ecological perspective. In D. Saleebey, ed., *The strengths perspective in social work practice*, 2nd ed., pp. 217–28. White Plains, NY: Longman.

Taylor, P. (1995). Power and authority in social work. In P. Taylor and C. Daly, eds., *Gender dilemmas in social work*, pp. 61–74. Toronto: Canadian Scholars' Press.

Taylor-Gooby, P. (1994). Postmodernism and social policy: A great leap backwards? *Journal of Social Policy 23*(3): 385–404.

Tester, F., and Case, R. (1999). *Critical choices, turbulent times, Vol. II: Retreat and resistance in the reform of Canadian social policy.* Vancouver: School of Social Work, University of British Columbia.

Thompson, N. (1993). *Anti-discriminatory practice.* London: BASW/Macmillan.

Titley, B. (1986). *A narrow vision: Duncan Campbell Scott and the administration of Indian Affairs in Canada.* Vancouver: University of British Columbia Press.

Titmuss, R. (1974). *Social policy, an introduction.* London: George Allen and Unwin.

Toseland, W., Palmer-Ganeles, J., and Chapman, D. (1986). Teamwork in psychiatric settings. *Social Work 31*(1): 46–53.

Trecartin, W., Tasker, R., and Martin, K. (1991). *Moses Coady.* National Film Board of Canada. (Videotape).

Tripodi, T. (1994). *A primer on single-subject design for clinical social workers.* Washington, DC: NASW.

Turner, F. (1999). The theoretical base of practice. In F. Turner, ed., *Social work practice: A Canadian perspective,* pp. 23–33. Scarborough, ON: Prentice-Hall Allyn and Bacon Canada.

Turner, J., and Turner, F., eds. (2001). *Canadian social welfare,* 4th ed. Toronto: Allyn & Bacon.

Tutty, L. (2002). The setting of objectives and contracting. In F. Turner, ed., *Social work practice: A Canadian perspective,* pp. 165–79. Toronto: Pearson Education Canada.

Valentich, M. (1986). Feminism and social work practice. In F. Turner, ed., *Social work treatment: Interlocking theoretical approaches,* pp. 564–89. New York: Free Press/Macmillan.

Valverade, M. (1991). *The age of light, soap, and water: Moral reform in English Canada, 1885–1925.* Toronto: McClelland and Stewart.

Van Den Bergh, N., and Cooper, N., eds. (1986). *Feminist visions for social work.* Silver Springs, MD: NASW.

Wakefield, J. (1996a). Does social work need the ecosystems perspective? Part 1: Is the perspective clinically useful? *Social Service Review 70*(1): 1–32.

———. (1996b). Does social work need the eco-systems perspective? Part 2: Does the ecosystems perspective save social work from incoherence? *Social Service Review 70*(2): 183–213.

———. (1996c). Does social work need the eco-systems perspective? Reply to Alex Gitterman. *Social Service Review 70*(3): 476–81.

Waldram, J. B. (1997). *The way of the pipe: Aboriginal spirituality and symbolic healing in Canadian prisons.* Peterborough, ON: Broadview Press.

Walt, G. (1994). *Health policy: An introduction to process and power.* London: Zed Press.

Walt, G., and Gilson, L. (1994). Reforming the health sector in developing countries: The central role of policy analysis. *Health Policy and Planning 9*(4): 353–70.

Walton, R. (1975). *Women in social work.* London: Routledge & Kegan Paul.

Waring, M. (1996). *Three masquerades: Essays on equality, work and human rights.* Toronto: University of Toronto Press.

Weick, A. (1983). Issues in overturning a medical model of social work practice. *Social Work 28*(6): 467–71.

———. (1992). Building a strengths perspective for social work. In D. Saleebey, ed., *The strengths perspective in social work practice*, pp. 18–26. White Plains, NY: Longman.

Weitz, R. (1996). *The sociology of health, illness, and health care: A critical approach.* Belmont, CA: Wadsworth.

Wendell, S. (1993). Toward a feminist theory of disability. In D. Shogan, ed., *A reader in feminist ethics*, pp. 223–47. Toronto: Canadian Scholars' Press.

Westhues, A. (2003). *Canadian social policy.* Waterloo, ON: Wilfrid Laurier University Press.

———. (2004). *MSW 2002 Employment Survey: Faculty of Social Work, Wilfrid Laurier University.* Paper presented at the CASSW 2004 Conference, Winnipeg.

Wharf, B. (1992). *Communities and social policy in Canada.* Toronto: McClelland and Stewart.

Wharf, B., ed. (1990). *Social work and social change in Canada.* Toronto: McClelland and Stewart.

Wharf, B., and McKenzie, B. (1998). *Connecting policy to practice in the human services.* Toronto: Oxford University Press.

White, D. (1994). The rationalization of health and social-service delivery in Québec. In B. S. Bolaria and H. Dickinson, eds., *Health, illness, and health care in Canada*, pp. 83–105. Toronto: Harcourt Brace and Company.

White, R. (1963). *Ego and reality in psychoanalytic theory.* New York: International Universities Press.

Wicks, R., and Parsons, R. (1984). Counseling strategies and intervention techniques for the human services. New York: Longman.

Wien, F. (1999). The Royal Commission Report: Nine steps to rebuild Aboriginal economies. *The Journal of Aboriginal Economic Development 1*(1): 102–19.

Williams, F. (1989). *Social policy: A critical introduction*. Cambridge, UK: Polity Press.

———. (1992). Women with learning difficulties are women too. In M. Langan and L. Day, eds., *Women, oppression and social work*, pp. 149–68. London: Routledge.

Wills, G. (1995). *A marriage of convenience: Business and social work in Toronto 1918–1957.* Toronto: University of Toronto Press.

Wolin, S. (1993). *The resilient self: How survivors of troubled families rise above adversity*. New York: Villard.

Yelaja, S. (1985). *An introduction to social work practice in Canada*. Scarborough, ON: Prentice-Hall Canada.

Yoder, J., and Kahn, A. (1992). Toward a feminist understanding of women and power. *Psychology of Women Quarterly 16*: 381–88.

Young, D., Ingram, G., and Swartz, L. (1989). *Cry of the eagle: Encounters with a Cree healer*. Toronto: University of Toronto Press.

Zastrow, C. (1995). *The practice of social work*, 5th ed. Pacific Grove, CA: Brooks/Cole.

———. (1996). *Introduction to social work and social welfare*, 6th ed. Pacific Grove, CA: Brooks/Cole.

Zieba, R. A. (1990). Healing and healers among the northern Cree. Unpublished master's thesis, Natural Resources Institute, University of Manitoba, Winnipeg, Manitoba.

Ziegler, O. (1934). *Woodsworth, social pioneer*. Toronto: Ontario Publishing.

Index

B

C

D

G

H

T

U

V